Philipp Caspar Koch

Optimizing Distribution Systems in Asset Management

Institutional Arrangements as Key Factor of Success

With a foreword by Prof. Dr. Claudia Fantapié Altobelli

GABLER EDITION WISSENSCHAFT

Bibliographic information published by the Deutsche Nationalbibliothek
The Deutsche Nationalbibliothek lists this publication in the Deutsche Nationalbibliografie; detailed bibliographic data are available in the Internet at http://dnb.d-nb.de.

Dissertation Helmut-Schmidt-Universität Hamburg, 2007

1st Edition 2008

Editorial Office: Frauke Schindler / Nicole Schweitzer

Gabler is part of the specialist publishing group Springer Science+Business Media.
www.gabler.de

Cover design: Regine Zimmer, Dipl.-Designerin, Frankfurt/Main
Printed on acid-free paper
Printed in Germany

ISBN 978-3-8349-1107-0

Philipp Caspar Koch

Optimizing Distribution Systems in Asset Management

GABLER EDITION WISSENSCHAFT

Foreword

The content of this book is dealing with distribution systems for mutual funds in Germany. The production and distribution for these investment vehicles is usually organised along multiple structural levels: The producers of investment funds avail themselves of banks and insurance networks as distribution agents, and consequently do not have direct access to the investors. Both groups, especially in the last couple of years, have expressed strong interest in optimising the marketing of these financial services. It has to be taken into account that in Germany – as well as in other countries in Continental Europe – the producers of investment funds usually are part of banks or insurance groups. This translates into a very strong integration of value chains related to producers and distribution agents, resulting in a tendency of banks to sell primarily their own products to their clients. However, the economic crisis at the beginning of this decade highlights that profitability in the mutual fund market requires growth (i.e. de facto the acquisition of new clients). As alternative distributions channels, like for example direct marketing or distribution via independent financial advisors, play only a relative minor role, this growth requires the optimisation of existing and exploration of new relationships in particular with the distribution channel of banks.

The objective of this book is to analyse alternative distribution systems – against the background of different institutional arrangements - in order to find out whether new, more open and, hence less-integrated, distribution systems contribute to efficiency in terms of economic success, in spite of expected problems like information asymmetry, conflict of interests, and so forth. At first, alternative distribution systems are analysed theoretically. By applying new institutional economic arguments, it then comes to the derivation of a sound framework of analysis for outlining optimised distribution systems.

In addition to the theoretical analysis, the author is conducting an empirical survey. He is falling back on the methodology of comparative case studies, where strategically relevant cases are made units of analysis. This approach facilitates the theoretical generalisation of the findings on the grounds of plausibility and logical reasoning. Deka is selected to represent the organisational form of „hierarchy", Julius Bär serves as an example for a hybrid governance structure, and Fidelity Investments represents the organisational form of a „market". For collecting data, the enquiry applies a mix of different methods, most notably qualitative interviews. The analysis turns to institutional economic arguments to examine how the above mentioned producers choose and design the organisational form for distributing mutual funds in the German private investors market. Following the comparative institutional analysis in chapter 4, the author discusses avenues towards optimising distribution systems for mutual funds.

All in all, this book represents a successful examination of a very topical subject, giving economic researchers valuable clues and providing various suggestions to professionals working in this field.

Prof. Dr. Claudia Fantapié Altobelli

Preface

With this publication I am proud for being able now to present my Ph.D.-dissertation submitted to the Faculty of Economics and Social Sciences of the Helmut-Schmidt-University Hamburg as a book to the wider public.

In applying new institutional economics approaches of management science (and organization theory) the focus of this book is clearly on finding out for the asset-management industry with a model-building intent the way in which measures to optimize distribution systems are going to improve the company´s success – in this case is contributing to a sustained improvement in net inflow streams from private investors. In putting down this work, I very much enjoyed the opportunity to fall back on the various practical experiences I have been able to pick up so far in doing consultancy work with McKinsey&Company when serving numerous international clients in the area of asset management. At the same time, however, there can be no denying that also in my own case only a strict adherence to the rules and routines of scientific work allows for generating results with a lasting or sustainable character. In following the "rules of the game", there is then the hope to present results not only enjoying and standing out for a high level of practical relevance, but also are proving to be tenable in the light of rigorous critique.

Since projects such as dissertations have turned into complex production processes, it goes without saying that also this effort has its "creditors". Without the support of a number of different institutions and partners, it would not have been possible to successfully accomplish this effort. In this regard, my thanks are firstly going to the mentors of my immediate professional working environment – most notably Dr. Martin Huber (McKinsey&Company) – but also to the representatives from those asset management companies, which I have been able to make units of analysis in the course of my comparative institutional analysis. They have not only provided the critical access but also made themselves available as thought and sparring partners. In addition, I very much would like to take the opportunity to express my gratitude to my Ph.D. advisor Prof. Dr. Claudia Fantapié-Altobelli, who throughout the entire process was extremely supportive and became an essential "driver" of this project. However, I would also like to thank Prof. Dr. Hans Koller for his support in the preparation of the final oral exams. Last but not least, I cannot deny that probably also the remaining traces of a fairly cosmopolitan as well as sports- and competition-focused "Kinderstube" continuously motivated me to face and enjoy not only the challenges but also the enticements which typically come with such a dissertation project.

Finally, I would like to also include Anika Mannig into my sincere thanks, as she has helped me to bring the whole manuscript in a printable shape.

Philipp Caspar Koch

Overview

Table of Contents

Table of Figures

Abbreviations

AuM	Assets under Management
BVI	Bundesverband Investment and Asset Management
CAGR	Compounded Annual Growth Rate
CHF	Swiss Franc
DEKA	DekaBank
DSGV	Deutscher Sparkassen- und Giroverband
EUR	Euro
FIL	Fidelity Investments
FoF	Fund-of-Funds
GmbH	Gesellschaft mit beschränkter Haftung
IFA	Independent Financial Advisor
JBAM	Julius Bär Asset Management
KAG	Kapitalanlagegesellschaft
NIE	New Institutional Economics
OHG	Offene Handelsgesellschaft
ö.K.	Öffentlich-rechtliche Körperschaft
PA	Principal-Agent-Theory
PLF	Private-label funds
PoS	Point-of-Sale
PRT	Property-Rights-Theory

Chapter 1: Institutional Arrangements as a Key Factor of Success

1.1 Outline of Problem

Distribution systems and questions relating to their choice and design are of significant relevance for firms in order to successfully compete in increasingly competitive markets. Coughlan et al. (2001, p. 111) view channel integration decisions as a critical component of any firm's marketing strategy with the choice of the right level of integration possibly making the difference between success and failure. Not surprisingly, for more than 20 years now, academics have analyzed and discussed the suitability of alternative institutional arrangements for distribution systems in a wide range of industries and service sectors. In this regard, the papers by Anderson and Schmittlein (1984) and Anderson (1985) mark a starting point. These investigate decisions by electronic firms to fall back on either a direct sales force or a network of manufacturer representatives to sell products to end customers.

In view of new organizational patterns for distributing asset management products in Continental Europe which have been emerging since the late 1990s, **the question of how to choose and design distribution systems for marketing mutual funds to private investors has become a matter of the greatest importance to asset management firms as well as to banking and insurance groups**. Asset management firms are in charge of the production function of mutual funds, involving the investment management activities for the funds' assets. Banks and insurance companies run the distribution function, which means that they perform sales and advisory activities to private investors through their proprietary distribution networks. This assignment of activities along the specialized set-up of the value chain for producing and marketing mutual funds in Continental Europe indicates that, in general, asset management firms do not have direct contact with the end customers. Within such a setting distributors typically tend to enjoy considerable freedom in guiding the direction of cash inflow streams from private investors into mutual funds. Over the last couple of years, product providers and distributing intermediaries have controversially debated on how to organize optimally their coordination at the interface of the value chain. In this context, especially the asset management firms are seeking solutions on how to structure and manage relationships with distributors in order to secure strong inflow streams for their product range. **Therefore, in following a pragmatic perspective, it will be the primary focus of this enquiry to produce practically relevant guidelines for asset management firms on how to organize distribution systems with banks in order to optimize the cash inflow streams for their mutual fund offering**.

Fig. 1: FOCUS OF ENQUIRY

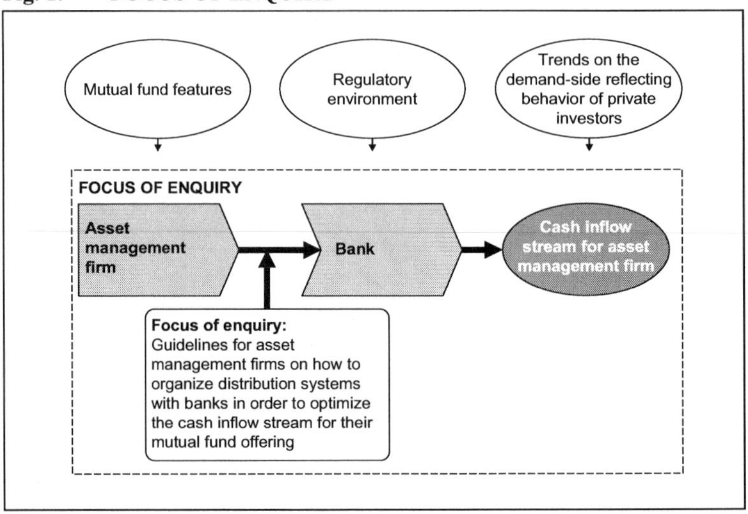

Source: Author

Without a doubt, as illustrated in Figure 1, a variety of elements such as particular mutual fund features, changes in the regulatory environment, and trends on the demand-side reflecting the behavior of private investors – just to name a few – can have an effect on the cash inflow stream. However, also in the light of the prevalent discussion in the asset management sector, **it is the overriding interest to explore the problem of how to optimally organize the relationship between asset management firms and banks to activate and ensure the desired actions of banks in order to strengthen the cash**

inflow stream for the asset management firms' product offering. As far as this analysis deals with this kind of organizational problem, it will mainly investigate in which way different degrees of decentralization have an optimizing effect on the cash inflow stream. With such an intended focus, this enquiry then clearly cannot control for the possible impact of all the other elements with a potential effect on the target. Nevertheless, by investigating in particular how to guide the behavior of the distributing intermediary, this enquiry will address indirectly in which way the supply-side of mutual funds can improve the interaction with private investors in order to come to an optimization of the cash inflow stream.

For outlining the problem facing asset management firms on how to organize the relationship with banks to market their products, it is imperative to turn back to the year 2001. After an incessant period of growth and strong profitability throughout the 1990s, **the asset management sector's average profit fell for the very first time in that year coinciding with the general economic slowdown**. As Huber, Leroy, and Saada (2003, pp. 10-11) explain, the dramatic nosedive of global equity markets led directly to the evaporation of assets under management [AuM] as well as to the strong movement of investors out of high-risk, high-margin products such as equity or sector funds into low-risk, lower-revenue asset classes such as fixed-income and money-market products. These shifts put significant pressure on the revenue side of asset management operations causing sector-average net revenues to collapse from 54 basis points [as 0.01% of AuM] in 2000 to 42 basis points in 2001. All in all, the dramatic fall in net revenues was not only contrary to the traditionally perceived economic attractiveness of asset management operations but also meant that 20 percent of European asset management firms operated at a loss. By 2003, it is true that profitability levels have more or less recovered and asset management firms are again searching for avenues to enjoy growth on a profitable basis. However, neither the expected future development of capital markets nor the demand of existing customer pools are regarded as being able to offer sustainable growth in terms of net inflows and AuM and, ultimately, in profitability. With these two potential sources unavailable, it still remains difficult for asset management firms to realize their aspirations without systematically rethinking the way distribution systems are organized. Therefore, **distribution strategies and the organization of distribution systems with**

distributing intermediaries have become top priority on the management agenda of most asset management firms.

Typically, the value chain for the mutual funds from the investment management activities to the distribution function has been highly integrated in Germany, as most asset management firms are a part of a larger banking/insurance group. Highlighting the implications of this integrated set-up, Heinemann et al. (2003, p. 39) cite that more than 80 percent of mutual funds distributed by banks are attributable to their in-house asset management firms. From the perspective of asset management firms, this integrated setting typically has meant that their products are sold primarily to the customer base of their in-house distribution channels. However, following the dynamics in the market environment, it is the expansion of customer reach that asset management firms consider a critical prerequisite to trigger sustained growth in distribution performance levels, rather than the increase in the "share of wallet" of the existing in-house customer base. Yet, establishing new or enlarging existing proprietary distribution channels to obtain access to new customer pools requires substantial financial resources and tends to offer adequate returns on investment only a long way down the road, if at all. Given limited customer movement in the form of switching between competing financial services providers, it is considered to be extremely difficult to attract new customer pools. Hence, **to achieve the aspired levels of profitable growth, it becomes imperative for asset management firms – irrespective of whether they are independent or part of a larger banking/insurance group – to successfully sell their products through external distributors.**

While asset management firms are increasingly feeling the economic pressure to expand customer reach beyond the limits of in-house channels, the opportunity to distribute mutual funds through external channels in Germany has surfaced on a larger scale since the beginning of this century. Banks in Germany have started to offer a wider choice [even] at the mass-market level by including products from external asset management firms in the offering they actively advise to their customers. By 2004, the majority of banks have adopted some form of branded third-party distribution with the identity of external product providers clearly visible to private investors. Different degrees of openness have emerged. Some banks offer products from over 20 external providers, while others have only granted access to a handful of asset management firms. Only a very small number have remained closed to external products.

This trend towards more open distribution systems provides asset management firms with access to new sources of inflow streams and revenues in domestic markets as well as in other European markets. **Some asset management firms, which traditionally relied almost exclusively on the in-house channel, are now generating a larger share of their inflow streams via external distributors**. At the same time, from the perspective of distributors, selling products of external asset management firms can be a lucrative option to bolster revenues as well. Heinemann et al. (2003, p. 55) point out that banks can sometimes earn more selling external products than by selling in-house funds. Moreover, the inclusion of external products tends to address the investors' need for more objective advice. This is expected to create the opportunity for distributors not only to retain existing customers but also to attract new ones, thereby strengthening market share (Handelsblatt 2004, p. 25).

In the face of these potential benefits, optimism with respect to the combined long-term [net] effect of a more open distribution environment prevailed even among integrated financial service institutions. Increased total revenues of the distribution function [due to the improved competitive positioning of the product offering with greater choice] and enhanced sales of the in-house asset management firm via external channels are expected to outweigh potentially lower sales of in-house products in the proprietary channel [due to increased competition]. In fact, the introduction of external asset management firms was initially considered as additional means to enhance the sales of the in-house provider rather to cannibalize them (Cameron 2002, p. 2).

All this explains why asset management firms [and their parent organization] have been increasingly pushing away from fully-integrated, high-control distribution systems towards more open systems. It seems that while in the 1990s a rather hierarchical organization of producing and marketing mutual funds was regarded as the profit-maximizing set-up, increased decentralization is now considered to be a more beneficial approach in the wake of the market dynamics at the beginning of this century. It allows asset management firms to expand customer reach beyond the limits of the in-house channel, while distributors may position themselves as more customer-focused (Skypala 2005, p. 6).

Accordingly, driven by developments in Germany the third-party fund ratio[1] in Europe more than doubled form 6 percent in 2000 to 14 percent in 2002 (Sector Analysis 2003a, p. 7). However, by 2004 the enthusiasm among asset management firms to be increasingly able to take this route to regain the performance levels of the late 1990s had vanished, as the progress towards more open distribution systems cooled down. Despite the potential economic benefits to both distributors and asset management firms, the third-party fund penetration not only stalled but in fact dropped to 12 percent in 2003 (Sector Analysis 2003a, p. 7). **While almost all distributors claim to have adopted a more open distribution system, there is the perception that they mainly offer their in-house products and only turn to external providers under duress** (Skypala 2004, p. 3). This has resulted in skepticism among asset management firms with respect to the growth prospects of more open distribution systems.

Reinforcing the **notion of fundamental challenges in implementing and managing more open distribution systems**, the recent empirical investigation carried out by Heinemann et al. (2003, pp. 52-57) accentuates a variety of obstacles facing asset management firms when marketing their products via external distributors. First and foremost, this study reveals that when asset management firms delegate the distribution function to external banks[2], they have learned that these banks and their sales staff at the point-of-sale demonstrate only limited willingness as well as lack the competence to carry out the distribution services appropriately. From the perspective of asset management firms, these relationships are perceived to be short on commitment on the part of distributing banks. Furthermore, turning to external distributors tends to entail

---

1 The third-party fund penetration measures the competitive positioning of external product providers to in-house providers relative to in-house providers by comparing the value of third-party mutual funds to the total value of funds distributed to private investors across Europe.

2 Banks then typically perform this activity for a number of external product providers besides their in-house provider.

substantial investments and considerable out-of-pocket expenses. Empirical studies reveal that asset management firms, which mainly sell through external distributors, suffer from sales and marketing costs four times higher than the asset management industry on average (Spence 2004, p. 7). This strongly indicates that while more open distribution systems may potentially benefit asset management firms to enjoy new sources of inflows, they may also give rise to considerable inefficiencies. **These inefficiencies, in turn, may not only jeopardize efforts to regain profitable growth but, in fact, leave many asset management firms still searching for the ideal distribution system** (McMeeken 2005, pp. 29).

In summary, these developments in organizing the distribution of mutual funds can be interpreted as deliberate moves by product providers [but also by their distributing owners] to strengthen inflows and, thus, revenues. However, **this tendency to move away from highly integrated organizational constructions towards new, more decentralized systems has been subject to severe impediments and disappointments**. As a consequence, there is substantial uncertainty and skepticism among asset management firms regarding the economic attractiveness of third-party distribution. The increasing use of external channels in addition to the traditional in-house channel does not necessarily offer the best of both the "make" and the "buy" world. It looks as if such an approach may entail substantial hazards and inefficiencies if the relationship to external banks is not adequately attuned (Frühauf 2002, p. 18). Hence, in an environment in which the majority of distributing banks claim to have opened up to external product providers, **asset management firms face the critical problem of how to optimally adapt their relationships to distributors**.

1.2 Derivation of Question and Objective of Enquiry

This complex relationship problem confronting asset management firms is an issue management science at large – and particularly the area of marketing – deals with quite regularly from a pragmatic point of view. Frequently, **research in marketing has approached the question of how organizational choices and designs affect the efficiency of interactions along the value chain** and, hence, determine economic success or failure. Therefore, in line with the overall epistemological orientation of management science, work in the area of marketing is interested in producing optimal solutions when exploring organizational choice problems. Accordingly, marketing research focuses on generating knowledge on how to achieve efficient solutions to practical organizational issues. In a more formal sense, the emphasis can then be put on producing propositions in terms of means-effect relations of varying complexity which can be deliberately applied in a controlled way to reach efficient solutions for practical distribution problems.

Therefore, in line with this basic epistemological orientation, **the problem facing asset management firms is going to be rephrased as an optimization problem**. Adopting such a practical orientation, it is essential to point out that, in the light of the general economic slowdown and the nosedive in customer demand for mutual funds, asset management firms and banks have dealt with the fundamental question of whether, with new and different organizational choices and designs for distributing mutual funds, the apparent negative trend of inflows could be turned around, or at least eased. In other words, **this enquiry conceptualizes the all-time low in sales of mutual funds to private investors as a problem of properly adapting the degree of decentralization of the distribution function in order to return to the distribution performance levels of the late 1990s**[3]. By rephrasing the practical challenge in this way, the enquiry aims to

3 As indicated above, the all-time low in mutual fund flows could also be conceptualized in a completely different fashion. A wide range of alternative perspectives are conceivable to address the problem outlined. For example, it is possible to state the problem as how asset management firms can optimize their investment management process to improve central features of their product offering (i.e., rate of investment return, ratings, pricing). Given the widely acknowledged relationships between product features and mutual fund flows, this approach would examine more from a more neo-classical perspective how to improve mutual fund flows. Alternatively, it also conceivable to put the private investor more into the center of the enquiry. In this regard, the analysis could ask for an explanation in which way the behavior of private investor has contributed the all-time low in mutual fund sales. While central building blocks of the concept of behavioral finance have only limited aspiration as a normative theory (Barberis and Thaler 2003, p. 1067), they have been quite successful in understanding and explaining how investors make their investment portfolio choices. Behavioral finance allows investments decisions to be subject to cognitive illusions (e.g., overconfidence, gamblers' fallacy) as well as to preferences that deviate from the subjective expected utility theory (e.g., loss aversion, regret aversion), as it relaxes the assumption of individual reationality. In this way, it is able to explain the phenomena of herding behavior (Shiller 2000, pp. 149-151), which may result in periods of "irrational exuberance" (Shiller 2000, p. 8) as observed during the "dot.com" bubble. Along those lines, arguments of behavioral finance also appear to be able to offer an explanation for the pro-longed hesistance among private investors to return to mutual funds as observed across Europe, despite indications of a recovery of capital markets. Nevertheless, as already pointed out above, according to the problem posed the enquiry's interest is to rephrase it from an organizational theory perspective, without neglecting other effects on the overall market level of demand for mutual funds in Germany. Therefore, as will be outlined in the following, the objective is to examine how asset management firms can strengthen the inflow stream into their mutual fund by way of adapting the degree of decentralization in relationships with distributing banks.

produce guidelines that will hopefully prove beneficial as a means of improving efficiency.

However, to give the main subject of enquiry the needed, more elaborate shape, this enquiry also has to bear in mind that all attempts to establish more open, in other words, decentralized structures for the distribution function [in particular in a service sector such as the asset management sector] are potentially subject to side-constraints. Therefore, what has to be highlighted later with the help of appropriate conceptual means, is that a range of likely negative side effects has to be successfully brought under control in order to benefit from the positive effects related to the use of external distributors. Thus, speaking already in some more conceptual terms, by turning to alternative, increasingly decentralized systems to organize the distribution of mutual funds, asset management firms most likely will be confronted with various motivation and coordination issues. These may in particular result from uneven distribution of relevant information, deviating interests, behavioral and environmental uncertainty, unclear contracts, or the [conventional] limits in standardizing service activities.

Therefore, following some conceptual view, it becomes evident that in order to enjoy the potential benefits of gradually less-integrated distribution systems, asset management firms have to find ways to deploy powerful instruments to adequately account for these latent hazards. From this view, **the structure of the relationship between the mutual-fund-providing asset management firm and the [external] distributing banks then gains critical relevance to achieve the targeted efficiency-improvement** as it facilitates the placement of these apparently necessary intervening measures. In line with this argumentation, questions about a more deliberately chosen set-up for their interaction with distributing banks are beginning to gain increasing consideration among asset management firms (Otto 2003, p. 3).

Hence, with this practical orientation, there can be no doubt that according to the stated challenges:

- This enquiry has to focus on identifying the **most efficient choice of a distribution system** from the range of given alternatives for organizing the distribution function. Therefore, in a rather general fashion the main question of enquiry aims at spelling out functional necessities as well as the problem-solving effects of the best possible choices **in terms of a degree of decentralization**. In more substantive terms, the study aims to clarify whether the utilization of external distributing banks or alternatively the application of some integrated, full-control distribution system is the optimal response to return to the distribution performance levels of the late 1990s.

- However, as indicated above, this choice potentially entails substantial negative side effects. Therefore, the rather general question regarding the optimal choice has to be further differentiated. Hence, the point is also to ask for an **efficacy assessment of the design of the chosen degree of decentralization** to control for the various hazards in relationships with distributing banks which, in turn, is anticipated to encourage the placement of productive investments to generate inflow streams. The more elaborate question has to explicitly consider the extent to which safeguards are designed in a way to secure an adequate handling of the situation-specific demands arising from possible coordination and motivation issues.

The above highlights, the overriding objective of identifying the optimal distribution system is in fact broken down into two interrelated questions. **The first question refers to a strategic system choice. The more refined version addresses the efficacy of designing those varying degrees of decentralization to set up adequate patterns of coordination to bring the latent negative side effects under control in more operational terms for boosting the level of net inflow streams.**

As this will be elaborated in more depth later from a theoretical perspective, this comes down to the question whether, through the choice and design of institutional arrangements, the relationship between asset management firms and distributing banks can be brought to full strength, implying a minimization of otherwise potentially significant inefficiencies. By falling back on an **empirical-normative approach**, this enquiry will be able to offer an answer to asset management firms on how a push-away from rather closed and fully integrated distribution systems towards more decentralized systems can bring about the desired strengthening of distribution performance levels, despite the presence of a variety of possible relationship hazards. In the light of this objective to offer support to this specific decision-making problem, **the enquiry intends to produce practically relevant guidelines on how to set up optimal distribution systems** in this service sector based on identified best- or better practice. In addition to this overarching practical objective, the more far-reaching ambition is to outline the derived results with respect to the choice and design of institutional arrangements in the form of a model-theoretical discussion. The goal is then also to produce an extension to the applied theoretical concept [given the particular characteristics of service firms] by offering new and relevant comments.

1.3 Concept of Enquiry

In order to carry out this study a theoretical concept is required which allows the creation of an understanding of the subject of enquiry in the way necessary to devise adequate answers to the questions raised. The conceptual approach needs to offer an adequate perspective of enquiry to transfer the practical problem into a scientific framework of analysis and ultimately to investigate it with refutable propositions. Thus, the selected concept needs to enable the enquiry to dissect the subject in terms of a set of arguments [i.e., single variables and interconnections] which supports the analysis and explanation of the practical problem of optimizing distribution systems. Equally important, it also has to provide the opportunity to exert guidelines with the highest efficiency improvement potentials. From a more formal perspective, the concept should be best suited for rethinking and/or arranging available alternatives to structure the coordination of the distribution function under the heading of an efficiency-enhancing choice and design problem.

From this view, in order to conceptualize an adequate framework of analysis this enquiry will fall back on recent developments in the area of marketing where a wider spectrum of organizational perspectives is gaining growing attention. Given its objective, this study will to a larger degree turn to the concepts underlying the New Institutional Economics (NIE), most notably principal-agent-theory (PA), transaction cost economics (TCE), and property-rights-theory (PRT). These concepts appear to be particularly suitable as they first of all pursue a **pragmatic-normative perspective**. Moreover, it appears that they offer an **adequate scope of enquiry** to appropriately conceptualize the practical challenges facing asset management firms, as they no longer view firms exclusively in neoclassical terms as technological constructions with production functions but as a particular institutional arrangement. As known, these concepts typically deal with **problems of optimizing the organization of economic activity** by analyzing the trade-off between the advantages of increasingly turning to decentralized systems and the latent dangers lurking in such rather discrete institutional arrangements.

As will be elaborated in more detail, this enquiry shows that NIE, which draws substantially on the work of Coase (1937), Hayek (1945), Chandler (1962), and Simon (1957), offers the necessary background in terms of contingencies, functional necessities, core arguments, propositions, and empirical soundness **to convert the practical challenge into a choice problem regarding the degree of decentralization**. However, as observed for the asset management sector, this practical challenge also tends to entail the question of how to deal with latent negative side effects arising with the chosen degree of decentralization. In this respect, further underlining its suitability, NIE's scope of enquiry explicitly acknowledges side-constraints related to each organizational choice, thereby stressing **the relevance of the organizational design** to bring these impediments appropriately under control. Hence, this theoretical background allows this enquiry to frame the practical challenges facing asset management firms into **a choice and design problem** with the opportunity to formulate refutable propositions on how to reach optimization of distribution systems. Moreover, this integrated conceptual approach also meets the enquiry's need for criteria to run a model-theoretical discussion of the framework of analysis. Central arguments of organizational theory and NIE provide **assessment criteria in terms of alignment/ fit requirements** [cost considerations] to examine alternative choice and design decisions. By enabling in this way the investigation to identify the most superior institutional arrangement, the concepts favor the enquiry's objective to address the choice and design problem from an **action-oriented decision-making perspective**. Hence, with the application of such a conceptual background this empirical study will be able to secure the intended **derivation of practical propositions** on how to achieve efficiency-enhancing solutions. All this already shows [and will be laid out in more detail later], an approach building on the core concepts of NIE without neglecting central arguments of organizational theory, exhibits not only the required **explanatory relevance** but also the desired **practical relevance** to adequately tackle the enquiry's question and objective.

By conceptualizing the framework with this theoretical guidance, this study rephrases the practical challenge into a purposively structured optimization problem. In doing so, this enquiry is in a position to offer guidelines to asset management firms on how to choose and design distribution systems to appropriately control for relationship hazards, which have their roots in latent opportunistic tendencies and specificity. In order to tame these negative side effects, this conceptual background offers a range of action variables, in more analytical terms, structure-shaping instruments as well as process-related measures. However, as will be discussed in more detail, in order to trigger strong performance levels, these instruments and measures have to be put in place at least to some extent in an internally consistent manner, while the overall configuration also has to be adjusted appropriately to the external environment (Chandler 1962, pp. 14-15, Mintzberg 1979, p. 219). Thus, by falling back on a combination of PA, TCE, PRT, and some arguments of contingency theory the stage is set to identify all the relevant and necessary prerequisites for taking best possible decisions regarding the choice and design of institutional arrangements. In this way, the enquiry will then be in a position to highlight the role of **institutional arrangements as a key factor of success for asset management firms** to achieve the aspired levels of cash inflow streams.

As far as practical relevant guidelines are concerned, these will be based on functional means-effect relations to be identified and confirmed between action variables available to choose and design institutional arrangements and the target efficiency [dependent] variables in the enquiry's framework of analysis. Thus, the comparative analysis will attempt to ascertain causal links to test already introduced and accepted arguments of NIE on how to manage marketing channels. To extend the already established findings of NIE, this study aims to derive propositions on the relevance of specific marketing levers to truly benefit from decentralized systems and the willingness to live with misalignments/misfits in arrangements for organizing the distribution function.

1.4 Method

An adequate research method is needed to allow the enquiry to systematically analyze the proficiency of alternative institutional arrangements against propositions, which will be derived on the basis of a theory-guided framework of analysis. Against the criteria outlined by Yin (1994, p. 6) for selecting the most suitable research strategies, a **comparative multi-case study research method** displays the best possible properties to adequately address the enquiry's question and objective. It is most notably the complexity associated with analyzing the functioning of entire social systems that suggests the appropriateness of this research method to clarify the contemporary research objective of "how" and "why" institutional arrangements matter in organizing the distribution of mutual funds. This method, at least in principle, offers the chance to get a good grasp of the subject of enquiry in far-reaching detail, in particular with regard to the different levels of evidence, the handling of different types of data, and the interplay between structural components and process-related elements within institutional arrangements. Moreover, a careful testing of theory-guided propositions can also be accomplished by means of this particular research strategy. It has been widely acknowledged that it does not necessarily require purely quantitative statistical procedures to accomplish this task (Bryman 1988, pp. 172). Therefore, by turning to this research strategy the stage is set to investigate the enquiry's propositions in both a reliable and valid manner.

To adequately confront the enquiry's proposition with the empirical realities, this study needs to ensure a sufficient definition and operationalization of the variables included in the framework of analysis. Therefore, as will be outlined in more detail later, a case study protocol-type of document and a standardized data-request/ questionnaire with an operational set of measures was prepared with great care to direct the investigation of the subject of enquiry. In essence, the aim of introducing this guide is to secure not only the **reliability** but also the **construct validity** of this examination.

To make full use of a comparative methodology to analyze the theory-guided propositions, on the one hand, the research design needs to ensure that case studies have a variety of critical contextual factors in common. On the other hand, in order to be genuinely able to discover the most suitable organizational means for distributing mutual funds to private investors, the case studies should also exhibit a conceptually relevant variance with regard to the action variables conceptualized in the framework of analysis. Thus, a **purposeful selection** is needed (Wollmann 2000, p. 208). In other words, to examine how different institutional arrangements prove able to operate under common challenges, this enquiry will follow some form of **theoretical sampling** (Glaser und Strauss 1967, pp. 48). Therefore, while solely focusing on the relationships of asset management firms with distributing banks in the German private investor market in the period between the late 1990s and the end of 2004, **this enquiry intends to cover the spectrum of alternative institutional arrangements as proposed by Williamson (1991a, p. 281) [i.e., market, hybrid, and hierarchy]**.

With the employment of such a comparative research design and its underlying selection of case studies, the enquiry is then, at least in principle, in the position to infer causal explanations regarding the way in which solely the impact of varying action variables results in crucial effects on the dependent variables. By controlling contextual influences [to examine observed co-variations of action and dependent variables across multiple case studies from a theory-guided perspective], the purpose is to single out the most efficacious means or at least to reduce alternative explanations. Therefore, on the basis of identified patterns and rigorous logical reasoning in deriving stringent causal relations, this enquiry strives to ascertain at least the necessary conditions to achieve desired effects. Moreover, as such a research design provides the opportunity to apply a **mix of data collection methods** (Hellstern and Wollmann 1983, p. 97), it favors the creation of an adequate picture of the cases as a whole and the large number of variables. This is expected to further help the enquiry to substantiate connections between means and effects within the framework of analysis, which ultimately further strengthens the **internal validity** of this enquiry.

As far as the generalization of the analysis of the enquiry's proposition is concerned, this can only be of theoretical rather than of statistical kind (de Vaus 2001, p. 237). In contrast to research efforts which rely on random sampling in order to generalize their findings to the wider universe of cases, this specific empirical study is then mainly able to develop, to refine, and to test theory-guided propositions on how to optimally choose and design the institutional arrangement for the distribution function of mutual funds in Germany. Yet, as the selection of the case studies follows the conceivable range of alternative distribution systems observed in the German asset management sector, it seems reasonable to assume that at least to some degree the identified functional/ causal relations exhibit sufficient levels of **external validity** to be recommended as best- or better- practices. Therefore, by falling back on such a research design, the enquiry seems to be able not only to make evident "how" and "why" differently chosen and designed institutional arrangements produce variations in cash inflow streams but also to explain the relevance of these finding for practical purposes.

1.5 Significance of Enquiry

To highlight the significance and relevance of the question and objective pursued by this particular enquiry from both a theoretical and a pragmatic point of view, it needs to be taken into account that a large number of efforts most notably in the area of finance as well as in marketing have addressed a similar objective: that is the identification of powerful factors, which drive distribution performance of asset management firms[4]. Most of these studies have mainly focused on the properties of individual mutual funds or the characteristics of the product range to identify variables, which explain cash inflow streams. These variables are recognized to be of considerable relevance to accomplish strong distribution performance at the level of a mutual fund or for an asset management firm as a whole.

In this regard, taking a pure **capital market perspective**, Sirri and Tufano (1998, pp. 1595-1605) for the US market as well as Krahnen, Schmid, and Theissen (1997, p. 15) for the German market find a positive correlation between [high] past investment performance and the cash inflows into mutual funds, indicating that this dimension of product quality is critical for eventually explaining economic success of asset management firms. The relevance of past investment performance is also reflected in the positive effect of fund ratings on inflows (Del Guercio and Tkac 2000, pp. 29-31; Bergstresser and Poterba 2002, pp. 404-407). Along those lines, it is also shown that the size of a particular mutual fund in terms of the already accumulated AuM tends to provoke further inflow streams (Fant and O'Neal 2000, p. 370). As far as pricing aspects are concerned, the empirical findings are somewhat mixed. However, Barber, Odean, and Zheng (2005, pp. 2106-2107) show that there is a negative influence on net inflows when combining different price-components to the so-called total shareholder cost. From a more **marketing-oriented point of view**, by falling back on various attempts to [in]directly question private investors as to which factors [hypothetically] play a central role in their purchasing decision, the study by Bauer, Sauber, and Werbick (2002, pp. 17) shows the relevance of investment performance and also emphasizes the accentuated role of brand strengths and reputation. Moreover, Kaas and Schneider (2002, p. 8) incorporate the role of experts and their opinions in influencing the purchasing intentions of private investors.

All these efforts, and many more, have shed light on relevant factors impacting distribution performance levels from an analytical but also from a practical point of view. However, it becomes apparent that these studies to a large degree tend to rely on some rather closed [neoclassical] decision-making models. They implicitly tend to presume either perfect competition, perfect distribution of information, or clarity of preferences in order to ascertain the significant drivers of distribution performance levels, in other words – the purchasing behavior of private investors.

In strong contrast, in addressing the similar question on how to secure strong inflows **this empirical study from a paradigmatic standpoint adopts a substantially different perspective of enquiry**. With the application of NIE, this enquiry takes into account this concept's central claim that institutional arrangements need to be purposively structured to govern efficiently the social process of exchange. In other words, by acknowledging rather high levels of uncertainty, unclear preferences, bounded rationality, and even opportunistic tendencies, **this effort emphasizes the functional importance of the actual way of organizing economic activities**. Although these questions of how to organize coordination between economic actors enjoy somewhat growing attention in this

---

4 See Dechow (2003, pp. 9-40) for an extensive literature review of current efforts from a capital-market and

field of research, the role of organization in this service sector in securing strong operational performance has so far been largely ignored. Moreover, the few existing studies focus almost exclusively on the production function of the value chain for mutual funds. These investigate the effect of incentives and career opportunities for portfolio managers (Chevalier and Ellison 1997, pp. 1186-1197; 1999, pp. 429-431), of organizing portfolio management teams (Chen et al. 2004, pp. 1276), of the allocation of decision rights (Cashman and Deli 2004, pp. 23-24), and of firm boundaries (Chen, Hong and Kubik 2005, p. 34) on investment performance. This underlines that questions of how to arrange the distribution function from the perspective of product-providing asset management firms so far have remained untouched not only by scholars with a finance-related background but also by academics in the area of marketing.

From this view, it becomes strikingly apparent that this particular empirical study with its subject of enquiry is entering an area in which academic literature until now has stayed virtually silent. Speaking in NIE terms, **the functional role of organizing the distribution function in this particular service sector to accomplish strong performance levels has so far been treated as what is commonly referred to as a black-box**. Therefore, by addressing this contemporary problem and the derived question from an organizational perspective, the significance of this enquiry rests on the attempt to substantially illuminate this black-box in an analytically as well as practically relevant fashion. With the adoption of such a perspective of enquiry, this study aims to close the apparent, but so far unaddressed gap regarding organizational levers and requirements that trigger an improvement in cash inflow streams.

1.6 Process of Enquiry

The process of enquiry is illustrated in Figure 2. In **Chapter 2,** this enquiry first of all intends to identify the relevance of alternative conceptual approaches for the question and objective of this empirical study. The most adequate conceptual background in terms of explanatory as well as practical relevance is then selected and applied for the derivation of the enquiry's framework of analysis. This discussion on the framework of

marketing-orientated perspective of enquiry.

analysis covers not only a detailed conceptualization of the different variables but also the derivation of refutable propositions with which the subject of enquiry will be investigated. This chapter concludes with an elaboration on the applied methodology, clarifying the sampling, the data collection, and the data processing.

After having outlined the concept and methodology for optimizing distribution systems, **Chapter 3** will introduce the asset management sector in some more detail. The focus is on highlighting recent developments in the German asset management sector, which are of relevance for the enquiry's optimization problem. This will be followed by a short introduction of the value chain for mutual funds, thereby outlining the activities along the major steps for producing and marketing mutual funds to private investors and the typical organizational setup in Germany. The underlying purpose of this chapter to bring forward the global characteristics of the contingency factors conceptualized in the enquiry's framework of analysis.

With a common understanding of the concept, the methodology, and the asset management sector, in **Chapter 4** this empirical study will turn to the comparative institutional analysis by examining the three case studies selected strategically. In line with the structure of the framework of analysis, for each case study this enquiry will first elaborate on the decision concerning the choice of the institutional arrangement. This is laying the ground for illuminating the design of the institutional arrangements in terms of the systemic configuration and the process-related measures before eventually coming to a more integrated assessment of the efficacy of choice and design with respect to the target variables. This chapter will conclude with a summary of the case studies highlighting the key properties from a comparative perspective along the single variables conceptualized in the framework of analysis.

These insights will then be applied in **Chapter 5** towards the identification of an optimized distribution system. In this chapter, the enquiry will produce answers to the research questions regarding the optimal choice and design of institutional arrangements for marketing mutual funds to private investors in Germany. Based on these results, the enquiry is then able to adequately address its propositions, thereby clarifying the relative importance of the different fit requirements for distribution systems. This final chapter will end with the theoretical implications of this enquiry.

Fig. 2: THE PROCESS OF ENQUIRY

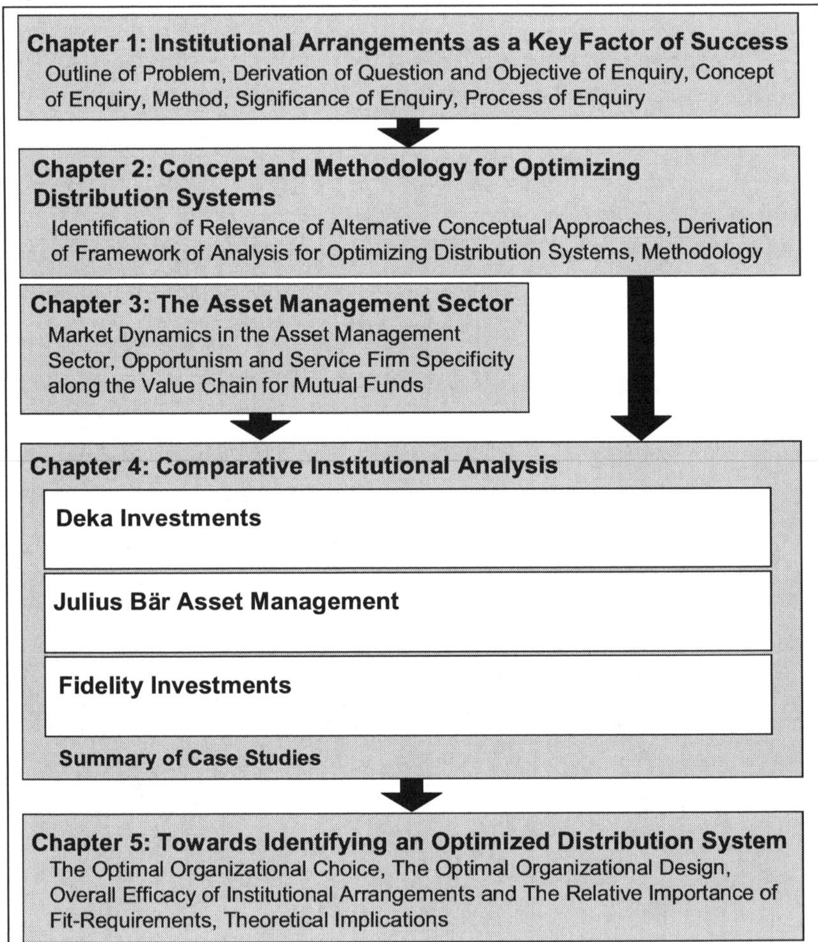

Source: Author

Chapter 2: Concept and Methodology for Optimizing Distribution Systems

Asset management firms face a complex relationship problem when they market their mutual funds to private investors through distributing intermediaries, most notably via banks. As outlined above, a move away from rather high control arrangements to enjoy the advantages of decentralization has been accompanied by substantial impediments and disappointments. Management science at large and research efforts particularly in the area of marketing frequently address these practical relationship challenges from a normative perspective to clarify the way in which organizational choice and design secure efficiency and ultimately economic success. In this regard, the challenges facing asset management firms at large can be rephrased as an optimization problem of how to minimize inefficient issues of coordination and motivation in order to achieve desired distribution performance levels.

However, there can be no denying that for this problem of choosing and designing distribution systems there is no such thing as one universal, optimal solution (Kieser and Welgenbach 2003, p. 43; Drazin and Van de Ven 1985, p. 514). Instead, to identify normative guidelines requires an analysis of the situation confronting asset management firms. Given this call for a contingency approach, to be elaborated in more detail later, this **enquiry then has to regard the relationships between asset management firms and banks as systems**, which need to be carefully managed with regard to the external environment but also internally in terms of structure and processes to secure aspired performance outcomes (Staehle 1999, pp. 48). In more substantive terms, this essentially highlights that asset management firms will need to adequately take into account situation-specific demands when choosing whether to increasingly turn to advanced degrees of decentralization or alternatively to primarily fall back on more integrated systems. Based on their choice, they then also have to design the relationship accordingly in order to enhance distribution performance in terms of net inflows.

In view of this subject of enquiry, a theoretical concept is required that provides best possible ways to establish a thorough understanding of this choice and design problem with all its facets. Furthermore, it has to provide adequate means-effect relations and assessment criteria to allow a systematic analysis of the decision-making problem, thereby offering propositions not only on when but also how a transition to more open distribution systems for mutual funds can lead to a sustained increase of distribution performance levels. By doing so, this enquiry is in a position to outline in sufficient detail that for this move to be successful it requires the adjustment of existing or the putting in place of alternative control and steering measures to minimize potential coordination hazards. Hence, to be able to adopt a contingency approach to appropriately pursue the enquiry's objective, the **selection of the theoretical concepts is based on their relative explanatory and practical relevance in dealing with the stated problem and question**.

Against these requirements, in the upcoming section the relevance of alternative conceptual approaches will be scrutinized. As will be explained now in more depth, an integrated background of concepts underlying NIE appears to be particularly adequate to address the enquiry's question and objective. It allows a detailed coverage of the peculiarities and implications of alternative organizational choices and designs for controlling potential hazards. In line with demands of the analytical philosophy of science (Hollis 1994, pp. 56), **this selected theoretical background is then applied to guide the construction of a framework of analysis**, which demarcates the study's focus. Based on the conceptually derived means-effect relations, it lays the ground for producing propositions on how to optimally choose and design distribution systems in this service sector to enjoy the potential benefits of decentralization. Moreover, these questions concerning the conceptual background and the framework need to be expanded by the question regarding the most adequate methodology to genuinely meet the objective of this enquiry. Therefore, this chapter will conclude by outlining how a comparative multi-case study approach with a selection of strategically relevant cases puts this enquiry in the position to appropriately tackle the central choice and design problem confronting asset management firms.

2.1 Identification of Relevance of Alternative Conceptual Approaches

A wide range of conceptual approaches has been applied to describe the current situation regarding distribution systems in the asset management sector. Therefore, it is more than reasonable to scrutinize which of these approaches is most adequate in dealing with the choice and design problem facing asset management firms. To illustrate the explanatory as well as the practical relevance of NIE, first of all two alternative approaches, namely Game Theory and Resource-Based-View-Theory will be discussed, before the core concepts of NIE are introduced in more detail to accentuate the pertinence of this specific perspective of enquiry.

2.1.1 Game Theory

With the purpose of describing the current status of third-party distribution across Europe, Promothee (2002, p. 35) refers to the **"Prisoners' Dilemma"** in order to stress the severe consequences of **limited cooperation within the relationship between asset management firms and distributors**. Such a framing of the present situation indicates that the problem with respect to the distribution of mutual funds to private investors can possibly be studied by applying the apparatus of Game Theory.

Game Theory deals with decision-making problems in situations of strategic interdependence, meaning that decision-makers who are motivated by self-interest need to take other parties' behavior into consideration when choosing their own course of action. Thus, the outcome from any decision is, in general, affected by the action of others. The main objective of a game theoretical analysis is to identify as well as to investigate the Nash Equilibrium of the game, which constitutes a stable outcome in which no single player wants to reconsider its choice, as each player's strategy is regarded as the best response.

A distinctive characteristic and key advantage of a game-theoretical approach is that it allows for the translation of complex issues into a rather simple setting of payoffs. This substantially facilitates the modeling of complicated strategic choice situations with the intention of deriving efficient coordination patterns among participants, thereby offering predictions and solutions for playing the game. Hence, it is not surprising to see that such approaches have been widely adopted (Jost 2001a; Dixit and Nalebuff 1991) to explain the evolution of cooperative arrangements under which the parties involved are better off than before.

Fig. 3: PAY-OFF MATRIX OF THE PRISONERS' DILEMMA

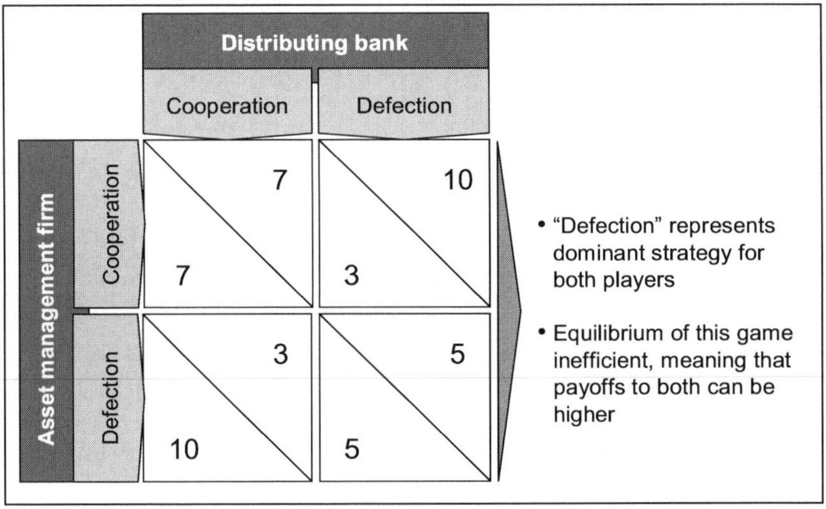

Source: Author

Within the area of non-cooperative Game Theory, the "Prisoners' Dilemma" is one of the most famous and studied strategic games. It refers to a situation in which each player pursues its dominant strategy, implying the optimal choice no matter what the counterpart does, but still ends up with an outcome that is both sub-optimal and inefficient. Figure 3 depicts the pay-off matrix often used to describe a game involving two players, with each of them having the choice between two strategies, namely "cooperation" and "defection". They will take their decisions simultaneously without any possibility of setting up a binding agreement or any other form of cooperative interaction. Moreover, the game is only played once. The dilemma is that both players will regard it optimal to choose "defection", which is the Nash Equilibrium, although the payoff is higher for both if they could somehow reach the cooperative outcome of the game. Thus, when this specific type of game is employed to describe the relationship situation between asset management firms and distributors, it indicates that in fact both could be better off if they reconsidered their strategic choices.

With respect to the suitability of a game theoretical approach for this particular enquiry, it is interesting to find that Milgrom and Roberts (1992, p. 138) apply the "Prisoners' Dilemma" to illustrate relationship problems arising from uncooperative behavior within the interaction between players. As far as recommendations are concerned to overcome this dilemma, Axelrod (2005, pp. 25) shows that by enlarging the shadow of the future, meaning that the interaction between the parties is repeated an infinite number of times, a cooperative outcome becomes a sustainable solution despite the assumed self-interest of players. The so-called "tit-for-tat" strategy prescribes "cooperation" as long as the other player cooperates but "defection" as soon as the other party deviates from "cooperation". By doing what the opponent chose the previous round, the "tit-for-tat" strategy provides the opportunity to punish as well as to forgive. As it never initiates defection, this guideline is recognized as a viable mechanism to induce cooperation, thereby offering and potentially reinforcing trust between exchange partners.

From this short elaboration on Game Theory, it shows that this theoretical perspective can model the relationship challenge as well as the decision-making problem facing asset management firms, insofar as it is capable of identifying and outlining the strategic choices available to asset management firms. As such, it strengthens the comprehension of the interactive character of this decision-making problem. Moreover, Game Theory appreciates the important role of trust-building measures to stimulate cooperative and, thus, efficient outcomes.

However, it also shows that a game-theoretical approach is not sufficiently sophisticated to cover the peculiarities of this specific decision-making problem. As Sydow (1992, pp. 169-171) outlines, Game Theory is not capable of fully acknowledging the dependencies within relationship structures. Apart from defining certain sequences within the interaction of the game, a further consideration of elements of power has not been conceptualized yet. Moreover, although the identity of players and their reputation regarding cooperation, as well as further interaction outside the actual game is starting to earn more recognition in game-theoretical approaches (Hill 1990, p. 505; Schrader 1993, p. 247), this background does not shed light on concrete steering measures for purposively coordinating activities. This highlights that a game-theoretical discussion is severely restricted in scope when approaching this central choice and design problem facing asset management firms. In line with this argument, North (1995, p. 20) summarizes that while Game Theory is an essential tool in helping to specify the problem at stake, it does not, however, tell players how to actively achieve [cooperative] results. Therefore, the focus of guidelines offered will be limited to the order of play, potential payoffs to parties as well as degrees of information sharing, implying that this conceptual approach is not sufficiently complex to produce the practically relevant guidelines required.

In summary, this theory is not sophisticated enough to advance an adequate handling of the choice and design problem. A game-theoretical examination can neither fully address the different dimensions underlying the relevant decision-making problem nor offer the much sought, detailed guidelines on how to purposefully control for potential relationship hazards. In other words, in the light of the problem and the optimizing objective of this enquiry, **Game Theory is only of limited explanatory relevance and lacks sufficient practical relevance**.

2.1.2 Resource-Based View

Another very appealing approach to analyze the current situation in the asset management sector concerning the distribution of mutual funds to private investors is the resource-based or capabilities-based view of the firm (RBV). It has its roots in the work of Penrose (1959) and Wernerfelt (1984) and addresses the fundamental question in the field of strategic management of "how firms achieve and sustain competitive advantage" (Teece, Pisano, and Shuen 1997, p. 509).

The RBV offers a perspective on when a firm will integrate activities and under which circumstances it sources these activities via the market. In general, this approach argues that **the reason an activity is conducted within the firm is not market failure**

but rather firm success (Madhok 2002, p. 536). This success, in other words, the competitive advantage a firm enjoys strongly depends on the strategic resources and capabilities it has access to. As Barney (1991, pp. 105-112) outlines, for resources and capabilities to be strategically relevant and, thus, to underpin a sustained competitive advantage, they need to be valuable, rare, imperfectly imitable, and difficult to substitute. In terms of a guideline for optimal degrees of decentralization, RBV proposes that firms will keep those activities in-house for which they have the strategic core competences (Prahalad and Hamel 1990, pp. 80), whereas they will attempt to outsource those parts of the value chain where they lack the strategically relevant capabilities.

Productive capabilities depend not only on the investments made in production factors such as equipment and personnel, but more importantly on tacit elements, in terms of the coordination of activities, the generation and transimisson of knowledge, and the development and learning of routines (Kogut and Zander 1996, pp. 507-510). As these soft factors evolve through individual path-dependent learning, they tend to lead to a significant degree of heterogeneity in productive capabilities not only across firms but also along stages of the value chain within firms.

This heterogeneity in turn constitutes a major factor in boundary decisions. For example, Jacobides and Hitt (2005, pp. 1219-1222) find in their empirical investigation of the mortgage banking industry that these banks are substantially heterogeneous, as each of them constitutes a unique bundle of resources and capabilities. They detect that this heterogeneity in capabilities drives the observed adaptive processes in this industry to optimize respective degrees of vertical integration. Latent gains from trade across firm boundaries along the different stages of the production process, in addition to the opportunity to enjoy benefits from specialization, induce firms to concentrate on those activities for which they possess superior capabilities. Therefore, taking on a RBV perspective, it is this difference in capabilities between firms that is recognized as the key determinant with respect to the optimal degree of vertical integration.

It is fair to claim that – similar to the mortgage banking sector – in the asset management sector significant differences in skills and knowledge exist as well, not only across firms but also along the two broad stages (i.e., production and distribution function) of the value chain for mutual funds. Bearing this in mind, the RBV perspective and its optimizing rule could then serve as an interesting approach to explain the emergence of new, more open distribution patterns in the asset management sector as moves to expand the pie of mutual benefits (Jap 1999, pp. 461). Yet, the question of this enquiry is not whether the increasing unbundling of activities along the value chain in the asset management sector can be explained in terms of attempts to realize competitive advantage. Instead, the objective is to clarify which choice and design of distribution arrangements is optimal in order to minimize inefficiencies resulting from encountered coordination and motivation problems. In this regard, as Conner and Prahalad (1996, pp. 482-484) argue, the competence perspective on boundary decisions of firms neglects inefficiencies due to relationship hazards. However, as already indicated, product-providing asset management firms are facing the apparent danger of limited willingness and commitment as well as rent expropriation on the part of [external] distributors. Thus, the application of a RBV perspective means that these latent challenges are not taken into account appropriately, which in turn indicates that RBV propositions are not adequate to deal with the specific problem at hand.

Moreover, Argyres (1996, p. 129) emphasizes that, unlike the NIE logic, the capabilities approach as yet cannot generate empirical predictions. Along these lines, Williamson (1998, p. 47) points out that RBV is preoccupied with ex-post rationalization of success. In other words, when falling back on such a theoretical perspective, this effort would only be able to provide a rationale as to why asset management firms and distributing banks have adopted new, less-integrated arrangements. However, it looks as if RBV would neither help to establish a sufficiently deep understanding of the different facets of the problem nor put the enquiry in a position to produce the intended practically relevant guidelines to the optimization problem at stake. Therefore, it seems that the application of a RBV approach would not facilitate an appropriate modeling of both the key dependent variable and the concrete design of the relationship. In other words, given the choice and designing problem and the objective of this enquiry, **RBV[5] lacks not only the required explanatory but also the practical relevance.**

2.1.3 New Institutional Economics

In the light of the decision-making problem confronting asset management firms, this enquiry aims at clarifying which of the emerging organizational forms for the distribution function can be recommended as the best possible means to secure operative growth in terms of net inflows while controlling for lurking coordination and motivation hazards. Given the recent trends in the asset management sector, the main area of interest is to find out which of the various ways to respond to the breakup of the hitherto highly integrated structures for marketing mutual funds into somewhat more decentralized systems is to be considered as most beneficial in generating strong distribution performance. To ensure these choice and design decisions are adequately conceptualized from a scientific point of view, it is essential to get a comprehensive grip of all the various types of [cognitive and motivational] challenges that occur when engaging in some more disintegrated relationships. Moreover, the perspective of enquiry needs to allow the production of propositions about which distribution system to choose and eventually how to optimally design the relationship to the distributing banks. Simply speaking, a theoretical approach is needed that favors an appropriate examination of choice and designing decisions made by asset management firms in terms of a fruitful framework of analysis.

As already indicated, the theoretical approaches of NIE offer the conceptual means to adequately address the problem and objective of this particular enquiry. As Wolff (2005) demonstrates, NIE is very much able to present explanations as well as to offer actionable guidelines on how to adjust distribution systems in a move towards more

---

5 Nevertheless, the once fiercely competing conceptual approaches have started to converge to some extent. While RBV scholars, for example Barney (1999, p. 143) and Jacobides and Winter (2005, p. 396), grant transaction costs the status of a moderating effect on decisions concerning vertical integration, NIE scholars, most notably Williamson (1999, p. 1103), recommend that the traditional TCE query, "What is the best generic mode (market, hybrid, firm) to organize X" be replaced by the question "How should firm A – which has pre-existing strengths and weaknesses (core competences and disabilities) – organize X?" Jacobides and Winter (2005, pp. 409) even go so far as to argue that transaction costs are catalysts in changing vertical scope. Along these lines, the explanatory relevance of NIE for this particular enquiry is affirmed even from the RBV point of view.

decentralized structures in order to enjoy the aspired levels of efficiency. Turning to NIE[6] now in more detail, it is essential to point out that it is not an integrated theory construction as it comprises a wide range of sometimes overlapping, sometimes complementing, and sometimes competing theoretical approaches. The three core concepts[7] of NIE as illustrated in Figure 4 are the principal-agent-theory (PA), the theory of transaction cost economics (TCE)[8], and property-rights-theory (RPT).

Fig. 4: OVERVIEW OF CORE CONCEPTS UNDERLYING NEW INSTITUTIONAL ECONOMICS

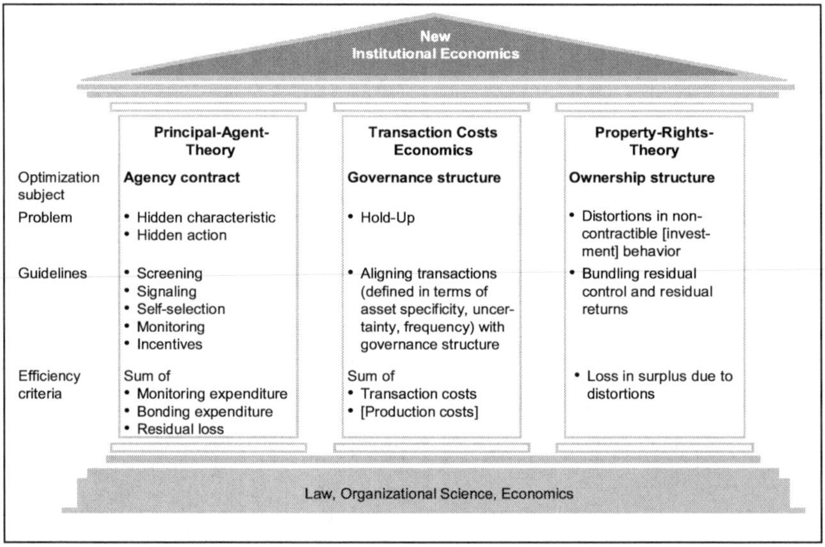

Source: Author

6 For a comprehensive discussion on these concepts of NIE, see Ebers and Gotsch (1999).

7 All three core concepts rest on methodological individualism, meaning that the findings, explanations, solutions, and propositions will be formulated in terms of goals, plans and actions of individual actors (Klein 1999, p. 457).

8 In particular TCE and PA have received a great deal of attention in the marketing literature that examines relationships between manufacturing and distributing units. For a comprehensive literature review, see Bergen, Dutta and Walker (1992), Shelanski and Klein (1995), Rindfleisch and Heide (1997), Boerner and Macher (2001).

As Wolff (1999, pp. 138-141) summarizes, all three concepts of NIE act on two very essential assumptions ascribed to behavioral attributes of economic actors:

- First of all, economic actors are presumed to be limited in their cognitive ability to plan for all likely contingencies in the future and to deal with the complexity and unpredictability of the world around them. The key implication of this **bounded rationality** (Simon 1959, p. 24) for studying institutional arrangements is that all complex contracts are unavoidably incomplete.
- On the other hand, economic actors are expected to engage in **opportunistic behavior** when it is in their interest and when given the chance to do so. Opportunism may take various forms and may occur at different points of time in the course of organizing economic activity. Simply speaking, it is viewed as "self-interest seeking with guile" (Williamson 1985, p. 47).

In the view of the simultaneous presence of bounded rationality and opportunism, different forms of relationship hazards are likely to emerge which tend to give rise to significant inefficiencies in economic activity. These may emerge as real costs but also in the form of opportunity costs in terms of valuable deals that are not done (Ghosh and John 1999, p. 134).

In this regard, although assuming slightly different perspectives, each of the three conceptual approaches of NIE offers guidelines to alleviate inefficiencies stemming from bounded rationality and opportunistic tendencies. As will be seen, these concepts go hand in hand to address the different motivation and coordination issues within economic interaction (Picot, Reichwald and Wigang 2003, pp. 38). Thus, already at first glance, NIE and its theoretical approaches appear most suitable as the conceptual background for the framework of analysis to be derived. Nevertheless, it still needs to be scrutinized in more detail as to why and in which way these approaches are able to frame the relationship issues as a decision-making problem as well as to produce actionable guidelines on how to solve the optimization problem. Along those lines, when introducing these core concepts, the intention is not to present an exhaustive literature review, but to point out why this integrated theoretical background is most appropriate for the subsequent conceptualization of the framework of analysis.

2.1.3.1 Principal-Agent-Theory

The PA has been successfully applied to analyze bilateral relationships in various fields. In the area of marketing, PA has provided an adequate frame to address relevant issues such as sales-force management and channel coordination (Jost 2001b; Bergen, Dutta and Walker 1992). According to Jensen and Meckling (1976, p. 308), agency relationships are defined as a contract under which one or more persons [the principal] engage another person [the agent] to perform some services on their behalf, which involves delegating some decision-making authority to the agent. Whenever one individual depends on the action of another, an agency relationship arises. In line with this perspective, Krauss (2004, pp. 50-51) describes **the interaction between asset management firms and distributors as an agency-relationship**. As Göbel (2002, p. 322) outlines, a number of different general perspectives are feasible regarding the relationship between product provider, distributing intermediaries, and end customers. Following this enquiry's perspective, **it is the asset management firm that is considered as the principal** that delegates the distribution activities to banks to sell mutual funds to private investors, while banks assume the role of agents.

The key objective of this conceptual approach is to pinpoint to the **most efficient contract to organize the specific relationship**. In general, efficiency is defined rather from the principal's perspective. Thus, the optimal contractual arrangement focuses quite extensively on the principal's objective to create the **appropriate incentive structure that induces the agent to advance the principal's interest**. However, the agent's preferences also need to be taken into account to appropriately motivate the agent to make choices, which will maximize the principal's welfare (Jensen and Meckling 1976, pp. 308-310). Hence, the efficiency criteria of **agency costs** are defined as the **sum of [monitoring] expenditures by the principal, [bonding] expenditures by the agent, and the residual loss**.

When designing the appropriate incentive structure to adequately motivate the agent, the principal needs to be aware of a variety of factors that complicate the designing of the optimal contract. Firstly, while the **principal** and the **agent** both pursue their own self-interest, they **commonly have diverging and conflicting goals**. Furthermore,

information regarding the characteristics, the quality, the behavior, and the performance of agents **tends to be asymmetrically distributed between principal and agent**. Typically, this is information the agent has. For the principal, however, it is either difficult and, thus, costly or even impossible to obtain (Barzel 1982, pp. 28). Moreover, in the light of **environmental uncertainty**, meaning that the outcomes of economic activity are beyond the full control of either principal or agent, both differ in their attitude towards risk. Whereas the principal is presumed to have the opportunity to diversify investments and is, therefore, regarded as rather risk-neutral, agents commonly are viewed as risk-averse and prefer some form of insurance against variations in their compensation. Last but not least, this environmental uncertainty also complicates the performance measurement of agents.

In this respect, it is of remarkable importance that the asset management sector is in fact a **prominent example of a service sector**. Establishing transparency of distribution efforts by turning to some performance measurement is already cumbersome as activities along the entire value chain for mutual funds, most notably the distribution function to private investors, can be best described in terms of intangibility, limited process standardization, outcome-induced quality, and the great pertinence of the integration of the external factor (Corsten 2001, p. 6). Environmental uncertainty then tends to aggravate the information asymmetry between the asset management firm and the distributing banks even further.

The presence of these complicating factors may give rise to two specific issues within the relationship between principal and agent:

- the hidden characteristic problem and
- the hidden action problem.

As will be outlined, these challenges in general need to be adequately addressed in order to reach an optimal decision for the choice and design of institutional arrangements, since they are indeed part of the relationship problems facing asset management firms.

The **hidden characteristic problem**, mainly associated with the work of Akerloff (1970, pp. 489) and his analysis of the market for "lemons", constitutes a problem that emerges due to prevailing **information asymmetries before the principal enters into a contractual agreement with an agent**. To be more specific, the principal lacks critical information to accurately evaluate the agent's qualification and motivation that are relevant for performing the delegated activity. Driven by self-interest, the agent may be reserved in sharing the relevant information or even attempt to send false information. As a consequence, the principal might be in the unfavorable position of selecting an unsuitable or unwilling agent. This risk of adverse selection, in turn, dramatically jeopardizes the realization of the principal's objectives.

When comparing this specific issue of PA with the impediments in the interaction between asset management firms and distributor, it is evident that the former are most likely exposed to this threat of asymmetric information. Hence, the solution mechanisms of PA are of great relevance to asset management firms when setting up optimal distribution systems to avoid or at least to ease the aftermath of this hidden characteristic problem before entering into a relationship. In general, at least three avenues are available in order to overcome this issue arising from information asymmetry:

- First of all, the principal may engage in some form of screening as an information-collecting effort to enhance the verification of the agent's qualification or motivation. Wathne and Heide (2004, p. 75) argue that these **screening** or qualification programs solve this specific issue as they facilitate the selection of suitable agents which are identified as more capable, more cooperative or less opportunistically inclined given the particular task. Although these screening activities may be very costly, they can still represent the most appropriate solution, particularly when differences in characteristics yield substantial variations in performance across agents and, thus, potentially have a significant effect on the resulting outcome for the principal (Bergen, Dutta and Walker 1992, p. 6).
- A second solution mechanism to master the risk of adverse selection is to establish a setting in which it is to the benefit of agents who own certain desirable capabilities to actively engage in some form of **signaling** (Spence 1973, pp. 358-368) that they possess the attributes the principal is looking for. This requires that signaling brings about advantages that the agents cannot otherwise receive,

thereby meeting the criteria of individual rationality. However, in order to accomplish the intended separation between capable and incapable agents, this signal must be significantly more costly for incapable agents than for capable agents. In other words, the costs of signaling for incapable agents must exceed the benefits, while for capable agents these benefits need to outweigh their costs. In more analytical terms, such a setting must be incentive-compatible not only for agents with the desired attributes to engage in signaling, but equally important also for the undesirable agents to refrain from it (Kirmani and Rao 2000, p. 68). Under the circumstance of such a separating equilibrium, the principal is then able to accurately identify those agents suitable for the activity.

- As a third solution mechanism to deal with the issue of opportunism, principals may offer agents opportunities for **self-selection** (Lal and Staelin 1986, pp. 189-192). Simply speaking, a principal may offer the agent a choice from a variety of different contractual arrangements. By making a choice, agents passively reveal their willingness to cooperate or their ability to perform the task. In this way, the principal has the chance to select the most suitable agents from a range of alternatives.

As the hidden characteristic problem generally faces asset management firms in their attempts to optimize distribution systems, these practical propositions of PA exhibit sufficient relevance to be taken into account in the development of a framework of analysis to appropriately address the enquiry's question and objective.

As is known, in contrast to the hidden characteristic problem, the **hidden action problem**, which is also commonly referred to as the problem of moral hazard (Holmstrom 1979, pp. 74), emerges **due to information asymmetry after the principal has delegated some activity**. In the light of the general assumption of divergent interest between principal and agent, this particular relationship problem describes situations in which the agent by pursuing their own interests shirks actions the principal would like the agent to perform. Due to environmental uncertainty, such aberrant behavior may remain undetected, as the principal faces considerable impediments in determining whether the agent has chosen a course of action that, in fact, deviates from the principal's objectives.

As in any other agency relationship, it is reasonable to argue that the hidden action problem also looms in the relationship between asset management firms and distributing banks. When asset management firms delegate the distribution activities for mutual funds to banks, they face substantial obstacles because of the general characteristics of the service activities in accurately assessing whether these intermediaries are actually behaving in their interests. Moreover, both parties are expected to have different goals. For example, consider a relationship in which the asset management firm may solely be interested in maximizing the revenue stream for its mutual fund offering, while at the same time the distributing bank will probably be more inclined to optimize the total revenue stream of its sales operations for a variety of financial services. This realistic situation in which the distributing intermediary is working on behalf of multiple principals and, thus, performs multiple tasks accentuates the likely presence of the hidden action problem. In this view, the guidelines of PA on how to overcome this type of opportunism tend to gain the greatest practical relevance to asset management firms.

Simply speaking, PA proposes that principals fall back on monitoring activities complemented by the deployment of incentive schemes (Wathne and Heide 2000, pp. 43-45). **Monitoring** potentially reduces the information asymmetry between two parties (Lal 1990, pp. 305; Stump and Heide 1996, p. 433) and, thereby, allows the principal to **match rewards and sanctions as part of the incentive system** to the agent's behavior in appropriate ways. These incentive systems, also referred to as self-enforcing agreements (Telser 1980, p. 27), aim to align interests by making the long-term gains from cooperation exceed the short-term payoff from opportunism. Therefore, as monitoring increases the probability of detecting opportunistic behavior, these efforts are expected to bring about a reduction in these tendencies. With respect to the focus of monitoring efforts, Celly and Frazier (1996, p. 201) show that different approaches are available to overcome this negative side effect of delegating activities:

- On the one hand, the principal may take actions to set up monitoring processes that involve information-gathering on **the agent's behavior**. With such processes implemented, the principal is in a position to establish a contract that specifies how the agent will be compensated based on the behavior observed. However, collecting this type of information may be either extremely cost-intensive or even simply impossible.

- The monitoring process and the corresponding contract design alternatively may primarily rely on observations of **performance outcomes** to address problems of moral hazards in their agency-relationship. In this way, the principal evaluates and rewards the agent's input based on the achieved output. Such incentive contracts, which meet the criteria of individual rationality and incentive compatibility, may essentially align the principal's objectives with the agent's interests, thereby overcoming the inherent motivation problem.

Yet, in consideration of the assumed environmental uncertainty, any link between unobservable actions and the monitored outcomes is imperfect. The most critical question from the principal's point of view is then to ascertain how much of the observable outcome is due to the agent's effort and how much is due to factors beyond the agent's control. At the same time, this process of inducing the desired cooperative behavior means that agents tend to be significantly exposed to random and uncontrollable factors. In the light of the assumed risk-aversion of agents, any transfer of risk from the principal to the agent, who by the introduction of outcome-based contracts unavoidably takes place, becomes costly for the principal. Hence, **the heart of this problem is to define an incentive contract design that secures an efficient trade-off between the costs associated with transferring risk and the likelihood of shirking**.

All in all, as hidden action problems tend to explain a facet of the relationship issues asset management firms face in their relationships with distributing intermediaries, propositions of PA regarding channel monitoring and associated designs of incentive schemes turn out to be of considerable practical relevance. From this view, it appears that these guidelines cannot be ignored when conceptualizing the enquiry's framework of analysis. Therefore, it seems that PA [in terms of assumptions, problems, core arguments, and proposition] displays the required explanatory as well as practical relevance to put this enquiry in a position to establish a good grasp of the decision-making problem at hand as well as to offer actionable guidelines on how to end up with optimal institutional arrangements for the distribution function.[9]

Although PA will play an important role when developing the framework of analysis, this conceptual approach falls short in appropriately taking into account the coordination aspects underlying the choice and design problem. Clearly, PA offers propositions on how to design the relationships to overcome specific types of opportunistic tendencies when delegating activities. However, this theoretical perspective does not clarify whether the recommended measures will need to be put in place in a hierarchically organized setting or whether their implementation is best secured in decentralized governance structures. As Klein (1999, p. 466) notes, the conceptualization of the firm as a particular governance structure for coordinating economic activity is not the subject of attention in the agency literature. Concluding from this, PA alone is not sufficient to exhaustively solve the optimizing choice and design problem confronting asset management firms. Insofar as asset management firms frequently have to cope with relationship hazards once specific investments are sunk in support of the transaction with distributors, this enquiry will clearly need to consider propositions offered by TCE. Hence, as will now be elaborated, the theoretical perspective of TCE will also play an important role when establishing the enquiry's framework of analysis.

2.1.3.2 Transaction Cost Economics

TCE, originally developed by Williamson (1975) and Klein, Crawford, and Alchian (1978) as the study of alternative institutions of governance, has been applied extensively and very successfully to examine choices and designs of institutional arrangements for the purpose of securing an efficient coordination of economic operations. As a basic insight of this theoretical concept, it is increasingly accepted that "transactions must be governed, and that certain institutional arrangements effect this

---

9 To pursue a more elaborated discussion of these various motivation issues underlying the central choice and design problem, the positive branch of PA in particular will be of great interest. Not only does it afford insights into the various avenues available to motivate agents, but this theoretical perspective has also tended to adopt the assumption that agents are rather risk-neutral than risk-averse, which is more appropriate to this specific enquiry. It seems reasonable to expect that asset management firms and distribution banks have a similar attitude towards risk and, in that respect, deal with each other on parity (Williamson 1998, p. 30).

governance better than others" (Shelanski and Klein 1995, p. 336). This conceptual approach regards governance as a means to induce order and, thereby mitigate conflict and realize mutual gains (Williamson 2002, p. 180).

Over the last 25 years, TCE has become an important theoretical paradigm in marketing. Its reasoning has been exploited extensively and its adequacy is widely accepted, particularly with respect to questions on the integration of distribution activities (John and Weitz 1988; Klein, Frazier and Roth 1990). As Anderson (1988, pp. 258-261) shows, taking a TCE perspective is remarkably suitable in investigating firms' decisions about when to fall back on an integrated distribution structure and when to use decentralized arrangements to market products.

In general, the objective of TCE is to identify the **optimal governance structure**, from a set of feasible institutional alternatives, which offers protection against opportunistic behavior at the lowest total cost. According to the classic TCE argumentation, boundary decisions are determined by relative costs of organizing transactions under alternative arrangements. More specifically, the optimal vertical organization is the one that minimizes the sum of technical and agency inefficiency (Williamson 1991b, p. 75). Decisions regarding the choice and design of institutional arrangements not only have to take into account the costs of initiating, negotiating, executing, supervising, and adapting governance arrangements, generally referred to as transaction costs, but also production costs. This shows that based on comparative cost considerations, this conceptual approach offers propositions to make-or-buy decisions, thereby addressing the famous question: why are there firms when there are markets? Underlining this normative character of TCE, Noordewier, John, and Nevin (1990, p. 80) argue that firms which follow prescriptions of TCE have in fact better performance [from lower costs] than those that do not adhere. **While the classic TCE underlying NIE focuses exclusively on a comparative cost perspective, alternative criteria have been frequently introduced and applied to pinpoint the optimal institutional arrangement**. In this regard, for example, Picot and Hardt (1998, p. 632) emphasize the strategic relevance, while Held and Nutzinger (2003, p. 129) highlight the importance of preserving norms to identify superior institutional arrangements.

These properties of TCE already indicate at this point its relevance to the optimization problem confronting asset management firms. In the course of deliberately introducing new distribution systems, implying the adoption of refined degrees of decentralization, asset management firms have encountered severe relationship problems. In the face of these experiences, asset management firms are now seeking guidelines on how to adjust their distribution systems to adequately deal with these substantial coordination and motivation issues. From this view, to outline the relevance of TCE to the enquiry's question and objective in more depth, a deeper understanding of the TCE reasoning and its practical guidelines is essential.

As far as the core argument is concerned, this theoretical approach of NIE argues that the optimal mode of governance is contingent upon the characteristics of the transaction to be governed. Three attributes are of substantial significance when describing the key unit of analysis of TCE (Williamson 1985, pp. 52-61):

- The most recognized attribute for the choice of institutional arrangements is the degree to which relationship-specific assets are involved in the underlying transaction. **Asset specificity** is defined as durable investments that are undertaken in support of particular transactions. These assets cannot be redeployed to another transaction without some sacrifice in their productivity and subsequently in their value, or additional costs are required to adapt them to new circumstances. In other words, once investments are made in relationship-specific assets they can reasonably be regarded as sunk. Generally six categories of asset specificity can be distinguished: specialized physical assets, specialized human assets, site specificity, dedicated assets, brand name capital, and temporal specificity.
- The second transactional attribute that is of pertinence to the choice of institutional arrangements is referred to as **uncertainty** (disturbances) as it gives rise to adaptive needs within the relationship. Besides behavioral uncertainty, parties to the transaction are exposed to environmental uncertainty as well (Walker and Weber 1984, p. 374).
- The third attribute to bear in mind is the **frequency** with which the transaction recurs.

In a world of incomplete contracts and the tendency towards self-interested behavior with guile, these transactional attributes, and most notably asset specificity, lead to the latent danger of the so-called hold-up problem. As Klein, Crawford, and Alchian (1978, pp. 298-299) outline, if the threat of being held up by the exchange partner is not adequately accounted for in the choice decision, it tends to lead to inefficient under-investment problems. In more detail, the hold-up problem represents an issue that arises after parties have entered into a relationship and investments with high specificity to support the interaction are sunk. As these specific investments, in general, yield significantly higher productivity relative to general purpose investments, they exhibit positive quasi-rents. This, in turn, entices exchange partners to engage in activities to appropriate those rents from their trading partners. Thus, in the face of incomplete contracts and subsequently imperfect protection, parties who lock themselves in by sinking their investment in relationship-specific assets are becoming increasingly vulnerable to being exploited. These investments that fundamentally transform the relationship from a "large numbers" bidding situation to a "small numbers" bargaining situation (Williamson 1996, pp. 16-17) give rise to a problem of social control, as investing parties expose themselves to the risk of not receiving an adequate reward for their capital outlay. Anticipating this unfavorable consequence, trading partners may then be reluctant to make these investments in the first place, in this way accepting the under-investment problem. In other words, if economically viable and productive investments to support a specific transaction are not sufficiently protected and, therefore, not placed, any decision regarding governance structures will be suboptimal.

When comparing this central relationship issue of TCE and its undesirable practical ramifications, it becomes evident that asset management firms, in fact, have to deal with the lurking threat of being held up. While the move to more advanced degrees of decentralization tends to require substantial investments (Heinemann et al. 2003, pp. 55-56), banks remain in the powerful position of being able to exert considerable influence on the purchase-decision of private investors and, thus, to guide the stream of inflows. This highlights the latent hold-up problem in the relationship between asset management firms and [external] distributing banks. Therefore, it appears as if this concept of NIE allows the enquiry to establish a good grasp of one of the key dimensions underlying the relationship problems facing asset management firms. Hence, propositions on how to come to the necessary safeguards in an efficient manner are of greatest relevance given the enquiry's question and objective.

Basically, the **guiding principle of TCE proposes to alleviate the ex post hazards of opportunism through the ex-ante choice of governance**. More specifically, the optimal [i.e., transaction cost-minimizing] choice [and implicit design] decision ensures that underlying transactions, which differ in their attributes, are brought in line with governance structures which differ in their costs and competences to alleviate the hold-up problem in a discriminating way (Williamson 1998, p. 37). This indicates that the classic TCE argumentation tends to assume that the choice [rather automatically] brings about a consistent design. However, recent developments in TCE-related marketing literature emphasize that there is also an explicit need to design the relationship (Heide 1994, p. 74-78) and to actively ensure alignment of marketing organizations with strategic choices that strengthens efficiency (Vorhies and Morgan 2003, Ghosh and John 2005).

Regarding the traditional argument of TCE, under the condition of high levels of asset specificity, the **autonomous spot market** as one extreme of the range of available governance modes becomes extremely costly in terms of negotiating, executing, supervising, and adapting the governance arrangement (i.e., the spot market contract). Therefore, with specific investments creating dependence (Heide and John 1988, pp. 23-24) and exposing investing parties to the threat of being expropriated, market control in general no longer provides an adequate safeguard to limit opportunism in a [transaction] cost-minimizing way. Typically, efficient protection is secured by moving away from an arm's-length market relationship to a **hierarchy** type of governance structure. More vertically integrated arrangements favor the introduction and execution of administrative control in order to mitigate potential opportunism. Although this organizational choice offers weaker incentives and entails substantial bureaucratic, out-of-pocket costs vis-à-vis more market-based arrangements, it is nevertheless still considered as the most efficient way to coordinate and adapt transactions in the presence of assets with high specificity. This central argument of TCE on how to appropriately account for latent ramifications of asset specificity is widely accepted. Anderson and Coughlan (1987, p. 78) find a positive relationship between specific investments and the use of integrated channel structures underlining that centralized structures offer adequate means to cope with the lurking hold-up problems.

As this empirical study covers a prominent example of a service sector, it is important to clarify how the central argument of TCE applies to **service firms**. In this respect, Murray and Kotabe (1999, pp. 802) underline the fact that the classic TCE argumentation needs to be modified as general characteristics of service activities, such as the inseparability of production and consumption, tend to moderate the positive relationship between high asset specificity and rather integrated arrangements. Moreover, Erramilli and Rao (1993, pp. 32-34) find that **service firms prefer high-control types of institutional arrangements even at low levels of relationship-specific investments**. In the face of the considerable [task] specificity already inherent in service activities, related to high levels of professional skills, specialized know-how, and the flexibility associated with customization, they argue that **service firms prefer to start with full-control modes and only tend to relinquish control in response to the rising costs of integration or diminishing ability to integrate.**

However, in order to secure efficient coordination, the transaction must not automatically be organized under a hierarchical setting. Instead, as is widely acknowledged, partners may find it optimal [i.e., transaction-cost minimizing] to choose some intermediate arrangement on the continuous spectrum between the extreme governance structures of market and hierarchy. Such **hybrid arrangements** may take the shape of long-term contracts (Joskow 1987), quasi-markets and joint-ventures (Osborn and Baughn 1990), partial ownerships (Pisano 1990), strategic alliances (Bleeke and Ernst 1991, 1995; Oxley 1997), and partnerships (Anderson and Narus 1990). With the purpose of bringing coordination issues under control, these arrangements offer the chance to blend high-powered incentives and autonomous adaptive properties of the market with the strengths of bureaucratically-shaped organizational characteristics.

In this regard, it is of particular interest that a variety of relational elements are applied in inter-firm relationships, which are recognized as very powerful in limiting opportunistic tendencies. Heide and John (1992, p. 42) show that **relational norms** such as **flexibility**, **bilateral information exchange**, and **solidarity** play a very significant role in structuring economically efficient relationships between independent firms. By way of stimulating commitment to the relationship, these norms of relational exchange are found to be effective in limiting opportunistic tendencies (Brown, Dev, and Lee 2000, p. 62) and, subsequently, result in lower transaction costs (Artz and Brush 2000, p. 356). Furthermore, Heide and John (1990, p. 25) propose that **joint actions** between independent parties can serve as a safeguard to curb opportunism. In line with this, Mohr and Spekmann (1994, pp. 144) find that **participation** is a powerful means to inhibit relationship conflicts. Moreover, it is widely accepted that **trust** plays a critical role in realizing satisfactory levels of cooperation among exchange partners (Dwyer, Schurr and Oh 1987, pp. 22-23). Consequently, trust-generating measures (Sydow 1991, p. 18; Doney and Cannon 1997, pp. 38-41) represent a prominent measure for securing efficient coordination of economic activities under decentralized, but intermediate regimes of governance.

Without neglecting the criticism with regard to this theoretical background in terms of its selective focus, the need for ad-hoc theorization, and its behavioral assumptions (Koch 2005, pp. 196-199), it seems that all the insights regarding the choice of governance modes – particularly its proposition relating to service firms but also the extensions regarding the need for actively designing relationships – are of remarkable relevance for the practical problem facing asset management firms. Hence, **TCE and its reasoning exhibit the required explanatory and practical relevance** to be selected alongside PA to establish a framework of analysis to approach the enquiry's question and objective in an appropriate fashion. However, the observed adoption of more open distribution systems not only portrays refined degrees of decentralization but also involves what NIE refers to as rearranged ownership structures. With PA as well as TCE remaining rather silent on the incentive implications of ownership, PRT as another core concept of NIE seems to be of relevance to the enquiry's optimization problem.

2.1.3.3 Property-Rights-Theory

Property-rights-theory (PRT) offers a conceptual approach, which places the institution of ownership at the center of the scope of analysis. Initially developed by Alchian and Demsetz (1972) and Furubotn and Pejovich (1972) and then formally designed by Grossman and Hart (1986) and Hart and Moore (1990), PRT holds the view that the ownership structure of productive assets and the according **allocation of property rights** play a critical role in **determining the efficiency level of organizational designs** for economic activity. This concept discusses and illustrates the incentive effects that alternative ownership structures have on the [investment] behavior of economic actors. In this regard, it offers the chance to address motivation issues which otherwise potentially breed substantial inefficiencies in organizing economic activity. From a formal point of view, the **optimal ownership structure** is the one **that minimizes the overall loss in surplus due to [investment] distortions** (Grossmann and Hart 1986, p. 697).

Ownership of a particular asset is defined as having control in terms of different categories of property rights[10]. Given the assumed incompleteness of complex contracts [for the reason of bounded rationality], which implies that some decisions are not contractible, ownership then essentially means having residual rights over assets. Moreover, the owner of an asset is generally entitled to claim the residual returns from the asset. Since it is this allocation of ownership rights that effects the distribution of returns, it gains a critical role in stimulating the undertaking of non-contractible [investment] behavior. In that respect, Milgrom and Roberts (1992, p. 291) emphasize that the **bundling of residual control and residual returns** is essential to the incentive effect of ownership. They argue that by properly linking these two aspects strong incentives are created to not only maintain but also to improve an asset's value. By tying together residual returns and residual control, the economic actor bears the full financial impact of the decision regarding the use of the asset under ownership.

---

[10] As will be illustrated later in more detail, Furubotn and Richter (1991, p. 6) distinguish four different categories of property rights: the right to use an asset, the right to appropriate the returns from an asset, the right to change its form, substance, or location, and the right to transfer any of these rights to a third-party.

Therefore, in case the residual claimant of returns possesses the residual decision rights as well, efficient decisions regarding investments, efforts, or other behavioral dimensions are most likely to occur as these are in line with the assumed self-interest of economic actors. Yet, once the possession of residual control is separated from the entitlement of residual returns, property rights become diluted and external effects emerge, as only part of the costs or benefits of a decision accrue to the economic actor actually taking the decision. This misalignment of residual rights and returns potentially leads to distortions of [investment] behavior as decision-makers most likely will be neither fully rewarded nor adequately punished for their actions.

With regard to practical optimization-problem confronting asset management firms, there can be no doubt that the move towards more decentralized distribution systems also involves some adjustments in the transfer of property rights to distributors. In this respect, it seems that misalignment of residual control and residual returns gives rise to the relationship hazards confronting asset management firms in their attempts to enjoy expanded customer reach via external banks. Hence, **the central proposition of PRT on how to deal with this type of motivation issue by way of allocating property rights appears to possess the required explanatory as well as practical relevance**. Thus, PRT can be selected in addition to the other two core concepts of NIE to develop an adequate framework of analysis for the empirical investigation.

2.1.4 Conclusion

Concluding from this elaboration of alternative theoretical concepts, it seems more than reasonable to claim that an integrated approach of NIE drawing on PA, TCE, and PRT appears most appropriate to allow this enquiry to perform the envisaged situational analysis of the outlined optimization problem. In comparison to alternative conceptual backgrounds, it shows that this concept puts the enquiry in a position to establish a sufficiently detailed understanding of the situational challenges facing asset management firms. Moreover, it offers a variety of conceptual means in terms of propositions and criteria to eventually produce practically relevant guidelines for the optimization objective at hand. In other words, **NIE as a whole exhibits the required**

explanatory and practical relevance for adequately dealing with the choice and design problem facing asset management firms.

Fig. 5: SUMMARY OF RELEVANCE OF ALTERNATIVE CONCEPTUAL APPROACHES

	Explanatory relevance	Practical relevance
Game Theory	(±) Lacks scope to cover peculiarities of enquiry's decision-making problem	(−) Offers only limited guidelines on how to actively achieve cooperative outcomes
Resource-Based View	(−) Gives reasons for break-up of value chains but neglects inefficiencies due to relationship hazards	(−) Provides only ex post explanations of success but no practical guidelines on how to handle inefficiencies
New Institutional Economics	(+) Covers various coordination challenges facing asset management firms	(+) Presents wide range of propositions on how to optimally choose and design institutional arrangements

Source: Author

As illustrated in Figure 5, regarding explanatory relevance, the concepts underlying NIE complement each other in providing a good grasp of the challenges facing asset management firms. In contrast to this, Game Theory offers only a rather narrow focus to absorb the practical problems of bringing distribution systems to full strength, while RBV hardly considers inefficiencies due to coordination and motivation issues at all. As far as practical relevance is concerned, NIE is able to supply this enquiry with a comprehensive repertoire of action-oriented guidelines and measures to optimize institutional arrangements with regard to both choice and design. On the contrary, the alternative theoretical backgrounds appear to be rather short of practically relevant propositions. While Game Theory appears to be not sufficiently complex to produce guidelines on how to control for relationship hazards, RBV does not generate empirical predictions at all. Therefore, it appears reasonable to turn to NIE as the theoretical backbone for a fruitful conceptualization of the choice and design problem. This paves the way for the situational analysis for comparing alternative institutional arrangements for marketing mutual funds to private investors in Germany.

2.2 Derivation of Framework of Analysis for Optimizing Distribution Systems

Having gone over an array of alternative theoretical concepts, the most adequate in terms of explanatory and practical relevance will now be applied to guide the construction of the enquiry's framework of analysis. As outlined already in some detail, this enquiry deals with the practical challenge facing asset management firms on how to optimize distribution systems in the wake of fundamental changes in the market environment at the turn of this century. To address this question according to the enquiry's own ambition, in the following section, NIE as the selected conceptual background will be employed to transfer the practical challenge into a framework of analysis. Before turning to the different groups of variables conceptualized in this framework and the dynamics for applying the framework in a model-theoretical discussion, its general structure with the underlying staged approach is going to be introduced.

2.2.1 General Structure of Framework of Analysis

In essence, the purpose of the derivation of a theory-guided framework is to convert the practical challenge into an action-oriented decision-making problem. In the light of the enquiry's practical-normative perspective, the intention is to establish a framework that allows the enquiry to simultaneously come to an analysis, an assessment, and an optimization of given ways to bring distribution systems to improved performance levels. Therefore, to examine existing practices from the perspective of efficiency-enhancing objectives, the framework needs to be structured in a way that facilitates a classification of variables as target variables, contingencies, and side-constraints, while also offering the chance to include action variables to conceptualize the means for achieving the desired optimizing effects. As far as the introduction of assessment criteria is concerned, the **aim is eventually to put the enquiry in a position to derive**

[contingency-specific] and analyze propositions regarding the superiority of particular systems for marketing mutual funds to private investors.

This discussion so far shows that this enquiry is dealing with the question of how to accomplish an optimization of distribution systems for mutual funds. This study will, therefore, address issues related to the decentralization of the distribution function in a prominent example of a service industry. To adequately unlock the practical challenge into a relevant set of means-effect relations, this enquiry to a large degree will fall back on the concepts of NIE. Therefore, in line with earlier discussion on the concepts underlying NIE, **this challenge of decentralization is going to be analyzed in the context of an agency-relationship** between the asset management firm and banks in which the **asset management firm is regarded as the principal** that delegates the distribution function to respective banks. Accordingly, this enquiry defines the practical issues facing asset management firms essentially as a problem of optimally organizing this agency-relationship. In this way, this **optimization problem becomes a steering and control problem of how to handle coordination and motivation issues in order to unleash the efficiency-enhancing potential available in increasingly decoupled agency-relationships**. Yet, as will be discussed later, in response to suggestions of more recent NIE-related marketing literature, there will be some considerable adjustments, in particular with regard to the conceptualization of relationship-specific investments (Gosh and John 1999, p. 134), as well as the application of decision-making criteria (Vorhies and Morgan 2003, pp. 110).

To tackle this optimization problem in a proper manner, the framework conceptualizes this optimization problem first of all as a problem of choosing the degree of decentralization for distribution systems in the asset management sector. Therefore, to appropriately unlock the optimization subject in terms of targets, contingencies, constraints, action variables, and decision-making criteria, this **first stage basically aims at positioning the choice of a degree of decentralization as a [strategic] decision**, which has to adequately account for some main contingency factors in its pursuit of realizing efficiency targets. However, as already pointed out, in line with the classic NIE standpoint, this enquiry will also spell out that each choice from the feasible range of alternative degrees of decentralization tends to give rise to control problems in a different fashion (Williamson 1991a, pp. 279-281). Besides the choice in favor of a particular type of institutional arrangement [in terms of the degree of decentralization], the framework then also declares the **actual design of the institutional arrangement as an important decision to bring choice-specific side-constraints, stemming from opportunism and the specificity inherent in the service activities, under control**. In this way, the design is assumed to be a functional prerequisite to achieve the desired efficiency targets. Therefore, as a means of analyzing, assessing, and ultimately optimizing distribution systems for mutual funds, this framework emphasizes that the optimization of an institutional arrangement simultaneously brings about the question on how to choose as well as how to design the degree of decentralization. However, as illustrated in Figure 6, **the structure underlying the framework puts the enquiry in a position to address the choice and design problem in a staged, rather step-wise approach**.

Fig. 6: GENERAL STRUCTURE OF FRAMEWORK OF ANALYSIS

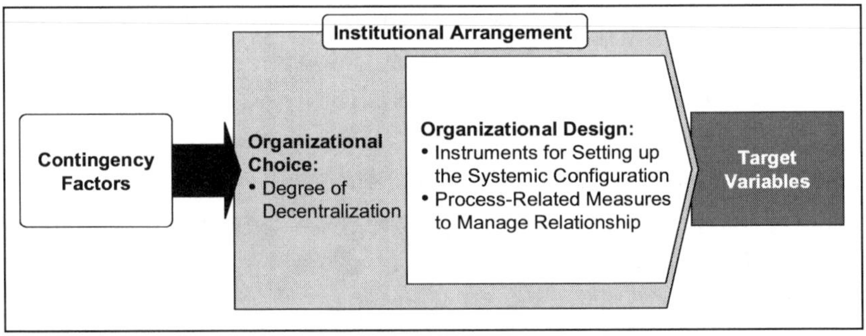

Source: Author

In more detail, in accordance with this envisaged structure of the framework of analysis, this enquiry will first of all introduce those variables for appropriately conceptualizing the choice decision. In the face of market dynamics at the turn of the century with the overall deterioration of demand for mutual funds at the market level, the point is to outline how the asset management firm fundamentally structures the agency-relationship by choosing a degree of decentralization [from a feasible range] in order to accomplish optimal distribution performance levels. The chosen coordination mode, which in its very essence is then ultimately reflected in the delegation of property rights, demarcates the key characteristics of the overall institutional arrangement for the relationship between asset management firm and banks as distributing agents.

Moving further to the right-hand side of Figure 5, thereby making some change in perspective, the purpose is to make clear that **with [or after] the choice the principal needs to carve out the organizational design of the agency-relationship in order to adequately control for varying side-constraints**. These, however, are assumed to be choice-specific at least to some extent, which underlines that once again there is no such thing as a free lunch. Hence, this enquiry argues that on the basis of the chosen degree of decentralization, the principal has to put in place a design in terms of both a systemic configuration and process-related measures in order to bring the institutional arrangement to full strength. In other words, to realize the desired improvements in distribution performance levels, this framework of analysis hands the institutional arrangement's design the crucial role of structuring the agency-relationship in detail as well as of establishing necessary cognitive and motivational prerequisites on the part of agents to appropriately take on the delegated [distribution] activities (Hill, Fehlbaum, and Ulrich 1994, pp. 61-71).

To derive propositions based on the framework of analysis, this study will fall back on purposively introduced decision-making criteria, in other words, assessment criteria. In this respect, the point is clearly to employ these criteria to facilitate a model-theoretical discussion of the framework and its conditional means-effect relations. As it will be outlined in more detail later, adjusted to wider NIE considerations **this enquiry will apply some fit-requirements to assess the efficacy of investigated institutional arrangements** to trigger strong distribution performance levels. In the light of the staged approach, this in turn means that these **fit-requirements are applied to both the choice-decision and the design-decision to reach optimization-relevant propositions and guidelines**. Following on from all this, **this enquiry will eventually pursue two interrelated general propositions**. First of all, this enquiry argues that, in the wake of fundamental market developments, more advanced degrees of decentralization for distribution systems in the asset management sector can in fact prove to be best at enhancing performance levels. Secondly, to truly activate desired improvements, this study claims that the institutional arrangements need to be not only in line with external contingencies confronting asset management firms but also designed in an internally consistent manner.

With all this in mind, it is now time to turn to the different categories of variables conceptualized in the enquiry's framework of analysis. The purpose is to introduce in some detail the single variables in each of the different categories and their [functional] relevance to the enquiry's choice and design problem. The discussion will then spell out how this framework is going to be applied in the envisaged model-theoretical discussion to pinpoint superior ways of organizing the distribution function in the asset management sector in Germany.

2.2.2 Variables of the Framework of Analysis

To appropriately decompose the optimization problem of how to truly unleash the advantages of decentralization while controlling for latent negative side effects, the conceptualization of the variables included in the enquiry's framework of analysis (please see Figure 7) will first of all focus on the target variables. Thereafter, the key contingency factor and the side-constraints to the choice and design problem will be introduced. This is followed by the categorization of the different [strategic] choices regarding the degree of decentralization of the institutional arrangements. Last but not least, in line with the slight change in perspective, the derivation of the framework of analysis turns to the action variables relevant to design the institutional arrangements.

2.2.2.1 Target variables

As this enquiry intends to deal with the question of how to enjoy the benefits of decentralization while accounting for the inefficiency-causing risks lurking in these ways of organizing distribution systems, the framework of analysis, in fact, exhibits two target variables. These, however, are intertwined/concorrelated to a great extent. The overriding objective of asset management firms when they aim to optimize distribution systems [in terms of the choice and design] is to generate a strong **"cash inflow stream"** for their product range. Yet, as mentioned, each choice tends to cause some form of control and steering problems, which potentially endanger that objective. From this view, the framework then argues that in order to secure the sought improvement in the "cash inflow stream", the principal essentially has to bring the latent dangers of **"hold-up"** on the part of the agent under control. Hence, for the reason of accurately evaluating the efficacy of choice and designing decisions from a practical decision-making perspective, this study has opted to separate the ultimate objectives into two targets, conceptualizing not only "cash inflow stream" but also "hold-up" as the framework's task variables.

2.2.2.1.1 Cash Inflow Stream

The emergence of more decoupled distribution systems in the asset management sector can clearly be acknowledged as a deliberate response by asset management firms to cope with the market dynamics in the wake of the nosedive of global capital markets in 2001. There can be no denying that in order to expand customer reach, asset management firms have turned to more advanced degrees of decentralization for the distribution function. They now increasingly rely on external banks for the marketing of their mutual funds to private investors. The aim is in this way to strengthen inflows for their mutual fund offering on a sustainable basis. Therefore, it is the "cash inflow stream" that is to be defined as the key efficiency variable within the framework of analysis. In the following:

- **"Cash inflow stream" will be measured in terms of the [net new] money the asset management firm [the principal] is able to collect from private investors [per year] for its mutual fund offering through the distribution channel of banks [the agent].**

The determination of this target efficiency variable, in turn, means that the framework has to include all the main [strategic] organizational choices, critical contingencies, powerful design variables, and their interconnectivities in order to pave the way for an adequate model-theoretical discussion. Only with such a comprehensive conceptualization is this enquiry able to ascertain optimizing solutions for the decision-making problem. Basically, optimization implies maximization of the "cash inflow stream".

Fig. 7: THEORY-GUIDED SPECIFICATION OF FRAMEWORK OF ANALYSIS

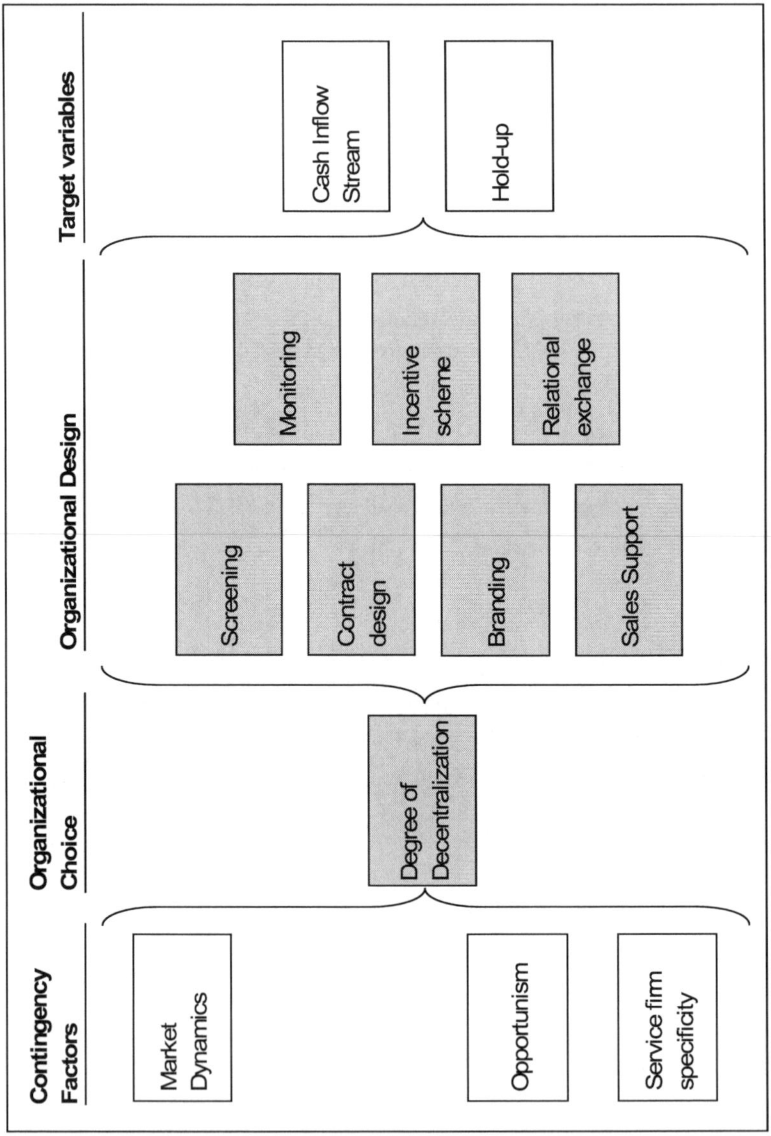

Source: Author

2.2.2.1.2 Hold-up

In the light of this main target variable, each choice for arranging the relationship between principal and agent tends to entail some form of control or steering problem. As already laid out, the concepts underlying NIE emphasize that the principal tends to relinquish some of the more explicit control measures to guide the agent's behavior when turning to more advanced degrees of decentralization (Williamson 1991a, p. 281). In case side-constraints stemming from latent opportunistic tendencies and the specificity inherent in the activities of the distribution function are not adequately controlled for by the design of the agency-relationships, they potentially lead to inefficient situations of "hold-up" (Besanko, Dranove, and Shanley 2000, pp. 154-160). These may ultimately threaten the generation of an optimal "cash inflow stream". Hence, when falling back on increasingly decoupled systems for the distribution function, this framework argues that asset management firms will need to successfully tame most notably the danger of "hold-up" to accomplish an improvement in distribution performance levels.

Therefore, with **the optimization of the "cash inflow stream" subject to the threat of "hold-up"**, to identify the optimizing solution to the enquiry's decision-making problem requires the conceptualization of "hold-up" in the framework of analysis. More importantly, this also underlines the relevance of the measures proposed by PA, TCE, and PRT on how to adequately account for sources of "hold-up"[11] to avoid these inefficient relationship hiccups of limited willingness, commitment, and possibly even insufficient competence on part of the agent. This indicates that these practical and action-oriented measures in their very essence then [at least indirectly] favor the improvement of the "cash inflow stream" and, therefore, need to find consideration in the enquiry's framework.

---

[11] This task variable, referred to as "hold-up", covers all the different relationship hazards possibly arising from information asymmetry, divergent interests, specificity of investments, task complexity, uncertainty, frequency, and incomplete contracts in the interaction between principal and agent. As discussed earlier, this may include the hidden characteristic problem, the hidden action problem, the problem of hold-up, and distortions in [investment] behavior. In more practical terms, "hold-up" refers to incidents in which distributing banks either are not willing, not truly committed, or not able to perform the distribution function for the principal's mutual fund offering. However, as this can only be measured by means of observation, this enquiry will infer the encountered level of "hold-up" from the handling of both the opportunism and service firm specificity.

2.2.2.2 Contingency Factors

To achieve the overriding target of an optimized degree of decentralization, this enquiry argues that the choice [and thereby eventually also the design] of the institutional arrangement for the distribution function needs to account for key contingency factors and side-constraints. Besides the fundamental changes in the market environment since the beginning of this century, NIE-related assumptions regarding the behavior of agents and the complexity inherent in the delegated activities of distributing mutual funds cannot be ignored in the decision-making problem confronting asset management firms. Therefore, this discussion will now conceptualize "**market dynamics**" as the key contingency factor and "**opportunism**" and "**service firm specificity**" as main side-constrains to the choice and design problem.

2.2.2.2.1 Market Dynamics

In order to analyze the optimization of the choice and design of distribution systems in the asset management sector from an adequate situational point of view, it is critical to clarify, as a starting point, the development of distribution performance levels the asset management firm under focus has experienced. From a conceptual perspective, it is of particular interest to explain to what extent and in which way "market dynamics" have resulted in a gap in distribution performance. A variety of trends in the private investor market in Germany emerged at the beginning of this century (Narat 2003, p. 262-264), most notably an overall deterioration of demand for mutual funds in Germany. **To quantify** the impact of these **"market dynamics"** in the selected case studies, the enquiry will take a close look at

- **the net inflow figures of the respective asset management firm in Germany and their trend over time vis-à-vis the overall market development [or groups of key competitors]**.

To relate these environmental forces to pressures to adjust institutional arrangements in terms of choice [and ultimately design], this enquiry will then consider these developments as raising challenges in securing strong distribution performance [by means of given distribution systems]. However, to appropriately investigate the [adjusted] choice, this analysis of implications of "market dynamics" must not be conducted from a purely objective point of view. Instead, **this study also needs to incorporate the interpretation of respective management** (Child 1972, pp. 11-12). Only with a thorough understanding of how management has conceived the impact of "market dynamics", the enquiry is able to elucidate if at all and in which way evolving performance levels provoke adaptations in the choice of institutional arrangements for the distribution function to raise the "cash inflow stream". Hence, to appropriately investigate "market dynamics" and its relation to the choice-decision of the degree of decentralization, this enquiry will consider not only the ramifications from an objective point of view but particularly the management's subjective perception of these developments.

2.2.2.2.2 Opportunism

One of the central behavioral assumptions of NIE is that economic actors are self-interest seeking, with opportunism as the strongest form. In general, "opportunism" is defined as "self-interest seeking with guile" (Williamson 1985, p. 47). In more substantive terms, opportunistic tendencies imply that, according to their very own utility-function, it is in the agents' interests to adopt some form of aberrant behavior (Jensen and Meckling 1976, p. 307) or to engage in calculated efforts to mislead and distort the principal. Whenever there is the chance to do so and whenever it is in their interest, agents behave opportunistically which, in turn, is assumed to carry the danger of being inefficient from the principal's point of view. Thus, in the light of the assumed agency-relationship between asset management firms and banks, it appears reasonable also in this framework to argue that the principal will be confronted with some form of opportunistic tendencies on the part of distributing agents. This may eventually take the shape of [external] banks [at the system-level of the relationship] or their sales staff at the point-of-sale demonstrating only limited willingness to perform the distribution function cooperatively on behalf of the particular asset management firm. However, in line with more recent developments in NIE-related literature, this enquiry acknowledges that not only extrinsic interests but also intrinsic considerations guide the behavior of economic actors (Osterloh and Frey 2000, pp. 539-540).

All this highlights the necessity to adequately account for this latent danger in the choice and ultimately in the design of the institutional arrangement. As is well known, each choice tends to give rise to this inefficiency-causing behavioral risk in a different manner. A swing from rather integrated distribution systems to more advanced degrees of decentralization entails trading off centralized coordinating instruments and administrative fiat for high-powered incentives and autonomous adaptive properties. Yet, in the absence of effective market control, such a move can lead to flaring issues of "opportunism" on the part of agents. Therefore, in order to adequately reach the framework's target variables, **this enquiry argues that with the choice-decision the principal needs to be aware of the efficiency-relevant requirement to bring these varying [choice-specific] forms of "opportunism" under control**. In this regard, as will be elaborated, on the basis of the organizational choice it is the design of the relationship that gains an important role in mitigating the side-constraints of "opportunism" in order to truly enjoy improvements in the "cash inflow stream".

2.2.2.2.3 Service firm specificity

The asset management sector is a prominent example of a service industry. Typically, the value chain for producing and marketing mutual funds to private investors displays not only a highly specialized set-up but also the typical characteristics of service activities. The sales and advisory activities of the distribution function can be best described by the inseparability of production and consumption, the intangibility, and the varying quality depending on the personnel involved in providing the services. Furthermore, these activities typically exhibit what Mennon and Varadarajan (1992, p. 61) refer to as **task complexity** in terms of the difficulties related to the delegated activity. Sales staff operating in direct interaction with private investors has to deal with **highly specific [product-related] questions** emphasizing the need for sufficient problem-solving skills in order **to build customer-specific solutions** (Johnson, Manyika, and Yee 2005, p. 21). From this view, as Erramilli and Rao (1993, p. 23) argue, these activities demand high levels of professional skills, specialized know-how, and the ability to perform customization. These are expected to favor a successful handling of the continuous stream and process of interaction with private investors (Lehmann 1998, p. 1733). Moreover, as these interactions are related to financial services they are particularly exposed to a **dynamic and uncertain environment** (Crosby, Evans, and Cowles 1990, p. 69). All this indicates that by their very nature these service activities related to the sales and advisory tasks delegated to the distributing bank entail substantial specificity and uncertainty, to which this enquiry will refer to as "**service firm specificity**".

Therefore, in order to improve the "cash inflow stream" on a sustainable basis, this enquiry argues that asset management firms at large have to adequately deal with this form of specificity inherent in the distribution function and its implications. In more detail, all these properties of the sales and advisory activities indicate that with the decision on choice and design the principal has to consider the efficiency-relevant requirement to ensure [relationship-specific] expertise and competence on part of agents regarding the principal's mutual fund offering, thereby setting the stage for sufficient levels of service quality (Corsten 2001, pp. 292). The asset management firm has to put distributors in a position to properly respond to private investors' needs in a flexible and specific manner. This is expected to benefit them in successfully completing the delegated sales and advisory activities. However, under advanced degrees of decentralization, the problem of coordinating efforts to build the necessary qualification usually tends to be aggravated. For example, an external bank's management may severely restrict or even deny access to staff operating directly at the point-of-sale.

At the same time, in particular in light of the external factor, this enquiry further stipulates that the choice and design of the institutional arrangement also needs to take into account the considerable ambiguity in performance measurement of the agents' distribution activities stemming from this "service firm specificity". From the principal's perspective, it generally appears to be difficult to clarify as to whether the distribution performance levels are driven mainly by the agents' cooperative behavior or by general market windfalls. In this regard, as a move away from rather full-control coordination modes towards a more advanced degree of decentralization tends to bring about a reduced scope for controlling this uncertainty, the "service firm specificity" in principle gives rise to the control and steering problem in the agency-relationship. Therefore, in order to achieve an optimized choice and design for the degree of decentralization, this enquiry pinpoints the necessity to adequately take into consideration the side-constraints associated with the "service firm specificity".

2.2.2.3 Degree of Decentralization

After having outlined the main target variables as well as the key contingency factors and the side-constraints, the purpose now is to conceptualize the variable still needed for the first stage of the optimization problem facing asset management firms. As discussed, this enquiry deals with the optimizing problem on how to set free benefits related to decentralization while controlling for the latent negative side effects. Therefore, as already indicated, this enquiry and its framework as a first step convert this challenge to strengthen the "cash inflow stream" into a **choice-decision regarding the "degree of decentralization"** in the face of "market dynamics" and side-constraints of "opportunism" and the "service firm specificity". At this point, the enquiry will define the range of organizational choices available to asset management firms in terms of the "degree of decentralization" to arrange the specialized set-up of the value chain for mutual funds.

Fig. 8: DEGREE OF DECENTRALIZATION REFLECTED IN TRANSFER OF PROPERTY RIGHTS TO DISTRIBUTORS

	Degree of decentralization →		
Type of Property Rights	**Hierarchy**	**Partnership**	**Market**
• Right to use a resource (usus)	✓	✓	✓
• Right to keep returns associated with the use of the resource (usus fructus)	✓	✓	✓
• Right to change form or substance of resource (abusus)	✓	✓	
• Right to transfer all or some of the above rights	✓		

Source: adapted from Furubotn and Richter (1991, p. 6)

In line with the selected conceptual background as well as recent developments in strategic marketing (Gosh and John 1999), this framework of analysis will distinguish three different choices regarding the **"degree of decentralization"** along the hierarchy-market continuum (Ouchi 1980, pp. 130-132; Williamson 1991a, pp. 277). In line also with ideas on modularizing property rights (Picot, Reichwald, and Wigang 2003, p. 259-260), each "degree of decentralization" is eventually reflected by a different allocation of property rights in the agency-relationship, which then demarcates the frame in which the design is put in place to adequately cope with choice-specific expressions of side-constraints.

- The enquiry assumes that the asset management firm may choose to turn to some highly integrated, **"hierarchy"**-type of institutional arrangement [under unified ownership]. As far as the distribution of property rights is concerned, this enquiry classifies this "degree of decentralization" as the one in which all four categories of property rights are assigned to the agent [to set up the systemic configuration of the institutional arrangement]. In more substantive terms, this choice basically implies that the banks integrate backwards into the asset management firm. This coordination mode appears to be particularly suitable for managing large, complex organizations (Jaques 1990, p. 129). It tends to provide the opportunity to reinforce [at least] compliant role behavior or demand adaptations on part of the distributing agents by means of authority, bureaucratically-shaped administrative control mechanisms, and internal dispute resolution procedures.
- Additionally, this framework of analysis conceptualizes the possibility that the principal may decide to choose neither market nor hierarchy but rather some hybrid, intermediate type of institutional arrangement (Powell 1990, pp. 300-305), referred to as **"partnership"** in this enquiry. Under the regime of this "degree of decentralization", besides the right to use the asset underlying the transaction [i.e., the right to distribute the mutual fund to private investors] and to appropriate some of the returns [i.e., compensation for distributing the mutual fund to private investors], the principal also hands the agent the right to get involved in decisions to change the form, substance, or location of the asset. Thus, this coordination mode rests on substantial participation along the value chain in interdependent fashion to secure mutual benefits (Johnston and Lawrence 1988, pp. 94). In the

light of the fundamental role of trust in the interaction within the agency-relationship (Bradach and Eccles 1989, p. 104), the principal may then even be able to activate extra-role behavior on part of the agent.

- Last but not least, the asset management firm may opt to choose a **"market"**-type of institutional arrangement to organize the distribution function. As illustrated in Figure 8, it comes to a rather restricted assignment of property rights on the part of distributors. From the view of such a discrete allocation of rights in the agency-relationship, the coordination mode to a greater extent relies on market forces to secure aspired performance levels (Klein and Leffler 1981, pp. 615-618). In more precise terms, in "market"-type institutional arrangements the principal tends to rely on the agents' [rather short-term] profit-maximizing interests to overcome side-constraints related to "opportunism" and "service firm specificity".

This classification of the different types of "degree of decentralization" appears particularly suitable to cover the different approaches to organize the distribution function in the asset management sector. As noted earlier, growing numbers of asset management firms in Germany, irrespective of whether they are domestic or foreign players, have turned to increasingly decoupled relationships with [external] banks to manage the value chain to produce and market mutual funds to private investors.

From a functional point of view, the framework of analysis argues that this choice is assumed to be made to bring in line the "degree of decentralization" with the "market dynamics" in order to produce positive effects on the "cash inflow stream". Simply speaking, a decision in favor of a more advanced degree of decentralization ultimately has to prove successful in securing strong inflow streams in an environment of declining demand for mutual funds. At the same time, in the light of side-constraints on the choice-decision, this framework spells out that each "degree of decentralization" tends to bring about a specific form of the control and steering problem. Therefore, from a system-level perspective, to enjoy improved performance levels the choice-decision needs to account not only for the ramifications of challenging sector developments but also the latent negative side effects of opportunistic tendencies and the specificity-inherent service activities of the distribution function. On the basis of the choice, following the staged approach of the framework of analysis [and the slight change in perspective], the design in terms of the systemic configuration and process-related measures then gains an important role in securing the efficiency-enhancing effects promised by the respective [advanced] "degree of decentralization".

2.2.2.4 Design Variables

As mentioned above, the enquiry's framework argues that the optimization of distribution systems in the asset management sector raises questions not only of organizational choice in response to changing market trends but rather simultaneously also of how to actually design the "degree of decentralization". With its staged approach, this enquiry stipulates that on the basis of the choice-decision the design of the institutional arrangement has to be set up [in a consistent manner] in order to ultimately realize the improvement in the "cash inflow stream". In this way, the principal is expected to be in an adequate position to cope with the choice-specific side effects related to "opportunism" and "service firm specificity".

To purposively manage distribution systems, the **design of the institutional arrangement contains** not only a **systemic configuration** but also **processes in order to secure the cognitive as well motivational prerequisites to activate the desired behavior on the part of agents**. In this view, it will become apparent that the conceptual background of NIE provides the principal with a wide range of functionally relevant means in terms of structure-shaping instruments and process-related measures to design the chosen coordination mode to enable and motivate agents to take on the delegated role in an adequately cooperative manner (Picot, Reichwald, and Wigand 2003, p. 534). Concerning the single **design variables** suggested by concepts underlying NIE, the upcoming **conceptualization will first of all focus on the variables relevant to set up the systemic configuration**. As these variables set up the structure of the agency-relationship, they also demarcate the frame for introducing processes to coordinate the interaction between principal and agent. The conceptualization **will then turn to the process-related measures** for making the distribution system run on a continuous basis.

2.2.2.4.1 Instruments for Setting up the Systemic Configuration

As far as the overriding optimization objective is concerned, this enquiry treats the systemic configuration as a decisive part in securing a consistent buildup of the design of the institutional arrangement given the [strategic] choice-decision, thereby unleashing the advantages related to the given organizational choice. In this regard, it is in particular the "**contract design**" with its assignment of property rights that fundamentally structures the interaction between principal and agent. In addition to this classic NIE perspective, the enquiry also considers investments in "**branding**" and "**sales support**" as prominent structure-shaping instruments to motivate as well as to enable agents to take on the delegated rights. Thus, investments in these capacities are regarded as additional levers to overcome the latent negative side effects stemming from "opportunism" and "service firm specificity". While this perspective is in line with more recent developments in NIE (Ghosh and John 1999) that treats the placement of productive investments in support of the transaction as endogenous, it is obviously in strong contrast to the classic NIE perspective. The classic NIE perspective views investments and their relationship-specific character as an exogenous variable explaining the choice of institutional arrangements (Anderson 1988; Anderson and Coughlan 1987; John and Weitz 1988; Klein, Frazier, and Roth 1990). In other words, **this framework is constructed in a way that considers investments and the degree to which these are specific to a particular transaction as a lever available to the principal to purposively structure the institutional arrangement**. While it is well-documented that [relationship-specific] investments may give rise to inefficient situations of "hold-up" (Besanko, Danove, and Shanley 2000, pp. 148), they also exhibit great functional relevance in guiding agents' behavior, thereby becoming another potentially important measure to cope with the latent negative side effects. Productive investments have proven to be powerful in balancing dependence (Heide and John 1988, pp. 24-25), creating bonding effects on the part of agents (Rokkan, Heide, and Wathne 2003, p. 221), and even in reducing transaction costs (Dyer 1997, p. 552). Therefore, as will be elaborated, this framework considers investments and their design particularly in the area of "branding" and "sales support" as functionally relevant structure-shaping instruments to unleash the advantages of an advanced "degree of decentralization". However, before it comes to the transfer of property rights or the placement of [relationship-specific] investments to set up the systemic configuration, the classic NIE suggests that the principal verifies the ability and motivation of potential agents. Therefore, the discussion about setting up the systemic configuration will commence with the "**screening**" efforts to be performed by the principal.

I) Screening

Before it comes to the delegation of property rights and the placement of productive investments to support the agency-relationship, NIE suggests carrying out some **"screening"** of potential agents in order to eventually select the most suitable agent for the activity to be assigned (Wathne and Heide 2004, pp. 75). Information concerning the agents' interests and qualifications tends to be asymmetrically distributed. This, in turn, exposes the principal to the hidden characteristic problem. The selection of an incapable and or uncooperative agent may be disastrous for the efficiency sought by moving to a more decentralized arrangement. Therefore, the introduction of a systematic "screening" mechanism is a viable lever to overcome this risk. Performing such verification or qualification efforts tends to reduce the information asymmetry, which is expected to facilitate the selection of less opportunistically inclined, trading partners. This potential to alleviate problems of "hold-up" underpins the general relevance of "screening" for asset management firms in their moves towards an advanced "degree of decentralization" to improve distribution performance.

Therefore, in the light of this functional role to control for ramifications of "opportunism" and "service firm specificity", "screening" deserves consideration in the second stage of the enquiry's framework of analysis to come to an optimized institutional arrangement for the distribution function for mutual funds. In this respect, the **intention of the empirical investigation is to clarify**

- **how and to what extent the verification effort covers the motivational aspects or whether they tend to center purely on clarifying the ability of potential distributors to offer customer reach and access to new sources of inflows**.

Stump and Heide (1996, pp. 432) highlight the need to verify the underlying motives, as the identification of parties with the appropriate skill-set does not necessarily guarantee that these skills will be applied in the agency-relationship in question. In this regard, the enquiry also intends to explore **to what extent the principal requires pledges from agents as indications of commitment** (Anderson and Weitz 1992, pp. 20). From this conceptual perspective, the framework of analysis views "screening" as a critical measure available to asset management firms when they craft the structure of increasingly decoupled agency-relationships. "Screening" tends to reduce the likelihood of "hold-up", thereby favoring the aspired improvement realization of a strong "cash inflow stream".

II) Contract design

An importance consequence of an advanced "degree of decentralization" is that contracts gain greater significance in structuring the inter-firm agency-relationship. However, as already indicated, in the light of the contractual incompleteness (Saussier 2000, pp. 190), they are widely accepted as imperfect tools to secure efficacious handling of opportunistic tendencies (Crocker and Masten 1991, p. 70). Nevertheless, contracts represent a central vehicle for transferring ownership, thereby assigning property rights for the asset underlying the transaction in the agency-relationship. This allocation is eventually expected to alter the efficiency of the relationship (Whinston 2001, p. 84), as it offers the chance to mitigate distortions in [investment] behavior stemming from a diluted distribution of residual rights of control and residual returns. In this view, **the distribution of property rights structuring the agency-relationship then appears to be of greatest functional relevance to the achievement of the optimization objectives**. Thus, by way of delegating these rights in the context of setting up the systemic configuration, the principal may then fundamentally activate desired, but non-contractible behavior on the part of the agents (Hart 1995, pp. 73). This ability to influence behavior, in turn, underlines the relevance of the **"contract design"** to asset management firms to accomplish a strong "cash inflow stream" when they distribute their mutual funds to private investors through the channel of banks.

Therefore, this framework considers the "contract design" in terms of the allocation of property rights as a key structure-shaping instrument for setting up a consistent design of the relationship based on the organizational choice. To investigate the efficacy of the "contract design" for mobilizing structure-driven motivation on the part of the bank to take on the distributing role on behalf of the asset management firm, the enquiry's framework will distinguish between the different categories of property rights, as suggested by Furubotn and Richter (1991, p. 6). In more specific terms, ownership consists of the right to use an asset [usus], the right to appropriate the returns from an asset [usus fructus], the right to change its form, substance, or location [abusus], and the right to transfer any of these rights to a third-party. As illustrated above, **the intention is to clarify**

- **whether the assignment of property rights adequately reflects the choice of the "degree of decentralization" in order to set the stage for a consistent design of the institutional arrangement**.

In this respect, the main aim is to ascertain to what extent the transfer of property rights is able to activate the desired role behavior on part of the distributing agents, thereby paving the way for a strong "cash inflow stream".

III) Branding

Investments in **"branding"** are expected to be of greatest pertinence to achieve aspired distribution performance levels. In the light of increasingly decentralized structures of value chains, "branding" activities give product-producing firms the means to reduce the information asymmetry between them and distributing intermediaries but most notably in their relationship to the end customer (Göbel 2003, pp. 324-331; Kay 1993, pp. 251). By way of making information available, the brand as an image in the mind of the [potential] customer about a product or service (Meffert and Burman 2002, p. 168) performs three critical functions to fuel demand. As Caspar, Hecker, and Sabel (2002, p. 13) summarize, brands ease information-processing as they offer orientation and recognition to customers. Moreover, they reduce the [perceived] risk among customers of taking wrong purchasing decisions by providing continuity and security. Last but not least, brands are in a position to create emotional appeal. These functional roles of "branding" are considered to be even more important for services than for goods. While Stauss (2004, pp. 103) pinpoints general implications for designing "branding" strategies in the face of the intangibility of services and the integration of the external factor, Jordan (2001, p. 23-24) highlights the need for asset management firms to strengthen the tangibility of their brand capacity by means of visualization, associations, physical presence, and documentation of quality in order to secure a differentiated positioning. Moreover, Jain and Wu (2000, pp. 950-956) show that advertising activities at the product level of open-ended mutual funds lead to improved distribution performance. All this then indicates the functional relevance of investments in "branding" also to asset management firms in their attempts to boost the "cash inflow stream" in the face of critically evolving "market dynamics".

Therefore, the enquiry framework conceptualizes "branding" as a variable available to the principal to design the chosen "degree of decentralization" in order to bring the choice-specific side-constraints of "opportunism" and "service firm specificity" under control. In this regard, first of all, the aim is to clarify

- **the intensity and the focus with which the respective asset management firm is engaging in brand-building measures.**

To allow a more elaborate discussion on how "branding" is able to guide the behavior of distributing agents under the regime of the given organizational choice, this enquiry is eager **to find out if these brand-building measures aim to reach the private investors and/or focus on communicating to distributors**. In more substantive terms, the purpose is to examine whether investments in "branding" are placed to enable private investors to impose some form of control on the agents' sales and advisory activities, [and] or whether these investments are mainly targeted at distributors in their role as gate-keepers and opinion-leaders (Kotler and Bliemel 1999, pp. 945) to mobilize their [profit-orientated] interests to take on the distribution function. Moreover, in line with classic NIE propositions, this enquiry will also **explore in which way these investments are in fact specific to a particular relationship.** For example, the asset management firm may engage in co-branding activities to offer the [external] banks the prospect of some differentiating image-transfer (Baumgarth 2004, p. 254-255).

IV) Sales Support

While "branding" activities by reducing information asymmetry may not only trigger some end-customer-driven control of distributors but also raise the banks' willingness to take on the distribution function, the asset management firm still needs to make sure that [external] distributors are adequately enabled to perform the sales and advisory activities for its product offering. According to Picot, Reichwald, and Wigand (2003, p. 534), it is crucial for the principal to [actively] ensure sufficient ability on the part of the agents to perform the delegated activities, in this way bringing the institutional arrangement as a whole to full strength. As outlined above, distributors for financial services have to successfully handle a so-called "process of truth" in their interaction with private investors (Lehmann 1998, p. 1733). Thus, banks and in particular their staff operating at the point-of-sale then need to be adequately empowered to successfully handle the relevant points of interaction in the sales and advisory activities in order to acquire, develop, and retain customers for a particular mutual fund offering (Beaujean, Davidson, Madge 2006, p. 66). In the light of this apparent need to adequately account for the "service firm specificity" inherent in the distribution function, investments in **"sales support"** capacities gain considerable relevance to asset management firms to establish the necessary cognitive prerequisite on the part of agents to eventually come to an optimized "cash inflow stream".

Following from all this, investments in "sales support" are assumed to play a critical role in shaping the design of the institutional arrangement to eventually reach the target variables of this enquiry's framework. To properly examine this action variable, the purpose of the upcoming empirical investigation is to clarify the **focus of these capacities** in the light of the organizational choice. In more concrete terms, the intention is to ascertain

- **whether these capacities are established mainly to deliver product-related information and some form of training or whether these investments in "sales support" aim at providing comprehensive sales concepts to the**

distributing banks and the sales staff in the respective branch networks in order to appropriately handle inefficiency-causing risks related to "service firm specificity".

The former approach tends to rely to a considerable extent on the ability to formulate instructions on how to execute the delegated sales and advisory activities with the product-related information provided. The latter rather aims to build qualification on the part of the distributing agents or [jointly] identify areas for value creation as an attempt to guide their behavior to successfully manage the "process of truth" for the principal's product offering. In general, this rather qualification-oriented approach is predicted to potentially activate extra role behavior, thereby setting the stage for the generation of a strong "cash inflow stream". Such an upgrade may even serve the [profit-maximizing] interests of distributors. The enquiry will then also investigate to what extent the principal is able to create some relationship-specific human assets on the part of the distributing agent, which potentially produces some **lock-in effect**. In line with the classic NIE perspective, all this indicates that the build-up of capacities in "sales support" may not only address efficiency-relevant risks related to "service firm specificity" but to some degree even tame issues related to opportunistic tendencies.

2.2.2.4.2 Process-Related Measures to Manage the Relationship

As Zaheer and Venkatraman (1995, p. 375) emphasize, it is not only the structure of the relationship but also the processes by which the relationship is managed that play a decisive role in bringing the exchange to the desired proficiency-level. Therefore, after having conceptualized the instruments available to the principal to set up the systemic configuration for the chosen "degree of decentralization", the enquiry will now introduce those measures suggested by NIE to manage institutional arrangements in an on-going manner to reach the framework's target variables. As is recognized in designing organizations (Galbraith 2002, p. 11-13), these process-related measures for ensuring agents' ability and motivation to take on the delegated role need to be carefully attuned to the structure [i.e., systemic configuration], which demarcates the frame for exerting influence on behavior on a continuous basis. In this regard, this enquiry will conceptualize NIE propositions on "**monitoring**", the "**incentive scheme**", and "**relational exchange**" in its framework of analysis. As already indicated earlier, these at least in general are expected to allow the principal to bring under control varying [but choice-specific] negative side effects stemming from "opportunism" and "service firm specificity" on a situational basis. In this way, these action variables potentially set the stage to accomplish the sought improvement in the "cash inflow stream".

I) Monitoring

Decentralized systems for coordinating economic activity are generally prone to situations in which relevant information is distributed asymmetrically. A shift away from hierarchically-organized exchange, therefore, may give rise to situations of "hold-up", as for example hired agents will be more likely to get away with exploiting the principal due to their information advantage. In this regard, **"monitoring"** provides the opportunity to reduce the information asymmetry in the agency-relationship (Lal 1990, pp. 305), which then assists the principal to overcome the hidden action problem by detecting uncooperative and, thus, aberrant behavior on the part of the agent. As this increase in transparency tends to induce agents to refrain from such behavior in the first place, "monitoring", in general, represents a key lever to exert influence on agents' activities. This ability to set the stage for some guidance of the distribution function underlines the general relevance of "monitoring" to asset management firms to manage the traditionally specialized set-up of the value chain for producing and delivering mutual funds to private investors.

Therefore, for the second stage of the enquiry's optimization problem, "monitoring" will be conceptualized in the framework as one of the process-related instruments to appropriately address issues stemming from "opportunism" and "service firm specificity". Of particular interest is to find out

- **whether a move towards a more advanced "degree of decentralization" is accompanied by a tendency to focus "monitoring" on the outcome of distribution efforts or if it centers around the agents' behavior** (Anderson and Oliver 1987, pp. 77-78; Celly and Frazier 1996, p. 201).

In this respect, this study also aims to explore at which level of the agency-relationship the asset management firm intends to establish transparency, as the assumed agency-relationship of this enquiry entails multiple levels (Mishra, Heide, and Cort 1998, pp.

278-280). The purpose is to clarify **whether** with the choice in favor of a more advanced "degree of decentralization" **the principal** then mainly **performs monitoring at the system-level of the relationship with banks or if these efforts are also carried out at deeper levels of the agency-relationship**. This can take the form of diving into breakdowns of "monitoring" data for example at the branch level of distributing banks. This enquiry will then also explore how the principal applies the established transparency to guide the agents' activities. For example, the asset management firm may pursue some form of direct intervention in the distribution function to secure the needed behavior for improving the "cash inflow stream".

II) Incentive scheme

As already pointed out, classic NIE literature argues that measures of monitoring need to be accompanied by appropriately designed incentives in order to bring rather decoupled systems to full strength. Kaufmann and Lafontaine (1994, pp. 439-444) outline that the generally divergent interests of independent parties in an agency-relationship can be harmonized by establishing an incentive scheme that makes the long-term gains from cooperative behavior exceed the short-term pay-off of opportunistic tendencies. The intention is to motivate agents to take actions that create long-run value for the principal and to avoid actions that destroy value (Jensen and Murphy 2004, p. 18). As far as the blueprint of an "**incentive scheme**" is concerned, the **use of different pay-components** play an important part in designing the institutional arrangement for guiding the agents' activities (John and Weitz 1989, p. 2) to favor the realization of aspired performance levels. In this respect, Katz (1971, pp. 578-581) argues that **system-rewards**, which are provided on the basis of membership and therefore are unrelated to respective performance levels, are effective in holding agents within the system. However, these do little to encourage behavior beyond the line of duty. To make agents to some degree bear the financial impact of their behavior, the principal may turn to some form of **performance-related pay** to mobilize cooperation of hired agents. All this highlights that the "incentive scheme" at least in general represents an efficiency-relevant lever available to asset management firms to mitigate latent problems of "hold-up", thereby achieving the desired improvement in the "cash inflow stream".

In the light of this functional relevance, this enquiry will, thus, consider the "incentive scheme" as a further process-related measure to design the chosen "degree of decentralization" to reach the framework's target variables. The intention is **to shed light on**

- **The compensation-components the asset management firms apply to adequately deal with the choice-specific situational demands arising from latent "opportunism" and "service firm specificity" in order to pave the way for strong distribution performance levels.**

In more detail, the purpose is to clarify whether in increasingly decoupled systems it comes down to more intensive use of performance-related pay and whether this is sufficient to bring inefficiency-causing behavior under control. Moreover, in the light of the multiple levels within the agency-relationship, the **purpose is also to clarify whether rewards are mainly provided at the system-level or if these are also deployed at individual levels**. At least in principle, the latter would indicate some more direct influence on the behavior of the banks' sales staff operating at the point-of-sale in direct contact with private investors.

III) Relational Exchange

Besides the classic NIE process-related measures to secure a consistent design of the institutional arrangement for a particular "degree of decentralization", this enquiry also acknowledges the efficacy of norms of "**relational exchange**" to cope with choice-specific side-constraints. As already point out before, with a shift towards less integrated institutional arrangements implying that coordination in the agency-relationship increasingly takes place at arm's length, parties to these transactions regularly attempt to supplant or at least to complement these [market-based, rather autonomous] arrangements by introducing elements of relational exchange. In this regard, Macneil (1980, pp. 38) argues that adherence to norms of role integrity, flexibility, and solidarity emphasizes the shared values in the continuous interaction between principal and agent. These norms as codes of conduct carry the potential to raise commitment, thereby bringing under control tendencies of opportunism on the part of distribution channels (Gundlach, Achrol, and Mentzer 1995, p. 81) and ultimately reducing negotiation costs (Artz and Brush 2000, p. 356). Heide and John (1992, pp. 35) argue that norms of "relational exchange" are capable of creating a mutually beneficial atmosphere in the agency-relationship, thereby alleviating the inefficient threats of "hold-up". All this highlights that norms of "relational exchange" also tend to display functional relevance to asset management firms in their attempts to boost the "cash inflow stream" by adjusting the choice and design of the distribution system in response to "market dynamics".

This enquiry will, therefore, include "relational exchange" as an additional process-related measure available to asset management firms to account for the choice-specific demands stemming from "opportunism" and "service firm specificity". As will be seen in the case studies, "relational exchange" covers various aspects of the continuous interaction in the agency-relationship. Of particular interest is to find out to what extent it comes to **multi-level interaction** across organizational boundaries to coordinate distribution activities (Brown, Dev and Lee 2000, p. 54), which is expected to facilitate the guidance of behavior. In this regard, the enquiry will also aim to illuminate whether the principal delivers **information in a flexible and proactive manner** as this is expected to strengthen the agents' role integrity in performing the delegated activities. As far as the information exchange is concerned, this enquiry furthermore intents to ascertain if at all and to what extent the principal leverages it for some **two-way communication** (Anderson and Weitz 1992, p. 21), in this way collecting feedback on how to create value for the agency-relationship as a whole. As this tends to raise the agents' involvement and commitment, such a design of "relational exchange" is assumed to inhibit "opportunism", thereby contributing to the generation of an improved "cash inflow stream". Last but not least, this enquiry will look at the **joint actions** between the asset management firm and the banks that go beyond the initial exchange and the way in which these potentially reinforce desired role behavior on the part of distributing agents (Heide and John 1990, p. 25).

2.2.3 Applying the Framework of Analysis to Derive Propositions on Optimizing Distribution Systems

So far, the derivation of the framework of analysis has focused on the introduction of the framework's general structure and the definition of the different groups of variables to unlock and transfer the practical challenge facing asset management firms into a choice and design problem. Now, the purpose is to arrange these groups of variables from a more interactive point of view in order to sketch out the conceptual dynamics underlying the framework of analysis. In this way, the enquiry will focus on putting forward the assessment criteria by which the choice and designing problem will be addressed from an action-orientated decision-making perspective. With these assessment criteria introduced, the enquiry is then going to find itself in a position to specify refutable propositions on how to capitalize on the advantages of an advanced "degree of decentralization", while simultaneously circumventing inefficient disturbances stemming "opportunism" and "service firm specificity". In other words, **the main aim of applying this framework is to spell out how to take best possible decisions regarding the choice and design of distribution systems** [in terms of the degree of decentralization] to realize improvements in the "cash inflow stream" in the face of critically evolving "market dynamics".

To make this framework operate according to the stated goals, an explicit criterion concerning decisions of that kind has to be introduced. In consideration of classic NIE propositions and in line with recent developments in strategic marketing literature (Ghosh and John 2005), this enquiry will turn to some form of fit-argument as decision-making criteria in order to apply the framework of analysis from the envisaged optimizing point of view. As will be laid out in more detail, by linking central arguments of NIE with core elements of organizational design concepts, **fit is going to be applied as explicit optimizing requirement in this comparative assessment of alternative approaches to organize the distribution function in the asset management sector**. In this regard, Zajac, Kraatz, and Bresser (2000, p. 432) illustrate that such a requirement plays an important role in normative models of strategy formulation. As is known, fit is considered to trigger desirable performance implications (Miles and Snow 1984, p. 22). Therefore, given its optimizing perspective, this study takes the view that a fit has to be realized between the organizational action variables and conceptually relevant contingencies to achieve optimized levels of the target variables. Yet, the way in which such a fit generates the desired effects still has to be specified in substantive terms by using conceptual arguments. To apply such a fit-criterion in outlining an optimal decision on the institutional arrangement for marketing mutual funds to private investors in

Germany, then demands that this claim of superiority can be proven on the basis of corresponding cause-effect relations.

Given the conceptual background of this framework of analysis, this enquiry, at least in principle, turns to the central arguments of NIE to define optimal, success-generating fit-constructions. Thus, at least in general, this study falls back on relative [transaction] costs reasoning to substantiate the proficiency of aligning institutional arrangements to changing environmental challenges and eventually bringing problems of "hold-up" under control by setting internally consistent designs. Yet, as Wolf (2003, p. 270-278) indicates, NIE-related argumentation already uses transaction costs in a rather implicit way, usually by rather vaguely translating the pros and cons of institutional arrangements and their behavioral ramifications into cost-performance relations. Accordingly, also in this study, the analysis cannot be reduced to the attempt to solely calculate the superiority of optimizing decisions in pure [transaction] costs terms. On the contrary, in line with some recent extensions of NIE (Vorhies and Morgan 2003), this enquiry will also have to make use of some information-processing arguments as well as behavioral science assumptions. These arguments and assumptions from organizational theory are implicitly applied to define optimal alignments with regard to both the environmental challenges and the internal control problems. Hence, as far as this study is concerned, the analysis itself from a system-perspective will then also draw on information-processing capacities and structurally induced behavioral effects in declaring "fit" to identify optimal solutions to the enquiry's choice and designing problem.

To specify in more detail in which way the fit-argument is used to outline the interconnectivity among the group of variables according to the framework's general structure, this enquiry will rely on central guidelines of the classic contingency perspective (Donaldson 1987, p. 2; 1996a, pp. 2-7). This perspective claims that [strategic] choice-decisions need to adequately take into account external, conceptually relevant contingency factors. This essentially means that individual organizations have to adapt their structure to their environment in order to regain and maintain performance levels. Treating asset specificity [in terms of investments] as an endogenous variable rather than as an exogenous factor, this enquiry, therefore, argues in a first step that, contingent upon the "market dynamics" and the rising need to adequately cope with the corresponding information-processing and motivational challenges, a choice concerning the "degree of decentralization" for the agency-relationship has to be made in order to establish the **external fit**. In this sense, this study alleges that such a fit will already lead to higher levels of distribution performance (Doty, Glick, and Huber 1993, p. 1239).

However, in addition to this fundamental decision with regard to the external adaptations, this enquiry simultaneously acknowledges that this choice has immediate implications for the internal design of the institutional arrangement. While classic NIE argumentation assumes the internal design rather automatically to be consistent (Williamson 2002, p. 175), recent marketing-related contributions highlight the explicit need to actively secure an internal consistent design to realize desirable performance implications (Olson, Slater, and Hult 2005, p. 59). Therefore, in line with most recent developments in the realm of design theories (Delery and Doty 1996, Wolf 2000), this framework of analysis explicitly stipulates as an optimizing-relevant requirement that the chosen institutional arrangement in terms of the coordination mode needs to be designed in an internally consistent manner. In other words, based on the organizational choice, instruments for setting up the systemic configuration and the process-related measures need to be carefully concerted and aligned to bring under control the choice-specific side-constraints of "opportunism" and "service firm specificity", thereby paving the way for the desired efficiency-enhancing effects. Thus, while this is something the central argumentation of NIE rather implicitly presupposes, this enquiry requires explicitly the design decision to recognize the motivational as well cognitive ramifications associated with the institutional arrangement in a choice-specific kind in order to meet this fit-criterion (Donaldson 1995, pp. 205). Regarding the placement of [relationship-specific] investments and its implications for the design, there can be no denying that central NIE arguments will have a central say in the formulation of this fit-requirement. Therefore, as far as the **internal fit** is concerned, given the risks associated with larger specific investments in "branding" and "sales support", this enquiry argues that these should generally be accompanied by stronger [explicit] control and steering mechanisms to minimize opportunities of rent-appropriation. This, in turn, indicates the synergetic interplay between the design's structure and process assumed in the enquiry's framework for optimizing the target variables.

With this conceptual grounding of the enquiry's framework, it appears feasible to derive at least broadly-defined **propositions on how to optimize distribution systems**. In the light of the conceptualized groups of variables and the introduced relations, there can be no doubt that both fit-requirements are of greatest functional relevance to produce adequate solutions to this enquiry's choice and design problem. By combining these fit-requirements, this enquiry, at least to some extent, follows some form of the **extended configuration hypothesis** (Henselek 1995, p. 50) as its central working proposition. In more specific terms, this framework of analysis generally proposes:

- **Those asset management firms that not only choose institutional arrangements for the distribution function in congruence with the rising "market dynamics" and the corresponding information-processing and motivational challenges but also design the chosen "degree of decentralization" in an internally consistent manner to guide distributors' behavior will enjoy a stronger efficacy in generating an optimized "cash inflow stream" than those that do not establish external and internal fit.**

However, while both fit-requirements are assumed to have a positive effect on the dependent target variables, this enquiry recognizes that these demands do not necessarily have to be of equal weight in impact. Nickerson and Silverman (2003, pp. 433) show that there are considerable constraints preventing organizations from immediately changing to the apparently optimal governance form. Given conflicting forces also at work in the enquiry's framework of analysis, this enquiry, in fact, accepts the notion of a dilemma which needs to be carefully managed (Remer 2001, pp. 356). While the "market dynamics" generally suggest a move towards a more decentralized system, the side-constraints of "opportunism" and "service firm specificity" at least in principle indicate the superiority of integrated institutional arrangements Therefore, and this is something the following empirical investigation intends to clarify, in line with the argumentation of Mintzberg (1981, p. 316) this enquiry argues that it is the internal fit that is possibly more relevant to the optimization of distribution systems than the external fit. In other words, the internal consistency may compensate for an external mismatch.

As far as the optimal choice [and ultimately the optimal design] is concerned, in the face of the competing forces conceptualized in the framework, this enquiry tends to suggest that, in the wake of the "market dynamics", a decision in favor of a more advanced "degree of decentralization" to organize the distribution function can prove to be best at increasing chances to regain distribution performance levels. However, while such an adaptation may open up attractive opportunities in particular related to expanded customer reach, at the same time it poses critical demands for the internal design of the agency-relationship to establish the necessary cognitive and motivational prerequisites to efficaciously guide agents' activities. According to the framework's general structure, adjustments in the design's systemic configuration and processes are essential to properly enable and motivate the agent to take on the distribution function, thereby addressing the danger of "hold-up".

In this regard, **taking a rather long-term perspective**, this enquiry is inclined to argue that – if designed consistently – a "**partnership**"-type of distribution system provides the principal with the opportunity to secure optimal [extra] role behavior on the part of distributing agents. Such an intermediate or hybrid type of institutional arrangement not only offers the chance to combine the incentive intensity of markets and the administrative control features of hierarchies to establish the necessary motivational and cognitive conditions but also tends to trigger extra role behavior, as it provides considerable scope of participation in the coordination along the value chain. Thus, from a comparative point of view, it appears that this particular coordination mode offers the best possible [i.e., most efficient] way in terms of systemic configuration and processes for dealing with side-constraints of "opportunism" and "service firm specificity" inherent in the distribution function. The way market discipline as well as internally provided incentives can be applied in a combined manner offers the chance to control the danger of "hold-up" without diminishing the necessary motivational prerequisites to achieve a strong "cash inflow stream" on a sustainable basis. Therefore, without neglecting other types of institutional arrangements that may in the short term provide strong distribution performance levels, this framework pursues a second working proposition:

- **Those asset management firms that set up a consistent design of a "partnership"-type of institutional arrangement are able to enjoy the**

advantages of an advanced "degree of decentralization", while simultaneously controlling for the latent negative side effects in comparison to those that do not establish the necessary prerequisites to cope with rising [choice-specific] challenges of "opportunism" and "service firm specificity".

In this respect, the framework of analysis intends to highlight the critical role of productive investments in activating appropriate role behavior on the part of agents [also in an advanced "degree of decentralization"]. If these are properly designed [i.e., mainly relationship-unspecific], they essentially have the opportunity to balance the dependence (John and Heide 1988, p. 24) and may even create bonding effects (Rokkan, Heide and Wathne 2003, p. 221) in increasingly decoupled agency-relationships. In this way, they may then prove to be productive in mitigating inefficiency-causing issues stemming from "opportunism" and "service firm specificity" and ultimately in bringing a "partnership" to full strength.

2.3 Methodology

Having set up the theory-guided framework of analysis, the purpose now is to present the selected research methodology in more detail. To identify better- or best-practice in the choice and design of institutional arrangements to market mutual funds to private investors, **this enquiry will turn to a comparative multi-case study research design**. In light of the complex observational task for the subject of enquiry, this research strategy appears to be particularly suitable to secure a scientifically adequate handling of the enquiry's question and objective in terms of the demand for validity and reliability (Bonoma 1985, pp. 203). Having already discussed the superiority of this research method in comparison to alternative approaches for this particular research purpose, the focus is now on outlining which case studies are sampled, which techniques and tools are developed for collecting data, and the method by which the data is processed to examine the truth of the framework's basic propositions.

2.3.1 Sampling

As far as the sampling of the case studies is concerned, it is of critical relevance to obtain the necessary data that allow propositions and statements to be generalized.

Therefore, as already indicated, this enquiry aims to sample strategically relevant case studies (Koch 1985, p. 260) in order to be able to identify and isolate the potential effects of the action variables. In more specific terms, in the light of the comparative multi-case study approach, the intention is to investigate a range of case studies that exhibit varying expressions among the variables conceptualized as choice and designing variables while having a variety of background factors in common. Hence, given the raised problem and question, **this enquiry selects the case studies according to their "degree of decentralization" of the institutional arrangement for marketing mutual funds via the banking channel to private investors in Germany**. By turning to such a sampling approach, which essentially secures the variation of the strategic choice variable, this enquiry is able to bring under control, at least to some extent, the assumed functional effects of these choice-decisions with regard to the design of the systemic configuration and process-related measures. In this way, the investigation is then, at least to some degree, able to isolate the impact of the choice from the design-decision on the framework's target variables.

Following the conceptualization of the choice variable and, thus, in line not only with the conventional NIE categorization of alternative institutional arrangements but also with recent trends in the German market, this enquiry is going to select three case studies which differ in their relative "degree of decentralization". Sampled and classified on the basis of publicly available information, these asset management firms will now be briefly introduced:

- **DekaBank** is selected for the analysis of the fully integrated organizational choice of the distribution system. Referred to as the **"hierarchy"**-type of institutional arrangement in this enquiry, DekaBank distributes its mutual funds to private investors exclusively through the proprietary in-house branch network of its parent organization, the German Savings Banks Financial Group.
- This enquiry selects **Julius Bär Asset Management** for the study of the rather intermediate mode of coordination along the value chain to produce and market mutual funds to private investors in Germany. The asset management arm of the Swiss-based private bank entered the German market in the early 1990s and has been at the vanguard of setting up collaborative approaches in the interaction with

external distributing banks. Therefore, Julius Bär Asset Management will be examined as the **"partnership"**-type of institutional arrangement, which offers considerable scope for participation along the different steps of the value chain for mutual funds.

- In this enquiry, **Fidelity Investments** represents the most far-reaching discrete, in other words, decentralized solution in structuring the relationship with external banks. The stand-alone US-based asset management firm entered the German market in the early 1990s and has traditionally engaged in relationships with external banks in Germany at arm's length to organize the distribution of its mutual fund range, while heavily emphasizing the quality of its investment products. From this view, Fidelity Investments is sampled as the asset management firm pursuing some **"market"**-type of institutional arrangement.

2.3.2 Data Collection

After having dealt with the identification and selection of strategically relevant case studies, Eisenhardt (1989, p. 533) proposes the development of adequate instruments and tools as preparation for the eventual data collection effort. The purpose is to ensure that this enquiry is based on reliable and valid information in performing the comparative case study analysis. As this empirical investigation deals with case studies that consist of various levels or components, a full picture of their complexity will only be established if data is collected at the holistic level but also from embedded units (Yin 1994, p. 41-44). In the light of its epistemological perspective on how to optimally organize the distribution function in the asset management sector, **this enquiry will have to deal with different "levels of reality", with some of these levels difficult to observe or directly ask about**. Therefore, a **mix of methods of data collection** is needed (Hellstern and Wollmann 1983, p. 97) in order to appropriately cope with the situations in which the unit of analysis of the case study is different from the unit of analysis as data collection source. When trying to handle data from the whole system-level as well as individual behavior, a combination of quantitative and qualitative techniques is necessary to [re]construct or proactively interpret properties of the subject of enquiry. Hence, to eventually carry out some form of triangulation (Stake 1994, p. 241), besides the analysis of newspaper articles, publicly available reports, archival records, internal documents, **this enquiry most notably collects evidence by means of qualitative interviews**.

The actual preparation of these different collection methods is based mainly on two workstreams. On the one hand, the sampled asset management firms were contacted. A first meeting with the key contact people is used to explain the study's objective, its conceptual background, and the framework of analysis demarcating the scope of empirical investigation. Moreover, in a joint-effort, relevant interview partners are identified. For all three case studies, this enquiry attempts to recruit relevant experts from various levels of the sales and marketing department who manage the interaction with the distributing banks in Germany on an on-going basis, as well as members of the management board as interviewees. Such a group appears to particularly insightful for the subject of enquiry as they tend to be deeply involved in setting up, managing, and revising the relationships with distributing banks in the German market. In this way, the stage is set to allow this enquiry to get not only a detailed but in particular a valid grasp on how the selected asset management firms [as principals] organize [in terms of choice and design] the central unit of analysis of the case study, that is the agency-relationship with the distributing banks for marketing mutual funds to private investors.

On the other hand, this investigation intends to establish an adequate **research plan**-type of document in the preparation of the data collection process. This document not only defines the questions to be examined in accordance with the enquiry's objective but also outlines probable sources of information in order to guide the actual gathering of data. The objective is in this way to reduce potential shortcomings stemming from errors and biases. Given the need for different data collection methods to systematically tap multiple sources and levels of evidence, the research plan first of all includes a detailed **interview guide** to carry out what Kepper (1993, pp. 43-44) refers to as problem-centered interviews. Focusing on the framework of analysis, this guide contains **two groups of open-ended questions**. While the first block intends to illuminate the interviewees' general perspectives and experiences in choosing and designing distribution systems, the second block focuses primarily on the single variables included in the framework of analysis, thereby facilitating a semi-structured interview process (Lee

1999, p. 62) to gather the relevant information. Besides this interview guide, the research plan also includes an **additional catalogue specifying the operationalized set of mainly quantitative information needs** along the conceptualized variables, thereby further attempting to limit subjective influences in the data collection process. By consistently applying such a standardized research plan in combination with the investigations at different analytical levels of the case studies to gather subjective perceptions as well as objective information, this enquiry is confident of reaching an acceptable level of reliable and valid data.

Regarding the actual data collection, each asset management firm was visited to carry out the qualitative interviews, as well as to collect and/or review internal documents, archival records, and quasi-statistics. The interviews with the relevant experts commonly lasted between 75 to 90 minutes and were recorded through the use of handwritten notes. **Immediately after each interview was completed, these notes were transformed into detailed interview protocols**, which were then amended by some further facts obtained from other sources as cross-references. This enquiry employs this method of recording as it creates an environment in which interview partners are more willing to share relevant information regarding choice and design decisions of institutional arrangements and the positive or negative impacts of these decisions on the target variables. Moreover, these comprehensive transcripts lay the groundwork for the analysis of the data that follows and also allow for more precise questioning in the course of further interviews, thereby increasing the prospects of achieving valid results. It almost goes without saying that a draft of the case study report is made available to key informants from the respective asset management firms to discuss and possibly to further refine the integrity of the empirical findings.

2.3.3 Data Processing

To generalize and reduce the information collected, due to the mainly open-ended nature of the questions, this enquiry will perform some kind of [systematic] classification and coding of the content gathered in the course of the interviews (Kepper 1993, pp. 56). As indicated before, regarding the examination of the framework of analysis and the proposed functional relations in more detail, this will not be achieved by means of statistical generalization, which is generally based on random samples. Instead, this enquiry will employ some form of theoretical generalization (de Vaus 2001, pp. 237-238; Yin 1994, pp. 30-32) that, to some degree, may involve some aspects of replication logic, which conventionally lies at the heart of generalizing from experiments. Bearing in mind that the selection of strategically relevant cases is in line with the range of alternative distribution systems observed in the German private investor market, identified causal patterns between conceptualized variables to reach the framework's target variables may then [still] exhibit a sufficient level of [external] validity to be positioned as better-practices. In other words, by falling back on such a comparative design with this systematic variation in variables, this approach is able to relate the superiority of institutional arrangements to varying expressions of action variables and the realization of fit, while keeping under control constant influencing contextual background factors. Yet, there can be no doubt, the exploration, the testing, and the possible refinement of the enquiry's propositions against the empirical findings **is only going to be accomplished on the grounds of plausibility and logical reasoning**.

Chapter 3: The Asset Management Sector

After having outlined concept and methodology for the comparative institutional analysis, the purpose is now to bring in relevant information concerning the asset management sector as a whole as well as the distribution environment for mutual funds to private investors in Germany. As elaborated, the objective of this enquiry is to identify best possible ways regarding the choice and design of institutional arrangements for marketing mutual funds to private investors in order to come to a sustained improvement in the "cash inflow stream" In this regard, the intention is to shed light on the global characteristics of the contingencies conceptualized in the enquiry's framework in order to set the stage for an adequate examination of the optimization problem across the three case studies. Therefore, the following introduction of the asset management sector will, first of all, turn to recent market developments in Germany to illustrate the general trends in overall distribution performance levels as well as the changes in the distribution environment. After **establishing a common understanding of those relevant "market dynamics" in Germany**, the enquiry will outline the key steps of the value chain for producing and marketing mutual funds to private investors. By bringing forward the typical organizational set-up along the different steps of the value chain, **the aim is also to illuminate the general expressions of the side-constraints stemming from "opportunism" and "service firm specificity" facing asset management firms** in their attempts to respond to the "market dynamics".

3.1 Market Dynamics in the Asset Management Sector

Asset management operations have become an important part of the German financial services industry. According to the statistics of the Bundesverband Investment and Asset Managament (BVI), at the end of 2004 the asset management sector in Germany has reached a size of EUR 1003 billion in terms of the Assets under

Management (BVI 2005)[12]. This total market volume managed by asset management firms can be divided into two central segments:

The so-called "Spezialfonds" accounting for EUR 543.1 billion [or 54 percent] of the overall market.

- The segment of the **"Publikumsfonds"** contributes the remaining EUR 459.9 billion [or 46 percent].

In order to shed light on the general "market dynamics" regarded as relevant for the choice and design of institutional arrangements for marketing mutual funds to private investors, **this enquiry is going to focus solely on the developments in the segment of "Publikumsfonds"**. This is the segment, which covers the market for open-ended mutual funds available to private investors, whereas "Spezialfonds" typically represent tailored investment vehicles for institutional investors. Therefore, whenever this enquiry outlines global characteristics of the "market dynamics" in the German asset management sector, it refers to developments in the arena of "Publikumsfonds".

Throughout the 1990s, the asset management sector experienced unprecedented growth in terms of AuM. Between 1990 and 2000, the market volume enjoyed a compound annual growth rate of almost 20 percent, in certain years growing by even more than 30 percent. To a considerable extent, the generally favorable capital market conditions at that time [and the resulting positive investment performance effect] spurred this boost. Additionally, from 1997 a growing stream of net inflows into mutual funds started to kick in, further contributing to the growth in total AuM. As outlined in Figure 9, the annual net inflows raised by distributing intermediaries from private investors increased from EUR 14.8 billion [in 1997] to a record high of EUR 58.8 billion [in 2000]. This implies an average annual growth of almost 60 percent in this key indicator for distribution performance levels.

---

12 Although the statistics provided by BVI represent the market dynamics in the German asset management sector in an accurate manner, it is important to point out that these only cover asset management firms that are members of BVI. Thus, these overall numbers do not include the figures of asset management firms, which distribute their mutual funds to private investors but are not members of BVI. This needs to be highlighted as Fidelity Investments, the enquiry's case study on a "market"-type of institutional arrangement", did not become a member of BVI until 2005.

Yet, in the wake of the general economic slowdown and the nose-dive of global capital markets [with the negative investment performance effects] at the turn of the century, this growth cooled down dramatically, inflicting serious damage on the profitability of asset management firms (McKinsey&Company 2003, p. 6). Since 2000, the asset management sector has only been able to grow at a moderate annual rate of 2 percent, reaching a total AuM of EUR 459.9 billion in 2004. As far as the development of net inflows in Germany is concerned, Figure 9 clearly highlights that demand for mutual funds has essentially evaporated. Private investors, to a great extent, have lost confidence in this particular investment vehicle, given the losses they incurred when the capital markets collapsed (Davies 2005, p. 3). As a consequence, net inflow figures in Germany have reached a level of only EUR 6.5 billion in 2004, **implying a decline in demand of more than 40 percent per year since the peak in 2000**. All these "market dynamics" show that, it has become increasingly difficult for asset management firms to sustain demand from existing customer bases for their mutual fund offering, pinpointing the expansion of customer reach as a promising avenue to strengthen growth.

Fig. 9: DEVELOPMENT OF NET INFLOWS IN GERMAN ASSET MANAGEMENT SECTOR

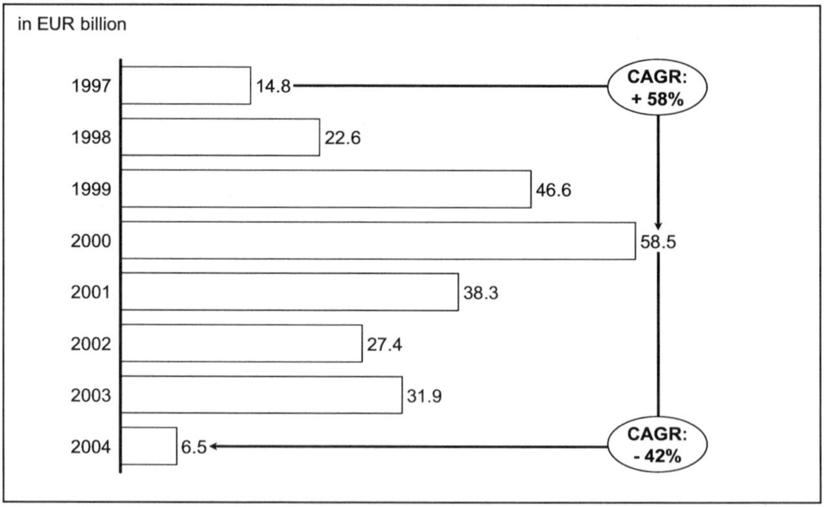

Source: BVI (2005), author's own calculation

To market mutual funds to end customers, asset management firms generally turn to a number of different distribution channels. Similar to the distribution environment across Europe [except for the United Kingdom], **in Germany the banking channel at large represents the most important intermediary, performing sales and advisory activities to private investors for mutual funds**. Recent market research efforts (BVI 2006) confirm that **73 percent of private investors prefer to purchase mutual funds via banks**, followed by the channel of independent financial advisors [16 percent], or directly from the asset management firm [15 percent].

Fig. 10: MARKET-STRUCTURE IN GERMAN ASSET MANAGEMENT SECTOR

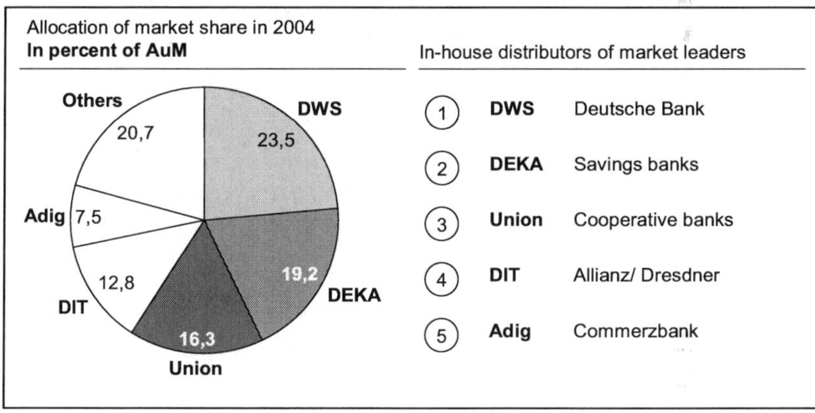

Source: adapted from Jenkins (2005, p. 3)

As banks in Germany almost exclusively sold the mutual fund offering of the respective in-house product provider throughout the growth period in the 1990s, it does not come as a surprise, as illustrated in Figure 10, that domestic asset management firms, which are part of a larger financial group, dominate the German asset management sector. According to the figures presented by Jenkins (2005, p. 3), DWS, the mutual fund management arm of Deutsche Bank, is the market leader with 23.5 percent [in terms of AuM]. DWS is followed by DEKA, the asset management firm within the German Savings Banks Financial Savings Group with a market share of 19.2 percent, and Union Investment as the central mutual fund provider of the cooperative banks in Germany [market share: 16.3 percent]. This, in turn, shows that **the market share of asset management firms is driven, to a considerable extent, by the distribution power of their in-house channel**.

However, in the wake of the nose-dive of capital markets and the declining overall demand for mutual funds, the distribution environment in Germany has been undergoing fundamental changes. Most notably, the majority of German banks have started to depart from exclusive distribution systems for their in-house asset management firms (Boos 2001, p. 28). Banks at the mass market level have increasingly opted to make shelf-space available for the mutual funds of external asset management firms. This trend can clearly seen as response to the mounting pressure from private investors demanding independent advice and greater choice at the point-of-sale, as well as the growing notion among distributors that they do not have all the necessary expertise in-house to offer a complete range of different mutual fund types (Cripps 2005, p. 14). In September 2000, HypoVereinsbank became the first large German commercial bank to offer third-party products to its end customers alongside the range of in-house mutual funds. By the end of 2004, most banks in Germany have introduced some form of [branded] third-party distribution, with a substantial share of the net inflow streams now going to external product providers (Handelsblatt 2004, p. 25). While banks increasingly consider this move to be essential to strengthen their long-term competitive positioning vis-à-vis distributing rivals [even if it means that means that, in the short-term, their in-house firm loses out on some of the net inflow streams] (Soop 2005, p. 28), it has favored non-domestic asset management firms in establishing a foothold in what used to be a relatively closed market (Narat and Renzer 2005, p. 21).

From all this, regarding the "market dynamics" relevant to the enquiry's choice and designing problem, it shows that first of all **asset management firms have to deal with an overall decline in demand for mutual funds**, highlighting the need to expand customer reach in order to boost distribution performance levels and ultimately to regain growth. At the same time, they also have to account for fundamental changes in the distribution environment, which offers opportunities but also poses considerable threats. The lasting trend towards **increasingly decentralized distribution systems in the**

banking channel, on the one hand, **may provide the aspired expansion of customer reach** and thus new sources for inflows and revenues. **However**, on the other hand, this trend **also gives rise to different forms of competition for market share between asset management firms** in Germany. There is an intense contest among [a large pool of] asset management firms to initiate and uphold agency-relationships with [a relatively small number of] distributing banks. Moreover, once access to the distributors' shelves is established, asset management firms still have to cope successfully with strong competition at the point-of-sale in order to realize the aspired levels of net inflows, as banks in Germany have typically granted access to a handful of external asset management firms alongside their in-house provider. To fully understand the implications of these "market dynamics," the enquiry will now turn to the value chain of mutual funds, thereby illuminating the global characteristic of latent side-constraints stemming from "opportunism" and "service firm specificity".

3.2 Opportunism and Service Firm Specificity along the Value Chain for Mutual Funds

In essence, **mutual funds are investment services** provided by a variety of financial institutions. As is known from literature on modern portfolio theory, **mutual funds are regarded as vehicles to pool investments** from a large number of [rather small] investors in order to purchase securities on their behalf (Grinnblatt and Titman 1998, p. 4). In this regard, they represent an attractive investment product for private investors[13], as they provide a relatively diversified exposure to global capital markets (Hughes 2002, p. 7).

To adequately mirror the involvement of economic actors to produce and market mutual funds to private investors in the context of the enquiry's optimization problem, the

13 In particular, the so-called "open-ended" mutual fund is a very attractive investment vehicle for private investors. This type of mutual fund allows private investors to buy and sell units [shares] of the fund at any time at the prevailing market rate, which is very closely related to the market value of the underlying securities in which the fund invests (Hughes 2002, pp. 8-9).

value chain contains two major building blocks[14]. As illustrated in Figure 11, this enquiry basically distinguishes between the production function and the distribution function for mutual funds. Along this typical, specialized set-up of the value chain, the asset management firm is responsible for performing the different [investment] activities of the production function to ensure strong investment performance levels for the mutual funds. The different distribution channels [banks, insurance agents, IFAs] – that own and manage the relationship to end customers – are in charge of carrying out the complex tasks of raising inflow streams for the mutual fund offering.

Fig. 11: THE VALUE CHAIN FOR MUTUAL FUNDS

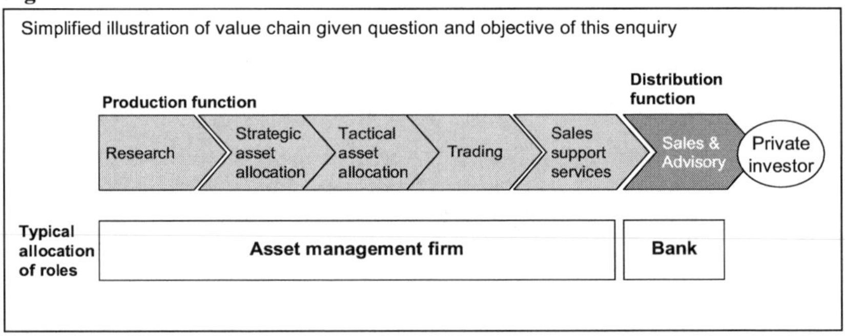

Source: Author

Given the subject of enquiry, with regard to the **production function,** it is of particular interest that the activities related to the actual management of the mutual funds'

14 Each mutual fund is, in fact, a legal entity consisting of the assets raised from investors and a board of directors to supervise the management of the fund's assets. From a formal point of view, the board of directors is responsible for allocating the responsibilities for the different activities related to the mutual fund. This includes not only the assignment of the asset management firm to run the investment activities for the fund but also the naming of the custodian [to physically hold the securities owned by the fund] and the transfer agent [to perform record-keeping services] in order to arrange the so-called middle-and-back office. In practice, it is the asset management firm that is in the driving seat for launching a new fund, collecting seed-money, assigning a portfolio manager, and appointing a board of directors (Siggelkow 1999, p. 4).

assets[15] are typically accompanied by the deployment of substantial resources to provide some form of support to the different distribution channels. In general, these sales support services cover not only the delivery of product information, the creation of sales materials, the provision of training, and the preparation of sales events but also the development of sales concepts and initiatives, the planning of branding efforts, and on-going relationship management with distributors. The intention is to assist the distributing intermediaries in generating inflow streams from private investors for the asset management firms' mutual fund offering.

The **distribution function** for mutual funds itself centers around the actual sales and advisory activities performed by the distributors' personnel at the point-of-sale, which usually takes place in direct contact with the private investors. In the light of the integration of the external factor, these service activities essential entail the complex task of building individual, **customer-specific investment solutions** from the mutual fund offering available. To adequately serve the respective risk profile and investment objective of private investors along a constant process of interactions, it is critical for the distributors' sales staff to have **specialized know-how** of the mutual fund offering in order to appropriately tailor the sales and advisory processes towards the needs of their end customers.

This short introduction of these central steps for producing and marketing mutual funds already indicates that these activities entail substantial **uncertainty in terms of both environmental and behavioral uncertainty**. This, in turn, gives rise to considerable concerns about information asymmetry between the parties involved along the value chain. For example, given the **far-reaching specificity** inherent in sales and advisory activities to match end customers' investment objectives with suitable mutual

---

15 Based on extensive **research** activities on macroeconomic trends [including prospects of economic growth, interests rates, inflation forecasts, business cycles, etc.] and industry and capital market data, this management of the funds' assets, in particular, involves the decision on the investment strategy in terms of the so-called **strategic asset allocation** for the respective mutual funds. This strategic asset allocation fundamentally defines the substance of the mutual fund as it determines the fund's proportions of the different asset classes [equities, bonds, money markets, derivates, etc.]. Within these proportions, the next step is then to fine-tune this strategy by selecting single titles in terms of the **tactical asset allocation** (Steiner and Bruns 2002, pp. 89) and, eventually, to implement this asset allocation for the mutual fund by executing the necessary **trading** in the capital markets.

fund offerings, it is difficult for the asset management firm to verify whether the level of the inflow stream is accountable to appropriate role behavior on the part of distributors, or driven solely by the explicit demand of private investors for the asset management firm's mutual fund offering, or just affected by general market developments. This, in turn, implies that any opportunistic tendencies of economic actors are likely to remain undetected and, thus, unpunished. Therefore, in line with service firm-related NIE literature (Erramilli and Rao 1993; Murray and Kotabe 1999), it is no surprise to see that the value chain for producing and marketing mutual funds has been traditionally set up in a relatively integrated manner in Germany [with distributors – most notably banks and insurance companies – having profoundly integrated backwards into asset management operations]. **In comparison to other industries in Germany, it is in fact the banking industry that overall exhibits traditionally the greatest depth of production** (Böhme 1997, p. 59).

Yet, as outlined above, the general characteristics of the "market dynamics" in Germany also included the attempts of distributors – most notably banks – to overcome the hurdles in differentiating intangible sales and advisory activities (Maier 1998, p. 1677) by offering more choice at the point-of-sale to their end customers. While this move of distributors towards rather decoupled distribution systems for mutual funds highlighted diminishing loyalty to in-house providers in order to pursue their own interests (Wittkowski 2003, p. 8), it also incited enthusiasm among asset management firms with regard to prospects of achieving increased customer reach through external distributors. However, from the viewpoint of asset management firms, it has become evident that **these advanced degrees of decentralization are increasingly prone to challenges stemming from "service firm specificity" and "opportunism"**, leading Sector Analysis (2003, p. 6) to conclude that the marketing of mutual funds via third parties has in fact "caught a cold".

To illuminate in more detail the general characteristics of those side-constraints on the enquiry's optimization problem, the findings of the survey conducted by Heinemann et al. (2003, pp. 52-57) are of particular interest. This study distinguishes between **three groups of obstacles confronting asset management firms in their**

endeavors to realize inflow streams through external distributors, with issues surrounding "knowledge, willingness, and commitment" considered as the most critical obstacle.

Fig. 12: MOST CRITICAL ISSUES IN THIRD-PARTY DISTRIBUTION

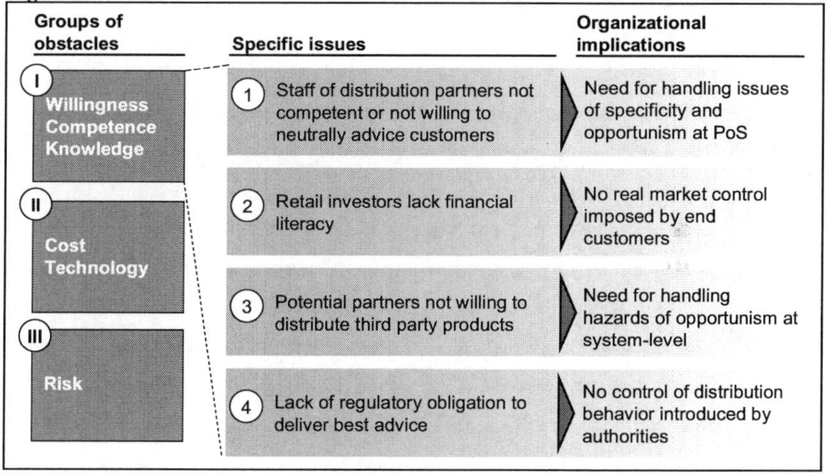

Source: adapted from Heinemann et al. (2003, p. 53)

With regard to the specific issues related to these most critical obstacles, as illustrated in Figure 12, asset management firms overall perceive the lack of willingness and insufficient competence on the part of external distributors' sales staff to offer objective advice as the largest barrier to realize the benefits of expanded customer reach. In line with this finding, Sherff (2003, p. 41) argues that distributors and their staff remain inclined to primarily sell the mutual funds of their in-house provider, despite making shelf-space available to external management firms in their bids for differentiation by offering more choice to end customers. This reflects not only strong self-interest seeking [profit-maximization] of distributors but also pinpoints troubles for the distributors' sales staff to adequately perform the complex sales and advisory activities for mutual funds on behalf of external product providers. There is the general notion that sales staff that have, so far, been trained only to sell in-house products, are having difficulties in making a transition towards using the offering of external providers in a flexible manner when they tailor individual investment solutions to private investors. All this underlines that asset management firms need to adequately account for these general side-constraints stemming from "opportunism" and "service firm specificity" in their decision-making on how to arrange the value chain to produce and market mutual funds to private investors.

Further highlighting this need is the general perception that private investors overall lack the financial literacy to be able to truly assess the mutual fund assortment offered by the distributor or even to genuinely control the actual sales and advisory activities performed at the point-of-sale. Although so-called fund-ratings by rating agencies such as Morningstar may provide some objective orientation to private investors [and, overall, are able to affect the inflow streams into mutual funds (Del Guercio and Tkac 2001, p. 29)], **it is still the actual advisory taking place at the point-of-sale within the banks' branches that substantially influences the investment decisions and, thus, the purchasing behavior of private investors** (Kramer 2004, p. 22). In other words, the distributors' sales staff are in the position to guide the inflow streams' direction into mutual funds to a considerable degree. It seems as if any lack of willingness and or specific know-how on the part of distributors and their staff for the mutual fund offering of a particular [external] asset management firm is not actively compensated – or only to some degree – by pressure from end customers. In this regard, it is important to mention that the financial services industry traditionally deals with a relatively loyal customer base, which usually shows only limited willingness to switch between competing financial service providers. In the wake of negative experiences, which covers incidents of inappropriate advice, it rarely comes to a complete breakdown of the relationship between distributor and private investors, with only 15 percent of end customers in fact switching their main bank (Beaujean, Davidson, and Madge 2006, p. 66). All this boils down to the impression that **an "invisible" hand of control from the demand side is not fully established** that – on the one hand – punishes inadequate distribution behavior but also – on the other hand – truly rewards objective, customer-orientated sales and advisory activities at the point-of-sale. In addition to the absence of fully developed competitive forces, asset management firms also regard the lack of regulatory obligation for distributing intermediaries to deliver best-possible advice to their customer as another obstacle to overcome the limited willingness of distributors at large and or know-how concerns at the point-of-sale. All this clearly shows, **to achieve desired distribution performance levels for its mutual fund offering** – be it via the in-house channel or in decentralized settings – **it is largely up to the asset management firm to adequately bring under control these side-constraints of "opportunism" and "service firm specificity".**.

Hence, all in all, the decision-making regarding the choice and design of institutional arrangements to coordinate the service activities along the specialized set-up of the value chain has to account for a number of contingencies. As elaborated, **asset management firms need to find best possible ways to respond to the "market dynamics" in Germany**. These include most notably the overall decline in demand from private investors for mutual funds as well as the intensified competition among asset management firms for shelf-space in distribution channels. Rearranging the choice and design of distribution systems becomes a crucial condition to tap additional sources of inflow streams. However, at the same time, given the general characteristics and circumstance surrounding the activities for the distribution function, **the institutional arrangement for the value chain also has to allow the asset management firm to establish the necessary cognitive and motivational prerequisites in order to successfully cope with the challenges related to "opportunism" and "service firm specificity"**. There can be no denying that it is essential that the choice and design of distribution systems for mutual funds successfully handle latent opportunistic tendencies on the part of distributors and the specificity typically inherent in the sales and advisory activities in order to succeed in regaining growth in distribution performance levels.

Chapter 4: Comparative Institutional Analysis

After having put forward both the theory-guided enquiry's framework of analysis and the asset management sector, the objective now is to investigate in which way the strategically selected asset management firms are approaching the central decision-making problem regarding the institutional arrangements for the marketing of mutual funds to private investors in Germany. Adopting a comparative perspective:

The intention is to assess whether and how the respective asset management firm deals with the two fit problems outlined in the enquiry's theory guided framework.

For each of the selected case study, the aspiration is to explain if and in which way the asset management firm is bringing into fit both choice and design for organizing distribution activities in Germany with the varying situational demands and objectives.

As far as the first – the external – fit is concerned, the ambition is to shed light with which organizational choice for the distribution system the asset management firm under focus accounts for the multiple challenges, including critically evolving distribution performance levels at the turn of century.

In a second step, with regard to the internal fit, the purpose is to elucidate whether and in which way the design is configured in consistence with the organizational choice in order to favor the optimization of distribution performance levels.

The overriding objective of the comparative institutional analysis is to assess the overall efficacy of the choice and design against the ability to capture net inflows raised from private investors, by appropriately controlling for latent negative side effects stemming from the specificity inherent in the sales and advisory activities and latent opportunistic tendencies.

4.1 The Case of DekaBank

4.1.1 The Choice of "Hierarchy" as Institutional Arrangement for the Distribution Function

To commence the comparative institutional analysis, the enquiry will first turn to DekaBank (DEKA)[16] to examine how this particular asset management firm is coping with the enquiry's central decision-making problems. Established by the merger of Deutsche Girozentrale and DekaBank GmbH in 1999, DEKA is the central financial service provider for the German Savings Banks Financial Group, the decentralized group of savings banks, landesbanks, public insurance companies, and mortgage banks. Integrated into this group, DEKA performs activities in segments of asset management, corporate banking, and capital markets.

As far as the asset management operations are concerned, DEKA distributes its range of investment funds exclusively through the German Savings Banks Financial Group, which has 477 different Sparkassen (which in the following will be referred to as savings banks) and more than 14,000 staffed establishments to reach private investors. By the end of the year 2004, DEKA as a whole has EUR 135 billion in AuM, with almost EUR 90 billion (or 67 percent) of this raised from private investors with capital market-based mutual funds as well as property-based investment funds. With this scale of operations, DEKA is the second largest asset management firm in the German asset management sector (Jenkins 2005, p. 3).

In the light of the enquiry's objective, it is of crucial significance that the German landesbanks and regional savings banks associations as a matter of fact hold an indirect and equal share of DEKA. Therefore, in view of this backward-type of integration, the enquiry considers the case of DEKA as the one in which the asset management firm falls back on the means of **"hierarchy"** to organize the distribution function in Germany. However, in line with the well known analytical distinction of current management

---

16 This empirical case study is based on four semi-structured interviews in March 2005 using the enquiry's standard questionnaire with management of DekaBank at Dekabank's headquarters in Frankfurt. Each interview lasted between 90-120 minutes. In order to meet the enquiry's information needs, additional information has been taken

science, it cannot be denied that, in this particular case study, a type of "hierarchy" is applied in the context of a multidivisional setting, rather than in a unitary form of coordination (McGuinnes 1991, p. 77). As will now be elaborated in more detail, DEKA management considers this integration into German Savings Banks Financial Group to be a key cornerstone for further increasing market share in the German asset management sector[17].

4.1.1.1 Emergence of Performance Gap

In line with the structure of the enquiry's framework of analysis, first of all, the intention is to ascertain to what extent and in which form the respective asset management firm is confronted with a performance deficit that, already from an objective point of view, can be regarded as critical. In other words, the aim is to clarify whether the asset management firm is facing unsatisfactory distribution performance levels and eventually increasing pressure to respond to disturbances to its organizational choice for arranging the distribution function. To adequately investigate the emergence of a performance gap, for all three case studies the examination of net inflow figures and their evolvement over time [either in comparison to the general market trend or selected competitors] appears to be most suitable. Reflecting the net new assets raised from private investors for the asset management firm's product range per year, this indicator

---

from DekaBank's annual reports 1999-2004. A draft of this case study has been made available to DekaBank management in order to further refine the empirical findings of this investigation.

17 Given the prominent role of the Sparkassen as distribution channel for this case study, it appears worthwile to outline briefly the pecularities of the savings bank group in the context of the wider German banking system. The German bank system can be best described by the so-called "three pillar system" (Hackethal and Schmidt, p. 15), comprising the private commercial banks, the cooperative banking group, and the savings bank group. The savings bank group itself consists of three tiers, as it contains the primary or local savings banks, Landesbanks and regional savings banks association, and DekaBank and the German Savings Bank Association (DSGV) (Hackethal and Schmidt 2005, pp. 9-11). The [public] savings banks are governed by savings banks laws of the respective German states. These laws usually oblige the savings banks to service the public interests of their region by facilitating individual savings and serving the credit demand of their local communities. This makes in particular employees, small and midsized companies, and public authorities their main target customers group. While the servicing mandate is under constant review and evolvement, it for example obliges savings banks to open a transaction account for every applicant. From all this, it then also does not come by surprise that profit maximization is not considered to be the primary business objective for savings banks, but rather assumes the role of a side condition (Kammlott, Mayer-Fiedrich and Schiereck 2005, p. 102). Instead, the public founding entity, which is typically a municipality or county, take a central role in bearing the responsibility for the economic activities of their savings banks. In the light of the so-called "maintenance obligation" ("Anstaltlast") and the "guarantee obligation" ("Gewährträgerhaftung") these public founding entities are essentially responsible to ensure that their savings banks are able to perform their operations or are liable without restrictions in the event of default of their savings banks. All this should be kept in mind, when his enquiry will examine the relationship between DEKA and the savings banks to optimize the cash inflow stream for DEKA's mutual fund offering.

appropriately portrays distribution performance levels. However, as Child (1972, pp. 11-12) points out, whether indications of unsatisfying performance development cause responses in organizational structures indeed depends on the managers' perception of these contingencies. Therefore, [in each of the three case studies] in order to specify the extent to which performance data reaches the level of a performance gap crying out for action, the upcoming elaboration will have to consider the way in which performance levels are classified from the view of respective management.

Looking at the development of DEKA's net inflows in more depth, it becomes apparent that this asset management firm achieved strong distribution performance in the late 1990s and at the turn of the century. Considering its entire investment product range[18] (including property-based funds) available to private investors, DEKA enjoyed record years in 1999 and 2000 with net inflows of EUR 12.6 billion and EUR 17.3 billion, respectively.

Fig. 13: EMERGING PERFORMANCE GAP CONFRONTING DEKA

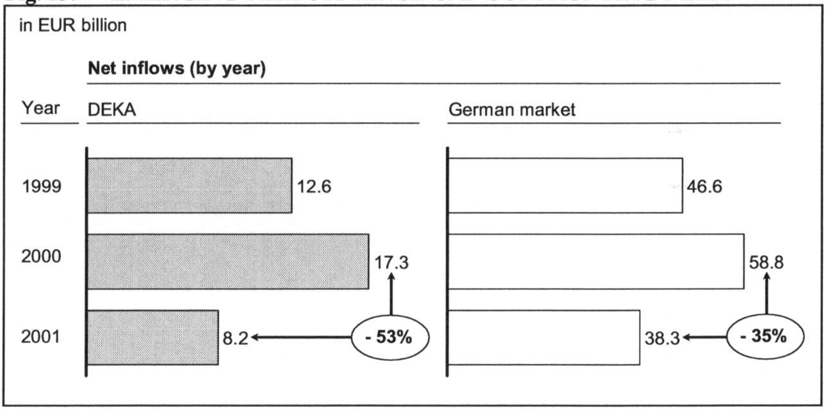

Source: DekaBank Annual Reports 1999-2001, BVI (2005)

18 Taking into account capital market-based mutual funds only, distribution performance reached even higher levels. In the year 2000, net inflows peaked with EUR 18.8 billion raised from private investors, allowing DEKA to obtain market leadership in Germany at that time.

However, as outlined in Figure 13, after this period of extreme growth, DEKA experienced a dramatic slump in distribution performance levels for mutual funds. In the year 2001, DEKA's net inflows plunged by more than 50 percent from EUR 17.3 billion to EUR 8.2 billion. This substantial drop highlights considerable impediments confronting DEKA to raise inflows for its product range. As net inflows at the market level only declined by 35 percent in the face of the overall challenging capital market conditions at that time, this slump indicates that DEKA, in fact, faced considerably greater difficulties in maintaining distribution performance levels relative to the overall market. This shows that the strong competitive positioning established in previous years was under growing pressure at the beginning of the century.

Hence, already from an objective point of view, given DEKA's aspiration to keep and even to extend its market leadership, there can be no doubt that **this deterioration indicates a very noticeable performance deficit**. In the light of the substantially stronger drop in net inflows vis-à-vis the overall market, it seems as if more than the challenging capital market conditions drive the decline in distribution performance at that time.

4.1.1.2 Perceiving and Interpreting Performance Gap

To shed light on whether an objectively perceptible deficit in performance levels ultimately results in adaptations to the institutional arrangement, it is crucial to elaborate how management interprets this gap. Management may be willing to absorb a decrement in performance and, thus, tolerate misfit and delay alterations for lengthy periods (Donaldson 1996b, pp. 60-61). Hence, it is important to clarify whether the gap has exceeded the management's subjective threshold to initiate reactions in order to restore [external] fit by altering most notably the organizational choice. Along those lines, the enquiry will therefore now elucidate how DEKA management has perceived the very noticeable gap.

Regarding the distribution strategy of DEKA, it is essential to point out that savings banks [and landesbanks] run the distribution function exclusively for DEKA's product range throughout the 1990s. In more analytical terms, **within the institutional**

arrangements the respective roles traditionally displayed what Fein and Anderson (1997, pp. 19) refer to as territory and brand exclusivity. Conventionally, DEKA has granted territory exclusivity to the distributing savings banks, underscoring that DEKA as the central mutual fund provider has committed itself to distributing its mutual funds solely via the distributing members of the German Savings Banks Financial Group. Traditionally, this was paired with brand exclusivity pledged by savings banks, meaning that they restrict their mutual fund offering to their in-house provider. In the view of the customer reach of savings banks and, thus, their remarkable distribution power, DEKA management is well aware that it was this vertically integrated character of its distribution systems underlined by the reciprocal exclusivity commitments that drove DEKA's success in realizing market-leading distribution performance levels in Germany.

However, as pointed out above, in 2001 growth in net inflows collapsed. Against the background of DEKA's aspiration to maintain its competitive position in Germany, DEKA management was already aware of this emerging gap in distribution performance at an early stage and regarded it to be of critical relevance. With regard to the root causes underlying this slump, DEKA management perceived, in particular, that fundamental changes in the distribution environment [in addition to challenging capital market conditions and the resulting decline in demand for mutual funds] aggravated the generation of inflows via an integrated setting.

As mentioned above, the distribution landscape in Germany experienced a lasting change at the turn of the century. In view of the growing request by private investors to offer mutual funds of external product providers alongside the banks' proprietary product offering, the majority of German banks increasingly turned to less integrated structures and essentially moved towards more open distribution forms. This trend did not spare the savings banks. A considerable number of them also started to offer shelf-space to external asset management firms. Underlining this movement away from brand exclusivity granted to DEKA, **up to 25 percent of the total net inflows raised by some savings banks from their customers are now going into mutual funds provided by asset management firms other than DEKA** (Rathmann 2004, p. 2). As one sales manager argued, DEKA found itself exposed to mounting competition in what used to be a closed distribution channel. Losing this status of being the sole product provider was viewed as substantially obstructing the aspiration of upholding distribution performance levels in what were already increasingly difficult market conditions.

Hence, concerning the interpretation and causal explanation of the perceived gap in distribution performance, **DEKA management learnt that its integrated arrangements for marketing mutual funds to private investors became increasingly vulnerable to coordination and motivation issues**. Besides the overall challenging [capital] market conditions, it was in particular the diminishing brand exclusivity commitment from savings banks that DEKA management regarded as a main obstacle to sustaining the distribution performance levels of previous years. In the light of the until then positive experiences regarding its integration within the wider German Savings Bank Financial Group, DEKA management considered the institutional arrangement to be of decisive relevance to remedy the performance deficit noticed.

In the light of DEKA's aspiration to cement its strong competitive positioning in the German asset management sector, management regarded the development to have reached such a critical extent already at an early stage of negatively evolving "market dynamics" that the broader [distribution] strategy was put under scrutiny. With the given organizational choice recognized as an important lever in allowing DEKA to have obtained market leadership, DEKA management sensed the necessity to examine the "degree of decentralization" and, thus, the question whether to turn to more decoupled structures to market mutual funds to private investors or, alternatively, to continue to pursue the route of a backward-type of integration for the set-up of the value chain.

4.1.1.3 Responding to Perceived Performance Gap

As far as the responses to perceived performance gaps are concerned, this enquiry will show, not only for this but in fact for all three case studies, that management tends to refrain from fundamentally [re]adjusting the organizational choice, in other words, the "degree of decentralization". Instead, it will show that management in reaction to unsatisfying performance evolvements focuses mainly on refining elements of structures and/or processes within given organizational choices to address challenges of coordination and motivation in order to bridge the performance gap. Therefore, speaking in more analytical terms, for all three case studies, the allocation of property rights underlying the organizational choice, in fact, remains unchanged.

Along these lines, for this case study, it becomes apparent that in the face of critically evolving performance levels, in the years 2000/ 2001 **management launched a broad-based strategic review, focusing in particular on DEKA's structures and processes as well its role within the German Savings Banks Financial Group**. As management stressed, the overriding objective of this refinement was not only to bring to a halt the apparent negative trend but eventually to further increase market share. Moreover, this strategy review was accompanied by an effort to articulate a cohesive corporate identity, which from the management's point of view became necessary and urgent given the profound changes in the German market environment.

Having enjoyed strong growth throughout the 1990s with relatively integrated distribution arrangements, DEKA management remained confident of overcoming this performance gap by continuing to distribute its mutual funds to private investors exclusively through the distributing members of the German Savings Banks Financial Group. **The newly established corporate identity stresses that DEKA's success is viewed as being founded on its membership of this group**. Hence, this reliance on the extensive customer reach and distribution power of savings banks to strengthen performance levels implies that DEKA management, in fact, clung to the already given organizational choice of backward integration. As indicated above, the adjustments in the distribution strategy mainly focused on modifying structures and processes, besides some additional changes in the mutual fund offering.

In more detail, given its overriding purpose to strengthen distribution performance levels within the existing organizational choice, **DEKA management most notably aimed at securing a stronger orientation to the distributors' needs to facilitate enhanced coordination** between DEKA as the central product provider and single savings banks. As a prominent cornerstone of this overall refinement, management decided to considerably streamline the interfaces to the savings banks. While distributors used to be assisted by six different DEKA units in performing the sales and advisory activities, **a single unit named "marketing and sales: retail and savings banks" is now providing bundled one-stop services for DEKA's entire product range**. In this structure, specialists from individual production units are called up selectively in order to provide further expertise if requested. Additionally, to be able to appropriately tailor the marketing "sales support" to the respective needs of individual savings banks, since the beginning of 2002 the three sales divisions, traditionally arranged along regions (i.e., north, center, and south), have been [further] adjusted according to segments. These are most notably defined by the size of the distributing banks. In this way, the provision of "sales support" for the largest savings banks from all regions has become bundled in order to facilitate a more segment-oriented servicing.

This brief illustration of prominent alterations in DEKA's distribution arrangements underlines that the strategic review mainly led to adjustments within the given organizational choice. As will now be elaborated in more detail, despite the unsatisfactory development of net inflow figures the choice in terms of the "degree of decentralization" remained unchanged. Hence, as one sales manager argued, although facing this pattern of contingencies, **DEKA management considered the comparatively integrated approach with savings banks to distribute mutual funds to private investors still to be the most attractive avenue to regain its strong competitive positioning.**

4.1.1.4 Upholding "Degree of Decentralization" for Distribution Function

Concerning the first, the external, fit problem, the preceding discussion has revealed that DEKA management still views the traditional choice in favor of "hierarchy"-type of arrangements to be appropriate for overcoming the drop in net inflow figures. Management regarded the maintenance of the existing "degree of decentralization" as the most promising route to remedy the gap in distribution performance. This, in turn, indicates that, in the face of critically evolving performance levels, **management viewed the implementation of the choice** in terms of the design of the agency-relationships **to be inadequate in order to accomplish DEKA's strategic aspirations, rather than the choice itself.**

All this underlines the fact that the bundled assignment of property rights on the part of distributing banks in fact remains unchanged. Therefore, corresponding to DEKA's given organizational choice, it shows that DEKA management intends to continue to fall back on bureaucratically-shaped administrative control mechanisms and internal dispute resolution procedures to guide the distribution function for improving inflows streams via the in-house distribution channel. In other words, management so far has remained confident that they can alleviate the ramifications stemming from growing coordination and motivation issues by turning to steering measures typically associated with the "hierarchy"-type of institutional arrangement. Hence, to bridge the noticed gap in performance levels, it shows that DEKA keeps on counting on the compliant role behavior of the distributing members in the German Savings Banks Financial Group to perform the assigned distribution activities for DEKA's mutual fund offering.

However, as observed for the other two case studies as well, but for different reasons, whether the aspired organizational choice will be realized appears to be moderated by the interests of the respective distributors. In this regard, it is important to point out that the savings banks operate with far-reaching autonomy and quite rigorously pursue their own profit-maximizing interests (Busse 2005, p. 27). Moreover, it cannot be stressed enough, that it is not DEKA that owns the distributing banks. Instead, it is the group of savings banks and landesbanks that, in fact, [indirectly] owns DEKA. Hence, from a pure ownership point of view, this is a **situation of a backward-type of integration, which is the common set-up of vertically integrated institutional arrangements in the asset management sector in Germany**. For the examination of the enquiry's forward-type of agency-perspective, this needs to be kept in mind. From this view, it then becomes strikingly evident that, even in "hierarchy"-type of arrangements, the distributing bank, at least in general, appears to be in the powerful position of quite independently deciding how to structure its mutual fund offering to end customers.

As far as the case study of DEKA is concerned, the recent developments highlight that savings banks possess and apply this decision-making autonomy to potentially include external asset management firms in their offering and, thus, are able to depart from brand exclusivity without being sanctioned. Nevertheless, from the enquiry's steering perspective, one sales manager remarked that the coordination along the value chain for mutual funds within the German Savings Banks Financial Group is secured to a relatively large extent by "hierarchy"-type steering measures. Hence, for the purpose of analyzing the enquiry's central decision-making problem, DEKA is classified as the case with the choice of some "hierarchy"-type of institutional arrangement for the distribution function in Germany. From a comparative point of view, as will be elaborated in more detail, this enquiry regards this case as the one in which at the system-level the asset management firm [the principal] allows the distributing bank [the agent]:

- to use the provided mutual funds for advisory activities
- to receive some form of compensation for performing the distribution function of the mutual funds
- to have a say on the form or substance of the mutual funds
- to transfer a single or all the above rights to a third-party

Thus, as DEKA management pointed out in its annual report in 1999, with this remarkably bundled transfer of rights and, thus, integration into the German Savings Banks Financial Group, **the objective is to further intensify the sales and advisory efforts of distributing members for DEKA's mutual fund range**.

4.1.2 The Design of "Hierarchy" as Institutional Arrangement for the Distribution Function

In the upcoming elaboration, the focus of the discussion is on the design of the institutional arrangement in the light of the chosen "degree of decentralization". The ambition is to examine whether and in which way a coordination mechanism is put in place that is consistent with the organizational choice. In more analytical terms, with respect to the second – the internal – fit problem of the enquiry's framework of analysis, the objective here is to ascertain if the design of safeguards and investments appropriately takes into consideration the situational demands arising with the chosen "degree of decentralization".

Therefore, framed as an agency-relationship between DEKA [principal] and the savings banks [agent], the main interest is to find out to what extent the design accounts for the challenges related to "service firm specificity" and "opportunism" latent in arrangements classified as the "hierarchy" mode of coordination for marketing mutual funds to private investors. In essence, the main interest is to shed light on the design's efficacy in favoring an optimization of the benefits associated with the far-reaching customer reach provided by the savings banks.

In the course of assessing the adequacy of the design of "hierarchy" as the chosen "degree of decentralization", it will show that already with the set-up of the **systemic configuration**, defining the main coordination mechanism and including the build-up of capacities, the attempt is made to account for side-constraints of the decision-making problem. Moreover, as will be acknowledged for the other two case studies as well, it will show that the system configuration is operating as the frame within which the **process-intervening measures** for [more directly] guiding distribution efforts are introduced. In the light of the optimizing perspective in the enquiry's framework of analysis, the efficacy of the design is evaluated most notably against the ability to generate a strong "cash inflow stream" from private investors. In other words, to regain distribution performance levels by way of bringing under control hazards stemming from specificity and opportunistic tendencies.

4.1.2.1 Systemic Configuration of "Hierarchy"

In the following discussion, the enquiry will shed light on the systemic configuration in which the agency-relationship between DEKA and the distributing savings banks is fundamentally structured. The objective here is to clarify by what means the organizational design already in structural terms is directed to control for issues related to the specificity inherent in the sales and advisory activities and the latent opportunistic tendencies on the part of distributing agents. As outlined above, these are also prevalent in systems of far-reaching specialization under an overall pattern of hierarchical control.

Fig. 14: SYSTEMIC CONFIGURATION OF "HIERARCHY"

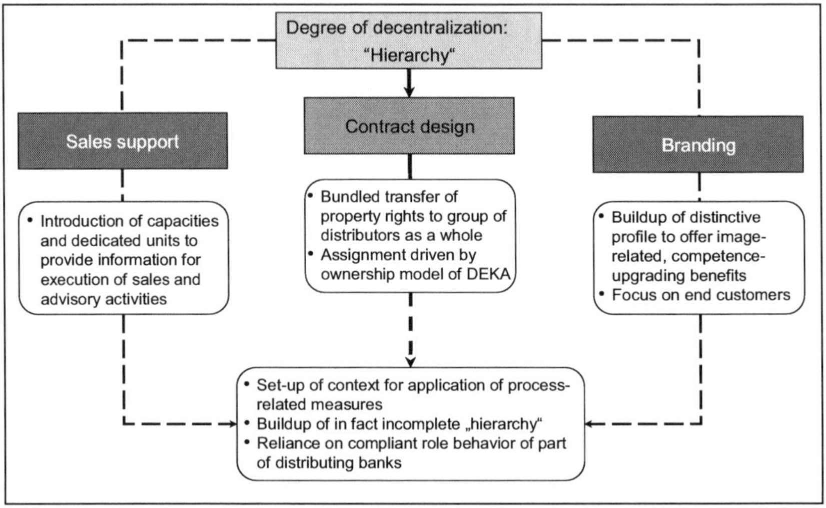

Source: Author

As outlined in Figure 14, regarding the systemic set-up for the "hierarchy"-type of arrangements, the discussion will make clear that, in line with the ownership model of DEKA, the agency-relationships are fundamentally configured by the comprehensive transfer of property rights to the distributing agents. Additionally, this examination of the design's structure intends to clarify what kind of capacities DEKA is putting in place to supplement the assignment of property rights. In this respect, the elaboration will take a detailed look at how DEKA is making investments in "branding" and "sales support" to cope with the latent hazards related to opportunistic tendencies and specificity in order to improve distribution performance levels.

As emphasized within recent discussions on hierarchical modes to coordinate economic exchange, **for this particular case study it will show that the transaction within the "hierarchy", in fact, takes place between essentially self-contained operating divisions**. Accordingly, as Eccles and White (1988, pp. 20) have already brought to light, it then cannot be ruled out that it deliberately comes to the employment of market-related instruments. As is known, economic actors may, for example, put in place some form of [transfer] pricing mechanisms (Holmstrom and Tirole 1991, pp. 201) in order to secure transactions within increasingly decomposed hierarchical modes of interaction. Along these lines, adopting features of markets then can even mean that members of the hierarchy possess full exchange autonomy with either external asset management firms or the central, in-house product provider. With savings banks increasingly reducing the brand exclusivity they have traditionally pledged to DEKA, it clearly shows that also this case study of a "hierarchy"-type of institutional arrangement displays traits of markets. Nonetheless, as will be outlined in more detail, in accordance with the classic properties of hierarchical governance, DEKA still attempts considerably to turn to the visible hand of administrative control, authority, and formal decision-making and planning procedures to coordinate the production and marketing of mutual funds. Hence, with the organizational choice of "hierarchy" at stake, the build-up of the systemic configuration focuses on both reinforcing and leveraging compliant role behavior on the part of distributing members in the German Savings Banks Financial Group to bolster the "cash inflow stream".

All in all, as will be put forward now in more detail, the systemic configuration operates as the contextual prerequisite to mobilize and secure desired distribution efforts on the part of savings banks for DEKA's product offering. Regarding the single action variables conceptualized in the enquiry's framework of analysis, the following elaboration will be touching on "contract design", "branding", "sales support", and "screening".

4.1.2.1.1 Assigning Property Rights to Set Up Governance Structure

The ownership model of DEKA with its underlying allocation of property rights considerably determines the design of DEKA's distribution systems. In line with the classic normative model of "hierarchy" and, hence, in strong contrast to the other two case studies of this enquiry, it will become apparent that there is no [bilateral, product-related] contractual agreement in place at the system-level of the respective agency-relationships specifying the terms, the process, and the rights associated with the exchange. Instead, it is the ownership model laying out the overall organizational structure that demarcates the frame for additional measures by which the transaction is then further coordinated.

Fig. 15: OWNERSHIP MODEL OF DEKA

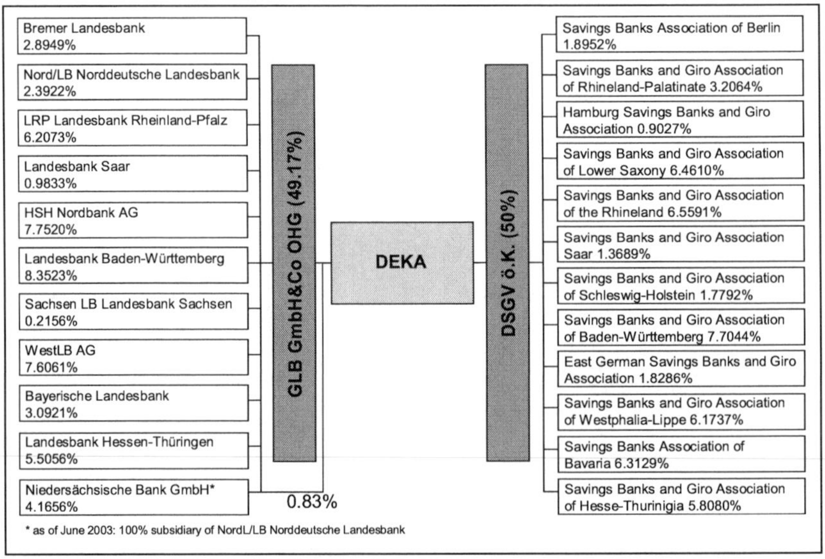

Source: DekaBank Annual Report 2004

As far as the ownership model of DEKA is concerned, with the merger of Deutsche Girozentrale and DekaBank GmbH in 1999, the main distributors of investment funds in the German Savings Banks Financial Group as a whole essentially integrated backwards into the production function for mutual funds. In more precise terms, since 2002, three shareholders directly own DEKA:

- The German Savings Banks and Giro Association [50 percent]
- The GLB GmbH & Co. OHG [49.17 percent]
- The Niedersächsische Bank GmbH [0.83 percent]

As Figure 15 shows, this structure implies that a group of 12 regional savings banks associations as well as a group of 11 German landesbanks hold an indirect and equal share in DEKA. Integrated into the Germany Savings Banks Financial Group to take on the role as the central mutual fund provider, it then also becomes apparent that DEKA performs no continuous "screening" efforts in order to verify the underlying motives of the respective exchange parties within the "hierarchy".

This ownership model with its organizational structure itself has a considerable impact on the allocation of property rights between the product-providing asset management firm and the product-distributing savings banks. In general, ownership is accompanied with the transfer of residual rights of control (Milgrom and Roberts 1992, p. 289). Therefore, from a genuine comparative point of view, it shows for this particular case study **that it comes to a comprehensive transfer of property rights to the distributors, which is, in fact, the defining characteristic of a backward integration-type of "hierarchy" for producing and marketing mutual funds to private investors**.

In more practical terms, as outlined in Figure 16, taking on the role as the central mutual fund provider within the specialized set-up of the "hierarchy", DEKA is in charge of the entire set of activities along the production function. However, there can be no doubt that the distributors at large are provided with rights that go beyond the mere performing of the distribution function. Thus, in terms of the property rights classified by Furubotn and Richter (1991, p. 6), the ownership model's implications for the enquiry's organizational steering perspective are, first of all, that DEKA is giving the savings banks the right to perform the distribution function for its mutual fund range (usus). Furthermore, savings banks are entitled to some form of compensation for offering DEKA's mutual fund range to their customers (usus fructus). In addition to these rights, savings banks have the authority to get involved in decisions concerning the production function (usus abusus). As will be outlined in more detail, a wide range of committees are institutionalized within the organizational structure. These give the distributing owners the chance to make use of this right and to influence, for example, the form and substance of the mutual fund range. Last but not least, highlighting the notion of ownership, the distributors in principle have the right to transfer any of those rights above to a third-party. This shows that while the value chain for mutual funds is organized in a specialized manner, with DEKA operating the production function and savings banks taking on the role of exclusive distributors, the distributors as a whole essentially receive a bundled set of rights. As ownership carries an incentive to maintain, develop, and improve an asset, it appears as if with this complete handover of property rights the attempt is made to appropriately account for the negative side effects of "opportunism" and "service firm specificity" lurking along such a specialized set-up of the value chain for mutual funds.

Fig. 16: ALLOCATION OF ROLES WITHIN "HIERARCHY"

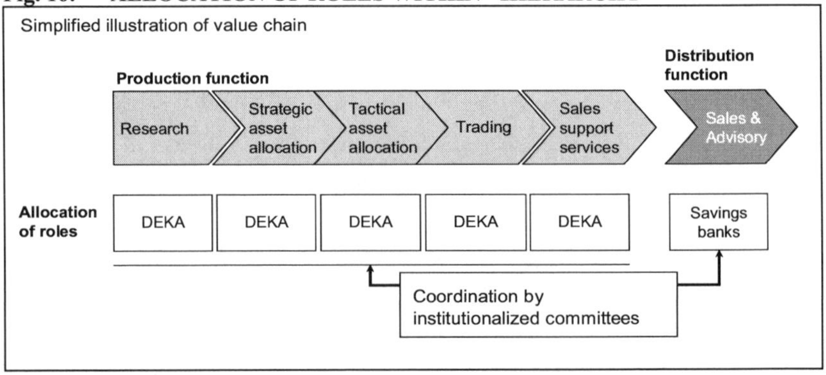

Source: Author

In this regard, as already pointed out, it also becomes apparent that **no additional contractual [service-level] agreements are in place to stipulate the sales and advisory activities for DEKA's product range**. As one sales manager explained, in the view of the ownership model, further contracts so far are considered to be only of limited functional relevance to tame opportunistic tendencies or to cope with the specificity inherent in the distribution function and, thus, to secure strong distribution performance levels. In other words, with distributors as the owner of the asset management firm, management senses no need to introduce additional contractual agreements to comprehensively regulate how the actual distribution services are supposed to be performed. As it is assumed that it is in their own interest to realize strong distribution performance for DEKA's mutual fund offering, sufficient commitment and, hence, at least standard role behavior on the part of the distributing members is expected. However, **this design of the agency-relationships also indicates that the range of sanctioning options available to DEKA is substantially narrowed for responding to specific incidents of opportunism**.

Furthermore, regarding the coordination of the interaction along the value chain, it becomes evident that DEKA, to a larger extent, relies on an administrative apparatus to agree upon instructions for subordinated members in the "hierarchy" [given the use of employment contracts]. It will show that a number of committees are institutionalized within the integrated structure. Involving management members of DEKA and the savings banks as well as the landesbanks, these provide the opportunity to discuss and work out plans, define sales targets, dovetail their activities, and eventually impose patterns of hierarchical control on the specialized set of activities along the value chain for mutual funds. In more substantive terms, document analysis reveals that besides the management and supervisory boards of DEKA, one investment fund committee, one fund sales advisory council, and 5 regional fund committees are in place to facilitate the coordination of otherwise fairly self-contained units within the "hierarchy"

However, although DEKA is handing over a comprehensively bundled set of property rights to the group of distributors as the defining characteristic of a backward-type of integrated "hierarchy", **from the agents' perspective the resulting distribution of the transfer seems to be rather diluted**. In the light of the dispersed ownership of DEKA, with 11 landesbanks and 12 savings banks associations [representing 477 savings banks] as [indirect] shareholder of DEKA, it appears unclear at this point of the enquiry whether a savings bank performing the distribution function will in fact bear the full financial impact of its behavior, in terms of the compensation it receives. Moreover, given the dispersed ownership it also remains somewhat in the dark to what extent an individual [indirect] shareholder is genuinely able to exercise influence on the form and substance of DEKA's product range. Therefore, while the assignment of property rights to autonomous distributing banks aims at strengthening their commitment and, thus, intensifying their distribution efforts, it seems as if it, in fact, gives rise to a situation in which there are clearly **collective interests among shareholders to increase the inflow stream into DEKA's product range, but possibly only limited individual interest of single banks to actually contribute strong distribution performance levels**. In other words, as will be discussed in more detail in the course of this enquiry, there are signs that this ownership model gives rise to some form of the **free-rider-problem** facing

DEKA. This may ultimately have severe ramifications with regard to an adequate handling of issues related to "opportunism" and the "service firm specificity".

4.1.2.1.2 Building Brand Capacity to Offer Competitive Advantage

"Branding" for asset managements firms is of great functional relevance to enhance distribution performance levels. As pointed out in the derivation of the enquiry's framework of analysis, at least two different but interrelated "branding" approaches are available by which asset management may attempt to boost net inflow figures. On the one hand, investments in "branding" bring about the prospect of providing image-related spill-over effects to distributors (Baumgarth 2004, p. 254-255), thereby mobilizing their motivation to take on the distribution function for the asset management firm under focus. In general, such spill-over effects carry the opportunity to favor the distributing bank in accomplishing a more competitive positioning vis-à-vis distributing rivals. Hence, these competitive benefits then potentially harmonize the interests and somewhat balance the dependence (Heide and John 1988, pp. 24-25). In this regard, "branding" offers DEKA the opportunity to reinforce the savings banks' willingness to perform the sales and advisory activities for its mutual fund range in a reliable fashion. On the other hand, by way of guiding expectations regarding the experience from purchasing the asset management firm's investment product, "branding" constitutes a means of dealing with the intangibility and variability associated with mutual funds (Keller 2003, pp. 16-19) and ultimately to generate demand from end customers. In this way, "branding" then offers the chance to mitigate the hazards related to the specificity in the sales and advisory efforts, as private investors increasingly become aware of a particular offering and potentially consider it in their purchasing decision. Therefore, along these lines, understood as an investment from an NIE perspective, the purpose now is to clarify in which way DEKA places investments in "branding" capacities in order to make provisions to curb issues of opportunism and specificity simultaneously.

Taking a comparative perspective, it clearly shows that **"branding" takes a very prominent part in DEKA's strategy to generate strong inflow streams**. Regarding the design of this action variable, it shows that DEKA management persistently places this kind of structure-shaping investment – yet in a slightly different way from the other two case studies – in order to establish a main [motivational] prerequisite for strong distribution performance levels. In more precise terms, following the organizational choice of "hierarchy" and the reliance on a compliant pattern of behavior from distributing members, DEKA's **"branding" efforts** for its [mutual fund] brand "Deka Investments" **predominantly aim at reaching private investors to carve out a differentiated profile in their mindsets**. It appears as if by creating close ties with end customers, DEKA intends to pave the way to stimulate demand for its product range. At the same time, as one sales manager emphasized, **the purpose of this "branding" strategy is also to provide competence-upgrading spill-over effects to the savings banks at large**. Thus, "branding" then also serves as a lever to control the potentially aberrant behavior of the distributing members of this group, as it is deployed to highlight the functional importance of DEKA to the German Savings Banks Financial Group in its endeavors to maintain a strong competitive positioning vis-à-vis other German banking and insurance groups.

To appropriately reach private investors (see Figure 17), DEKA runs a "branding" strategy in Germany that relies on a combination of communication channels. In more precise terms, DEKA traditionally turns to daily newspapers as well as to the larger weekend papers, magazines, and most notably television for its "branding" campaigns. In the principle, this media mix seems to be adequate to cover the wide-spread target group as these channels have the advantage of remarkably high reach. Moreover, television is widely acknowledged as the most powerful medium not only to demonstrate product attributes and persuasively pinpoint the related costumer benefits but in particular to establish a distinctive brand personality. Complemented by print media, DEKA is then also in the position to communicate more detailed product information. While this mix of communication channel facilitates the buildup of an image as an asset management firm and also provokes a lot of attention, the actual spending level on these "branding" efforts tends to be relatively high. Therefore, as one sales manager remarked, in comparison with competing asset management firms in Germany, DEKA has been the top spender on "branding" investments. Since 2000, DEKA's [above-the-line] expenditures have consistently topped more than EUR 10 million, in some years even more than EUR 20 million.

Fig. 17: BUILDUP OF "BRANDING" CAPACITIES IN "HIERARCHY"

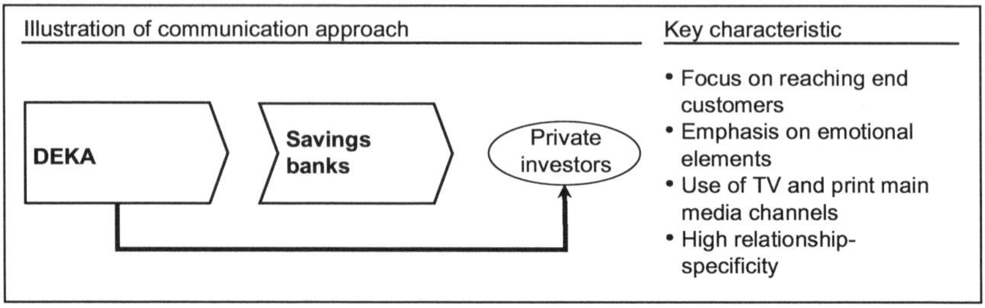

Source: Author

With regard to the actual content of these efforts, Jordan (2003, p. 26) points out that DEKA has so far pursued a relatively strong emotional focus[19] to differentiate itself vis-à-vis competitors. Moreover, in order to secure lasting recall as well as unambiguous recognition, DEKA persistently includes the "red scarf" as the key visual in its "branding" approach. Last but not least, in correspondence with salient features of "hierarchy"-type of institutional arrangements, it becomes strikingly clear that **investments in "branding" are in fact designed in a relationship-specific manner**. In each of its "branding" efforts, DEKA highlights its role as the central mutual fund provider of the wider savings banks organization as well as the exclusive availability of its product offering in the savings banks' branches.

As far as the result of these measures is concerned, it cannot be denied that **DEKA overall has managed to established strong "branding" capacities**. On the one hand, as a result of comparatively high investment levels on a consistent basis, it shows that **from the perspective of investors DEKA is the leading asset management brand in Germany**. Various market research efforts reveal that DEKA has achieved an aided awareness of more than 90 percent. Thus, end customers, to a large extent, are not only aware of and familiar with DEKA and its product offering but are also more likely to

---

19 As the larger share of private investors perceive the actual purchasing decision for mutual funds to be very complex, it appears as if DEKA intends to stimulate demand for its product range by provoking emotional associations. It seems that the aim of "branding" efforts is to appeal to end customers by addressing their fundamental needs, desires, and objectives. For example, recent "branding" activities of DEKA refer to the financial resources required to fund a child's education, thereby highlighting the suitability of a particular product offering.

actually consider it in their purchasing decision. In this way, "branding" is then expected not only to stimulate demand but, in fact, to enable private investors to control at least to some degree the actual distribution services at the point-of-sale. Therefore, it seems as if this buildup of "branding" capacities has the potential to mitigate issues of specificity likely to appear in the course of sales and advisory activities.

On the other hand, as DEKA management stresses, another result of this design of "branding" is that the end customers' perception of DEKA belonging to the savings banks has been remarkably strengthened. Since the very center of DEKA's "branding" strategy is to support the savings banks in carving out their investment expertise, it is laid out in a way that provides positive spill-over effects to its distributing owners. In view of this objective, one sales manager referred to end customer market research that highlights that private investors, who know about the close relationship between DEKA and the savings banks, regard savings banks as more competent in questions requiring investment expertise in comparison with private investors who are not aware of this relationship. This perceived competence-upgrade clearly underscores the positive spill-over effects DEKA's brand capacities provide. These are likely to reinforce the compliant role behavior at large within the German Savings Banks Financial Group and, thus, are predicted to alleviate, at least to some extent, growing opportunistic tendencies among the distributing owners.

In summary, given the comparatively extensive magnitude of investments, there can be no doubt that "branding" plays a very prominent part within DEKA's systemic configuration. By primarily targeting the end customer, it seems that the relatively strong buildup of "branding" capacities aims at establishing the necessary motivational prerequisite to strengthen the commitment on the part of the distributing owners via competence-based, image-related spill-over effects. Additionally, the brand capacity also appears to be deployed with the purpose of bringing challenges related to the specificity inherent in the distribution function under control. Therefore, even if the "branding" investments predominately focus on emphasizing the emotional and physical proximity of DEKA to private investors, thereby somewhat neglecting more rational elements, it looks as if the required provisions are made to take advantage of the substantial customer reach that the savings banks offer.

4.1.2.1.3 Setting up Sales Support Capacities to Secure Sales Success

The build-up of "sales support" capacities represents an additional measure of great functional relevance to asset management firms to secure strong inflow streams for their product range. The sales and advisory activities for mutual funds performed by the distributors' sales staff at the point-of-sale require a complex and continuous stream of interaction with private investors to build costumer-specific solutions, while being exposed to a dynamic and uncertain environment (Crosby, Evans, and Cowles 1990, pp. 69). From this view, "sales support" aims to serve two different, but interrelated, objectives. First and foremost, investments in "sales support" capacities intend to establish the prerequisites to appropriately enable the agents to perform the distribution function. Furthermore, the purpose of introducing these capacities with systemic configuration is to secure sustained commitment from the distributors to actively take on the sales and advisory activities for the principal's product offering.

As far as the first case study of this enquiry is concerned, DEKA has introduced comprehensive capacities to support the actual sales and advisory efforts performed by distributing members of the German Savings Banks Financial Group (Langer 2003, p. 100). In this regard, a sales manager pointed out that DEKA has a catalogue in place, which includes more than 200 different elements and items of "sales support" [ranging from giveaways and sales materials to office equipment] to assist savings banks in their efforts to raise net inflows. In substantive terms, it becomes apparent extensive capacities are available to supply relevant information on a regular basis. **The main objective is to equip savings banks with the necessary material to successfully perform the distribution function on behalf of DEKA**. Additionally, DEKA has also deployed capacities that facilitate the build-up of qualifications of the sales staff of savings banks. Within the unit "market and sales: retail and savings banks", which is responsible for managing the interface to DEKA's distributors, **a sub-unit is included that is specialized in conducting training programs to build the skill-set and know-how of the savings banks' staff operating at the point-of-sale**. Furthermore, an **additional sub-unit is in**

place, which plans and carries out sales events together with [individual] savings banks to more intensively promote selected product offerings to end customers. Therefore, with these different "sales support" capacities to account most notably for hazards stemming from the specificity inherent in the distribution function [but also the growing incidents of opportunism], DEKA's aspiration is to establish the necessary [cognitive] prerequisites to improve inflow streams for its mutual fund offering on a sustainable basis.

In more detail, to secure the **regular delivery of information to savings banks**, DEKA turns to a variety of vehicles. As observed for the other two case studies of this enquiry, a wide range of publications are available to continuously update distributing agents with product-related, rather quantitative but also qualitative type of information. Within this range, the so-called "Deka Investmentfonds Spezial" takes a prominent position, as it covers DEKA's entire mutual fund offering in full detail. Additionally, based on extensive fund research covering also mutual funds produced by competing asset management firms, DEKA provides annual and monthly product profiles and investment recommendations, as well as opinions and reports on capital market themes. These may then also slip into the so-called "Fonds Magazin" and other sales-orientated brochures. As some of the material provided is meant to be employed by the savings banks' personnel located at the point-of-sale in the course of the sales and advisory activities and eventually to be passed on to private investors, **this form of "sales support" aims at enabling the distributors' personnel from a purely informational point of view**.

As far as the actual way of delivering those capacities is concerned, similar to the other two case studies, **DEKA increasingly turns to electronic media in addition to the conventional ways such as hardcopies**. The implementation of this more flexible mode allows sales staff to respond more appropriately to the different information requests that may arise in the sales and advisory activities for DEKA's product range in the 14,257 branches of savings banks in Germany. However, in the face of increasingly limited exclusivity granted to DEKA, it appears as if this form of making available this comprehensive capacity of "sales support" also depicts an attempt to retain control over the information actually reaching the point-of-sale. Hence, such an approach may represent another attempt to account not only for the latent hazards of specificity but also to narrow the opportunities for opportunistic behavior.

Furthermore, as indicated above, DEKA additionally introduces **capacities to provide training programs** to distributors' personnel operating in direct interaction with private investors as well as to conduct [joint] sales events to promote a specific product offering to the banks' customers. From this view, the training programs entail the chance to transfer or upgrade the skill-set required of the savings banks' sales staff. From a comparative point of view, given the relatively integrated structure, it is easier to obtain the much desired access to single savings banks and their branches to conduct these training programs. As will be seen in the other case studies, asset management firms in more decentralized settings usually face substantial obstacles to directly interact with the distributing banks' personnel operating at the point-of-sale. This access, in turn, allows DEKA to familiarize the sales staff with the so-called "investment story" for a specific mutual fund of DEKA's product range in order to highlight the key advantages and selling points related to a particular offering. Moreover, these sessions tend to carry the opportunity to outline rather general routines and methods with which the savings banks' personnel is in a better position to adequately cope with possible challenges arising in the complex interaction with private investors. Thus, **this capacity of "sales support" seeks to provide relevant sales expertise in order to enable the members of distributors' sales staff, from a qualification point of view, to successfully perform the distributing role**. In line with fundamental characteristics of "hierarchy", it seems though as if these training programs mainly focus on transferring the required skill-set for executing the assigned role. Nevertheless, these training modules may still strengthen the distributors' identification with the agency-relationship in which DEKA positions itself as the central product provider. Hence, while the introduction of this form of "sales support" mainly aims at addressing challenges related to the specificity in advising mutual funds to private investors, it potentially provides the opportunity to mitigate opportunistic tendencies as well. Speaking more in NIE-terms, there is the tendency that this kind of "sales support" facilitates the buildup of relationship-specific know-how, in this way reinforcing some sort of lock-in effect on the part of the distributing members of the

German Savings Banks Financial Group, which is expected to curb opportunistic behavior.

Regarding the **capacity to offer [joint] sales events** to promote specific product offerings to the savings banks' end customers, it shows the purpose is two-fold. On the one hand, these events allow DEKA to guide the way in which product-related information is presented to the end customer, thereby controlling for challenges related to the specificity inherent in the distribution activities. On the other hand, they may strengthen the commitment on the part of the savings banks to actively perform the advisory activities for their central in-house provider, as there is the tendency that these events almost immediately stimulate demand for the promoted mutual fund offering.

In summary, following from this discussion it becomes apparent that the aspiration is to set the stage not only to enable the distributing savings banks from an informational point of view, but also to strengthen identification with DEKA as the central mutual fund provider by means of know-how transfer as well as more immediate pay-offs through [joint] sales events. Therefore, similar to the two following case studies – yet with some distinctive differences – DEKA has a comprehensive range of "sales support" capacities in place to favor the generation of strong inflow streams by bringing the latent hazards associated with specificity and opportunism under control.

4.1.2.1.4 Systemic Configuration as Context

After having discussed in which way DEKA designs the structural set-up of the "hierarchy"-type of institutional arrangements to produce and market mutual funds to private investors in Germany, the enquiry's goal now is to explain how this systemic configuration functions with regard to the optimization objective. With the systemic configuration being a critical ingredient of the internal fit, the purpose is now to elucidate in which way "screening", "contract design", the capacities in "branding" and "sales support", and their interplay lay the ground to mobilize standard role behavior on the part of distributing members of the "hierarchy".

From the view of the preceding elaboration, it becomes apparent that the **systemic configuration as such mainly lays out the frame within which more process-based measures are applied in order to govern the actual distribution activities**. Therefore, even if the stage is already set to bring under control hazards of specificity and opportunistic tendencies, process-related means are still required to deal appropriately with these situational demands arising in this organizational choice. In this regard, means of indirect or direct, more ad-hoc type of interventions are available to exert influence on the distribution behavior of savings banks. In other words, the systemic configuration constitutes a necessary rather than a sufficient condition to accomplish a substantial improvement in net inflow figures and, thus, to overcome the gap noticed in distribution performance levels.

Therefore, with the systemic set-up regarded as outlining the context for the subsequent employment of rather process-related instruments, it becomes evident that, in the face of the bundled transfer of property rights to the distributing banks, the specialized agency-relationships essentially turns out to be configured as a relatively integrated, "hierarchy"-type of institutional arrangement. Hence, in comparison to the other two case studies, consistent with the normative model of "hierarchy", **the visible hand of administrative control, authority, and formal decision-making and planning procedures are expected to take a prominent role in further efforts to coordinate the activities along a specialized set-up of the value chain**. In this regard, as one sales manager explained, coordination relies greatly on the commitment of the distributing banks related to their ownership of DEKA. Thus, contrary to the other two case studies, [in which participation and competitive pressures, respectively, play a central part in guiding activities along the value chain,] it shows that this asset management firm counts considerably on the ownership-driven interests among savings banks to take on the distribution function in a compliant way. However, as already pointed out, given the dispersed ownership model, it looks as if the far-reaching transfer of property rights leads, in fact, to a diluted assignment of these among the distributing banks. From this view, it then seems as if commitment on the part of the savings banks may not be as strong as initially assumed.

Moreover, it has become evident that DEKA management has deliberately implemented further capacities to establish the necessary motivational and cognitive motivational prerequisites to strengthen the savings banks' willingness and ability to take on the distributing role. In that respect, "branding" capacities with a comparatively specialized design aim at providing competence-upgrading, image-related spill-over-effects. At least in principle, these are expected to strengthen the notion among savings banks that it is in their very own interests to actively perform the distribution activities for their central product provider, thereby mitigating impediments stemming from opportunistic tendencies. Furthermore, with these "branding" efforts [almost] exclusively targeting private investors, the purpose is also to impose some [indirect] control through the end customer and to restrict scope for issues related to specificity and opportunism at the point-of-sale. Moreover, as an additional attempt to cope with the side-constraints on the central decision-making problem, "sales support" capacities are introduced to appropriately enable savings banks and their sales staff from an information as well as a qualification point of view to perform the distributing role in compliant way. In that respect, it was also highlighted that capacities for carrying out [joint] sales events are implemented, which, when put into practice, include the opportunity to offer immediate pay-offs to serve the ownership-driven interests of the savings banks. However, at this point, it remains inconclusive whether the capacities of "branding" and "sales support" are sufficient to overcome the latent deficiencies related to the somewhat diffused ownership model of DEKA mentioned earlier.

4.1.2.2 Process-Related Measures of "Hierarchy"

After having elaborated on the systemic configuration within the organizational design, the enquiry will now turn to the processes the principal applies on a regular basis to account for the coordination needs arising in the institutional arrangement in a situation-specific manner (Galbraith 2002, p. 11-13). Thus, with regard to the second fit problem, the ambition is to bring to light to what extent, in the context of the systemic configuration, the process-related measures facilitate the adequate handling of the latent hazards stemming from "service firm specificity" and "opportunism". Therefore, the purpose is now to clarify for the enquiry's first case study **which process-related**

measures DEKA deliberately employs to guide the distributing banks' behavior to achieve the desired boost in distribution performance levels.

For this case study, it will show that the coordination processes mainly rest on a bureaucratically-shaped administrative apparatus with the chance in principle to impose decisions and instructions on how to carry out the distribution function for mutual funds. Accordingly, from a genuinely comparative point of view, DEKA mainly turns to a range of institutionalized committees to exert influence on the behavior of the distributing members, rather than relying on procedures of participation or competitive pressures. Moreover, in such a relatively integrated set-up, it will become evident that DEKA brings into play the extensive capacities of "branding" and most notably "sales support" to directly intervene in the sales and advisory activities to guide distribution behavior also in a more ad-hoc manner. However, despite the assumed harmonization of interests and, thus, commitment on the part of the savings banks, it will become apparent that extra motivational means are introduced at the system-level in order to encourage strong distribution performance levels.

Adopting a more functional perspective, it appears as if DEKA's intention of introducing process-related measures is to further mobilize and reinforce the savings banks' willingness and ability to adhere to compliant patterns of role behavior as the [in-house] distributor for DEKA's product range. In line with the classic model of "hierarchy" and, thus, in remarkable contrast to the other two case studies, it shows that DEKA, to a large extent, puts into play and relies on processes to articulate instructions and directives on how to carry out the sales and advisory activities for DEKA's mutual fund offering. However, given the considerable autonomy of distributing agents and the in fact somewhat diluted assignment of property rights among these agents, it appears unclear if the organizational design in terms of those processes is adequate to curb the agency-relationships' latent dangers of opportunistic tendencies and specificity.

Regarding the upcoming empirical investigation, as for the other two case studies, within the group of process-related measures to guide the distributing banks' behavior, the enquiry distinguishes between **information-processing means** and **motivational**

means. In line with classic hierarchical patterns of coordination, this particular asset management firm falls back on instruments that guide distributors not only in an indirect but also in a rather direct way. These direct, rather ad-hoc intervening measures will be primarily discussed within the group of information-processing means as these procedures are mainly based on information flows taking place between principal and agent. In terms of the single action variables conceptualized in the enquiry's framework of analysis, besides the already discussed, structure-shaping variables, the investigation will now also touch on "relational exchange", "monitoring", and "incentive scheme" in order to illuminate the way in which DEKA aims to regain distribution performance levels by marketing its product offering exclusively via the distributing members of the German Savings Banks Financial Group.

4.1.2.2.1 Information-Processing Means for Process-Intervention

The purpose is now to discuss in more detail the information-processing means the principal employs to guide the agents' distribution effort in a more situation-specific manner to secure an improvement in the "cash inflow stream". In general, these information-processing means can be applied at least in three different, but interrelated ways. As mentioned before, the provision and exchange of information within the agency-relationship allows the principal to **formulate instructions** in which way to execute the distribution function, to **build qualifications** on the part of distributors, and to **collect feedback** to identify value-added potential. Therefore, it is of great interest to ascertain how DEKA designs these information-related measures in its "hierarchy"-type of institutional arrangements in order to exert influence on the distribution behavior.

Fig. 18: OVERVIEW OF INFORMATION-PROCESSING MEANS IN "HIERARCHY"

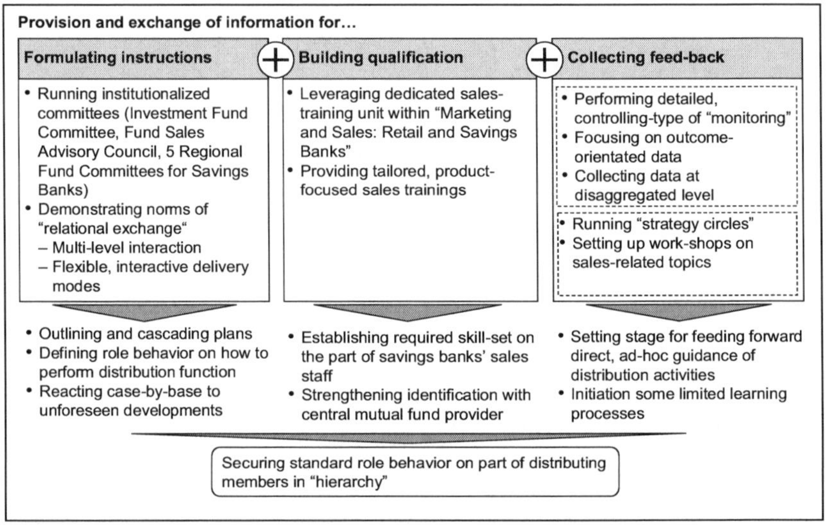

Source: Author

As summarized in Figure 18, it will become evident that DEKA falls back on all three information-processing means on a continuous basis, thereby putting into action elements of the systemic configuration, most notably the bundled transfer of property rights and the capacities of "sales support". In line with the classic assumptions for "hierarchy"-type of arrangements, from a comparative perspective it clearly shows that DEKA extensively turns to a wide range of institutionalized committees to guide distribution activities by way of formulating instructions. Secondly, in a supplementary approach, DEKA employs the wider process of providing information also for running tailored sales training programs in order to ensure an adequate skill-set on the part of the savings banks' sales staff to follow the instructions. Thirdly, DEKA also runs procedures to collect information from the distributing agents on how distribution performance is actually evolving. As will be elaborated in more detail, consistent with the very idea of a "hierarchy", the focus is mainly on establishing sufficient transparency on the actually realized performance levels. In principle, this transparency is then at hand to enter into rather direct guidance of the distribution behavior. While distribution agents are also invited to submit constructive ideas, feedback procedures and the joint-identification of value-added potential tend to play only a comparatively minor part in the wider collection of information from distributing agents [particularly vis-à-vis the case study on "partnership"]. Therefore, this brief introduction already shows that, with this integrated approach of indirect and direct guidance, **DEKA most notably aspires to secure an appropriate standard in the execution of the distribution function in terms of committed role behavior by savings banks and their staff**.

I) Formulating instructions

As far as information-processing means are concerned in agency-relationships for marketing mutual funds, it is known that norms of "**relational exchange**" bear the chance to limit opportunistic tendencies in distribution channels (Brown, Dev and Lee 2000, pp. 53-54). Against this background, it is therefore of particular interest to this enquiry to find out with which norms the principal seeks to support the formulation of instructions and recommendations on how to perform the distribution function, as well as to stimulate compliance on the part of distributing agents. Beginning with the more detailed empirical investigation of the design for the information-processing means, similar to the other two case studies, it clearly shows that the provision and exchange of information between the mutual fund providing principal and the mutual fund distributing agents occurs across a large number of organizational levels. In other words, also in this case study, the **asset management firm seeks to adhere to multi-level interaction as norm of "relation exchange"** in the process of delivering information to distributors, involving not only management at the upper levels but also staff at operational levels. Yet, as a salient characteristic of arrangements of "hierarchy", this multi-level interaction between DEKA and the distributing banks takes place in a much more institutionalized manner. Thus, from a comparative point of view, the exchange of information resembles more a bureaucratic-type of character in order to facilitate the formulation of instructions on how to appropriately perform the distribution function.

Regarding the interactive process of providing and exchanging information at the upper levels of management, it becomes evident that a number of **committees are installed as institutionalized interfaces between the asset management firm and the**

[distributing] owners. Besides the conventional supervisory board of DEKA, it shows that,

- the "Investment Fund Committee",
- the "Fund Sales Advisory Council", and
- five "Regional Fund Committees for Savings Banks"

take a prominent role in allowing DEKA's upper management to present information to the top management of the distributing members within the German Savings Banks Financial Group. The "Investment Fund Committee" under the leadership of one board member of a savings bank and a landesbank each [and consisting of 18 board members of savings banks or landesbanks] tends to focus on product-related topics. The "Fund Sales Advisory Council" [which includes 25 board members from savings banks only] deals to a larger extent with advisory-specific aspects of marketing mutual funds to private investors. Additionally, the five "Regional Fund Committees for Savings Banks", each comprising around 40 savings banks as members and the overarching savings banks associations with the status of so-called "Further Members", ensure that a large number of distributing members is involved and potentially offers a remarkable control span.

The regular meetings [at least on a semi-annual basis] of all these committees provide DEKA management with the opportunity to bring up topics that are of particular relevance to DEKA's distribution performance in a rather reactive, case-by-case approach. This clearly favors the detailed formulation of instructions on how to appropriately respond to specific situations. Moreover, these meetings also include the determination of a so-called "Master-Plan", outlining the input required to reach defined sales targets for DEKA's product offering. Quite in line with classic features of "hierarchy", **the coordination of activities then essentially relies on the authority of senior management of the respective distributors to accept these plans and to impose instructions on their subordinates to realize the intended levels of inflows streams into DEKA's mutual fund offering.**

Equally important, besides this range of committees, a sales manager explained that there is also an **information exchange of a rather bilateral kind between the upper management of DEKA and single savings banks**. This additional interaction, which tends to take place on an [semi]annual basis, allows DEKA management to further cascade the sales targets according to the overarching plan, thereby attempting to reinforce commitment on the part of distributing banks. Another sales manager stressed that it is this backing from distributors' top management that is critical for establishing an appropriate coordination of activities at the operational level. Hence, even if it absorbs substantial resources on the part of DEKA, this interaction at the upper management level is regarded as being of great functional relevance to mobilize compliance not only at the system-level of the agency-relationship but also at the point-of-sale. It, therefore, is considered as a critical lever to improve the cash inflow stream.

As far as the multi-level interaction is concerned, there is also a remarkable flow of information in a bilateral way at the rather operational level. The so-called **"Gebietsleiter"**, taking on the role of local relationship managers, are in fact in charge of the more frequent, rather on-going provision and exchange of information to savings banks. Around 60 "Gebietsleiter" are in direct and continuous contact with the so-called "Vertriebssteuerer" of single savings banks. Typical of "hierarchy"-type of arrangements, according to the formulated instructions and/or plans passed down from upper management, they together then dovetail the input in support of the actual sales and advisory activities performed at the point-of-sale. This clearly underlines that for this case study "relational exchange" in the form of multi-level interaction plays a prominent part in the process of formulating instructions to ensure compliant patterns of role behavior and, thus, mitigate hazards stemming from opportunism and specificity.

Last but not least, the interaction between DEKA and the distributors is accompanied by so-called **"strategy circles"**, which were introduced in 2001. A sales manager explained that this is a platform where second level management gets together to share their thoughts on product-related as well as on marketing-focused trends. Thus, there appear to be first signs that the wider process of information flow is also leveraged to engage in an exchange of constructive ideas on how to improve the arrangements' overall proficiency. As these "strategy-circles" tend to strengthen the savings banks' involvement in the agency-relationship, they potentially reinforce commitment and, thus, stimulate appropriate role behavior. Moreover, as will be elaborated in more detail, they may even trigger mutually beneficial search-behavior on the part of the distributing agents, which is, in fact, beyond the classic properties of "hierarchy"-type of arrangements as it represents behavior that goes beyond the line of duty.

As mentioned before, DEKA is increasingly turning to interactive and more flexible formats of making information available on a continuous basis to savings banks, and most notably to the point-of-sale. Though it is typical for classic models of "hierarchy" to provide information in rather standardized ways, it clearly shows that for the transfer of product- and or sales-related material DEKA increasingly falls back on electronic media in addition to the traditional approach of hard-copies to adequately reach the sales staff that interact with private investors. To a large extent, the "Gebietsleiter" coordinates this flexible approach of providing information and material. However, it may also involve DEKA's fund research unit, located in DEKA's headquarter in Frankfurt, in case more detailed product information is requested. In this regard, it is important to point out that the main purpose of this fund research unit is, in fact, to support the production function for DEKA's structured investment products, as it covers not only DEKA's product range but most notably more than 2,500 external mutual funds. Therefore, from a comparative point of view, although this fund research unit offers the positive side effect of being selectively called up to provide more detailed, product-related information, its employment appears to be somewhat different to the approaches pursued in the other two case studies. In these, as will be seen, dedicated positions or units are introduced with the explicit purpose of handling situation-specific interaction with distributors regarding rather technical information requests. Nevertheless, it cannot be denied that there are strong indications that **DEKA goes to great lengths to respond in a flexible manner to information needs arising at the point-of-sale in the savings banks' branches**. In turn, the adherence to this norm of "relational exchange" is expected to provoke the same kind of behavior on the part of agents, in particular with regard to instructions on how to carry out the distribution function.

As far as the third prominent norm of "relational exchange" is concerned, distributing banks in general very much appreciate it if they are provided with

information in a proactive way especially with respect to two different kinds of information:
This first of all includes proactive updates regarding changes in key personnel responsible for the production function of mutual funds.
Distributing banks also value if asset management firms indicate proactively the emergence of key investment performance issues for particular mutual fund offerings.
All this allows the distributing banks to appropriately adjust their sales and advisory activities to private investors, which eventually favors their endeavors to strengthen the quality of their relationship with their customers.

In this respect, it shows that in the course of the earlier mentioned strategic adjustment in structure and process at beginning of this century, DEKA increasingly engages in **proactive information-sharing** in areas that are regarded as having considerable impact on savings banks' operations at the point-of-sale. However, from a comparative point of view and quite in line with bureaucratically-shaped processes in arrangements of "hierarchy", it appears as if DEKA's design exhibits this norm of "relational exchange" only to a limited extent. This, in turn, has proven to have dramatic ramifications for the efforts to dovetail activities with distributors. There can be no doubt that communication to the savings banks was inadequate in the wake of the critical [investment] performance development of one of DEKA's larger property-based mutual funds in 2004 that eventually required a correction of more than EUR 700 million to the fund's value. As DEKA management acknowledges, a main consequence of this hesitance to proactively inform the savings banks in this particular situation is that the trustworthiness of DEKA in the perception of the distributors as well as end customers has been fundamentally shaken (Balzer and Jakobs 2005, p. 122-127), which ultimately has weakened their receptiveness for instructions and recommendations, respectively.

Therefore, as far as the provision and exchange of information for formulating instructions is concerned, it becomes evident that DEKA's design exhibits a critical deficiency. Given the autonomy of the distributing members in the "hierarchy", the definition of binding commitments and plans in the form of sales targets paired with directives on how to actually execute the distribution activities is already a challenging task. The application of multi-level interaction and flexibility in principle facilitates this goal and encourages at least standard role behavior on the part of the savings banks and their sales staff. However, the shortcoming in proactively providing information potentially jeopardizes the entire procedure of instructing savings banks and, thus, DEKA's efforts to control for challenges arising from specificity and opportunism. In more analytical terms, although some norms of "relational exchange" are embedded in the organizational design, some other necessary standards of conduct in the interaction appear not to be sufficiently emphasized. As a consequence, this may give rise to obstacles and even overshadow other process-related measures in support of the overriding objective of strong inflow streams.

II) Building qualification

The wider process of proving and exchanging information within the agency-relationship to distribute mutual funds may also be employed to transfer relevant expertise to the distributing banks' and their sales staff. The main purpose is to ensure that they are adequately enabled to perform the distribution function. In this regard, **DEKA is putting into action the "sales support" capacities introduced with the systemic configuration to transfer sales-relevant know-how to distributors**. As mentioned above, a dedicated unit is in place that solely focuses on running tailored training programs for savings banks' sales staff who operate in direct contact with private investors. As will now be elaborated, in comparison to the other case studies, the main objective is to ensure that savings banks are put in a position to take on the role as distributors for DEKA's mutual fund offering and essentially to follow instructions on how to execute the distribution function. In this way, the attempt is made to control for the specificity inherent in the sales and advisory activities at the point-of-sale and the latent opportunistic tendencies and, ultimately, to accomplish strong distribution performance levels.

In the light of the "hierarchy"-type of institutional arrangements, DEKA as the central mutual fund provider in the German Savings Banks Financial Group is able to run these programs on a comparatively more regular basis, as access to the savings banks' sales staff is usually granted. In general, DEKA's "Gebietsleiter" together with the

"Vertriebssteuerer" of respective savings banks identify the need for training and, thereupon, arrange the training sessions. As far as the content of those know-how-transfer programs is concerned, they tend to primarily focus on a detailed presentation of particular mutual funds in DEKA's product range, highlighting the key selling points of how the product offering matches the needs of particular segments of end customers. Thus, it seems as if this training mainly aims at establishing the skill-set necessary for the savings banks' sales staff to appropriately carry out the sales and advisory activities for DEKA's mutual fund offering, thereby mitigating hazards related to specificity. As a sales manager added, DEKA leverages these training programs, at least to some extent, to also share positive experiences [other] savings banks have made in the course of marketing DEKA's product offering. This clearly represents an attempt to outline rather general methods and routines on how to appropriately cope with possible obstacles arising in the interaction with private investors. Being prepared with these different but complementary types of information, the savings banks' sales staff is expected to be appropriately enabled to handle the [general] challenges inherent in the distribution function. Since these training programs with the transfer of specific as well as rather general information tend to help sales staff to successfully complete the sales and advisory activities for mutual funds, they are also expected to further strengthen the identification with DEKA as the central mutual fund provider. In other words, commitment is expected to increase in terms of a general aptitude to comply with instructions. Hence, by potentially increasing solidarity on the part of the savings banks' personnel operating at the point-of-sale, running such tailored training programs may then also bear the upside of alleviating issues of opportunistic tendencies. However, from a comparative point of view, as indicated already in the discussion on the "sales support" capacities, it appears as if in line with classic features of "hierarchy the scope is mainly on transferring the specific skill-set to execute the distribution function rather than on building qualification by way of thoroughly educating sales staff.

All this shows that great efforts are made to employ the provision and exchange of information to put the savings banks in a position to take on the role as distributors for DEKA's product offering. Thus, the main intention of this cornerstone of DEKA's information-processing is to appropriately prepare the savings banks' sales staff to successfully complete the sales and advisory activities. From this view, this information-related measure is of great functional relevance to achieve desired levels of "cash inflow stream".

III) Collecting feedback

Besides the employment of information-processing means in order to formulate instructions as well as to transfer specific know-how to the distributing banks' personnel, the wider process of providing and exchanging information additionally carries the opportunity to collect information. In more specific terms, the flow of information between principal and agent offers the chance to gather information on how distribution performance levels actually evolve. As far as the enquiry's first case study is concerned, similar to the other two case studies, it becomes apparent that DEKA turns to two collection procedures that allow to exert influence on the distribution behavior of savings banks in an indirect as well as in a rather direct way.

As will be discussed later in more depth, on the one hand, DEKA gathers data regarding the savings banks' actual distribution performance for DEKA's product range. Consistent with classic properties of "hierarchy", it turns out that it is this established transparency that in principle puts DEKA in a position to impose control on the distributors by way of performing a relatively extensive **"monitoring"** of distribution efforts. On the other hand, it shows that distributing members of the German Savings Banks Financial Group are invited to submit innovative ideas, in other words, some form of feedback. Hence, even under the regime of hierarchical patterns of control and the prominent role of standard role behavior, **there are first attempts to initiate some form of learning processes**, thereby at least to some degree encouraging search-behavior on the part of distributing agents in support of the agency-relationship.

In general, "monitoring" serves the principal as a key lever to reduce the information asymmetry within the agency-relationship, thereby increasing the chance of detecting aberrant behavior of agents. This, in turn, is expected to prevent this type of activity in the first place (Lal 1990, pp. 308). Regarding the design of "monitoring", like the other two asset management firms under focus in this enquiry, **DEKA primarily**

focuses on outcome-oriented data. DEKA particularly pays attention to the net inflow figures and the total volume of AuM to evaluate the actual distribution performance for its product range against the plan agreed upon within the various committees mentioned above. In line with expectations concerning hierarchical control, DEKA has comparatively far-reaching transparency, with access to a breakdown of this performance data at the level of the savings banks' single branches and even beyond that. As a sales manger pointed out, it would be possible for DEKA to trace back the realized performance levels to individual members of savings banks' sales staff performing sales and advisory activities in interaction with private investors. Moreover, as another sales manager remarked, this data tends to be available on at least a monthly basis, if not even at a weekly frequency.

Following on from this, it seems as if DEKA runs administrative processes in order to dive into this disaggregated information to actively detect issues arising from "opportunism" and "service firm specificity". Conducting extensive benchmarking of the savings banks' respective distribution performance allows DEKA to spot those branches that appear to encounter greater difficulties than others in generating strong inflow streams for DEKA's product range. In this regard, it further shows that the intention of this approach to controlling is neither to purely give rewards to savings banks or single branches nor to simply inflict sanctions. Instead, **the "monitoring" of outcomes exhibits such a design that, at least in general, allows the principal [in a positive way] to selectively feed forward suggestions to distributing agents on how to adjust their efforts in order to come to improved distribution performance levels**. In more substantive terms, in the face of unsatisfactory performance developments, there is the tendency that DEKA's "Gebietsleiter" together with management and "Vertriebssteuerer" of savings banks define some type of intervening measures in order to generate desired levels of inflow streams. For example, these measures can take the form of tailored training programs or sales events in support of critically performing bank branches or even corrective instructions on how to execute the sales and advisory activities, in this way aiming at reinforcing standard role behavior. Thus, "monitoring" offers the chance to adequately tame issues related to opportunistic tendencies and specificity.

However, a sales manager indicated shortcomings in the design of "monitoring", stressing that the consequent application of this transparency to demand adjustment in distribution activities appears unclear in the wake of critically evolving performance levels. Therefore, given the backward integration with its underlying assignment of property rights, there are indications that the "monitoring" processes are not fully leveraged to launch a more determined attempt to directly guide the distribution function in rather short circles. From this view, a sales manager also mentioned that there are no distribution performance targets imposed [internally] on DEKA's personnel who are responsible for managing the relationship with the distributing banks.

In addition to "monitoring", as mentioned above, there are indications that **the wider process of exchanging information is also leveraged at least to some extent to initiate learning processes more explicitly**. In other words, there are first signs that savings banks are invited to submit their opinions and suggestions on how to create additional value for the agency-relationship as a whole. In this way, this process offers the opportunity to increase their involvement and ultimately their commitment to the agency-relationship. Besides the institutionalized "strategy circles", which facilitate considerable information exchange between savings banks and DEKA, it shows that DEKA additionally runs a number of workshops to discuss various topics on how to create value-added to the agency-relationships at large. The focus of these interactive exchanges covers product-related aspects but tends to center mainly on distributing-related topics. As a result of these two-way communication processes, a sales manager pointed out that it may then come to the definition of additional, tailored "sales support" measures to assist distributors in realizing mutually beneficial improvements in inflows streams for DEKA's product range. From all this it appears as if DEKA demonstrates willingness to some degree to engage in search-behavior to discover further value creation opportunities and eventually to realize the potentials identified, thereby triggering the same kind of behavior on the part of the in fact autonomous savings banks. This, in turn, is expected to ensure that savings banks carry out the distribution function in a reliable fashion on a sustained basis. Therefore, by running such processes to improve the agency-relationships' proficiency, **it appears as if this interactive exchange**

is also employed as an additional method to indirectly guide the behavior of the distributing members of the German Savings Banks Financial Group.

Yet, from a comparative point of view and quite analogous to classic properties of "hierarchy"-type of relationships, it looks as if **the interactive learning processes are not of such a far-reaching character as it will be observed in particular in the case study of "partnership"**. With 477 savings banks performing the role as distributor for DEKA's product offering to private investors, one sales manager hinted at difficulties in getting all of them adequately involved in the learning process. In other words, there seem to be indications that the exchange of information, which in fact is assumed to be implemented much more easily in "hierarchy"-type of institutional arrangements, is not fully leveraged to trigger search behavior beyond the line of duty. Consequently, it appears as if the principal potentially forgoes a functional-relevant measure to strengthen the agents' solidarity and commitment.

Overall, from this discussion on the design of information-processing means under the regime of "hierarchy" it shows that these serve different purposes in order to support the principal's overriding objective of achieving a strong "cash inflow stream" through the in-house distribution channel. In line with the very idea of "hierarchy" to organize economic transactions, it becomes evident that the information-based processes are shaped in a rather bureaucratic manner in order to arrive at the formulation of instructions on how to actually perform the sales and advisory activities for the principal's mutual fund offering. Moreover, this discussion has brought to light that these procedures are also employed to transfer specific skills to distributing agents to enable them to follow these instructions, to control the agents' distribution activities by means of "monitoring", and even to activate to some degree learning processes and search-behavior. It clearly shows that this blend of procedures to indirectly as well as directly guide distribution activities aims at reinforcing standard role behavior of in fact considerably autonomous distributing members. However, in this regard it also becomes apparent that this organizational design of "hierarchy" not only absorbs substantial resources to run these information-processing means but, as a matter of fact, exhibits critical shortcomings to exert influence and, thus, authority on the distributing banks. It appears as if critical norms of "relational exchange" are neglected, "monitoring" processes are not adequately applied and [joint] learning processes and search-behavior are not fully initiated to establish a design, which paves the way to overcome the challenges of "opportunism" and "service firm specificity" lurking in this organizational choice. Hence, along these lines it seems as if the overriding objective of improving distribution performance levels is put at risk.

4.1.2.2.2 Motivational Means for Process-Intervention

Concerning the second, the internal fit problem, the elaboration so far has illustrated how DEKA designs the systemic configuration as well as information-processing means in order to strengthen net inflow in the context of the organizational choice of some type of "hierarchy". Although DEKA's design in terms of structure and process appears to entails classic properties of hierarchical patterns of coordination, it exhibits deficiencies with some of these stemming from inconsistencies. Now, the intention is to shed light on the additional measures the principal employs to [further] activate the agents' willingness to generate a strong "cash inflow stream" for the principal's product range.

As highlighted in the discussion on the systemic configuration, the salient feature of this type of "hierarchy" is a bundled transfer of property rights to the distributors as a whole. In general, such a far-reaching handover of property rights to the distributing agents is predicted to ensure substantial harmonization of their interests with those of the product-providing principal. By way of bestowing ownership, in other words, membership to all the distributing banks, it is typically expected that the members of the "hierarchy" tend to demonstrate reliability in meeting performance standards according to the plan when they carry out the assigned tasks. Thus, it appears as if by simply prescribing role behavior the principal could then count on compliance on the part of the distributing banks. However, there are indications that the assignment of property rights, in fact, turns out to be somewhat diluted among distributing members, highlighting that continuous efforts to reinforce commitment are of the greatest functional relevance to accomplish the envisaged improvement in inflow streams. In line with a regular hierarchical setting, it shows that the principal turns to a wide range of formal information-processing means to outline and forward instructions to ensure adequate role behavior and, in this way, to achieve adequate handling of the challenges related to "service firm specificity" and "opportunism". However, due to the apparently incomplete type of "hierarchy", **some extra motivational means are deployed to make distributing agents adhere to the assigned role** [despite already established levels of compliance].

As illustrated in Figure 19, it turns out that once again DEKA brings into play capacities already introduced with the systemic configuration to further activate the distributing agents' willingness to perform the sales and advisory activities. In more practical terms, DEKA leverages capacities in "branding", but most notably in "sales support", to trigger extra motivation on the part of savings banks to comply with the assigned role. In the following section, these activities will be referred to as **joint actions**, as these actions tend to involve substantial interaction between the principal and agent within the respective agency-relationship. Yet, in accordance with the classic model of "hierarchy", these joint actions tend to be more of a bureaucratic-instructive character and less of a participative nature. Besides these joint actions, DEKA also falls back on an **"incentive scheme"** comprising a blend of different instruments, with some of them mainly operating at the system-level of the relationship while one particular element aims to directly reach the individual staff operating at the banks' point-of-sale. With regard to the financial incentives at the system-level, only in this case study it shows that the "incentive scheme" includes some form of [system] reward, which accrues to distributing banks at large by virtue of their ownership of the system and, thus, are not [directly] related to their individual efforts and performance levels. At the same time, similar to the other two case studies, some performance-pay is also in place at the system-level of the agency-relationships in the form of some [internal] transfer pricing. In addition to these instruments at the system-level, something that can only be observed in this case study, DEKA provides incentives that are, in fact, directly awarded to the distributors' sales staff operating at the point-of-sale. Already this brief preview of motivational measures highlights DEKA's attempts to overcome latent opportunistic tendencies primarily in a positive way so as to eventually secure strong distribution performance levels.

Fig. 19: OVERVIEW OF MOTIVATIONAL MEANS IN "HIERARCHY"

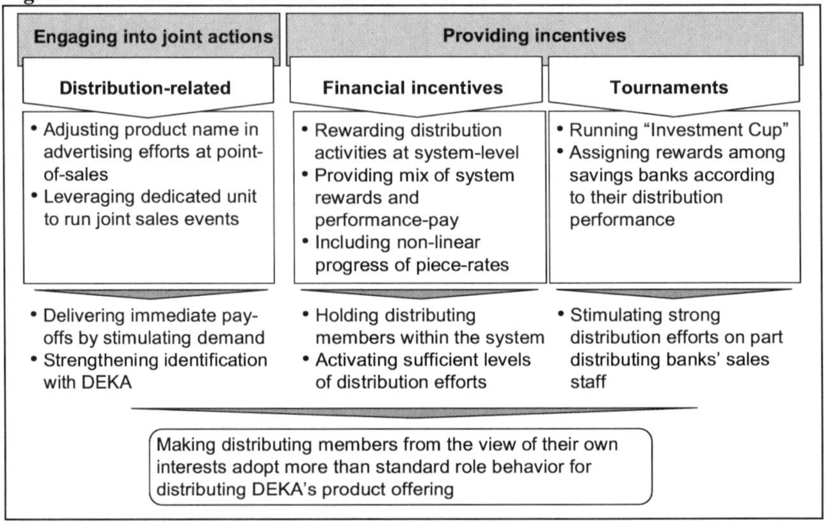

Source: Author

I) Engaging into joint actions

Following the general argument that formal procedures may serve as a motivating means, Heide and John (1990, p. 24) emphasize that the principal to some degree is able to tame opportunistic tendencies by undertaking activities together with the agent. As far as joint actions are concerned in this particular case study, it turns out that these **joint actions mainly center on activities to support the actual marketing efforts at the point-of-sale**. Therefore, besides some additional "branding" measures, DEKA most notably puts into play its "sales support" capacities. In this respect, as will be discussed in more depth, the main emphasis of these attempts to guide distribution behavior is not on creating involvement and sound commitment through participation but mainly on stimulating demand for DEKA's product range in a rather instructive, hands-on type of support. In this way, DEKA then finds itself in a better position to serve the profit-maximizing interests of the autonomous savings banks. All this, in turn, indicates the reinforcement of the distributors' role integrity through offering extensive participation in on-going [product-related] decision-making processes play a comparatively minor role.

As indicated above, in the face of the already extensive relationship-specific buildup of "branding" capacities, additional "branding" initiatives in the form of co-branding efforts assume a rather minor role to further mobilize willingness on the part of the distributing members. Nonetheless, for some agency-relationships, **there is a tendency for DEKA to slightly modify the name of a particular mutual fund in advertisements placed directly at the point-of-sale as an attempt to strengthen the distributor's identification with the agency-relationship** and ultimately to realize stronger inflow streams. As one sales manager explained, this modification can take the form of adding the name of the relevant savings bank to the typically rather technical name of the product. In this way, these **"branding"** measures, at least in principle, have the chance to substantially raise the commitment of the distributors' staff and, thus, to trigger distribution efforts beyond the mere standard level of compliance.

In addition to that, as mentioned above, DEKA most notably turns to its **"sales support"** capacities to engage in joint actions. As already indicated in the discussion on information-processing means, DEKA's "Gebietsleiter" together and in direct contact with management and "Vertriebssteuerer" of single savings banks identify the need for additional "sales support". **This "sales support" can then take the form of [joint] sales events to further stimulate demand for DEKA's mutual fund range**. This may be economically beneficial not only to DEKA itself but, in fact, also to distributing members, as will be elaborated in the discussion on the "incentive scheme". With the decision to stage such an event, they then normally in a rather formal manner turn to the aforementioned DEKA's centralized sub-unit, which is specialized in preparing and carrying out [joint] sales events. Thereupon, this unit in some interaction with the single savings banks is in charge of arranging the event, which can take the form of dinners with a number of selectively invited end customers. In their very essence, these events provide DEKA with the opportunity to put forward its mutual fund offering directly to savings banks' end customers, thereby gaining control on how product-related information is presented. In more substantive terms, DEKA is in a position to highlight the attractiveness of specific mutual funds and explaining as how those match with the private investors' specific investment objectives and needs. As far as the **impact of the sales event** is concerned, one sales manager stressed that there is significant **empirical**

evidence that these efforts translate into substantial demand from investors in the form of inflow streams within weeks of the event. Therefore, by providing [rather] immediate pay-offs to distributors, these joint actions offer the opportunity to reinforce the notion among autonomous and profit-orientated savings banks that it is in their very own interests to take on the role as distributors for DEKA's product offering. Moreover, another positive side effect is that these events potentially serve as an additional lever to provide competence-upgrading and image-benefits in a more tailored fashion to savings banks, which may strengthen their relationships with their customers. All this, in turn, is predicted to further mobilize the willingness of savings banks to execute selling and advisory activities appropriately, thereby allowing the principal to inhibit opportunistic tendencies.

It shows that the principal turns mostly to **distribution-related joint actions** to strengthen [at least] the compliant role behavior of the distributing agent in the "hierarchy" but possibly even to motivate behavior beyond standard levels. Therefore, these joint actions then essentially carry the opportunity for DEKA to trigger strong inflow streams for its product range by alleviating issues related in particular to lurking opportunistic tendencies. From a comparative point of view, however, in line with very idea of "hierarchy", it appears as if these measures to a large degree follow rather formal, standardized ordering procedures, in other words, bureaucratic processes. In this regard, it then seems as if these procedures are exposed to the danger of failing to raise the involvement of the distributing members and their sales staff. This in turn implies, at least to some extent, that these activities may miss out on strengthening commitment and, thus, on encouraging more than standard role behavior on a sustainable basis. With regard to **product-related joint actions**, in the institutionalized multi-level interaction between DEKA and savings banks it clearly comes to various discussions on product-focused topics. Though, given the assigned roles along the specialized set-up of the value chain in these "hierarchy"-type of arrangements, as indicated above, **on-going participation in single steps of the production function for mutual funds is only of minor relevance in motivating the distributors**.

II) Providing incentives

Besides joint actions, the classic approach of providing incentives within agency-relationships serves as a further means to guide the behavior of agents, thereby at least in principle influencing them to make choices in such a way that will maximize the principal's interests (Jensen and Murphy 2004, p. 18). Along these lines, the introduction of an "incentive scheme" at least in general gives the asset management firm the chance to further align interests, thereby inhibiting opportunistic behaviors of distributing agents and eventually strengthening inflow streams:

- For the first case study of this enquiry and quite in line with classic properties of "hierarchy", it shows that at the arrangements' system-level the "incentive scheme" first of all includes what commonly is referred to as a **system-reward** in order to keep members within the "hierarchy".
- Furthermore, the "incentive scheme" also contains **performance-related rewards** at the system-level in the form of transfer-prices with the aim of encouraging some extra role behavior on the part of the distributing banks. In addition to these instruments at the system-level, DEKA seeks to give rewards more individually to the distributors' personnel operating directly at the point-of-sale.
- Unique in this enquiry, for this particular case study it shows that DEKA is able to run some type of **tournament** (Lazear and Rosen 1981, p. 844) among savings banks, in this way reaching out to their sales staff in a more direct approach to secure desired levels of motivation.

In more detail, in the face of the systemic configuration and the underlying ownership model for DEKA, the distributing banks as [indirect] shareholders are entitled to receive some form of financial reimbursement by virtue of their ownership, in other words, due to their membership in the "hierarchy". In correspondence with the classic properties of "hierarchy", this typically takes the shape of some share of the profit-stream generated by DEKA. This share of the profit-stream each distributing bank receives, in turn, tends to be determined by their respective share of ownership. Therefore, this compensation resembles some form of **system-reward**, as it is not allocated on the basis of differential performance levels but on the grounds of their membership. However, as is known, while system rewards may be effective in holding members within the system they tend to do little to inflame behavior beyond the line of duty. In other words, as the share of profit-stream tends to be unrelated to individual performance levels, savings banks are not held fully accountable for their individual distribution efforts. Thus, while this form of compensation may be able to keep the distributing members within the "hierarchy", it becomes apparent that the allocation of the profit-stream among distributors is somewhat diluted. Consequently, the agency-relationships may be exposed to the danger of weakened commitment on the part of the savings banks, in this way potentially giving rise to incidents of "opportunism" and, hence, putting the overriding objective of improving inflow streams at considerable risk.

Therefore, in addition to this type of system reward, a sales manger pointed out a transfer pricing system that comes into play before the profit-stream is calculated in order to account more accurately for the distribution performance actually realized by respective savings banks. In other words, similar to the other two case studies of advancing degrees of decentralization, the "incentive scheme" also aims at rewarding distributors more directly according to the outcome of their efforts. In this regard, calculated bottom-up across the mutual funds for which the respective distributing bank has successfully completed the sales and advisory activities, the **performance-related compensation** first of all includes [a share of] the load fee, which end customers are charged when investing in a mutual fund. Additionally, the distributing banks also receive a share of the management fee, which represents the main revenue stream related to the production and marketing of mutual funds to private investors. Both fees charged to private investors, are in fact a function of the assets they have invested, defined as basis points of AuM. Thus, the respective savings bank's absolute level of compensation tends to increase with the total of volume it has raised from its customers. This, in turn, highlights that even in "hierarchy"-type of arrangements, similar to the other two case studies, the principal turns to some form of **piece-rate based** compensation (Stiglitz 1975, pp. 557-558) to activate strong distribution performance levels.

Furthermore, as will be observed for the other case studies as well, the performance-related compensation **includes a non-linear slop in piece-rates**. The actual share of the management fee transferred to each distributing bank increases every time the total level of AuM it has collected from its end customers surpasses a specific threshold. All this shows that the actual reimbursement grows progressively with increased sales performance, which underlines that it is supposed to be in the profit-maximizing interests of the autonomous distributing members to achieve strong distribution performance levels on behalf of their in-house mutual fund provider.

Moreover, a sales manager explained that the "incentive scheme" entails an additional financial bonus for distributors. In case they are able to enhance their net inflow stream for DEKA's product range in comparison to the stream they generated in the previous year, savings banks receive extra compensation. In this way, an additional means is in place to make the distributing agents continuously strive to improve performance levels. Yet, as net inflows figures are compared against the level realized the previous year [and not against the agreed-upon plan], it remains inconclusive to what extent this additional instrument is able to stimulate at least standard role behavior.

Overall, as far as these financial instruments at the system-level of the "hierarchy"-type are concerned, it shows that with this design of the "incentive scheme" an attempt is made to account for both the necessity to hold the distributing members within the institutional arrangement and the requirement to reward optimal role behavior in order to truly leverage the extensive customer reach provided by savings banks. **However, it remains somewhat in the dark whether this "incentive scheme" is able to overcome the latent free-ride problem in the face of the dispersed ownership model**. In other words, given the performance-unrelated system-rewards, it appears unclear to some extent as to whether the performance-related components are sufficiently strong to drive optimal patterns of distribution behavior. While these elements of the "incentive scheme" play a functional relevant role at the system-level of the agency-relationships, they barely reach the distributing banks' sales staff operating in direct interaction with private investors. As a sales manager remarked, it is in the scope of the savings banks in which way and to what degree to pass on this kind of compensation to single branches or even to individual staff operating at the point-of-sale. In this regard, it is important to point out that in this particular distribution channel the salary of the personnel actually performing the advisory activities usually includes only a relatively small proportion of pay related to their individual distribution performance. As will be observed for the other two case studies, **there is a tendency that these financial incentives provided at the system-level have a rather weak direct influence on the issues of "opportunism" and "service firm specificity" occurring at the point-of-sale**.

Observed only in this case study, it becomes apparent that **DEKA leverages the relatively integrated structure of its arrangements of "hierarchy" to run some form of a tournament** among savings banks to more individually reward the personnel carrying out the distribution function. In more detail, a sales manager explained that at the beginning of each year DEKA tends to launch the so-called "Investment Cup" for a particular period of time of 3 to 4 months as a further measure to stimulate strong distribution efforts for its product range. With regard to the prize of this tournament, a sales manager emphasized that it is not a monetary reward but takes the form of an event sponsored by DEKA. It shows that DEKA turns to what de Ruiter and Koch (1991, pp. 1030-1031) refer to as incentive trips. For example, referring to an event declared as the prize in previous years, this has been a week-long trip to the Mediterranean for a fixed number of seats available to the distributing banks' sales staff. As a sales manager explained in more detail, these seats are allocated at the level of savings banks according to the overall tournament ranking. This ranking is based on the net inflows the respective savings banks have raised for DEKA's mutual fund offering within the time period of the "Investment Cup". In this regard, it becomes apparent that it remains in the scope of single savings banks, which have managed to obtain a number of seats for this event, to define how to distribute these among their personnel. As another sales manager noted, there is a tendency that this assignment follows the individual contributions of the sales staff.

Hence, in the light of this design on how the prize is created and eventually distributed to their sales staff, the tournament, at least in principle, imposes some social pressure on the sales staff to adopt appropriate role behavior to successfully complete the sales and advisory activities. It promotes some competition among the sales staff for prestige, which is predicted to further reinforce appropriate role behavior. Hence, while the "Investment Cup" introduces explicit rivalry between savings banks, it, in fact, provides DEKA with the chance to hold the savings banks' sales staff accountable to a greater extent for their individual distribution performance. Regarding the functional relevance to strengthen the net inflow stream, a sales manger pinpointed the empirical evidence that between 60 to 70 percent of the annual net inflow stream realized by savings banks is accomplished in the period of the "Investment Cup". This strongly indicates that the application of this kind of motivational lever within the "incentive scheme" allows DEKA to alleviate to some extent the latent issues related to opportunism as well as to specificity arising at the point-of-sale, in this way favoring the realization of desired distribution performance levels.

Therefore, by deliberately turning to a variety of motivational means operating not only in different ways but also at different levels, DEKA makes great efforts to secure [at least] standard role behavior on the part of the distributing members in the face of rather incomplete "hierarchy". In this regard, it has been brought to light that DEKA turns to some form of joint actions. However, in line with a rather hierarchical design, it appears as if these activities are not carried out in a truly participative manner, but rather follow a bureaucratic procedure. Moreover, it has been ascertained that DEKA also falls back on an "incentive scheme" which includes not only financial components at the system-level but also rather non-monetary elements to more individually reward the distributors' sales staff for strong distribution results. While the non-monetary rewards tend to mobilize desired role behavior on the part of sales staff, regarding the financial incentives at the system-level it seems somewhat unclear whether they are in the position to activate the appropriate behavior to realize at least standard distribution performance levels for DEKA's mutual fund range.

4.1.2.3 Towards the Efficacy of the Design of "Hierarchy"

Regarding the second – the internal – fit problem, this enquiry claims that it is the consistent configuration between the design of the arrangement and the choice of the "degree of decentralization" that is of crucial importance to realize the optimization objective. In other words, along the enquiry's conceptualization, the design for the agency-relationship of "hierarchy" needs to be set up in a consistent manner to activate efficiency-enhancing effects. In this respect, **the preceding elaboration indicates, that while the organizational design to some degree seems to be in line with various classic properties of "hierarchy", it looks as if it exhibits considerable shortcomings, of which some are related to signs of inconsistency.**

The second fit problem pinpoints the optimizing-relevant condition that the design adequately accounts for the situation-specific challenges stemming from "service firm specificity" and "opportunism" lurking in the respective organizational choice. The choice of "hierarchy" to a considerable extent relies on the compliant role behavior of members of the "hierarchy" to coordinate activities along the value chain. Hence, according to the internal fit requirement, in order to be consistent, structure and process need to be designed in a way to ensure the desired role behavior to achieve optimal distribution performance levels. In more specific terms, to be consistent with the fundamental idea of "hierarchy" the design has to secure the agents' on-going compliance to take on as well as their ability to actually execute the distributing role by means of hierarchical coordination. Therefore, in order to achieve an adequate handling of the latent hazards stemming from opportunism and specificity, for this case study it shows that the **bundled handover of property rights portrays the most prominent feature within the design's systemic configuration. However**, as indicated above, in the light of the underlying diffuse ownership model, the impression is that **the distribution of property rights in fact turns out to be somewhat diluted among the distributing banks**. This implies that these can then neither bear the full reward of strong distribution performance nor the financial consequences of unsatisfactory performance levels. Hence, it appears as if the design is inclined to be substantially vulnerable to coordination challenges stemming from "opportunism" and "service firm specificity" and, thus, potentially lacks optimal role behavior on the part of in fact autonomous distributing members in the "hierarchy".

Against this background, it shows that it is this systemic configuration, which also includes substantial capacities in "branding" and "sales support" that sets the tone for the employment of process-related measures. These processes then bring into play those capacities in order to secure desired levels of willingness and ability on the part of the distributing banks on an on-going basis. In this view, as elaborated in some detail, it becomes evident that DEKA turns to information-processing means and even to motivating measures with the intention of exerting influence on the distribution function in an indirect manner but also in a more direct, ad-hoc type of approach. As far as the **information-related procedures** are concerned, the purpose is mainly to make sure that the banks and their sales staff are adequately enabled to carry out the distributing role for DEKA's mutual fund offering, and in this way achieve the aspired strengthening of the inflow stream. In this context, with regard to internal fit the discussion brings to light the following points:

- In line with the very idea of "hierarchy" DEKA adheres to norms of "relational exchange" for the provision of information. In particular, by way of bureaucratically-shaped multi-level interaction paired with some flexibility the aim is to formulate instructions on how to perform the distribution function. While rather limited proactive information delivery is in fact in line with classic arrangements of "hierarchy", it appears as if this feature of the design then tends to considerably jeopardize efforts to devise the input-focused instructions for coordinating activities along the value chain.
- By bringing into play the dedicated "sales support" capacities in a more tailored fashion, the attempt is made to build qualifications of the distributing banks and their sales staff. In order to adequately enable the personnel at the point-of-sale to perform the distributing role as instructed, these training programs tend to mainly aim at establishing the required skill-set [though proven routines and methods are also shared].
- The wider exchange of information is also employed to collect data on how distribution performance levels are actually evolving. It looks as if this process is laid out in such a way that it puts DEKA in a position to perform some controlling-type of "monitoring". Although this transparency sets the stage for feeding forward some rather direct guidance on how to adjust distribution activities, its systematic and consequent application appears to be somewhat inconclusive.

- There are first signs that the information exchange is also leveraged for some form of feedback to initiate learning processes and possibly even search-behavior. While this is, in fact, not common in a classic type of "hierarchy", this exchange has the potential to raise commitment of distributing members of the "hierarchy".

Hence, it shows that these information-processing means potentially set the informational stage for guiding arrangements of "hierarchy" to improved performance levels but partially also offer the chance to mobilize the commitment of the agents. Moreover, with regard to the internal fit, it has further become evident that DEKA simultaneously runs some extra **motivational means** with the purpose mainly of securing compliance and membership on the part of the banks and to trigger patterns of behavior even beyond the call of duty. In this regard, this enquiry shows:

- For some agency-relationships, DEKA alters the name of the mutual fund in the advertisements placed directly at the point-of-sale. This constitutes an attempt to strengthen the distributing banks' and their personnel's identification with the "hierarchy" und ultimately their motivation to comply with their supposed role.
- DEKA intends to assist the distribution activities by putting into action its capacities in "sales support" to stage [joint] sales-events. These rather hands-on types of activities not only offer the prospects of some image-related competence-upgrade but there is the empirical tendency that they stimulate strong demand from end customers rather immediately. In this way, these events offer the chance to boost the willingness of autonomous distributors to execute the distribution function in solidarity, thereby curbing potential opportunistic tendencies.
- In line with salient features of "hierarchy", DEKA provides rather performance-unrelated system-rewards within the "incentive scheme" to distributing members in order to keep them in the system and to secure standard levels of motivation to take on the distributing role for DEKA's product range.
- DEKA further provides performance-related pay in the form of transfer-prices and some additional bonus at the system-level of the agency-relationship with the purpose of appropriately compensating strong distribution outcomes. The aim is in this way to stimulate performance levels that may even surpass the standard targets. Yet, it appears unclear to what extent this revenue-sharing within the

"incentive scheme" is able to sufficiently mitigate issues of opportunism and specificity.

- Additionally, DEKA runs a tournament on a regular basis to introduce some competition between savings banks regarding their distribution performance for DEKA's product range. By imposing social pressure and competition on distributing members' sales staff in a positive way, it looks as if DEKA is able to stimulate strong efforts to raise substantial inflow streams from private investors.

All in all, while it is the systemic configuration that aims to bring into play the rather fundamental reliance on compliant role behavior of the distributing members of the "hierarchy", it clearly shows that additional process-related measures are applied on a day-to-day basis as an attempt to secure in fact both ability and willingness to perform the assigned role in an appropriate manner. However, in the context of the structural set-up, it appears inconclusive if the interactive relation between providing and exchanging information on the one hand and stimulating motivation, on the other hand, is able to put the principal in a position to appropriately guide the "hierarchy" to the desired distribution performance levels.

As it is the foremost purpose at this point of the case study to assess the criterion of consistency, this enquiry argues that **this particular design suffers considerably from two ramifications of the given approach of transferring property rights underlying the backward-type of integration**. As indicated before, **the bundled transfer appears, on the one hand, to have resulted in a diluted allocation of property rights among the distributing members**. From the perspective of a single distributing bank, this then has critical implications. While the distributing bank does not enjoy all the positives from its strong distribution performance, it also does not suffer all the negative consequences in case of non-compliant role behavior. Thus, the institutional arrangement tends to face a structure-driven, latent deficit in commitment on the part of the distributing members and, hence, considerable impediments to truly activate desired levels of motivation. **On the other hand, there are strong signs that, at the same time, the extent of the handover of property rights is in fact far-reaching enough to substantially narrow the options for DEKA to respond to situation-specific**

challenges by means of classic steering instruments of hierarchical patterns of control. For example, it becomes evident that it is not within DEKA's scope to discipline aberrant role behavior with sanctions or even to take the decision to exclude single distributing members from the system. Hence, taking these two ramifications together, it is then not surprising to see inconsistencies in the design vis-à-vis an ideal type of "hierarchy". In fact, it is reasonable to expect that management deliberately turns to measures atypical of classic patterns of hierarchical coordination in its attempts to bring hazards of opportunism and specificity under control. With regard to the enquiry's optimization perspective, however, all this may boil down to a situation in which, already **with the design's systemic configuration, DEKA faces a self-blocking situation in its arrangements of "hierarchy"**. Eventually, this incomplete "hierarchy" tends to severely hinder the generation of strong inflow streams by way of efficiently leveraging the extensive customer reach offered by the distributing members.

There can be no doubt that this particular design as a matter of fact absorbs substantial resources, in terms of extensive [transaction] costs. These costs stem not only from the structure-shaping investments in capacities of "branding" and "sales support", but most notably from the on-going management of the "hierarchy" to guide the distributing members. The heavy, rather bureaucratic interaction between DEKA and the distributing members as well as the situational application of capacities in order to intervene more directly in a hands-on type of approach drive these costs considerably. At the same time, however, these processes typically are expected to limit the danger of inadequate ability and willingness on part of the distributing agents. Therefore, with regard to the classic trade-off between efficiency and risks, it is the move to engage in instructive guidance and control of the distributors that is assumed to bring about at least standard patterns of role behavior, thereby reducing tendencies of "hold-up", which would otherwise give rise to further transaction costs.

This then clearly underlines that even within this design of a rather incomplete "hierarchy", the set-up and quality of single action variables still plays a relevant part in the assessment of the institutional arrangement's efficacy to accomplish the aspired improvement. However, given the far-reaching autonomy for distributors, the enquiry also has doubts whether such a coordination mode for guiding the distribution function is able to efficiently deal with hazards of opportunisms and specificity. Therefore, to what extent the design is able to truly prevent situations of "hold-up" and, thus, to trigger the aspired strengthening of inflow streams under the regime of "hierarchy" will be discussed in the following section.

4.1.3 Efficacy of Choice and Design of "Hierarchy"

Having discussed both choice and design regarding the institutional arrangement for the distribution function so far in a rather isolated, but interrelated manner, the objective now is to assess in a more cumulative way to what extent distribution performance levels are improved. Hence, the **decisive question to answer is how the external fit and its interplay with the internal fit favor the arrangement's efficacy in turning around the gap noticed in the "cash inflow stream"**. In view of the enquiry's central optimization objective, the purpose is to find out whether and in which way the chosen "degree of decentralization" in combination with the design in terms of structure and process trigger a considerable improvement in performance levels. The intention is to clarify if the overall arrangement is not only consistent but also congruent (Mintzberg 1981, p. 316). Thus, speaking more in terms of the enquiry's framework of analysis, of particular interest here is to ascertain whether the institutional arrangement adequately takes into consideration not only the "market dynamics" but also the general hazards arising from the "service firm specificity" and "opportunism". From its normative perspective, the enquiry intends to assess whether the external choice in combination with the internal design are bringing about the aspired improvement in the arrangements' efficacy in realizing strong "cash inflow streams".

As summarized in Figure 20, the analysis brings to light that DEKA makes the attempt to remedy the noticed deterioration in performance levels through clinging to its strategy of "hierarchy"-type of institutional arrangements for organizing the distribution function. However, from a comparative point of view, it looks as if such an organizational choice for arranging the relationships to savings banks [and landesbanks] fundamentally lacks critical ingredients to adequately take into account the "market dynamics" and the strong self-interest seeking of distributing members. With private investors increasingly demanding and appreciating more choice in the product offering of distributing banks and a great number of economically attractive external providers being available to distributors, the mere reliance on classic steering instruments and safeguards

Fig. 20: SIMULTANEOUS ASSESSMENT OF CHOICE AND DESIGN OF "HIERARCHY"

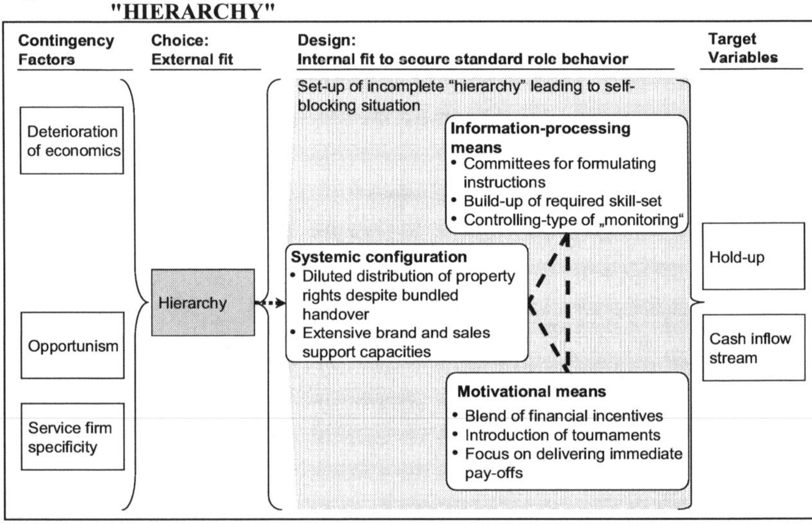

Source: Author

of a coordination mode of "hierarchy" appears rather unsuitable to bring the challenges arising from opportunistic tendencies and specificity under control on a sustainable basis. In other words, from a comparative point of view, the enquiry argues that this choice even with an internally consistent design would encounter considerable obstacles to genuinely activate efforts according to plan or even beyond the line of duty on the part of the distributing banks. A classic-type of "hierarchy" would be short of elements to encourage more than the standard role behavior. Such a choice, therefore, appears inefficient to deal with the growing scope for opportunistic tendencies [prevalent in this choice] and the specificity traditionally inherent in distribution activities for mutual funds. Moreover, in the light of the underlying backward type of integration, this enquiry has already hinted at further critical deficiencies related to the bundled handover of property rights in the organizational design. Thus, while in the face of the contingencies a classic hierarchical mode of coordination appears to be somewhat inappropriate in the first place, it also seems difficult to establish in a consistent design to ensure the desired distribution behavior. Therefore, even in the light of the extensive customer reach provided by distributing members of the German Savings Banks Financial Group, this enquiry tends to argue that DEKA's external response with regard to coordination mode is incoherent.

Hence, as far as the cumulative assessment is concerned, this enquiry gains the impression that **this constellation of external and internal adjustments does not properly account for the development noticed in the market environment to appropriately leverage the enormous distribution power of the savings banks**. Thus, this investigation of DEKA's institutional arrangements along the enquiry's framework of analysis argues that there is a tendency to regard the choice and design to be inadequate to regain strong distribution performance levels, although the extensive distribution power of the savings banks may possibly outshine some of the mentioned deficiencies.

Along those lines, concerning the efficacy of the "hierarchy"-type of institutional arrangements, it becomes apparent that DEKA in Germany is facing considerable challenges to maintain performance levels:

- With respect to the total AuM DEKA has gathered via the savings banks, it shows that DEKA has enjoyed only moderate growth since the year 2001. AuM raised from private investors grew from EUR 85 billion in 2001 to EUR 90 billion in 2004. This implies an annual growth of 1.9 percent, while the German market as a whole produced at least an annual rate of 3.3 percent. This moderate growth was primarily fueled by a strong development of property funds [from EUR 13 billion in 2001 to EUR 23 billion in 2004]. AuM in DEKA's capital market-based mutual funds have, in fact, considerably depleted from EUR 72 billion in 2001 to EUR 66 billion in 2004, despite the recovery of capital markets.
- As far as the "cash inflow stream" is concerned, it becomes apparent that after the dramatic drop between 2000 and 2001, DEKA's overall distribution performance levels have continued to deteriorate further. As illustrated in Figure 21, this trend

hit its low in 2004, when DEKA for the first time faced outflows for its product offering available to private investors via savings banks, while at the market level inflows remained positive throughout 2004.

- Diving deeper into DEKA's "cash inflow stream" it shows that this incessant slump was primarily caused by poor distribution performance for capital-market based mutual funds [which in fact fueled the growth in the late 1990s]. After the record year in 2000, when DEKA collected more than EUR 18 billion for these mutual funds, the "cash inflow stream" essentially evaporated in the following years. In 2004, DEKA experienced an outflow for this product group of almost EUR 2 billion. In this regard, it is important to point out that in particular for this product group a large number of outside-options are available to savings banks.

Fig. 21: DEVELOPMENT OF NET INFLOWS RELATIVE TO MARKET TREND

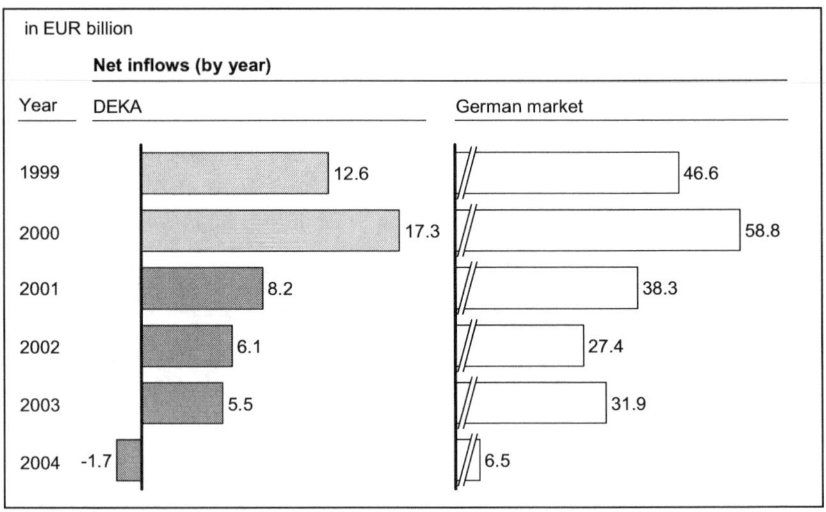

Source: DekaBank Annual Reports 1999-2004, BVI (2005)

Therefore, in the light of this clearly unsatisfying development of the "cash inflow stream", there can be no doubt that the external fit, the internal fit and their interplay show critical deficiencies for truly leveraging the customer reach available through savings banks. As mentioned before, this elaboration indicates that a classic coordination mode of "hierarchy" in terms of choice and design appears to be inadequate for coordinating activities with distributors that, in fact, enjoy considerably autonomy to decide which mutual funds to put on their shelves. Consequently, for this particular case study **this enquiry hints at the need for a change in paradigm regarding the institutional arrangement for the distribution function in order to rebuild distribution performance levels on a sustainable basis.** It appears as if not all organizational options for the relationship with savings banks have been fully explored yet. However, adaptations in choice and design should not necessarily imply that DEKA gives up its exclusive focus on marketing its product range to private investors via the distributing members of the German Savings Banks Financial Group. Instead, as a concluding remark, in order to achieve the desired increase in inflow streams this enquiry holds the view that these adaptations should more strongly consider, in particular, participation-type of elements to more appropriately address issues of opportunism and specificity.

Fig. 22: SUMMARY OF CASE STUDY ON DEKA IN GERMANY

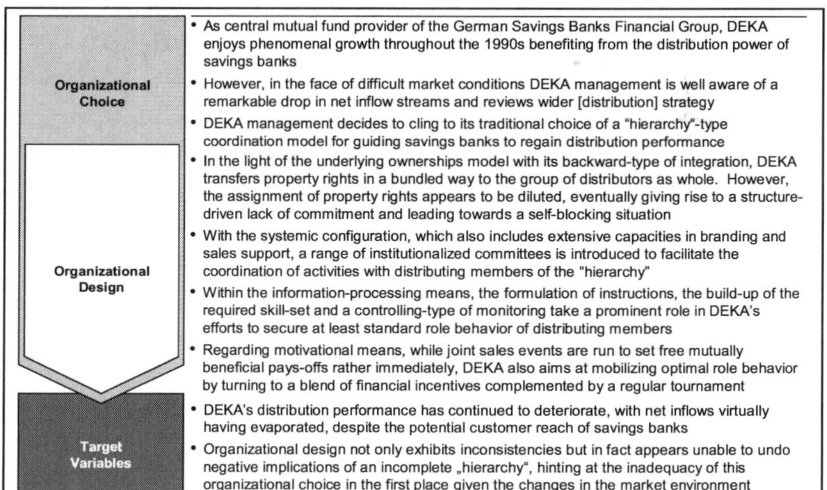

Source: Author

4.2 The Case of Julius Bär Asset Management

4.2.1 The Choice of "Partnership" as Institutional Arrangement for the Distribution Function

Now, this enquiry will turn to its second case study in order to examine how Julius Bär Asset Management (JBAM)[20] handles the central decision-making problem concerning the choice and design of institutional arrangements for the distribution function. In the light of the general constraints outlined for this optimization problem, the intention is to analyze whether and in which way JBAM is coping with the two fit requirements conceptualized in the enquiry's framework of analysis. As for the previous case study, the main focus is to clarify to what extent JBAM decisions regarding choice and design favor the strengthening of the "cash inflow stream" by accounting for the "market dynamics" and by bringing negative side effects of "opportunism" and "service firm specificity" under control.

JBAM is a core business line of the Julius Bär Group, which is one of the leading Swiss private banking institutions with a total of CHF 135 billion in AuM in 2004. By offering asset management products and services to retail as well as institutional clients, JBAM contributed CHF 74 billion in AuM to this group total, with CHF 45 billion (or 61 percent) of this raised from retail clients with a product range comprising 203 mutual funds. The production function for these products is carried out by JBAM out of its investment centers in Zurich, London, and New York. Due to its relatively small scale in comparison to other European asset management firms, JBAM is mainly perceived as an international niche player. Concerning the services in support of the actual sales and advisory activities to private investors, distributors of mutual funds view this asset management firm to be one of the most innovative in the entire asset management sector.

---

20 This case study is based on seven semi-structured interviews along the enquiry's standard questionnaire with management of JBAM in August 2004 at JBAM's headquarters in Zurich. Interviewees included management from Zurich as well as sales managers from JBAM's local sales team operating in Germany. Interviews lasted between 90-180 minutes. In order to meet the enquiry's information needs, access to internal documents was provided. Additionally, this study turned to the Julius Bär annual reports. A draft of this case study was made available to JBAM management. Findings of this study were presented to the management committee and discussed with single committee members.

As will be elaborated in more detail, this enquiry classifies JBAM as the case study, in which in some form of **"partnership"** is chosen to organize the agency-relationship between JBAM and external distributors in Germany. JBAM management overall is convinced that the chances of successfully generating inflows abroad are better with an established local distribution partner.

4.2.1.1 Emerging Performance Gap

With the aforementioned general assumptions concerning the adjustments to the organizational choice, the enquiry now attempts to clarify to what extent and in which form this particular asset management firm has been confronted with a performance gap that can be regarded as critical from an objective point of view. Thereafter, the discussion will turn to the respective interpretations and explanations by JBAM management. Hence, by outlining the performance development in terms of AuM and net inflows raised from private investors in Germany, the purpose is to ascertain if JBAM has been exposed to an increasing gap and, thus, to growing pressure to respond to unsatisfactory distribution performance levels.

Throughout the late 1990s, JBAM enjoyed phenomenal growth in Germany. However, at the beginning of this century growth in AuM started to cool down and eventually collapsed by 31 percent from CHF 2.5 billion [EUR 1.7 billion] to CHF 1.7 billion [EUR 1.1 billion] in 2002. This was not only in strong contrast to the development in previous years but, in fact, indicated the emergence of critically evolving performance levels for JBAM in Germany. Clearly, this severe drop and the resulting significant negative deviation between the actual realized and targeted AuM figures can be related to the nosedive of capital markets at that time, which significantly reduced the volumes of mutual funds, leaving many asset management firms across Europe with evaporated levels of AuM.

However, taking a look at the net inflow figures realized in Germany (Figure 23), which in fact is a more accurate indicator for distribution performance as it measures the net new assets raised from per year, it already shows from an objective point of view that since 2000 the generation of inflow streams from private investors has become increasingly difficult for JBAM in Germany. Although net inflows also started to decrease at the market level in Germany, they declined much more strongly for JBAM. In 2001, JBAM experienced a drop of net inflows by 39 percent in comparison to a decline of 35 percent at the market level. More dramatically, in 2002 JBAM's net inflows literally crashed by 77 percent to only EUR 0.1 billion, while the market in total faced a drop of only 28 percent. This clearly underlines that JBAM encountered greater difficulties maintaining distribution performance levels than competitors in these difficult market conditions.

Fig. 23: EMERGING PERFORMANCE GAP CONFRONTING JBAM

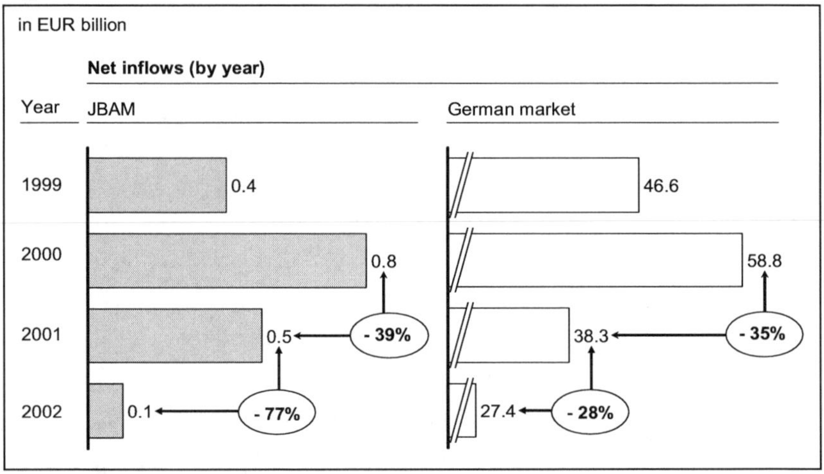

Source: JBAM Controlling, BVI (2005), author's calculation

The observed negative trends in AuM and net inflows highlight critically evolving performance levels facing JBAM. Moreover, it appears as if this deterioration of the distribution performance hints at aspects, other than the mere challenging capital market conditions at that time, that may have caused this objectively very observable deficit confronting JBAM in the German asset management sector.

4.2.1.2 Perceiving and Interpreting Performance Gap

To elaborate in which way such a performance gap eventually has led to decisions concerning the organizational choice and, thus, possibly to adjustments of the "degree of decentralization" for the distribution function, it is essential to shed light on how such a gap has been perceived and interpreted. The aim is, therefore, to ascertain whether the magnitude of this deficit surpassed a subjective threshold among JBAM management, initiating reactions to revise distribution arrangements in the German market.

In that respect, it is important to point out that already in the early 1990s the Julius Bär Group took the fundamental strategic decision that the in-house asset management division should increasingly turn to decentralized structures for marketing its mutual fund range to private investors. To capture the growth opportunities emerging in the asset management sector in the 1990s, the intention was to increasingly rely on external distributors in addition to the proprietary private banking channel. Therefore, **in the mid 1990s**, to achieve scale in terms of AuM and revenues, **JBAM started to pursue the strategic route of selling its asset management products via non-proprietary networks by entering into sales agreements with external distributors** in both its domestic Swiss market but also in other European markets, most notably Italy and Germany.

As part of this strategy to leverage existing customer pools of local distribution partners, JBAM targeted the generation of inflow streams with different types of products. Besides branded sales of JBAM products as the more intuitive form of third-party distribution [as well as the repackaging of JBAM products in fund-of-funds solutions produced by the asset management in-house divisions of external distributors], so-called private label funds [also referred to as white label funds] constitute another important source of inflows and revenues. Within these decentralized structures, after a period of strong growth by 2002 the latter product category contributed CHF 11 billion in AuM, thereby accounting for more than 40 percent of JBAM's total AuM raised from retail investors. Tailored individually to the distributor's needs, private label funds generally tend to be sold under the brand name of the distributing organization, while the production function or parts of it remain under the responsibility of JBAM. Such a set-up of the value chain for this particular product category calls for frequent in-depth interaction, with the positive side effect that it allows JBAM to establish close relationships with many of its distributors. A sales manager noted that in the 1990s these relationships exhibited strong links as JBAM in many cases held the position of being the unique external product-providing asset management firm. Therefore, **having already in the early 1990s foreseen the limits of selling solely through its in-house channel, JBAM was one of the first European asset management firms to strategically turn to decentralized structures for marketing its mutual funds to private investors**. In this way, JBAM overall – but also in Germany – was in the position to accomplish strong growth, similar to the levels the asset management sector as a whole enjoyed in the late 1990s.

However, as pointed out above, at the turn of this century growth in both AuM and net inflows not only stalled but eventually collapsed. The emerging distribution performance deficit within these decentralized organizational designs did not remain unnoticed and drew the attention of JBAM management. In the face of the traditionally high strategic priority of the German market to JBAM, **it considered the emergence of this performance gap to be of critical relevance to JBAM's overall performance**. With respect to the root causes underlying this deterioration, JBAM management perceived in particular the fundamental evolution of the distribution landscape in Germany at the turn of the century to be considerably worsening the generation of inflows via external banks.

As already illustrated, the distribution environment in Germany underwent a lasting change at the beginning of this century. The majority of German banks increasingly started to open their shelves for external products by granting access to a lager number of external asset management firms. This trend towards more open distribution systems allowed and enticed non-domestic asset management firms to enter into the economically attractive German market without having to incur considerable capital-outlays for setting up a customer base by themselves. Following from this, JBAM increasingly found itself exposed to intensified competition within its decentralized agency-relationships for the distribution function. A sales manager argued that in the light of this significant change, JBAM experienced in some cases the loss of its status as the [unique] external product provider with relationships in general becoming more discrete. Resulting from this loosening of its relationships, the realization of inflows in fact turned out to be considerably encumbered. This unfavorable implication of these "market dynamics" at the turn of the century was further aggravated by some JBAM-internal management scandal in Germany.

Therefore, with regard to the interpretation and causal explanation of the noticed deterioration of distribution performance levels, **JBAM management learnt that the decentralized arrangements in Germany, which had spurred the growth in the late 1990s, increasingly became prone to intensified coordination and motivation issues**. Along this recognition, the obstacles arising in managing these decoupled arrangements stemming from increasingly weakened relationships were seen as a major difficulty in upholding the distribution performance levels of previous years. In the face of this interpretation, JBAM management regarded the choice [and the design] of institutional arrangements for marketing mutual funds to private investors as a key lever to regain performance levels. By means of reconsidering or at least refining the choice of institutional arrangements for the distribution function in Germany, JBAM management saw the opportunity not only to reduce but eventually to overcome the gap in net inflows provoked by intensified competition for access to distributors' shelf-space.

All in all, given the high strategic relevance of the German market, already at an early stage of the emerging deficit in net inflow streams, JBAM management regarded this negative trend to have reached such a critical level that the successful distribution strategy of the 1990s was in fact under scrutiny. In other words, with organizational choices being considered as efficacious in bringing under control varying coordination and motivation issues, JBAM management felt the urgency to review its "degree of decentralization" for the distribution of its product range to German private investors.

4.2.1.3 Responding to Perceived Performance Gap

In response to these "market dynamics" and in anticipation of the resulting negative consequences for performance levels, in 2001 and 2002 JBAM management reacted by introducing a variety of measures with the overriding goal to systematically [re]build robust relationships with external distributors. Having experienced both the upside of employing non-proprietary distribution networks but also glaring issues of coordination and motivation in decoupled systems, **JBAM management at that point remained confident that it would be able to overcome the deficit by sticking to decentralized arrangements**. In other words, management was optimistic that it could reestablish strong distribution performance by clinging to its strategic route of falling back on external distribution partners. Expanded customer reach by gaining access to already established customer pools was considered to be the most promising route to improve inflow streams.

Yet, the use of non-proprietary distribution channels does not only offer the advantages of leveraging broader access to private investors. Given the "service firm specificity" inherent in sales and advisory activities as well as the danger of "opportunism", it can give rise to situations in which asset management firms are held up in agency-relationships to market mutual funds. In that respect, following the fundamental change in the distribution landscape in Germany, one sales manager confirmed that in some cases JBAM has faced the situation in which at the beginning of a relationship a lot of promises were made, but ultimately not much happened in terms of inflow generation. In the view of this pattern of side-constraints, JBAM management was well aware of the necessity to complement its intended choice in favor of rather decoupled governance structures with refined steering instruments to secure the distributors' ability and motivation on a sustainable basis to overcome the performance gap. Therefore, as observed for the other case studies, **the aspired organizational choice and the corresponding adaptations in response to the gap noticed represent a refinement of the existing "degree of decentralization"** rather than a fundamental rearrangement. This essentially implies that the allocation of property rights within agency-relationships remains untouched.

In line with this overriding aspiration to strengthen inflow streams from private investors in Germany by initiating and [re]building more robust decentralized agency-relationships, **one main step was to establish a local sales team in Frankfurt** to allow the personnel directly interacting with the distributing banks in Germany to create closer and more robust relationships. Being in charge of relationship management, this team is responsible for the acquisition of [new] external distributors, subsequent business development as well as their retention. Complementary to these activities performed by the local sales team, centralized sales support units located in JBAM's headquarters in Zurich provide further assistance.

Moreover, corresponding to this overriding objective, another responsive measure to the perceived performance gap was to further fine-tune the process of optimizing decentralized structures by **systemizing the identification of most compatible distribution partners [upfront]**. The compatibility of external distributing organizations and, thus, their suitability for constructing the intended, more robust relationships is in general evaluated along four groups of criteria. JBAM management attempts to perform this appraisal from a strategic as well as a product range related point of view. Additionally, JBAM takes into account service level requirements of potential distributors and, last but not least, considers economic aspects in order to assess the chance of building the aspired more stable agency-relationships. One sales manager summarized that this refined approach of initiating institutional arrangements in the hands of the local sales team is not only much more sophisticated in comparison to how it used to be but also focuses much more on the sustainability of potential decentralized distribution systems.

4.2.1.4 Refining "Degree of Decentralization" for Distribution Function

With regard to the external fit problem, it turns out that **the emerging gap in distribution performance in the German private investor market became a concern of critical relevance to JBAM management already at an early stage**. In the light of the main root cause, the dynamics in the distribution environment, management regarded the organizational choice for arranging the distribution function as an essential means to improve inflow streams. Therefore, in response to this deficit, JBAM management was confident of bolstering distribution performance by falling back on decentralized – yet more robust – agency-relationships. To be more specific, JBAM management intended to overcome the slump encountered by aiming to set up arrangements of "partnership" with external distributing banks.

However, in the case of JBAM, it shows that while asset management firms are in a position to aspire to such a mode of coordination as the desired "degree of decentralization" for the distribution function, whether this aspired [decentralized] choice actually turns out to be the realized one appears to be moderated by the interests of distributors and by the relative attractiveness of JBAM vis-à-vis competing asset management firms. In other words, the menu of available alternatives to choose from seems to be somewhat narrowed. As mentioned earlier, after a first move towards more open distribution systems, major distributing banks in Germany have remained rather restrictive in permitting entry to their distribution platforms. Being in the powerful position to own and, thus, to control the relationship with private investors, it is, in fact, the distributing bank that has a fundamental say which asset management firm gets access as a mutual fund provider, thereby moderating screening efforts of asset management firms to search for suitable [meaning compatible] distributors. In this regard, the major distributing banks have put in place increasingly professionalized and sophisticated selection procedures to pick external asset management firms from a growing pool of most notably cross-border entrants seeking access to German private investors. This underlines that the choice sought by asset management firms regarding the "degree of decentralization" might not necessarily be attainable. In more practical terms, for this case study, it becomes apparent that these entry hurdles limit the opportunities to bridge the distribution performance gap in the Germany, as in some cases JBAM finds itself not being selected as a [preferred] provider.

Underlying this moderating restriction to the actual choice, it seems that in the face of the intensified rivalry to obtain access to distribution networks, JBAM sometimes has trouble in successfully holding its own in comparison with other competing asset management firms within these increasingly professionalized selection procedures. While JBAM is regarded as one of the leading asset management firms in Europe with respect to the quality of its sales support services to distributors, the brand strength in terms of awareness among private investors in the German market is fairly moderate. With one sales manager acknowledging the importance of a competitive brand in such a guided distribution environment, another sales manager noted that while JBAM in general enjoys a good reputation among distributors, private investors in Germany rarely consider or even demand JBAM's product offering explicitly. Thus, JBAM's overall attractiveness in this contest for getting access to non-proprietary networks is somewhat reduced. As a third sales manager remarked, even if a competitive brand triggers willingness on the part of distributors to grant access and to perform the sales and advisory activities, JBAM still feels the consequences of currently not having a so-called blockbuster-product in its range of mutual funds. In the asset management sector, a blockbuster-product is referred to as a mutual fund with an impeccable investment performance track-record in combination with substantial media attention, which already has and still is achieving a remarkable growth in terms of AuM. Another sales manager argued that products with this informal status of being a blockbuster are a critical prerequisite for increasing the likelihood of being invited to guided, non-proprietary distribution networks, as these are more readily sellable to private investors. As JBAM currently does not have such a product, its positioning relative to competing asset management firms for becoming a preferred provider is further weakened.

Therefore, given the importance of this relative attractiveness to get access to external distribution networks, it shows that the envisaged choice concerning the "degree of decentralization" may not always be achievable, as autonomous banks leverage their powerful position to determine with whom to enter into agency-relationships. In other words, in such a competitive surrounding, like almost all other asset management firms, JBAM is not always in the position to initiate the decentralized arrangements to market its product range to private investors as intended. Among the total number of around 70 decoupled agency-relationships, a prominent example of the intended and actually realized form of "partnership" is the institutional arrangement between JBAM and Union Investment. Union Investment, the third largest fund provider [in terms of AuM] in the German private investor market, is the in-house asset management production platform of the German cooperative banks. This preferred "partnership" between JBAM and Union Investment centers around the "SwissRubinum", a mutual fund-based investment solution, which was launched very successfully in 2001. In Germany, this wealth management product is exclusively available to customers through the extensive distribution network of cooperative banks.

For the purpose of investigating the enquiry's decision-making problem on the choice and design of institutional arrangements for marketing mutual funds to private investors in Germany, JBAM is classified as the case study of "partnership". From a comparative perspective, it will become apparent that JBAM offers considerable scope to its distribution partners to participate along the value chain in the otherwise decentralized agency-relationship. Therefore, as will be elaborated in more detail, this enquiry regards the case as the one in which the asset management firm [the principal] allows the distributing bank [the agent]:

- to use the mutual funds provided for advisory activities
- to receive some form of compensation for performing the distribution function of the mutual funds
- to have a say on the form or substance of some mutual funds

In this way, the external distributor is given the right to get involved in areas beyond the sales and advisory activities of the distribution function, which essentially constitutes the defining characteristic of the "partnership"-type of institutional arrangement.

4.2.2 The Design of "Partnership" as Institutional Arrangement for the Distribution Function

In the following section, the point now is to take a closer look at how JBAM designs the agency-relationship based on its choice of the "degree of decentralization" to fully capture the advantages of "partnership" for arranging the distribution function in Germany. Of particular interest is to determine whether and in which way JBAM falls back on the variables conceptualized in the enquiry's framework to establish a coordination mechanism that is consistent with this overarching organizational choice. In other words, concerning the internal fit requirement, the purpose is to clarify if JBAM's design in terms of the systemic configuration and process-related measures adequately considers the side-constraints arising with the chosen "degree of decentralization". Therefore, against the background of the agency-relationship between JBAM [principal] and its external distribution partners [agent], the question now to elaborate on is to what extent JBAM with its overall design of such "partnership" arrangements is able to come to an optimization of distribution systems for its mutual funds by bringing under control challenges stemming from "opportunism" and "service firm specificity".

When examining the adequacy of the design of this "degree of decentralization", it will become apparent – as for the other two case studies – that already with the **systemic configuration** by laying out competencies, roles, and authorities JBAM attempts to account for risks related to specificity and opportunism arising with its organizational choice. Furthermore, it will be brought to light how this systemic configuration operates as the context of governance within which JBAM subsequently applies **process-related measures** in order to guide the behavior of the autonomous, external distributors. As this will be analyzed from the view of an optimizing perspective, the efficacy of JBAM's design of the chosen "degree of decentralization" is then mainly assessed against its ability to raise a "cash inflow stream" from private investors for its mutual fund range.

4.2.2.1 Systemic Configuration of "Partnership"

In view of its normative context, the discussion will now turn to the systemic configuration by which the relationship between JBAM and the distributing banks is structured in order to set the stage to improve the distribution performance levels for JBAM's mutual funds. The purpose is to ascertain whether and in which way this configuration takes into consideration the issues related to the "service firm specificity" and the gradually rising threat of "opportunism".

Fig. 24: SYSTEMIC CONFIGURATION OF "PARTNERSHIP"

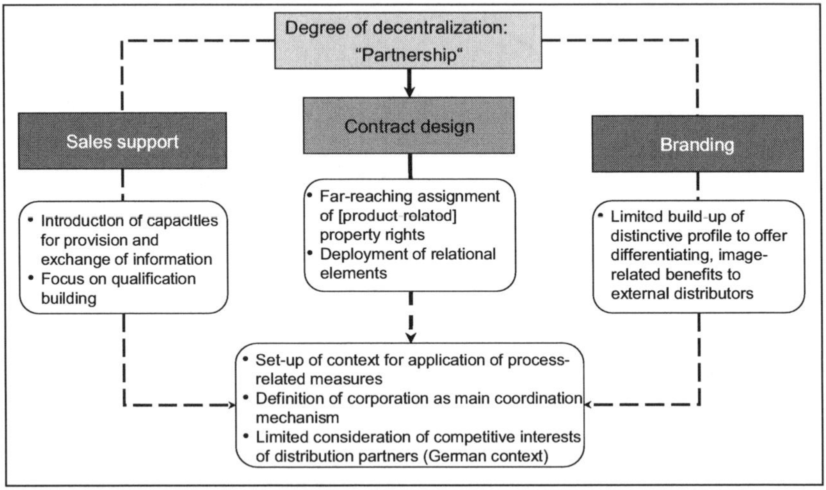

Source: Author

With regard to JBAM's design of the systemic configuration, as summarized in Figure 24, this enquiry will bring to light that the agency-relationships between JBAM and the external distributors are typically structured by the application of a specific pattern of assigning property rights. In addition to this, this part of the enquiry will also outline to what extent JBAM has the capacity in place to offer image-related benefits to its distributing partners, which allows them to [further] improve their competitive positioning. Last but not least, this elaboration will additionally bring to light how and to what degree capacities are also made available to facilitate the build-up of qualification and relevant knowledge on the part of the agents with the intention of empowering them to appropriately deal with sales and advisory problem.

In elaborating on this systemic configuration, it will turn out that these properties aim to set the context for dovetailing activities between JBAM and the external distributors on a continuous basis. As will be seen from this case-study, the actual coordination of interactions along the value chain relies to a considerable degree on specific forms of cooperation. Therefore, with this organizational choice of "partnership" at stake, this specific range of features is introduced as a means to eventually facilitate the introduction of the cognitive and motivational prerequisites to secure the desired [extra] role behavior of external distributors. This, in turn, underlines that **this overall structure of governance for arrangements of "partnership" ultimately constitutes the contextual frame for generating strong net inflow streams**. In this way, it represents a critical ingredient for bringing distribution systems of "partnership" to optimal distribution performance outcomes. Speaking more in terms of single variables conceptualized in the framework of analysis, this elaboration on the systemic set-up will touch on "screening", "contract design", "branding", and "sales support".

4.2.2.1.1 Assigning Property Rights to Set Up Governance Structure

When initiating the intended decentralized agency-relationships for the distribution function in Germany, as any other asset management firm turning to decoupled forms of organizing sales and advisory activities, JBAM engages in efforts to lay down a contractual agreement that defines the terms and process of exchange with the external distributing bank. In this way, the rights for both parties of the transaction are specified. As will be illuminated now in more detail, these agreements underlying the agency-relationship of "partnership" tend to entail a **far-reaching bundling of property rights on the part of the external distributing bank**. Following from this approach of assigning competencies, these legal contracts set the stage for introducing participation and, thus, for relying on cooperation as the central mechanism to coordinate activities along the value chain for producing and marketing mutual funds to private investors.

Before these property rights are assigned, as indicated above, JBAM intends to perform some form of **"screening"** of the external distributor. However, as already mentioned, in the light of the allocation of power between asset management firms and distributing banks, which own the relationship to private investors, the opportunities for the former to conduct a systematic "screening" are limited. Thus, with a great deal of information concerning the distributors' qualification such as the size of the branch network, the number and type of end customers, the size of the sales force and its quality being readily available, the negotiation to lay out the systemic configuration represents one of the very few chances to verify the underlying motives of distributors. One sales manager hinted at a situation in Germany where a distributing bank demanded comprehensive assistance but was not willing to include JBAM in the group of preferred providers. Based on this signal of limited prospects of strong inflow generation, JBAM opted against entering into the agency-relationship. This, in turn, highlights that is the **information exchanged in the process of setting up the systemic configuration that is used for some [rather situational] "screening" of potential distribution partners**.

Regarding the content of a typical contract to regulate the exchange, each of the bilateral relationships with external distributing banks has its very own specific agreements. As far as the "contract design" is concerned, it becomes apparent that these agreements are employed to fundamentally structure the interaction along the value chain for producing and marketing mutual funds to private investors. From a genuine comparative perspective, **it shows that in this case study it comes to a far-reaching transfer of property rights to the distributor, which constitutes the defining characteristic of a "partnership"-type of distribution system** and, thus, gains functional relevance in controlling for lurking negative side effects stemming from specificity and opportunism.

With regard to a typical contractual agreement for a "partnership", according to the classification of property rights by Furubotn and Richter (1991, p. 6), JBAM gives the distribution banks the right to use its mutual funds for their advisory services (usus) as well as to receive some share of the management fee in the form of retrocession (usus fructus). Moreover, while JBAM usually retains the authority to change the investment focus or other features of its mutual fund products within the limits of the respective fund prospectus[21], in selected relationships of "partnership" JBAM even assigns some of those [product-related] property rights to the autonomous distributor (usus abusus). As illustrated in Figure 25, **JBAM invites the distribution partner to get involved beyond the mere distribution function**. In practical terms, for some arrangements JBAM deliberately hands over the competence to decide upon the strategic asset allocation for a

[21] A fund prospectus is classified as a legal publication to specify the characteristics of a mutual fund. The scope of information covers supplementary information for investors, the investment objectives of the fund, the investment policy and limits, special investment techniques, and financial instruments.

particular mutual fund [underlying the relationship] to the distribution bank [and the respective in-house asset management], while JBAM remains in the position of performing the actual fund or stock selection. Additionally, participation may also take place along other areas of the production function.

Fig. 25: ALLOCATION OF RESPONSIBILITIES WITHIN "PARTNERSHIP"

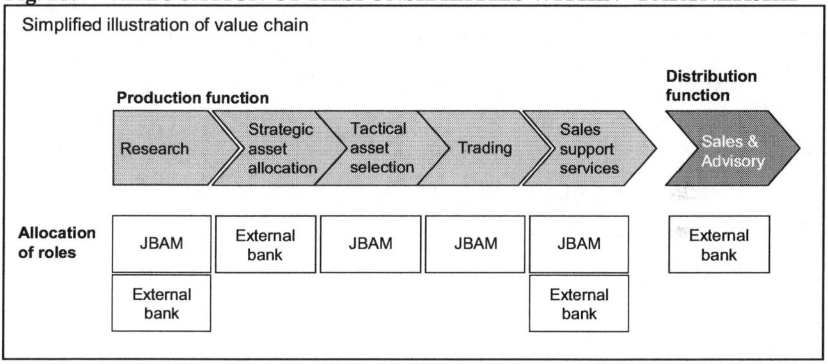

Source: Author

Moreover, in this particular case study these authorities are increasingly allocated by the application of elements of a relational contract. Given partners' participation in decisions concerning the form and substance of investment products, JBAM faces the imminent need to secure cooperation. Therefore, besides the "classical" elements such as the price for performing the distribution function [in terms of the retrocession], **the "contract design" predominately stipulates rather general behavioral guidelines**. In essence, JBAM makes an appeal to the distributor to act cooperatively. In this regard, document analysis reveals that the duration of a typical contract is declared to be infinite, thereby signaling continuous willingness to cooperate which in turn is expected to have a cooperation-encouraging effect on the part of distributing partners. Furthermore, in the face of significant specificity inherent in the distribution function, the contractual agreement generally does not seek to comprehensively regulate the way in which the actual sales and advisory activities are supposed to be carried out. Hence, distributors in fact are given substantial scope to perform the distribution function in accordance with the needs of time and place. Consequently, with respect to the obligations imposed on external distributing banks, JBAM simply stipulates that the external banks are responsible for maintaining as well as for taking care of their pool of end customers in an "appropriate" and "accurate" manner. Moreover, JBAM points out that it will hold the distributor liable in case the information and sales material provided is knowingly used in an incorrect or misleading way. Although the detailing of the contract can last for almost a year or more, this design indicated that **these contract agreements only offer some form of sanction function in situations of crude misconduct**.

This increased application of elements of a relational contract within its "contract design" already underlines that JBAM intends to stimulate the cooperative behavior of external distributors by strengthening their willingness to participate rather than by relying on the explicit, protective functionality of formal agreements. In that respect, one sales manager confirmed that JBAM has never taken legal action in response to noticed situations of hold-up. Another sales manager added that if a relationship with the external distribution partner is severely interrupted, the legal contract will not help to secure or [re]establish commitment.

From all this, it shows that JBAM hands over substantial [product-related] property rights to its distribution partner as a salient feature to arrange the distribution function under the regime of "partnership"-type of systemic configuration. This structural set-up is flanked by the employment of some form of relational contract outlining the exchange relationship. In this way, JBAM aims to appropriately cope with lurking issues of specificity and opportunistic tendencies. Therefore, with the purpose of ensuring the external distributor's willingness to cooperate, this structural set-up, on the one hand, facilitates participation beyond the mere distribution function. On the other hand, it signals trust in the cooperative intentions of its distributing partners by giving them considerable scope. This, in turn, shows that by attempting to align possibly diverging interests in this manner, **JBAM's systemic configuration predominantly turns to some motivation-enhancing means rather than to external enforcement mechanisms to strengthen inflows for its mutual fund range**.

4.2.2.1.2 Building Branding Capacity to Offer Competitive Advantage

Achieving a relevant and differentiating value proposition by way of **"branding"** is widely regarded among asset management firms as a further lever to strengthen the inflow stream raised from private investors and, thus, to overcome the deficits encountered in distribution performance. As outlined in the enquiry's framework of analysis, an appropriate design of the **"branding"** strategy, at least in two different but interrelated ways, is able to contribute to the aspired improvement in distribution performance. On the one hand, by guiding and, thus, managing expectations concerning the experience from purchasing the asset management firm's mutual funds, investments in "branding" offer the chance to stimulate demand directly from private investors (Keller, pp. 16-19). On the other hand, with a relevant and differentiated image firmly established in the mind of end customers, the asset management firm increasingly finds itself in the position to offer some form of positive image-transfer to its distributors (Baumgarth 2004, pp. 254-255). This, in turn, potentially benefits them in succeeding to take on a more competitive positioning vis-à-vis distributing rivals. In this regard, investment decisions in "branding" carry the opportunity to establish structural prerequisites with the systemic configuration in order to align interests as well to balance the dependence within agency-relationships.

Therefore, in the light of the choice of "partnership" and the subsequent necessity to secure the sustained willingness of distributors to cooperate, "branding" as a structure-shaping investment is clearly of functional relevance to achieve the strengthening of inflows streams collected from investors. Thus, following the remarkably bundled assignment of property rights as well as the handover of substantial scope on how to perform the distribution function, of particular interest now is to clarify to what extent and in which way JBAM deliberately deploys capacities of "branding" within its governance structure as a measure to induce cooperation, thereby taking precautions against the latent issues of opportunism and specificity.

From a comparative point of view, however, it becomes strikingly evident that **JBAM management makes this type of investment to strengthen distribution performance only in a very restrictive way**. As one sales manager confirmed, concerning the design of its "branding" strategy [in Germany], JBAM management overall remains rather reserved in introducing brand-building measures in the first place or even more relationship-related co-branding activities. Highlighting this diffidence, relative to the other two case studies as well the wider group of competitors in the German asset management sector, JBAM is in fact a far cry from being among the top spenders on brand investments, irrespective of whether targeted at the private investor segment or the distributing intermediaries. For example, while DEKA consistently spends more than EUR 10 million per year in terms of media spending, the amount of resources JBAM devotes to these activities in Germany is negligible.

As far as the result is concerned, it does not come as a surprise that in particular from an end customer perspective, JBAM's brand lacks awareness and a thoroughly established, distinctive image as a product-providing asset management firm vis-à-vis German and other foreign asset management firms competing in the private investor market. One sales manager pointed out that JBAM's brand does not enjoy a pull effect from private investors in Germany. Contrary to the situation in Switzerland where JBAM benefits from the strong brand[22] of the Julius Bär Group [most notably in terms of awareness], this [self-]appraisal indicates that in Germany the brand is in fact experiencing difficulty in directly stimulating demand. This, in turn, means that end customers in Germany hardly impose control on the distribution activities at the point-of-sale, indicating that in this case study "branding" is not fully leveraged to cope with the specificity inherent in the sales and advisory activities.

This limited brand strength also indicates that this lever to serve distributors' aspirations to achieve a more differentiated and, thus, more competitive positioning overall is not available to JBAM in the German context. As it is JBAM's brand strength relative to the respective distributor's that considerably drives the degree to which the deployment of JBAM's name or logo can deliver positive spillover effects to the distributor, it looks as if the chances for JBAM to offer those image-related benefits are

22 A recent market research effort in Switzerland with regard to the private investor market segment reveals that the Julius Bär Group is one of the leading Swiss private banks with an aided awareness of more than 90 percent.

limited. Despite the general positive perception of its Swiss origin and the exclusiveness associated with its private banking background, **JBAM is missing critical prerequisites to introduce "branding" on a larger scale as a move to activate sufficient levels of cooperation**. Due this deficit in brand awareness and the fairly blurred image [as a mutual fund producing asset management firm], it appears as if JBAM lacks sufficient "branding" capacities to adequately serve the competitive considerations of [potential] distribution partners.

Hence, JBAM together with respective distribution partners decides to put in place, only in a rather moderate manner, branding investments specific to their arrangement. These decisions are taken most notably for those agency-relationships in which respective brand profiles have been identified to actually complement each other. It clearly shows that the purpose is two-fold. While these investments [anchored with the outline of the systemic configuration] aim to make private investors aware of JBAM's mutual fund offering and their availability at the distributing bank's point-of-sale, they are also introduced to provide image-related benefits in order to reinforce the distributors' willingness to cooperate.

Therefore, in summary, as institutional arrangements of "partnership" rely considerably on willingness to cooperate, it becomes apparent that at least to some degree JBAM aspires to trigger distributors' self-interest to participate by means of these structure-shaping instruments. It shows that the principal for some of its agency-relationships deploys "branding" as a functionally relevant lever to capture the advantages associated with this differentiated approach to arranging the distribution function. However, it cannot be denied that **the extent of these investments in "branding" is not sufficient to secure adequate handling of challenges stemming from "opportunism" and "service firm specificity"**, indicating that **this design for "partnership"-type of institutional arrangements apparently lacks a critical ingredient to bring such decoupled agency-relationships to full strength**. Instead, and this is something that will be elaborated now in more detail, JBAM puts greater

Strongly driven by the group's value proposition "true to you.", the group brand image profile exhibits strengths with regard mainly to advisory relevant associations such as trust, competence, sympathy, and reliability.

emphasis on the provision of comprehensive "sales support". Capacities for structurally assisting the advisory activities are offered through the local sales team in Frankfurt as well as the additional sales support units located at its headquarters in Zurich.

4.2.2.1.3 Setting-up Sales Support Capacities to Create Specific Know-How

The provision of "sales support" is widely regarded as a further measure that potentially has a positive effect on improving inflow streams raised from private investors. In the light of the overriding optimizing objective, **"sales support"** in fact serves two purposes. On the one hand, the objective is to enable the external bank to take on the distribution function. On the other hand, the aim is also to secure desired role behavior to cooperatively perform distribution activities on behalf of JBAM. Therefore, at least in principle, "sales support" represents a key lever to properly address the perils of specificity and latent issue of opportunism. Following from this then, there can be no denying that investment decisions concerning the capacities to provide adequate "sales support" gain functional relevance already with the structural setup of decentralized arrangements.

From a genuine comparative perspective, as indicated above, it turns out that JBAM has a comprehensive set of capacities in place in order to assist the actual sales and advisory efforts of the external distributing banks. First of all, capacities are available to provide "sales support" in the form of a regular supply of relevant and accurate information. By seeking to overcome the likely asymmetric distribution of information within agency-relationships of "partnership", the primary objective of this form of "sales support" **is to equip distribution partners with the necessary material to actively sell and advise JBAM's mutual funds to their customers**. Additionally, in support of selected relationships, already with the systemic configuration, JBAM intends to pave the way to **facilitate the buildup of qualification of the distributing partners' sales staff**. Through tailored training programs as well as product presentations, the aim is to [further] upgrade the expertise of the distributors' personnel operating in direct contact with private investors, which is expected to be mutually beneficial. Following on from this, by already outlining these two different but complementary ways of assisting distribution activities with the structural set-up, JBAM intends to establish the prerequisites to improve inflow streams.

Like the other two asset management firms under focus in this enquiry, JBAM has a **variety of vehicles in place for the regular provision of information to distributing banks**. With regard to publications made available to distribution partners, the extensive choice ranges from periodical reports, such as for example fact-books and fact-sheets, outlining rather technical and quantitative features of JBAM's product portfolio, to more qualitative aspects in additional professional fund information. These materials are mainly targeted at distributors and their sales staff to enable them from an informational point of view, thereby facilitating a deeper understanding of JBAM's mutual fund range with regard to the respective investment focus, past investment performance, and the underlying investment process, etc. Additionally, this form of "sales support" also includes brochures and booklets to be used and passed on by distribution banks to private investors when they perform the sales and advisory activities for JBAM's mutual fund offering.

With regard to the actual way of making these capacities available, besides the conventional ways of hard copies and road-shows, **JBAM was one of the first asset management firms in Europe to implement a web-based extranet-solution**, called JBfundnet®. In this way, external distributing partners are given the chance to further tailor the information provided to their individual advisory needs. While offering greater flexibility as well facilitating easier access to advisory-relevant information for the actual sales staff in the banks' branches, it also becomes apparent that this structural set-up of delivering information also constitutes a move to retain control of what and how information related to JBAM's mutual fund offering is presented at the point-of-sale.

Furthermore, complementing this type of "sales support", as indicated above, **JBAM is generally willing to dedicate further capacities to offer dedicated sales training programs as well as product presentations**. While this form of assistance allows JBAM to make clear what kind of sales and advisory behavior is considered as cooperative, it in particular offers the chance to build up know-how and capabilities on the part of the distributors' sale staff. Gaining the much sought direct access to the distribution partners' sales staff, this mode of "sales support" gives JBAM the opportunity to further professionalize their skill-set and expertise. In the light of JBAM's private banking background, this form of assistance bears the potential of lasting improvement in the quality of the distributing bank's advisory efforts overall. With respect to the individual sales staff, JBAM is in this way able to familiarize them with additional techniques to appropriately handle issues arising at the point-of-sale in the course of the interaction with private investors. If respective sales staff members apply them successfully, thereby raising their self-esteem, this interactive "sales support" at the end of the day may strengthen their identification with the agency-relationships. This, in turn, favors the internalization of JBAM's product offering. Therefore, this kind of support for the actual advisory activities potentially bears the chance to reinforce the distributors' perception, at both the system-level and also at the level of individual sales staff, that it is in their own interest to cooperate.

Additionally, these training programs typically entail the transfer of relationship-specific know-how, as they centered around JBAM's mutual fund range. In case the distribution arrangement is discontinued, this know-how loses [some of its] value to the distributing bank and its sales force. Hence, this form of "sales support" constitutes a relationship-specific investment also to the external distributor [not only to JBAM]. Following on from this, it becomes apparent that by offering the prospect of know-how- and qualification-building JBAM also stimulates the **placement of an idiosyncratic investment by external distributors**. As is known, this in turn is expected to set the stage to further strengthen the commitment and motivation of the distributor to cooperate on a continuous basis.

Moreover, similar to the other two case studies, it shows that further capacities of "sales support" are introduced with the systemic configuration for "partnership"-type of agency-relationships. These capacities eventually take the form of **jointly-conducted sales events** for a JBAM mutual fund offering in order to assist distribution partners in their interaction with private investors. This kind of assistance entails the opportunity to enable but also to motivate the external bank to cooperatively take on the distribution function on behalf of JBAM. While the principal is in the position to guide the way in which and what kind of information is presented, the external distributing agent is expected to enjoy not only immediate economic benefits from a boost in demand for JBAM's product offering but also image-related benefits related to the glossiness and exclusivity of JBAM's Swiss private banking background in their interaction with their own customers.

In summary, it shows that by attempting to anchor these forms of "sales support" already with the set-up of the systemic configuration for its arrangements of "partnership", JBAM aims at ensuring that its distributing partners are appropriately applying the property rights assigned on their part. This deployment of "sales support" capacities aspires not only to enable distributing agents to actively sell and advise JBAM's mutual funds through equipping them with the relevant information but also to activate sufficient levels of self-interest to perform the distribution function on behalf of JBAM. In other words, it shows that JBAM in selected relationships introduces further measures of "sales support" with the purpose of being able to adequately account for the latent issues of specificity and opportunistic tendencies in order to improve cash inflow streams.

4.2.2.1.4 Systemic Configuration as Context

Having illustrated in which way JBAM intends to lay out the systemic configuration for its decentralized distribution arrangements of "partnership" in Germany, the purpose here is to discuss how this structural set-up operates with regard to the optimization objective. Therefore, as far as the second fit problem is concerned, the purpose is to clarify in which way the design of ["screening"], "contract design", "branding", and "sales support" and their interplay supports JBAM in handling negative challenges related to specificity and opportunism arising with the choice of "partnership" for the distribution function.

The discussion so far shows that the **systemic configuration itself primarily serves the purpose to set the context for the introduction of additional rather process-related measures to guide distribution activities**. In more specific terms, the structural set-up of governance for its arrangement of "partnership" in fact outlines the frame in which JBAM then deploys further instruments in order to react to situational demand through some form of intervention. In this sense, the systemic configuration with its defining properties constitutes the necessary rather then the sufficient element in order to come to an optimization of distribution performance levels.

Hence, as far as the systemic configuration as a context-setting device is concerned, in comparison to the other two case-studies, it shows that in this case study it is the far-reaching assignment of property-rights to external distributors that demarcates the degree to which JBAM puts in place additional, rather process-intervening measures. By considerably bundling product-related competencies on the part of the distributing bank in conjunction with the application of various elements of a relational contract, the decentralized agency-relationship essentially becomes structured as a distribution arrangement of "partnership". Such an arrangement by definition relies on the **participation** of the external partner, which requires sufficient levels of **self-interested cooperation** in order to successfully coordinate the process-oriented interaction between JBAM and the distributing bank.

Therefore, JBAM deliberately includes two additional measures in the systemic configuration to ensure that external distributing agents cooperatively use the rights granted and scope when performing the distribution function. As elaborated,, JBAM has a comprehensive set of capacities ready for delivering information and know-how as well as for building qualification on the part of external distributors. Additionally, though only to a comparatively limited extent, JBAM considers the opportunity to offer the prospects of some differentiating and, thus, competitiveness-enhancing spill-over-effects by means of branding activities as a way to further encourage the willingness to cooperate. Consequently, it seems as if only partially the function relevant capacities are in place to establish the necessary cognitive and motivational prerequisites to bring to full strength the "partnership"-type of distribution systems with their far-reaching transfer of property rights. Since this systemic configuration is regarded as the frame for the introduction and design of rather process-related instruments, this enquiry will now outline how in the face of this structural set-up JBAM is applying further process-related measures in order to come to an optimized "cash inflow stream".

4.2.2.2 Process-Related Measures of "Partnership"

In the following section, the purpose is now to illustrate the way in which JBAM attempts to guide the behavior of its external distributors to achieve a sustained strengthening of cash inflow streams from private investors. The objective is to find out which process-related instruments JBAM applies to manage the agency-relationships on an on-going basis. From an analytical point of view, under the condition of a "partnership"-type of systemic configuration, the main interest is, therefore, to find out the extent to which process-related measures are taken in order to bring the lurking side effects of "service firm specificity" and "opportunism" in this "degree of decentralization" under control.

As already indicated, it is the far-reaching assignment of [product-related] property rights that sets the context for designing and applying available measures to steer distributors' activities. In more precise terms, following this transfer of [product-related] property rights, **cooperation constitutes the main coordination mechanism within these decoupled agency-relationships**. Therefore, with participation as the main instrument to guide behavior, it will also become evident that JBAM does not, in fact, rely on directly intervening measures. In contrast to the other case studies, JBAM to a considerable extent employs indirectly intervening means to raise the external distributors' ability as well as to encourage their willingness to take on the assigned role. The enquiry will now outline that JBAM in this way aspires to appropriately account for situational impediments arising from specificity and opportunistic tendencies.

Consequently, from a functional point of view, **JABM's aim in deploying additional process-related means is to further promote self-motivation on the part of the external distributor to perform the distribution function.** As opposed to especially the more conventional "arm's length" type of interaction between autonomous exchange partners, for this case study it becomes obvious that this envisaged mobilization of self-interest is approached by offering extensive participation in decision-making processes along the value chain. In other words, in comparison to the other two case-studies, it is this transfer of rights to selected external distributors to participate in more depth and beyond the mere distribution function that sets the stage to trigger the desired levels of self-interested cooperation. As this chance for involvement tends to reinforce commitment, the ground seems to be laid to secure that the distribution activities on behalf of JBAM are performed in a cooperative manner. Being motivated in this way, the external agents eventually may even actively engage in some form of search-efforts to further improve the overall proficiency of the agency-relationships. These efforts to develop the agency-relationships are assumed to be mutually beneficial and favor the further alignment of goals.

As for the other two case studies, within these process-related measures for guiding distribution activities, this enquiry will distinguish between **information-processing means** and rather **motivational measures**. In the course of the following elaboration, in terms of the single action variables conceptualized in the framework of analysis, this enquiry will touch on "monitoring", "incentive scheme", and "relational exchange", besides the context-setting variables, in order to outline the way in which JBAM attempts to bring its distribution systems to full strength.

4.2.2.2.1 Information-Processing Means for Process-Intervention

The enquiry's focus now is to shed light on the information-processing means JBAM applies in its decentralized agency-relationships in Germany. Against the already sketched-out, structurally given capacities of "sales support", this elaboration will point out that JBAM in three different, but nonetheless interrelated, ways intends to establish the informational prerequisites for strengthening distribution performance. In discussing these three ways of guiding the external distributors' behavior, as summarized in Figure 26, it will be made clear that JBAM, in the first place, focuses on **formulating instructions** on how to perform the distribution function. Secondly, within its processes of supplying information JBAM additionally puts up training capacities in order to transfer know-how to **build qualification** of its external distributors. Thirdly, it will become apparent that in line with the very idea of "partnership", JBAM heavily engages in two-way communication processes to **collect feedback** from its external partners, in this way facilitating the joint identification of areas to create additional value for both parties. Clearly, this integrated approach of rather indirectly exerting influence on the distributors' sales activities highlights the fact that JBAM attempts to tackle the challenges of both specificity and opportunistic tendencies also with information-processing means.

Fig. 26: OVERVIEW OF INFORMATION-PROCESSING MEANS IN "PARTNERSHIP"

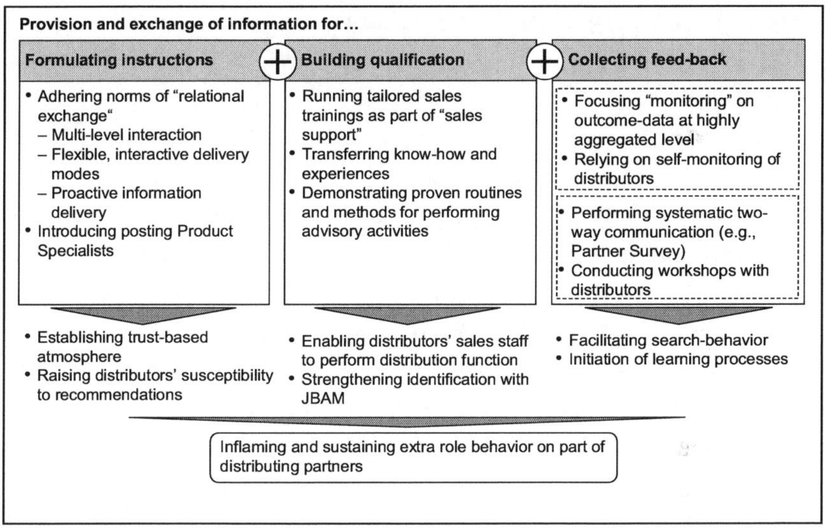

Source: Author

I) Formulating instructions

First of all, a salient characteristic of its distribution arrangements of "partnership" is that the actual processes of providing information take place across all the organizational levels of both the mutual fund producing principal and the distributing agent. From a comparative point of view, it shows that JBAM puts great emphasis on comprehensive **multi-level interaction** to deliver information to its external distribution partners. In practical terms, the adoption of this norm of "relational exchange" for its decentralized agency-relationships implies that information is not only exchanged at upper levels between JABM and the external distributing banks but also at the operational levels.

With regard to the interactive exchange at the upper level for most of its arrangements of "partnership", this can mean that meetings between management committee members take place at least on a semi-annual basis. These regular meetings give top and senior management the chance to address impediments experienced as well as to devise action plans to strengthen the proficiency of the agency-relationship. Complementing this interaction at upper levels, a more frequent, ongoing supply of information also takes place at the operational level with so-called **Liaison Officers** in charge of this process. It includes the involvement of staff from different areas of respective value chains. In more precise terms, in the light of the participation already illustrated of the external distributors along the conventional asset management activities, it becomes apparent that not only personnel of respective marketing and sales units participate in these interactive exchanges but that also members of portfolio management teams attend these processes. In line with the systemic configuration, this allows JBAM and their distributing partners to further orchestrate their activities in areas such as the strategic asset allocation and fund selection [for the investment products underlying the relationship] as well as to initiate marketing programs in support of the actual distribution activities. Overall, this discussion underlines the fact that JBAM aims at getting external banks more deeply engaged as active partners in the coordination of the agency-relationship by interacting not only at management-committee level but particularly in various areas at the operational level.

As far as the regular delivery of information is concerned, JBAM is increasingly confronted with a functionally relevant issue. As already illustrated, the characteristic of activities along the value chain for mutual funds typically performed by the asset management firm demand specialization and usually result in an internal separation of the value chain between the investment management activities, on one side, and the marketing and sales activities in support of the actual distribution function, on the other side. Generally, the latter is responsible for handling the direct interaction at the interface to distributors, which also includes managing information-processing means. Yet, external distributors across the board increasingly prefer to deal directly with members of the portfolio management team to obtain the information relevant for their advisory activities first hand (Sector Analysis 2003b, p. 41). In other words, in general, external banks would like to see the quality and authenticity of the information provided to be improved. Therefore, in response to this growing demand, JBAM management has deliberately introduced the posting of so-called **Product Specialists**. The potential benefit of having those product specialists involved in interactive processes of providing and exchanging information, in addition to personnel primarily from marketing and sales, is in fact twofold. As product specialists are supposed to possess the rather technical know-how of JBAM's mutual fund range, with their introduction JBAM finds itself in a more credible position to meet the increasingly professionalized demand for more sophisticated technical information from distributing banks. At the same time, JBAM's portfolio management teams are freed up to focus on their main objective, which is the management of the investment performance of mutual funds.

Concerning the actual procedure to provide relevant sales information to external banks, similar to the other two asset management firms under focus in this enquiry, JBAM does not only rely on one-way traffic to deliver the necessary materials. As a matter of fact, JBAM is increasingly falling back on more **interactive formats**, in reaction to the growing request by distributing banks for on-demand-modes of information delivery. In more precise terms, to a greater extent JBAM now turns to the vehicle of electronic mail to supply the information requested in a specifically tailored manner. Additionally, JBAM uses its web-based extranet platform JBfundnet® or the conventional, rather standardized forms of hard copies. In this way, **JBAM displays flexibility in responding to changes in information needs on the part of external distributing agents**. Hence, in the light of the participation offered and the resulting blurring of organizational boundaries, it cannot be denied that JBAM then also aims to indirectly stimulate cooperative behavior on the part of its distribution partners by demonstrating flexibility as a prominent norm within its "relational exchange".

Additionally, supplementing the on-going process of delivering information, it seems that **JBAM adheres to the norm of sharing or delivering information in a**

proactive manner in its decentralized arrangements of "partnership". In other words, the external banks performing advisory efforts to their customers on behalf of JBAM can expect to be supplied with unforeseen information that may affect their operations. JBAM takes great care to ensure that they are informed of crucial developments as soon as these emerge. Particularly with respect to two sensitive fields JBAM adopts this norm of "relational exchange". On the one hand, JBAM's sales managers make great efforts to actively let external distributors know already at the planning stage about changes in the personnel within the portfolio management teams responsible for the quality of mutual funds in terms of investment performance. For instance, in case a portfolio manager in charge of a particular mutual fund is going to be replaced, JBAM launches a communication procedure to inform its distribution partners before the actual substitution takes place. Furthermore, on the other hand, in situations where fundamental issues concerning the investment performance of individual mutual funds start to surface, external distributors are made aware of those tendencies proactively. In this way, JBAM gives its distribution partners the opportunity to switch its customer base into other mutual funds before the emerging deficits gain critical status. By deliberately adopting this norm within the process of delivering information, **JBAM aims to position itself as a reliable exchange partner, thereby engendering trust on the part of external distributors**. As one sales manager argued, this standard of conduct is of considerable relevance to be viewed as a trusted business partner. Hence, in order to avoid distribution arrangements being in relationship-threatening turmoil, JBAM notifies its partners proactively about changes in portfolio management personnel or deficits emerging in product quality.

With respect to the overall design of providing relevant information and material, it becomes evident that in fact JBAM is laying the ground for transferring instructions on how to carry out the distribution function by engaging in multi-level interaction, in combination with a sufficiently flexible and proactive delivery of information. In such a trust-based atmosphere, agents are assumed to be more susceptible to the principal's recommendations on how to perform the distributing role for the mutual fund offering. In other words, by raising the receptiveness of external distributors through the application of these norms of "relational exchange", JBAM seems to be in a position to indirectly guide the distribution partners' sales and advisory activities at the point-of-sale. This potentially allows JBAM then to gain some control over the lurking negative side effects in the "partnership"-type of institutional arrangements. **Hence, by way of embedding these norms into the design of its arrangements, which facilitate the formulation of instructions and encourage cooperative behavior, there can be no doubt that JBAM attempts to control for challenges of "opportunism" and the "service firm specificity" inherent in the distribution function.**

II) Building qualification

In such a surrounding, JBAM employs the wider process of delivering information to also transfer expert knowledge which is potentially helpful for [further] upgrading the external distributors' advisory capabilities. **It seems that by sharing its own experiences made in the course of marketing its mutual funds through the in-house channel, JBAM intends to make external partners' sales staff familiar with established routines on how to successfully sell mutual funds to private investors**. In other words, JBAM leverages the delivery of information not only to articulate instructions for the sales behavior but particularly to outline methods on how to improve the actual advisory activities overall. Therefore, in the light of JBAM's private banking background, this sharing potentially provides distributors with the chance to further improve [their sales and] advisory services and, thus, to strengthen their own competitiveness.

With regard to the extent to which JBAM is able to employ this approach within the informational procedures of indirectly guiding the autonomous partners' behavior, one sales manager pinpointed a particular agency-relationship of "partnership" for which JBAM has been able to conduct more than 150 sales training sessions with partner's sales staff. Having the much-aspired direct contact with the distributors' sales staff, JBAM takes the opportunity to pinpoint encountered challenges at the point-of-sale in its proprietary channel and to highlight proven actions on how to overcome these issues. Being supplied with this kind of information in a preparatory way, the distributors' sales staff are expected to be better able to cope with interferences possibly arising in the course of carrying out advisory activities to private investors. Therefore, the demonstration of these routines and methods carries the chance to raise the identification of external banks' sales staff with JBAM's mutual fund offering and possibly even its internalization.

Yet, for some arrangements this opportunity to stimulate self-interested cooperation is severely restricted. One sales manager remarked that in some cases the autonomous distributing bank refuses access to sales staff to conduct these programs. In other words, JBAM is not allowed to interactively inform them about proven routines and methods on how to successfully advise private investors regarding mutual funds in general, but particularly with respect to its own offering. Thus, JBAM in some agency-relationship misses out on this highly relevant form of indirect guidance.

Still, for its arrangements of "partnership", it shows that JBAM also intends to indirectly encourage the external distributors' willingness to cooperate by attempting to build up their expertise and qualification. The resulting enhanced qualification for performing the distribution function for mutual funds in general is not only potentially beneficial to JBAM but particularly to the external distributors, as it offers them the chance to strengthen their competitiveness vis-à-vis distributing rivals.

III) Collecting feedback

In addition to the already sketched-out application of information-processing means for formulating instructions as well as building distributors' qualifications, it turns out that **JBAM also falls back on two-way communication processes** (Anderson and Weitz 1992, p. 21). These are supposed to give its distribution partners the opportunity to submit some form of feedback. With regard to this way of indirectly guiding the external distributors' behavior, two slightly different procedures for exchanging information come into play. On the one hand, JBAM gathers data concerning the actual performance levels of respective external distributors. Thus, with the application of such an information exchange, JBAM finds itself in the position to perform some form of **"monitoring"** on how the distribution function is in fact carried out. Corresponding to a "partnership"-type of structure, it will show that the focus of "monitoring" is primarily on highly aggregated data. This highlights once again the principal's reliance on agents' self-interested willingness to cooperate, thereby counting on the self-control of distributors. On the other hand, it will also become evident that **JBAM systematically collects partners' opinions with respect to various fields of its operations to initiate learning processes**. By aiming at the joint identification of areas for creating additional value, JBAM lays the ground for triggering continuous search-behavior on the part of external distribution partners. As will be outlined now more comprehensively, in this context of a "partnership"-kind of systemic configuration, the application of **these feedback-related procedures tends to facilitate cooperative behavior on the part of external distributors that goes beyond the line of duty**.

As is widely accepted, **"monitoring"** in general gives the principal the chance to control for issues arising from information asymmetry, most notably aberrant activities on the part of agents (Jensen and Meckling 1976, p. 307). Yet, for this particular case study, it seems as if "monitoring" is adjusted to the salient characteristics of a "partnership" Therefore, from a comparative perspective, it shows that **JBAM mainly focuses on outcome-oriented data of a highly consolidated nature for performance "monitoring" purposes in such trust-based relationships**. In more substantive terms, JBAM concentrates on aggregated net inflow figures [for a particular period of time] and the total volume in terms of the AuM the respective external distributors have raised from their private end customers for JBAM's mutual funds. Focusing on these total figures highlights that JBAM deliberately abstains from intervening more deeply in the distribution function by requiring the external banks to provide some more disaggregated distribution figures. For example, JBAM refrains from asking for a breakdown of performance data at the level of the banks' branches for its mutual funds. The application of such a "monitoring" indicates that JBAM is already content to obtain notification on possible interferences in achieving strong distribution performance level. Hence, by controlling the distribution function on the grounds of global results figures rather than engaging in efforts to identify opportunistic tendencies, it shows that **JBAM relies on the self-control of distribution partners to a considerable extent.**

By running monitoring processes on outcome figures of this sort, it becomes evident that this kind of feedback is mainly used to disseminate positive signals to assess the actual ways of performance delivery. The purpose of this information exchange is clearly not to inflict sanctions but rather to give rewards. Strictly speaking, even in those few relationships in which specific distribution performance targets are defined, this kind of data is generally not used to exercise the contractual option to fine the autonomous distributor in case of underachievement. Instead, while this information is also applied to link the distributors' compensation with their respective performance levels, the approach is in fact setting the stage to identify [additional] avenues to accomplish strong distribution performance levels. All this then indicates that by way of employing of this process of "monitoring", JBAM aspires to encourage the distributors' willingness to cooperate in a positive way rather than by imposing control. Hence, already in this regard, it shows that the exchange of information for **"monitoring" is designed to reinforce external distributors' self-motivation to bridge possible distribution performance gaps**.

This salient characteristic of "partnership" becomes even more apparent, as the wider process of exchanging information is also designed in a way to initiate some form of learning processes. In that respect, external distributors are invited to hand in suggestions on how to create additional value. In other words, **external distributors are explicitly asked to contribute their experiences to these learning processes**. By establishing opportunities to submit this kind of feedback, parties to exchange are given the chance to engage in search-behavior, which is expected to raise overall performance levels of the agency-relationships.

In a remarkably systematic approach, JBAM applies a variety of different measures to identify areas for which it can add value to its external distributors:

- Within the pattern of collecting and processing this type of feedback, the so-called **Partner Survey represents the backbone of JBAM's efforts**. This survey, which is carried out on an annual basis, covers not only JBAM's external distributors in Germany but all the geographic markets in which JBAM operates. Although the focus of this information exchange varies slightly each year, it generally centers on questions concerning the quality and use of the wide range of available publications, web-based delivery formats, the appropriateness of proactive communication, JBAM's range of investment products, relationship management in general, and particular elements of sales support such as the training programs for the distributors' sales staff.

- In addition to this regular procedure, JBAM also runs processes of gathering information with a focus on one specific topic. A prominent example is the so-called **Service Landscape Review** JBAM carried out between October 2003 and March 2004. By collecting opinions from more than 40 external distributors across 5 different countries, JBAM intended to ascertain the most valued elements of its "sales support" as well as those elements, which needed to be overhauled. The way in which the information exchange actually takes place ranges from standardized questionnaires with mainly closed questions to in-depth interviews in a rather workshop-type of interaction. In particular these more interactive discussions with external distributors are considered as essential to bring to light the areas where JBAM potentially can add value. In this regard, a sales manager made it clear that a mere interrogation tends to be viewed as rather disturbing.

The derived results of these processes and the synthesized recommendations on how to create value-added for external distributors are presented to the JBAM top management. It is then the management committee that to a great extent is involved in the decision making on how to adjust the design of distribution arrangements. In that respect, one sales manager pointed out that a couple of years ago the Partner Survey revealed that a specific type of information which clarifies why a particular mutual fund is outperforming or underperforming its benchmark is of the greatest benefit to distributing banks. Being provided with such an attribution of the actually realized investment performance to single steps of the JBAM's investment management activities, distributing partners indicated they would feel more competent in the sales and advisory activities for JBAM's mutual fund offering. Subsequently, JBAM decided to devote great effort to make this kind of information available, thereby demonstrating its willingness to search for and to eventually realize mutual benefits in support of the actual distribution activities. With regard to the recently conducted Service Landscape Review, the insights gained have helped JBAM to initiate steps to further enhance its "sales support" offering. Thus, by way of this particular information gathering, JBAM has made attempts to actually realize further benefits for its distributing partners. From all this, once again it becomes apparent that **the information received via these exchanges is not used to directly intervene in the distribution function but rather to continuously improve the overall design of the agency-relationships, in terms of structure and/or processes to eventually realize an improvement in the "cash inflow stream".**

In summary, the information-based interaction between JBAM and its external distributors is not only employed to formulate instructions on how to perform the distribution function or to transfer expert knowledge relevant for the sales and advisory activities. Instead, information-related processes are also applied to receive some form of feedback on the quality of the respective agency-relationships. From a comparative point of view, in accordance with classic features of a "partnership", JBAM runs these procedures in a way to mainly focus on highly consolidated performance-related feedback, thereby relying to a great extent on the self-interest of distribution partners to overcome possible distribution performance gaps. At the same time, in contrast to the other two case studies, JBAM leverages this exchange to facilitate search-behavior, which goes beyond the standard role behavior related to the distribution function. In this way, the attempt is made to realize further value-creating opportunities assumed to be mutually beneficial. In other words, JBAM applies the collection of information for more than the mere assessment of performance levels of respective distributors. This interaction is leveraged, in particular, to learn how to further develop and improve the design of its decentralized agency-relationships for the distribution function. Hence, these information exchange processes with the aim of finding mutually beneficial ways to strengthen the proficiency of distribution arrangements are expected to favor the harmonization of possibly diverging interests and carry the opportunity to account for the lurking negative side effects of "service firm specificity" and "opportunism".

4.2.2.2.2 Motivational Means for Process-Intervention

For this case of "partnership", it cannot be denied that management seems to be aware of the repercussions of an advancing "degree of decentralization" for the distribution function. So far the discussion has brought to light, already with the design of the systemic configuration and the application of information-processing means, that the principal attempts to establish the necessary cognitive and motivational prerequisites in order to bring "partnership"-type of institutional arrangements for marketing mutual funds to private investors to full strength. Now, the aspiration is to outline how in the face of such a structure and information-based processes the principal relies on further means to motivate agents in order to come to optimization of the "cash inflow stream" for its mutual fund range.

As illustrated in the elaboration on the systemic configuration, corresponding to the very idea of "partnership", it is the far-reaching assignment of [product-related] property rights that considerably demarcates the way in which the coordination of activities takes place. This fairly bundled assignment, implying the granting of considerable participation and decision-making authority, highlights the critical role of cooperation as the main coordination mechanism for dovetailing activities along the value chain. Therefore, given such a structural design, it then becomes evident that the principal aims to bring under control the lurking challenges arising from possible opportunistic tendencies or specificity by influencing agents' behavior in a rather indirect manner and not in the form of directly intervening measures.

Along these lines, in response to the imminent need to strengthen the distributing agents' cooperative behavior, as already pointed, a variety of information-based measures are taken to further promote the distributors' self-motivation to participate cooperatively in what are increasingly becoming agency-relationships of equal partners. As it is then assumed to be also in their interest to alleviate inefficient impediments, the application of these information-based processes primarily aim to empower external distributors to cooperatively take on the distribution function on behalf of JBAM. Moreover, it also becomes clear that while these information-processing means aim at enabling external distributors by establishing the cognitive prerequisites to run decentralized arrangements successfully, they also trigger the mobilization of distributors' self-motivation to do so in a cooperative way. Yet, as will be elaborated now in more detail, additional attempts are made to further harmonize possibly diverging interests to trigger the desired levels of cooperation.

Fig. 27: OVERVIEW OF MOTIVATIONAL MEANS IN "PARTNERSHIP"

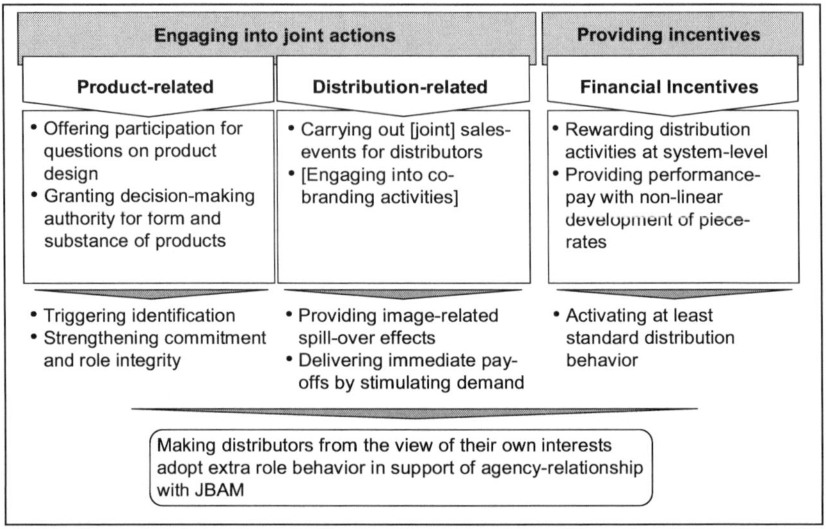

Source: Author

As summarized in Figure 27, for this case study it will become apparent that JBAM most notably turns to the opportunities of **engaging into joint actions** to promote self-interest among external partners to perform the distribution function. In addition to this, JBAM also intends to motivate distributors through **providing incentives**, thereby explicitly accounting for economic considerations in the external distributors' behavior. Already this overview of measures indicates that JBAM aims to achieve the aspired mobilization of self-interested cooperation in a positive way.

I) Engaging into joint actions

As far as the joint actions are concerned, it turns out that it is once again the "contract design" with the far-reaching assignment of [product-related] property rights that considerably demarcates the frame within which JBAM can trigger motivation to cooperate on the part of external distributors. From a comparative point of view, given the considerable transfer of decision-making authority and the scope offered for participation, JBAM and the respective distributors are expected to engage in joint actions not only across multiple levels but, in particular, for a large set of activities. This is likely to strengthen the distributors' commitment to the agency-relationship, which, in turn, tends to facilitate controlling for issues arising particularly from opportunistic tendencies.

As already previously illustrated, **this can lead to the situation in which the distributing bank [and its in-house asset management division] becomes deeply involved in important questions concerning the product design**. In practical terms, in some selected institutional arrangements of "partnership", the external partner is in charge of taking decisions concerning the strategic asset allocation defining the weights of each asset class for the investment product [underlying the relationship]. Subsequently, JBAM picks the individual security-titles within each asset class. This interaction shows that in line with salient features of a "partnership" **the organizational boundaries become increasingly interpenetrated**, implying that the **traditional roles of the product-providing principal and the distributing agent are no longer narrowly defined but in fact become increasingly integrated**.

As **these joint actions underline the notion of "relational exchange"** (Heide and John 1990, p. 24), they are assumed to be efficacious in strengthening the distributors' as well as their sales forces' identification with the particular agency-relationship. This process is then supposed to further develop their self-interest to willingly cooperate in arrangements of "partnership". Such a strengthened association facilitates the opportunity that the respective sales staff is more likely to internalize JBAM's mutual offering, which, in turn, is predicted to help in the interaction with private investors directly at the point-of-sale. Ultimately, the undertaking of these product-related joint actions with greater levels of involvement bears the potential to strengthen the external distributors' role integrity and commitment. Hence, the far-reaching assignment of property rights offers JBAM the chance to promote self-motivated willingness to cooperate among distributors, thereby accounting for the lurking negative side effects stemming from "service firm specificity" and "opportunism".

However, not only the agent gets involved in activities that are traditionally considered to be in the principal's area of responsibility but, in fact, **joint actions also increasingly take place with regard to a distribution-related focus**. This type of joint actions then aims to further induce the self-motivated cooperation of distributors by offering the prospect of immediate pay-offs and some differentiating, image-related spill-over-effects to attain an even more competitive positioning. This interaction can take the form of **jointly conducted sales events** or **co-branding activities** as part of the principal's "sales support" or "branding" strategy, respectively.

Thus, in this context, it becomes apparent that in some arrangements of "partnership", **JBAM and the respective autonomous distributor jointly plan, prepare, and carry out joint actions in support of the actual advisory activities at the point-of-sale**. One sales manager pinpointed a particular agency-relationship for which a series of events was staged, some of them attended by more than 600 invited customers of the external partner. At these events, JBAM put forward in more detail its offering of mutual funds and explained under which circumstances this offering suits the investors' objectives and needs. These jointly-conducted presentations tend to stimulate strong demand from private investors for this offering, which clearly is of benefit to both. Moreover, it further gives the external distributor the opportunity to enjoy a possibly differentiating image-transfer. In principle, such positive spill-over-effects are potentially beneficial for the distributors' future interaction with their own customers, which, in turn, is expected to promote their self-interest to cooperate with JBAM. Additionally, although only for selected relationships, JBAM and respective external distributors engage in relationship-specific co-branding activities in order to stimulate mutually beneficial demand for JBAM's mutual fund offering available in the distributors' branch network. These activities entail the potential side effect of providing further image-related benefits.

Following on from this, it shows that by engaging in these forms of joint actions with its external distribution partners, **JBAM aims to mobilize the distributors' self-interested cooperation** in different but still interrelated approaches. Intensified participation along the traditional activities of the production function for mutual funds potentially triggers motivation via the avenue of building the distributors' identification with and internalization of JBAM's product offering. This is expected to strengthen their role integrity and commitment to the agency-relationship. Additionally, JBAM also intends to secure desired levels of self-interest by providing more tangible pay-offs and competitiveness-enhancing benefits through joint actions in support of the actual distribution activities. It seems as if these more immediate benefits further reinforce the distributors' identification with the agency-relationship.

Yet, in the German context it seems as if JBAM is only regarded to be able to provide these more tangible benefits in a comparatively restricted manner. As already mentioned in the elaboration of the structure-shaping investments in "branding", from the distributors' point of view, in comparison to competing asset management firms, JBAM's image lacks strength not only in terms of awareness among end customers but also in terms of a distinctive profile to support their endeavors for differentiation. Thus, **in the light of this deficit, only for selected agency-relationships is JBAM able to offer prospects of these image-related spill-over-effects, be it in the form of jointly conducted sales events or co-branding**. Hence, only in a few relationships is JBAM in a position to further develop self-interested willingness to cooperate on the part of external distributors by means of joint actions in "branding" or "sales support".

II) Providing incentives

Besides these different forms of joint actions, additional attempts are made to indirectly exert influence on the agents' behavior. With the provision of adequate incentives for the agent, the principal is in the position to harmonize interests and, thus, to limit aberrant behavior on the part of agents (Jensen and Meckling 1976, p. 307). As far as the **"incentive scheme"** in this case study is concerned, it will become evident that JBAM predominantly falls back on some form of **performance-related financial incentives** to guide external distributors' sales and advisory behavior. Moreover, as will be illustrated in more detail, there can be no doubt that corresponding to the way with which JBAM performs the "monitoring" of performance levels of respective external distributors, the "incentive scheme" tends to be mostly of a rewarding character. In that respect, as aforementioned the information exchange processes for "monitoring" purposes mainly focus on outcome-orientated data of a highly aggregated nature in terms of the total net inflows raised for JBAM's mutual funds [for a particular period of time] and the total volume of AuM accumulated over time. Last but not least, in the view of the "degree of decentralization" for its distribution arrangements it turns out that **incentives are predominately provided at the system-level** of the respective agency-relationships.

In more detail, in addition to the **load fee**, charged to end customers when they purchase shares of a mutual fund, distributors receive some form of compensation mainly in the form of retrocession for performing the distribution function on behalf on JBAM. In general, this retrocession, which is **a proportion of the management fee**, is calculated according to a standard fee-table. Usually, the level of the compensation tends to be a function of the total AuM the external distributor has contributed to JBAM's entire mutual fund range, which means that the absolute level of compensation increases with total volume. Hence, it shows that JBAM intends to strengthen the distributor's self-interest to cooperate with the application of this **piece-rate type of compensation** that rewards higher levels of distribution performance, thereby also exposing the agents to some form of risk.

Further emphasizing this rewarding character, one sales manager added that for most of its distribution arrangements, **the "incentive scheme" includes some form of progression in piece-rates**. This highlights that with higher levels of AuM raised on behalf of JBAM, the compensation increases not only in absolute terms but in relative terms as well, with a greater percentage of the management fee being transferred to the external distributor. Concerning the actual level of compensation, one sales manager remarked that from a comparative point of view JBAM pays more or less the industry average. Following on from this, it shows that in this case study the principal turns to some performance-related pay to further align possibly diverging interests, thereby attempting to account for the lurking negative side effects arising with its choice for institutional arrangements of "partnership".

In line with this advanced "degree of decentralization", it further becomes evident that the "incentive scheme" establishes primarily the financial incentives at the system-level of the agency-relationship. In other words, it remains in the scope of the autonomous banks to decide in which way and to what extent this compensation is transferred to the actual sales staff interacting with private investors at the point-of-sale. The salary for the individual sales staff of distributing banks usually includes only relatively small distribution-performance-related components. This indicates that, in this particular distribution channel [product-related], property rights are passed on to the personnel operating at the point-of-sale only in a very diluted manner. In this respect, it then appears as if the use of **financial rewards at a highly consolidated level intends to primarily maintain rather than intensively stimulate distributors' self-interested willingness to cooperatively perform the distribution function**. Thus, the efficacy of such financial incentives appears to be somewhat limited for improving the inflow stream on a sustainable basis as they influence behavior only at the system-level. Along these lines, one sales manager pointed out that **the fee split needs to be competitive but plays only a minor role in sustainable improvement in distribution performance levels**.

In summary, this elaboration has outlined how in the face of the systemic configuration for the "partnership"-type of agency-relationships, JBAM also falls back on motivating measures in order to facilitate an adequate handling of challenges related to "opportunism" and "service firm specificity" To influence the behavior of the autonomous distributor JBAM engages in joint actions in a variety of different areas as well as positions incentives at the system-level of the "partnership". As far as these different forms of joint actions are concerned, it turns out that these not only bear the potential to strengthen the distributor's [intrinsic] commitment to the agency-relationship but also offer the prospects of more tangible, competitiveness-enhancing [extrinsic] benefits to the distribution partner. However, with regard to the latter, from a comparative point of view, the discussion has highlighted that JBAM faces deficits in mobilizing the distributors' self-interested willingness to cooperate, which may jeopardize the efficacy of other attempts to activate the desired behavior on the part of the external distributor. Concerning the employment of incentives to harmonize interests, the elaboration has outlined that JBAM primarily turns to performance-related, financial rewards to encourage cooperation. Yet, for stimulating strong inflow streams, the enquiry has also indicated that their provision encounters difficulties in mobilizing the individual sales staff operating at the point-of-sale in this particular distribution channel for mutual funds, as these financial incentives are rewarded at the system-level of agency-relationships.

.

4.2.2.3 Towards the Efficacy of the Design of "Partnership"

With regard to the second, the internal fit requirement, it is the consistency between the ideal type of design of the chosen "degree of decentralization" and the actual design of the institutional arrangement for coordinating activities along the value chain that is of functional relevance to actually achieve the optimization objective. Thus, the enquiry's framework of analysis argues that based on the choice of "partnership", the design of the agency-relationship needs to be set up in a consistent way in order to realize the aspired efficiency-enhancing effects. In this respect, the preceding discussion illustrates that while the design of the process-related measures and the far-reaching transfer of property rights is consistent with a typical "partnership"-type of coordination mode, **the design's systemic configuration with regard to the structure-shaping investments in "branding" appear to exhibit some critical shortcomings, giving rise to inconsistency in the design**.

The second fit problem emphasizes the optimization-relevant requirement that the design has to adequately account for the situational challenges of "service firm specificity" and "opportunism" arising with the organizational choice. As the choice of **"partnership"** offers considerable scope for participation, this type of an institutional arrangement predominately **relies on cooperation as a means to coordinate activities** between principal and agents. Therefore, according to the second fit problem, in order to be consistent, the design for arrangements of "partnership" [in terms of structure and processes] needs to aim at securing both the agents' ability and willingness to cooperatively apply the property rights granted. In other words, to be in line with the very idea of "partnership", the design is required to establish the necessary cognitive and motivational prerequisites to secure self-interest to cooperate on the part of the agents. In this regard, to activate appropriate levels of cooperation, the purpose of the buildup is not to directly intervene in the actual advisory activities but to induce adequate levels of self-steering behavior. Yet, a fact that cannot be neglected is that the decisions of autonomous agents, whether to get involved at all and to what extent, are driven by their own utility function, which clearly includes [short-term] profit-maximizing interests. This highlights that such a design remains substantially exposed to the danger of the lack of the agents' willingness [or ability] to take on the distribution role as assigned in the context of arrangements of "partnership". Therefore, the principal will have to turn to context-setting systemic configuration, as well as rather process-related measures, in order to appropriately respond to this imminent pressure to adequately serve the agents' diverse set of interests.

Against this background, JBAM has set up an overall design within which the systemic configuration sets the framework for the subsequent application of process-related measures. In this respect, as indicated already above, **given the rather limited capacities of "branding" at least in the German context, it appears as if the structure does not adequately account for the competitive interests of external distributors in these decoupled agency-relationships**. Given the assumed interplay of structure and process in the organizational design, this may then substantially moderate the efficacy of the information-processing means and motivating measures JBAM employs as an attempt to indirectly guide external distributors' behavior. With regard to the **information-related processes**, the objective is primarily, yet not exclusively, to enable the external banks to actively distribute JBAM's mutual fund offering in an appropriate manner. Thus, in this rather cognitive context, it becomes apparent that:

- by adhering to norms of "relational exchange" to deliver information relevant for performing the distribution function, JBAM strengthens its position to articulate instructions on how to actually carry out the distribution function
- by running procedures within its "sales support" to transfer expert knowledge and experiences, JBAM gives its distribution partners and their respective sales staff the opportunity to acquire routines and methods that have proven successful in direct interaction with private investors
- there is also a regular exchange of performance–related information, triggering a critical assessment of the relationship quality that goes beyond the mere "monitoring" of distribution performance levels. In this way, these two-way communication processes of collecting feedback encourage the willingness

among distributors not only to maintain but in fact to actively develop the agency-relationship

As these means facilitate the adequate provision of information, the buildup of qualification, and even a positive change in attitude towards the agency-relationship, they set the informational ground to run the arrangements of "partnership" successfully and to promote the distributors' self-interested motivation to cooperate. Furthermore, with regard to the second fit problem, it has become apparent that JBAM also applies additional **motivational means** as an attempt to further align possibly diverging interests within the institutional arrangements. As illustrated, JBAM aims at activating the desired role behavior of distributors not by imposing more or less mechanical procedures of control but rather in an encouraging way. In this respect, to cement the insight on the part of external banks that it is in fact in their own interest to cooperatively take on the distribution function on behalf of JBAM, the elaboration outlines that JBAM:

- attempts to strengthen the notion of "relational exchange" by engaging in joint actions together with the respective external bank in activities that traditionally are JBAM's exclusive responsibility. This participation, in turn, is expected to ultimately strengthen their role integrity within the relationship and their identification and internalization of JBAM's product offering
- also aims to offer differentiating spill-over-effects to its external distribution partners through joint actions in areas of "branding" and "sales support", which have the potential not only to provide immediate pay-offs but also to favor external distributors in attaining a more competitive positioning vis-à-vis distributing rivals
- applies an "incentive scheme" that provides primarily performance-related financial rewards at the system-level of its agency-relationships. Focusing exclusively on the global results of the actual distribution activity, this revenue-sharing mainly intends to account for the profit-orientated motives on the part of external distributors rather than to mobilize the banks' sales staff that interact with private investors at the point-of- sales

Hence, while the systemic configuration accentuates the role of cooperation as the main coordination form, the principal also falls back on these motivating measures in combination with the more information-related means to secure the needed levels of self-interest to cooperate from its autonomous agents. It appears as if this interplay of providing and exchanging information on the one hand, and mobilizing motivation on the other hand, bears the potential to strengthen the agents' attitude that it is in their very own interest to become involved in the relationship and to accept the participation offered.

However, for the upcoming overall efficacy assessment, it needs to be borne in mind that JBAM's design, in fact, exhibits some severe shortcomings pinpointing some inconsistencies. This enquiry argues that in the German context JBAM is confronted with difficulties concerning the provision of differentiating spill-over effects to its distributors, indicating that the design's systematic configuration lacks decisive ingredients to activate the external banks' self-interest to cooperate. Moreover, it shows that JBAM is not always able to build qualification by transferring routines and methods. The direct access to the distributors' sales staff in some relationships is severely restricted, highlighting that the design is possibly missing critical parts of information-related processes.

It cannot be denied that such a design entails [transaction] costs. However, there are indications that the out-of-pocket expenses are comparatively low, given the focus of process-related measures to mainly guide the agents' behavior in an indirect manner and the restrictive approach regarding the buildup of capacities in "branding". With this renunciation of more directly intervening measures for this type of arrangement, which otherwise would give rise to considerable out-of-pocket [transaction] costs to manage the distribution systems, the principal remains exposed to the danger of a lack of ability and/or willingness to cooperate on the part of the agents. Emphasizing the conventional trade-off between efficiency and risk, it is the move not to intervene that gives [further] rise to the threat of "hold-up" [and, thus, to considerable inefficiencies], as decoupled agency-relationships are traditionally prone to aberrant activities of agents. Along those lines, as to whether "partnership" will bring about the envisaged optimization of distribution performance levels or not, is then driven by the quality of the overall configuration in terms of structure and process and thus, by the set-up of the single action variables employed to govern autonomous agents.

In summary, the principal attempts to build a design for its arrangements that in terms of the process-related measures is largely consistent with the choice of "partnership" as coordination mode. Participation takes an optimization-relevant role to bring the challenges of opportunities tendencies and specificity under control. Moreover, as the principal to a great extent relies on the insight of agents that it is in their own interest to cooperate, it mainly comes to the application of indirectly-intervening measures. Yet, it also becomes evident for the German market that, in particular, the **systemic configuration exhibits some deficiencies in activating the willingness to cooperate as it partly fails to fully address the competitive considerations of autonomous banks**.

Therefore, this enquiry tends to argue that only to a moderate extent does this organizational design facilitate the triggering of the advantages associated with "partnership"-type of institutional arrangements. Nevertheless, by stimulating and maintaining self-interest among autonomous agents to take on the distribution function, implying also sufficient levels of self-monitoring on their part, the design appears to be laid out in a way to account for the lurking negative side effects at least to some degree. Hence, in an agency-relationship where the principal is able to serve the agents' competitive interests [in particular by means of differentiating spill-over effects through "branding"], the expansion of customer reach via the distribution networks of external distribution partners is generally expected to bring about the desired improvement in inflow streams. To what extent this turns out to true for JBAM will be discussed next.

4.2.3 Efficacy of Choice and Design of "Partnership"

Having elaborated on both fit requirements concerning the institutional arrangement for the distribution function so far from a fairly isolated but still interrelated view, the aspiration now is to assess in a more integrated manner to what extent distribution performance levels are, in fact, optimized. Thus, the question to address is how the decisions on choice and design in a cumulative way favor the arrangement's efficacy to achieve enhanced proficiency levels. In the light of the overriding optimization objective, the intention, therefore, is to ascertain how under the conditions of changing "market dynamics", the chosen "degree of decentralization" and the build-up of the structural and process-related design positively impact the generation of "cash inflow stream". Given the organizational choice and the overall configuration of the agency-relationship, the point is to clarify whether it allows for an adequate consideration of not only a changing market environment but also of the challenges stemming from "opportunism" and "service firm specificity" inherent in the distribution function. From a normative perspective, the ambition is also to shed light on the extent to which the external adaptation in combination with the internal design result in reinforcement of the arrangements' efficacy to generate an enhanced "cash inflow stream".

With regard to this central choice and design problem, as far as the case of JBAM is concerned as summarized in Figure 28, this enquiry puts forward in quite some detail that the attempt is made to accomplish the overriding objective by falling back on a "partnership"-type of institutional arrangement. **With reference to the outlined choice and design requirements, this assessment brings to light somewhat mixed results**. In more specific terms, in the face of the "market dynamics" in Germany at the beginning of this century, this enquiry ascertains that overall JBAM accomplishes appropriate external adjustments to the distribution arrangements. Turning to external distributors, while activating their self-interest to cooperate, appears to be an efficient organizational solution to bring distribution systems to full strength, given the absence of fully established market control. Yet, as far as the internal design is concerned, for this case study it looks as if the systemic configuration to some degree lacks decisive capacities to trigger and maintain self-interest among distributors to cooperatively take on the assigned role. The process-related measures, however, appear to be in line with the very idea of a "partnership"-type of institutional arrangement. From this simultaneous assessment, **all this indicates that this constellation of external and internal adaptations properly accounts for the changes noticed in "market dynamics" but does not necessarily fully capture the opportunities inherent in these developments**. Therefore, this enquiry assumes a circumscribed perspective by arguing that that only for those agency-relationships for which capacities in terms of "branding" and "sales support" are sufficiently strong to unleash extra role behavior, JBAM's choice and design decisions are suitable for achieving an improvement in distribution performance levels. Only under these conditions is this enquiry inclined to claim that the requirements are met to efficaciously control for challenges of opportunism and specificity, which otherwise give rise to situations of "hold-up".

Fig. 28: SIMULTANEOUS ASSESSMENT OF CHOICE AND DESIGN OF "PARTNERSHIP"

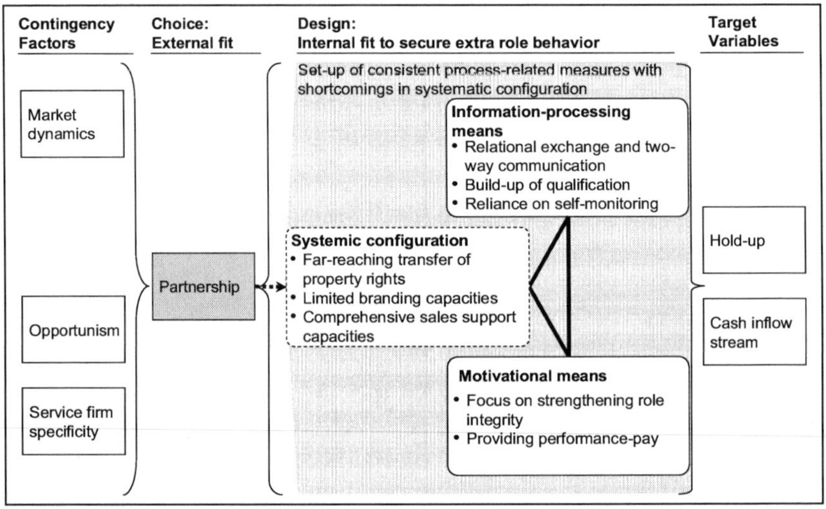

Source: Author

Accordingly, concerning the efficacy of the "partnership"-type of institutional arrangement, it becomes apparent that JBAM, overall, has been enjoying a strong revival since 2002. It seems that at the global level, particularly in markets in which JBAM's Swiss origin and the exclusiveness related to its private banking background is highly appreciated, this way of arranging the distribution function adequately accounts for challenges arising from recent market developments but also facilitates overcoming performance gaps:

- In this regard, it shows that the declining trend of JBAM's total AuM at the beginning of this century has been turned around. AuM raised from private investors has grown significantly from CHF 26 billion in 2002 to CHF 45 billion in 2004

- While the moderate recovery of global capital markets and, thus, the asset management sector in general may have favored this development, this strong positive trend can be traced back in particular to substantially enhanced distribution performance levels. In 2004, JBAM managed to collect a total of CHF 16.6 billion of net inflows from private investors worldwide, in comparison to only CHF 2.8 billion in 2002
- Moreover, as outlined in Figure 29, it cannot be denied that the increase has been accomplished by means of decentralized agency-relationships. In 2004, the share of AuM generated via external distribution partners of total AuM raised from private investors increased to 84 percent from the low 70s at the beginning of this century

Fig. 29: IMPORTANCE OF THIRD-PARTY DISTRIBUTION FOR JBAM

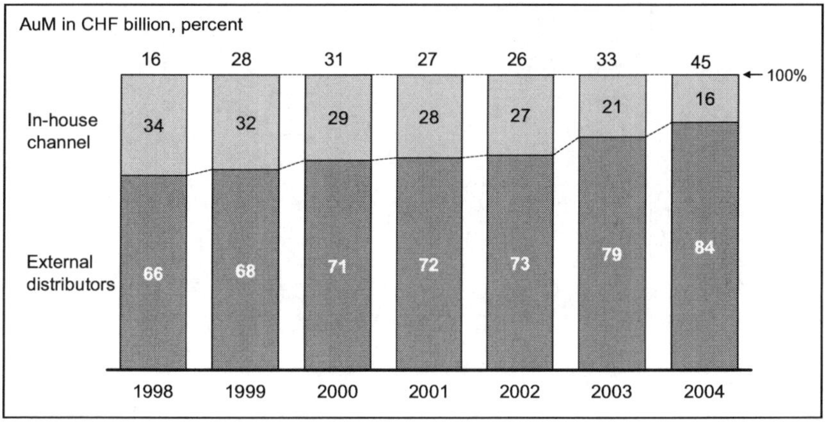

Source: Julius Bär Annual Reports 1999-2004

Yet, as far as the German development is the subject of analysis, it becomes apparent that the realized choice and design has not been efficacious in producing a turn-around in distribution performance levels to the same extent. By 2004, JBAM only managed to stabilize the level of AuM at CHF 1.8 billion (EUR 1.2 billion), after its strong evaporation in the period between 2000 and 2002. However, it also shows that the actual distribution performance levels have, in fact, deteriorated further. While the decline of JBAM's development of net inflows at the beginning of this century was more or less in line with the overall trend in the German private investor market, it is now deviating considerably from the overall market movement. As outlined in Figure 30, since 2003 JBAM has been facing outflows for its mutual fund range in Germany, whereas at the market level inflows remained positive throughout 2004.

Fig. 30: DEVELOPMENT OF NET INFLOWS RELATIVE TO MARKET TREND

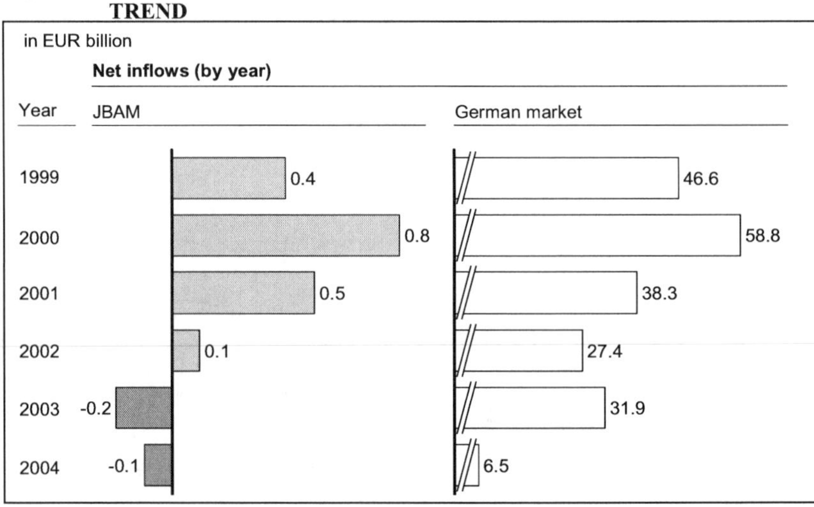

Source: JBAM Controlling, BVI (2005), author's calculation

Therefore, in appreciation of the salient features of "partnership" arrangements which, in principle, are considered efficacious in bringing about the envisaged efficiency-enhancing effects [as recognized at the global level for this case study], this elaboration argues that this way of arranging the distribution function in Germany has at least helped to prevent a more severe deterioration in net inflow figures. Taking a closer look at the development of distribution performance, it shows that those agency-relationships in Germany are still contributing positive net inflow streams for which JBAM is able to serve the distributors' competitive considerations, thereby reinforcing their self-interest to cooperate. Hence, there is the assumption that without its existing "partnership"-type of arrangements with external banks, the distribution performance would even be worse.

Thus, this enquiry argues that that the choice and to some extent also the design of "partnership" have softened this pressure.

Nevertheless, given this unsatisfactory trend, in the competitive context in Germany, there can be no doubt that from a comparative perspective JBAM's structure and process show critical shortcomings that aggravate a sustained turn-around of distribution performance levels. As mentioned before, this elaboration indicates that structure-shaping investments are not adequate to establish a truly differentiating positioning. Consequently, it seems somewhat unclear in which way distributing banks realize image-related and, thus, competitive benefits from performing the distribution function for JBAM's mutual funds. Moreover, concerning the qualification-building measures, the quality of proven routines and methods appears to be insufficiently pronounced and positioned as sales concepts, which would allow distributors to distinctively upgrade their sales and advisory activities. Hence, in the view of the results outlined, it shows that JBAM is encountering difficulties in mobilizing desired levels of self-interest to cooperate across a large set of German distributing banks. Therefore, as a concluding remark, while at the global level the positive efficacy of distribution arrangements becomes evident, it cannot be denied that in order to enjoy a similar revival in the German context, optimization-relevant adaptations remain to be put in place, most notably to the design's systemic configuration.

Fig. 31: SUMMARY OF CASE STUDY ON JBAM IN GERMANY

- Throughout the 1990s JBAM enjoys strong growth in German market by mainly entering into "partnership"-type of institutional arrangements with external distributors
- However, at the beginning of this century JBAM management notices slump in distribution performance levels, with changes in distribution environment aggravating generation of strong inflow streams
- JBAM management remains convinced chances of successfully generating inflows are better with "partnership"-type of relationships with established local distribution partners

- In selected "partnership"-type of institutional arrangements JBAM assigns far-reaching property rights to the autonomous distributors, thereby offering considerable scope for participation and bringing into play distributors' self-interest to cooperate
- This coordination mode is flanked by comprehensive capacities of sales support. At least in the German context only limited "branding" capacities are introduced to support distributors' endeavors for improving their competitive positioning
- Strong focus on norms of relational exchange and two-way communication efforts take prominent part in information-related processes to activate desired [extra] role behavior, thereby also relying to a considerable extent on distributors' self-monitoring
- Besides some of forms of joint actions [product-related and distribution-related] to strengthen distributors' role integrity as well as to serve their competitive interests, JBAM relies on performance-related compensation to activate desired distribution behavior

- At the global level, since 2002 JBAM enjoys revival in distribution performance by falling back on "partnership"-type of institutional arrangements
- However, in Germany the net inflow stream continues to deteriorate, leading to outflows in 2003 and 2004
- Organizational design appears to exhibit inconsistencies in the systemic configuration to bring organizational choice to full strength

Source: Author

4.3 The Case of Fidelity Investments

4.3.1 The Choice of "Market" as Institutional Arrangement for the Distribution Function

After having analyzed the case studies of "hierarchy" and "partnership", the comparative institutional analysis now intends to examine how Fidelity Investments (FIL)[23] handles the enquiry's central decision-making problem concerning institutional arrangements for marketing mutual funds to private investors in Germany. The purpose is to assess whether and how FIL deals with the two fit problems conceptualized in the enquiry's theory- guided framework. Hence, the following discussion aims to clarify whether and in which way FIL brings into line choice and design for the distribution function in Germany with the particular situational demands and targets confronting this

[23] This case study is based on five semi-structured interviews in October 2004 along the enquiry's standard questionnaire with management of FIL at FIL's German headquarters in Kronburg. These interviews lasted between 90 to 150 minutes. In order to meet the enquiry' information needs in particular with regard to quantitative information, three internal documents were provided. A draft of this case study was made available to FIL and discussed intensively with management to further refine and specify the results of this empirical study.

asset management firm. As far the other two case studies, the main objective is to assess in a cumulative manner the efficacy of FIL's choice and design to strengthen "cash inflow stream" in the face of "market dynamics" and possible negative side effects stemming from "service firm specificity" and "opportunism".

FIL in Germany is part of the Fidelity International Limited, which together with Fidelity Management & Research Cooperation is the world's largest independent asset management firm. By the end of 2004, Fidelity as a whole had USD 1,286 billion in AuM. With more than 35,000 staff, including 480 portfolio managers and analysts, Fidelity serves more than 19 million clients around the world. Founded back in 1946 in Boston, Fidelity has remained under private ownership ever since. In the light of a strong market positions obtained most notably in the US and in the UK, **Fidelity as a whole is regarded as one of the leading players in the global asset management sector**. Accentuating this notion also in the wider European context, Fidelity has earned a variety of high-profile awards from independent rating agencies, for example being named the "Best Overall European Fund Manager" by Standard & Poor's. In Germany, by mainly serving the private investor segment, FIL contributes EUR 9.39 billion to the group total. Although FIL set up a Kapitalanlagegesellschaft (KAG) in Germany at the beginning of 2005, the actual production function for [most of] the product range offered to private investors in Germany is, in fact, carried out outside of Germany.

For the purpose of investigating the central decision-making problem, this enquiry classifies FIL as the case that tends to turn to some form of **"market"-type** of institutional arrangements for arranging the distribution function in Germany. FIL management is confident that market forces and distributors' competitive interests will favor the strengthening of its distribution performance levels in terms of net inflows raised from private investors.

4.3.1.1 Emergence of Performance Gap

The aspiration now is to clarify to what extent and in which form this particular asset management firm is facing a performance gap that, already from an objective perspective, can be considered as critical. Then, the discussion will turn to the interpretations and explanation from FIL management in order to bring to light how this deficit is perceived. In this regard, by outlining FIL's distribution performance development in terms of net inflows raised from private investors in Germany vis-à-vis major German competitors, the purpose here is to ascertain whether and to what extent FIL has been confronted with an increasing gap and, in turn, with mounting pressure to react to unsatisfactory distribution performance levels.

For the case of FIL, it will become apparent that the **performance deficit as such is of a considerably different nature than those noticed for the other two case studies of this enquiry**. As will be seen, given FIL's overriding ambition to establish a strong position in one of the most attractive European markets, management viewed the distribution performance in comparison to domestic competitors to have room for improvement, despite the continuous growth FIL enjoyed in terms of AuM since entering the German market in 1992. Against the background of its own ambitions, FIL management ultimately felt the pressure to adjust its wider distribution strategy in Germany at the turn of this century.

After entering the market in 1992, FIL managed to establish some traction, having accumulated EUR 1.4 billion in AuM by the end of 1997. In the following years, from this established, albeit rather small, foothold FIL's expansion in Germany continued at a remarkable rate. At the end of the year 2000, the level of AuM collected from private investors reached a total of EUR 5.2 billion. This implies an annual growth of more than 50 percent since 1997. Comparing this growth with the overall market development for that period of time, it becomes apparent that FIL was in fact growing at a stronger rate. This growth was not only fueled by the favorable capital market conditions at that time but also by a considerable stream of net inflows FIL managed to raise for its product offering each year. In precise terms, FIL collected EUR 0.8 billion in the year 1999 and EUR 1.4 billion in 2000. Thus, **overall it cannot be denied that FIL management, in**

fact, faced a generally positive development of its operations in the German private investor market.

However, the comparison of the net inflow figures FIL raised from private investors in Germany with the distribution performance levels of major domestic competitors pinpoints a performance gap confronting FIL, regardless of the progress made in establishing some traction in the German market. As illustrated in Figure 32, looking at the net inflow figures of the years 1999 and 2000, it becomes clear that the market-leading asset management firms [in terms of AuM] captured extensively stronger inflow streams at that point of time. In more detail, throughout the year 1999, Union Investments managed to raise net inflows of EUR 10.9 billion relative to FIL's net inflows of EUR 0.8 billion. In the following year, the difference to the most successful local competitor in terms of net inflows widened even further. While FIL succeeded in increasing its inflow stream to EUR 1.4 billion in the year 2000, DEKA Investment was able to collect EUR 18.9 billion for its entire product range. Hence, in the light of this very observable disparity it seems as if FIL encountered considerable impediments to match the domestic rivals' distribution performance levels and, thus, to achieve similar levels of scale in the German market[24].

24 As far as this comparison is concerned, it is important to point out that FIL's product range mainly focuses on the segment of high-margin asset classes such as **equity-based mutual funds**. In contrast to that, domestic players tend to offer a more diversified range of mutual funds, with fixed-income or money-market-related mutual funds which tend to carry relatively lower margins usually receiving a large share of their inflow streams.

Fig. 32: EMERGENCE OF PERFORMANCE GAP CONFRONTING FIL

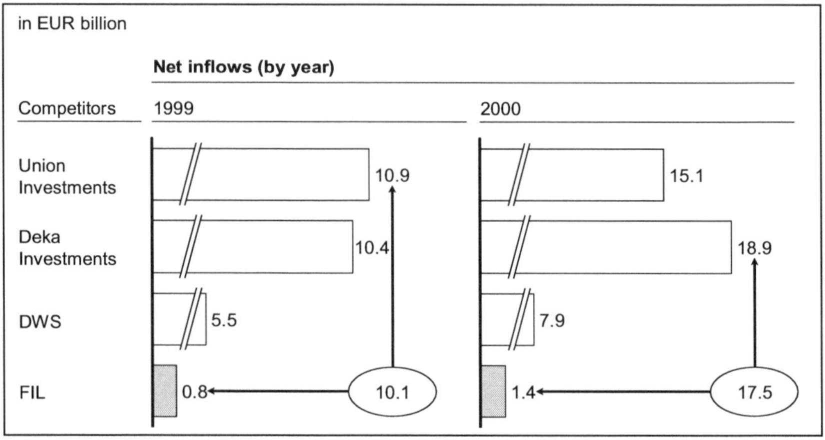

Source: Fidelity, BVI (2005)

Therefore, already from an objective point of view, in the light of FIL's usual goal to obtain a leading competitive position in a market it has entered, **this difference then unarguably hints at a very observable performance discrepancy**. In other words, in spite of the strong progress FIL has made since entering the German market, it is this difference to the larger incumbent players that constitutes the gap in this enquiry. In this regard, it will become apparent that FIL is facing structural challenges to accomplish the aspired competitive positioning, as the positive market trend in Germany at that time also favored FIL's progress.

4.2.1.2 Perceiving and Interpreting Performance Gap

In order to discuss how this gap in distribution performance levels has eventually led to adjustments in the institutional arrangements and particularly concerning the organizational choice, it is essential to elaborate on how this gap has been perceived and interpreted by FIL management. In more precise terms, the purpose is to elucidate to what extent this deficit has exceeded a subjective threshold and, in this way, initiated responses to adjust agency-relationships to market mutual funds in the German market. In that respect, it is important to highlight that, in Europe, FIL mainly tends to pursue the strategic route of falling back on decentralized distribution structures to capture market share by leveraging already existing customer pools of local distributors.

Having established leading competitive positioning not only in the US but also in the UK, **the expansion of its operations on the European mainland and particularly in Germany has been a key priority on the agenda of FIL management** (Ferber und Narat 2002, p. 26). Hence, regardless of the growth in AuM throughout the 1990s, the disparity of net inflows vis-à-vis major German competitors did not remain unnoticed to FIL management. Given the overriding strategic importance of this particular market to FIL management, it viewed this difference as a critical performance deficit.

With regard to the root causes underlying this noticeable discrepancy in performance levels, FIL management acknowledged not only the different focus in the product offering but, in particular, perceived the **mix of distribution channels** it applied in the German market to raise inflows from private investors to be **unsuitable for keeping up with domestic competitors**. As a sales manager pointed out, after entering Germany FIL primarily relied on autonomous IFAs to perform the distribution function. Reflecting the prominent role of the segment of IFAs within FIL's distribution strategy in the late 1990s, this channel accounted for 62 percent of FIL's total AuM by the year 2000. The wider banking channel, which is the most important channel segment for marketing mutual funds to private investors in Germany, contributed only 16 percent to FIL's total volume of AuM. This is in strong contrast to the distribution approaches of the group of domestic competitors as these incumbents were in the position to predominantly rely on their respective proprietary banks. For raising strong inflows streams and, thus, for achieving scale these banks relative to IFAs bring about the advantage of remarkable customer reach as that their pools of end customers tend to be considerably larger.

From all this, FIL management learnt that a distribution strategy of primarily falling back on discrete arrangements with IFAs was not sufficient to match or to narrow the difference in performance levels to main competitors. Therefore, although IFAs unarguably spurred FIL's growth throughout 1990s, **FIL management regarded the avenue of setting up distribution arrangements with the larger German universal**

banks as a very promising route to overcome the gap noticed. In other words, it was in particular the initiation of agency-relationships with banks that FIL management perceived as strategically critical to substantially bolster the inflow stream raised from private investors. Nonetheless IFAs still remain a cornerstone of its wider distribution strategy in Germany. This indicates, as for the other two case studies, that **it was not a reconsideration of the "degree of decentralization" that was viewed to be the most decisive in order to strengthen distribution performance levels**. Instead, hitherto having achieved a strong competitive position in many countries by relying on rather "market"-type of institutional arrangements, **the intention was to transfer this proven organizational choice to the distribution channel of banks in Germany**. Thus, management was optimistic of bridging the deficit through adhering to its conventional choice for arranging distribution relationships.

Yet, in this regard FIL management was confronted with a particular pattern of obstacles. The banking channel as a whole showed traditionally only limited enthusiasm to perform the distribution function for asset management firms other than its in-house provider. In more specific terms, in the late 1990s particularly the larger German banks tended to demonstrate strong loyalty to their respective in-house asset management division and its products by solely offering these mutual funds to their customers. As a sales manager explained, banking groups in general were afraid of a reduced market-share for their asset management division in the course of opening up their shelves to external competitors. This in turn implies that the most important distribution channel for mutual funds in Germany in general turned out to be more or less impregnable for external asset management firms. Therefore, concerning the interpretation and causal explanation of the gap from the view of FIL management, it was this limited willingness among banks to take on the distribution activities on behalf of FIL that was regarded as a key obstacle to bridge the observed difference in distribution performance. Hence, **to accomplish the aspired change in strategy, FIL management sensed the pressure to intensify its endeavors to activate external banks' motivation to actively perform the distribution function for FIL's mutual fund offering**.

In summary, the discussion shows that management considered the nevertheless positive development of its performance levels to have room for improvement. This perceived deficit is in elementary contrast to the ones of the other case studies of this enquiry, where in fact performance levels had deteriorated. In view of the strategic aspirations to establish a strong foothold in the German market, FIL management regarded the difference in distribution performance vis-à-vis main competitors to have reached such a status that it required an adjustment in its wider distribution strategy. Despite the growing inflow stream in the late 1990s management felt the urgency to introduce a change in strategy in order to set the stage to continue FIL's expansion in Germany.

4.3.1.3 Responding to Perceived Performance Gap

In response to this interpretation, FIL management reacted at the turn of this century by introducing changes to its distribution strategy. Having made the experience that discrete distribution structures prove to be economically attractive to both the product-providing asset management firm and the distributing bank, FIL management aims at gaining increased market access and, thus, at achieving greater scale by way of exciting motivation among banks in Germany to enter into considerably less integrated agency-relationships. With getting access to customer pools of these banks being identified as the most promising route to overcome the gap, FIL management **further intensified its efforts to initiate distribution arrangements with external banks**.

All this underlines, as for the other two case studies, that **the response to the noticed gap in terms of the intended organizational choice represents an intensification of the conventional "degree of decentralization" rather than a fundamental change**. From a comparative point of view, once again it turns out that management tends to cling to its already given organizational choice, implying that the allocation of property rights remains untouched. In other words, it will show that FIL management regards FIL's conventional approach of "market"-related structures as adequate to overcome the performance deficit. However, it will become apparent that FIL aims to successfully introduce this choice in the channel segment of banks. This alteration in strategy to increasingly fall back on banks [in addition to the segment of

IFAs] as the distributing agent offers FIL the opportunity to substantially enlarge customer reach, which is expected to facilitate the strengthening of distribution performance levels. Thus, this strategic change entails the prospect of enjoying economies of scale and scope by way of bolstering the inflow streams for its product offering. However, choosing to fall back on rather "market" type of arrangements in the channel segment of banks not only provides the chance to leverage enlarged customer reach, but also brings about remarkable challenges of securing motivation and coordination. Hence, although opting to rely to some extent on the invisible hand of markets as a coordination mechanism, FIL management recognizes the necessity not only to bring in to play but also to adequately serve the self-interest of banks in optimizing their product offering to end customers.

Therefore, following this intended change in strategy FIL management has deliberately taken a variety of measures. First of all, as part of its strategy of gaining sustained access to the private investor market through "market" type of arrangements with the banking channel, FIL management has intensified its endeavors to promote these types of distribution systems for mutual funds in Germany. It cannot be denied that **FIL has been and still is at the vanguard of the group of asset management firms highlighting to distributing banks the benefits of less integrated distribution structures**. Applying various communication media, such as articles in professional journals, interviews in the business press as well as speeches and presentations at conferences, FIL management consistently stresses the optimizing character these distribution arrangements possess. In this respect, referring to examples in the US as well as in Germany, FIL's European managing director, Balk (2001, p. 21), emphasizes the chances for banks to unleash growth potential and ultimately to [re]gain market share by moving away from purely bilateral arrangements to increasingly multilateral and, thus, decentralized structures for producing and marketing mutual funds to private investors. Along those lines, FIL's managing director in Germany, Baum (2005, p. 24), provides additional empirical evidence that the inclusion of external product providers, in addition to the bank's in-house mutual fund offering, is highly appreciated by end customers and allows the bank to attain a more competitive positioning. These examples clearly indicate that FIL top management has been very active in emphasizing the advantages associated with increasingly decentralized agency-relationships for marketing mutual funds.

As another part of the strategy, FIL has also dedicated resources to further systemize the process to assist external banks in actually realizing the benefits associated with an advanced "degree of decentralization" by taking into account their specific needs. Thus, following the main objective to increase net inflows, as will be elaborated in more detail, **FIL is going to great lengths to outline sales concepts that aim to support the autonomous distributing banks in strengthening their competitive positioning**. These concepts [focusing on FIL's range of mutual funds] intend to assist the external bank in the acquisition of new customers, their subsequent development, and ultimately their retention. In that respect, one sales manager emphasized that the introduction of these concepts carry the potential to facilitate the bank's bid for differentiation vis-à-vis distributing rivals. Clearly, the aim of these concepts is to encourage the external banks' willingness to take on the distribution function on behalf of FIL.

Complementing these measures to overcome the deficit in distribution performance, since the beginning of this century **FIL has been substantially adjusting its staff size and composition in Germany in order to be able to appropriately interact with external banks within decoupled arrangements**. In particular the sales and marketing teams have experienced a substantial increase in personnel, with many of them recruited directly from the wider mutual fund-distributing community in Germany. By the end of 2004, this adjustment implies that almost 50 staff were primarily involved in the sales and marketing-related activities. First located directly in Frankfurt, in the meantime having moved to prestigious premises in Kronburg near Frankfurt, which further signals FIL's commitment to the German market, these teams are in charge of the management of the agency-relationships to distributing intermediaries. This entails the acquisition and the following business development as well as the retention of distributors. Further assistance is provided by FIL's European headquarters in London.

4.3.1.4 Intensifying "Degree of Decentralization" for Distribution Function

Concerning the first, the external, fit problem, it becomes apparent that despite the positive development of its operations, FIL management identified the organizational set-up of the distribution function in Germany as being unsuitable for realizing its overriding strategic goal in this European market. Thus, in response to the noticed difference vis-à-vis domestic asset management firms in the late 1990s, management considered the organizational choice to be an essential means within its altered distribution strategy to enhance inflow streams.

In the light of the positive experiences made with discrete arrangements for the distribution of its product offering in various markets, FIL management aimed to adhere to its traditional choice in order to close the gap in performance levels, yet with intensified focus on the most important channel segment in Germany. Having primarily relied on the channel of IFAs to perform the distribution function for FIL's product range throughout the 1990s, distribution relationships with external banks are viewed as the essential route to bridge the noticed difference. From this, it becomes evident that this aspired **external choice of "market"-type of institutional arrangements then pinpoints a horizontal adaptation in terms of the channel segment rather than a reconsideration of the "degree of decentralization".** As already indicated above, this then also highlights that the extent of transferring [product-related] property rights to distributors remains unchanged. Hence, FIL management in general remains optimistic of accomplishing the expansion in the German market through continuing to rely to a large degree on the self-interest of distributing intermediaries to optimize their product offering to end customers. In other words, FIL aims to improve inflow streams by focusing more strongly than before on the coordinative efficacy of the rather invisible competitive mechanisms [with their considerable incentive intensity] imposed by the demand-side for mutual funds.

Yet, as outlined before, this had to be achieved in a challenging environment. Despite a first move to more open distribution systems, the banking channel overall has remained fairly restrictive in granting access to their shelves, resulting in a distribution environment commonly referred to as "guided architecture". Hence, whether the aspired choice actually turns out to be the one realized appears to be restrained by the interests of distributing banks as well as FIL's relative attractiveness relative to other asset management firms in the bidding for shelf space. For this case study, though, it seems that **FIL has been quite successfully in bearing the comparison with other asset management firms in the contest to obtaining shelf space from distributors**. It appears as if FIL finds itself in a favorable position to establish the intended organizational choice of "market" type of distribution arrangements. With distributing banks in Germany applying in particular brand strength as a key criterion to select their external product providers (Sector Analysis 2003b, pp. 16-20), it looks as if FIL appropriately meets this requirement by having one of the strongest brands in the asset management sector with spikes in capabilities and size. Moreover, at the same time, FIL's product range includes one of the main blockbuster-products. Taking on the distribution for such an asset management firm then allows banks in principle to optimize their competitive positioning vis-à-vis distributing rivals.

Hence, following from this ability to support external banks in this way, it shows that **for the external fit relation, FIL is more or less able to realize the intended organizational choice in response to the noticed gap in distribution performance**. One sales manager highlighted that by 2004, FIL had been able to set up decentralized distribution arrangements with the majority of the larger universal banks and even some savings banks as well as cooperative banks. When the banking channel in general started to move to less integrated and, thus, to more "market"-related distribution structures, in a considerable number of cases FIL found itself in the selected group of asset management firms granted access to the distribution networks' shelves (Ferber 2003, p. 24). This highlights that FIL at large has managed to introduce its organizational choice as intended in order to respond to the situational demands arising in the late 1990s, although in some cases in Germany FIL still was not able to initiate an agency-relationship with banks for marketing its mutual fund offering.

Overall, for the purpose of investigating the enquiry's central decision-making problem, FIL is classified as the case study with the choice of a "market"-type of institutional arrangement for the distribution function in Germany. From a comparative point of view, it will become evident that while turning to decentralized arrangements, in line with its founding culture, FIL intends to pursue a strategy of remaining in control of its own destiny. Thus, as to be discussed in more detail, this enquiry regards the "market"-type of distribution arrangement as the one in which the asset management firm [the principal] allows the distributing bank [the agent]

- to use the mutual funds provided for advisory activities
- to receive some form of compensation for performing the distribution of the mutual fund.

4.3.2 The Design of "Market" as Institutional Arrangement for the Distribution Function

In the following discussion, the point is to elaborate how FIL designs the overall structure of governance for its chosen "degree of decentralization", classified by this enquiry as a "market"-type of institutional arrangement. In this respect, the intention is to examine whether and in which way FIL has introduced a coordination mechanism that is consistent with its fundamental organizational choice. Regarding the internal fit problem, the aspiration is to elucidate if FIL's design of structure-shaping instruments and process-relation measures appropriately accounts for the situational demands arising with chosen "degree of decentralization" and is efficacious in optimizing the benefits of this way of marketing mutual funds. It is of particular interest to find out by which means FIL's design brings latent issues of "service firm specificity" and "opportunism" under control, given the general notion of in fact limited market control imposed by end customers or regulatory authorities (Heinemann et al. 2003, pp. 52).

In the process of analyzing the adequacy of the design for the chosen "degree of decentralization", it shows that, already with the set-up of the **systemic configuration** which includes the layout of the central coordination mechanisms and the buildup of capacities, FIL attempts to account for specificity and the growing risk of opportunism related to this organizational choice. As for the other two case studies, this systemic configuration is operating as the frame within which FIL then puts into place **process-intervening measures** to exert influence on the actions of otherwise autonomous, external banks. Adopting an optimizing perspective, the efficacy of FIL's design is largely evaluated against the ability to raise a "cash inflow stream" from private investors and, thus, to bridge the difference in distribution performance relative to main domestic competitors.

4.3.2.1 Systemic Configuration of "Market"

In the following, from a normative point of view, the enquiry will now elaborate on the systemic configuration by which the overall agency-relationship between FIL and the distributing bank is structured before turning to rather process-related measures. The purpose here is to illuminate in which way the organizational design already in structural terms intends to curb issues of specificity and opportunistic tendencies.

Fig. 33: SYSTEMIC CONFIGURATION OF "MARKET"

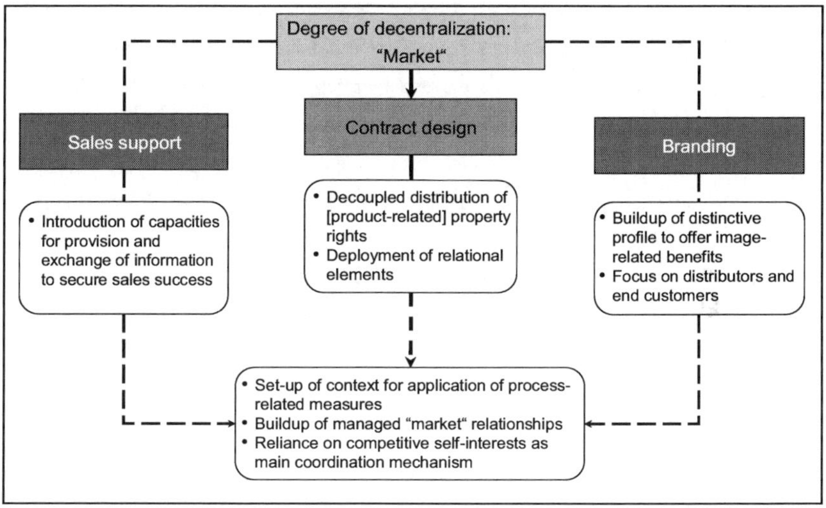

Source: Author

As outlined in Figure 33, similar to the other two case studies, the enquiry will bring forth that once again it is the transfer of a specific pattern of property rights that fundamentally structures the agency-relationships between FIL and external banks. Moreover, this elaboration on the structural set-up will aim at ascertaining in which way and to what degree FIL is establishing capacities to account for the latent challenges of opportunism and specificity. It is of interest to clarify whether and in which way FIL is making investments in "branding" capacities, on the one hand, and what kind of "sales support" capacities are introduced, on the other hand, for handling negative side effects lurking in this organizational choice.

Turning to the empirical analysis, as is known from the more recent discussions on markets for organizing economic transactions, also for this case **it will become apparent that the transaction via the "market" tends to be in some form socially embedded** (Granovetter 1985, pp. 482-483) and that the parties to the exchange still face various types of information asymmetries. Moreover, it may also come to the application of rather hierarchical instruments within "market"-type of structures. Along those lines, **it will show for this case study that there is an aspiration to set the context for coordinating actions in more continuous relationships**, indicating that this asset management firm under focus in fact pursues a strategy, Heide (2003, p. 26) refers to as **"managing" a "market".** Nevertheless, consistent with the rather classic assumptions of markets, the actual coordination between principal and agent will still rely predominantly on the individual self-interest in optimizing profits from economic activity. Therefore, with the organizational choice of "market" at hand, the buildup of the systemic configuration is focused on facilitating the optimization of competitive objectives in order to induce and maintain the agents' willingness to take on the distribution function.

Overall, it will become apparent that this systemic configuration represents the contextual prerequisite for generating strong inflow streams from private investors and for additional process-related measures to account for the latent challenges arising from specificity and opportunistic tendencies. Speaking more in terms of the action variables included in the enquiry's framework of analysis, the upcoming discussion will touch on "contract design", "screening", "branding", and "sales support".

4.3.2.1.1 Assigning Property Rights to Set Up Governance Structure

As for any other asset management firm turning to external banks to perform the selling and advisory activities for its product offering, FIL engages in efforts to lay down a contractual agreement. In general, as a sales manager explained, FIL falls back on a **menu of contracts** that includes mainly **two different but complementary agreements to set up decentralized agency-relationships**. As this will be brought to light

- the **main contract**, setting up the "market"-type of arrangement, purely defines the terms of the exchange,
- while the **complementary agreement** intends to lay out the process of interaction within the exchange.

It will show that the former is more of a spot-market type of agreement, whereas the latter – referred to as the Letter of Intent by FIL management – underlines the relational nature of the exchange. Still, regarding the specification of rights to both parties of the transaction, it will become apparent that this menu of contracts entails a fairly decoupled transfer of property rights to the external bank.

Before entering into this kind of agency-relationship, FIL intends to clarify the underlying motivation of the external bank by running some form of "**screening**" effort. As already mentioned in the previous case study, a great deal of the information concerning the distributors' qualification to facilitate market access to private investors as well as the quality of the respective in-house asset management division to identify possible areas of compatibility is more or less available. Yet, information concerning the banks' genuine willingness to actively sell mutual funds on behalf of external product providers tends to be asymmetrically distributed. Therefore, **the negotiation to set up the systemic configuration and the inherent exchange of information is one of the very few opportunities to verify to some degree the underlying interests of external distributors**. In that respect, a sales manager remarked that the parties to the exchange are keen on having an agreement that includes not only the spot-market type of contract but in particular the Letter of Intent. This letter gives both the external banks and FIL the chance to reduce the asymmetric distribution of information relevant for the agency-relationship. As one sales manager made clear, in case such a Letter of Intent cannot be established, as experienced in some negotiations, FIL management tends to recognize this as a signal of limited willingness and in some cases tends to abstain from entering into the agency-relationship. All this shows **that the interaction with the external bank to**

set up the systemic configuration is also employed to perform some "screening", thereby at least in principle gaining relevance for avoiding situations of opportunism.

Regarding the agreements within the menu of contracts, there can be no doubt that they substantially differ in content. With respect to the rather spot-market type of contract, one sales manager pointed out that this agreement purely stipulates the terms of the exchange. Although each bilateral relationship has its own specific contract, it is generally structured as follows. After naming the parties involved in the transaction, the contract mainly focuses on the specification of the level and components of compensation to the external bank for performing the distribution function as well as on the definition of the products to which this agreement applies. Additionally, it outlines the settlement of the exchange and declares the duration of these terms. From this, it then becomes evident that it is this agreement that defines the competencies on the part of the external bank. Moreover, from a genuinely comparative point of view, **it also shows that it comes to a relatively restrictive assignment of [product-related] property rights on the part of distributing banks, which constitutes the defining characteristic of the "market"-type of institutional arrangement**.

Regarding the transfer of [product-related] property rights in this typical "contract design" according to the classification of Furubotn and Richter (1991, p. 6), FIL gives the distributing bank the right to use its mutual fund offering within sales and advisory services to private investors (usus). Moreover, in connection with this assigned role, FIL is entitling the distributor to some form of compensation for carrying out the distribution function (usus fructus). Therefore, given this extent of assigning [product-related] property rights to the external distributor, it becomes evident that FIL retains full authority for the activities related to the production function along the value chain for a mutual fund. As illustrated in Figure 34, the **responsibilities along the value chain** for producing and marketing mutual funds to private investors **are allocated in a comparatively discrete manner**. In practical terms, in such a specialized set-up the asset management firm is primarily in charge of the activities along the production function, while the bank is mainly responsible for the activities of the distribution function. As already observed in the other case studies, this in turn also underlines that the agreement does not aspire to comprehensively regulate the way in which the actual sales and advisory activities are supposed to be performed. In the view of this strong reliance on the banks' competitive interests, the principal provides the agent with considerable scope on how to tailor the distribution activities to the peculiarities of time and place.

Fig. 34: ALLOCATION OF RESPONSIBILITIES WITHIN "MARKET"

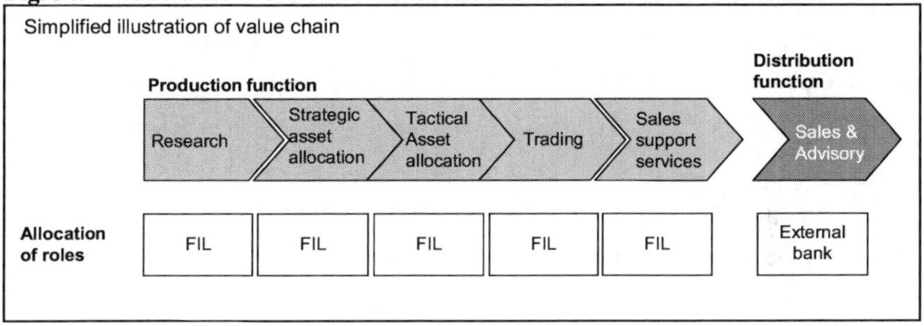

Source: Author

In some deviation from the normative model of "market", for this particular case it shows that **the assignment of [product-related] property rights is increasingly complemented by elements of a relational contract**[25]. Therefore, it seems as if FIL management has learned that a mere spot-market type of agreement specifying the classic dimensions of the "market" exchange [such as the price of performing distribution services] is not sufficient to appropriately account for the issues of specificity and the latent danger of opportunism. In other words, despite the fundamental reliance on self-interested profit-orientation guiding the action of external banks, FIL also asks the bank to demonstrate its willingness to take on the distribution function by additionally introducing a so-called Letter of Intent. All this indicates that a formal agreement specifying purely the terms of the "market" exchange tends to be considered as insufficient to bridge the performance difference to domestic competitors on a sustainable basis.

---

25 The relational contract not only serves the principal to overcome latent challenges related to asymmetric distribution of information but also helps the agent to verify the principal's objectives and intentions. Therefore, as a sales manager pointed out there is a mutual interest to introduce such an additional agreement.

Concerning the content of such a Letter of Intent, one sales manager stressed that it is not a legal document offering sanctions in case of crude misconduct. Instead, **such a letter primarily serves the purpose to articulate both parties' individual expectations related to the decentralized distribution arrangement at stake**. This, in turn, reduces the asymmetry regarding the respective, underlying motives. Moreover, as a sales manager stressed, **considerations regarding reciprocity** within the institutional arrangement is increasingly gaining attention in drafting such a relational contract. All this is expected to strengthen the spirit of the agency-relationship and to have a stabilizing-enhancing effect on the relationship as whole. Within such an atmosphere, parties to the exchange are expected to refrain from deliberately holding up each other. Thus, it appears if this Letter of Intent is purposively introduced as a measure to mitigate challenges related to opportunistic tendencies. Furthermore, there is a tendency that these agreements also include **the definition of sales targets**. With top management generally involved in defining these targets, a sales manager remarked that this underlines the bank's commitment to actively take on the distribution function on behalf of FIL. Another sales manager added that the mere determination of goals itself is not a guarantee these are in fact accomplished. However, it provides the opportunity to enter into discussion not only on the aspiration levels but also the avenues on how to get there. Additionally, these agreements tend to entail a common understanding with regard to the intended interaction that goes beyond the initial scope of the exchange. As one sales manager emphasized, these interactions may include discussions concerning product development or the derivation of sales concepts.

Nevertheless, the defining characteristic of FIL's systemic configuration for "market"-type of decentralized arrangements overall remains the discrete allocation of responsibilities along the value chain. Even in the light of this menu of complementary contracts, it shows that with this "contract design" it only comes to a rather decoupled distribution of [product-related] property rights. In such a fairly specialized set-up, the competitive interests of banks in optimizing their service offering to end customers then assumes a crucial role to bring challenges related to "service firm specificity" and "opportunism" under control. However, while counting on the self-interests of banks, it also shows that FIL turns to some form of relational contract as an additional move to account for latent negative side effects arising in such an advanced "degree of decentralization" Thus, it seems as if FIL management regards the contractual agreement with a mere focus on the exchange's economic terms as not exhaustive for laying the ground for a sustained strengthening of inflows streams. Instead, it becomes evident that explicit pledges (Anderson and Weitz 1992, pp. 20-21) in the form of a Letter of Intent are viewed to have a functional-relevant role for accomplishing strong distribution performance levels so that in some cases FIL management refrains from setting up a decentralized arrangement with an external bank if these commitments are not made.

4.3.2.1.2 Building Brand Capacity to Offer Competitive Advantage

"Branding" for financial service firms is of great functional relevance to address challenges related to the specificity and opportunism. Therefore, "**branding**" also for asset management firms represents an important measure to enhance distribution performance levels. As outlined in the enquiry's framework, there are least two different but still interrelated "branding" approaches available with which asset management firms are in a position to strengthen the inflow stream raised from private investors. On the one hand, investments in "branding" entail the chance to mount the pressure on distributing intermediaries to take on the distribution function, in particular by way of offering the prospects of image-related spill-over effects (Baumgarth 2004, pp. 254-255). Therefore, by way of providing these competitive benefits to harmonize interests and balance the dependence within those discrete agency-relationships, "branding" tends to possess the ability to mobilize the external banks' motivation to actively take on the distribution function and to push FIL's product offering to their end customers. On the other hand, by way of managing the expectations concerning the experience from purchasing the asset management firm's mutual fund, investments in "branding" have the potential to deal with the intangibility and variability related to mutual fund offerings (Keller 2003, pp. 16-19) and to pull private investors to the point-of-sale. Thus, "Branding" also bears the chance to alleviate issues related to the specificity inherent in the distribution function. Following on from this, it is of particular interest in which way and to what extent FIL builds up "branding" capacities in order to establish prerequisites to capture the efficiency-advantages typically associated with such discrete arrangements.

From a comparative point of view, it becomes evident that **"branding" takes a prominent role in FIL's strategy of falling back on "market"-type of agency-relationships in order to realize strong inflows streams for its mutual fund offering**. As far as the design of this action variable is concerned, FIL management places this kind of structure-shaping investment with the predominant purpose of increasing the pressure on the part of distributing agents to actively take on the distribution activities for FIL's product range. In more precise terms, although FIL turns to a blend of those two approaches outlined above, one sales manager pointed out that the emphasis clearly rests on inducing the distributing community and especially banks to push FIL's mutual funds to their end customers. The purpose is to strengthen the notion that it is in their very own, competitive interest to perform the sales and advisory activities on behalf of FIL. Thus, following the organizational choice to turn to rather "market"-type of agency-relationships **FIL's "branding" efforts particularly aim to reach distributing intermediaries and their staff**. These are not only gatekeepers restricting access to private investors but also take the critical role of opinion-leaders influencing the actual purchasing decision of private investors. With a considerable share of private investors in Germany believed to need the endorsement of the distributing banks' sales staff in order to eventually purchase a specific mutual fund, it seems as if FIL focuses its brand-building measures on establishing a distinctive brand profile as an asset management firm in the perception of these professionals, without neglecting the ultimate end customer.

Fig. 35: BUILDUP OF BRANDING CAPACITIES IN "MARKET"

Illustration of communication approach

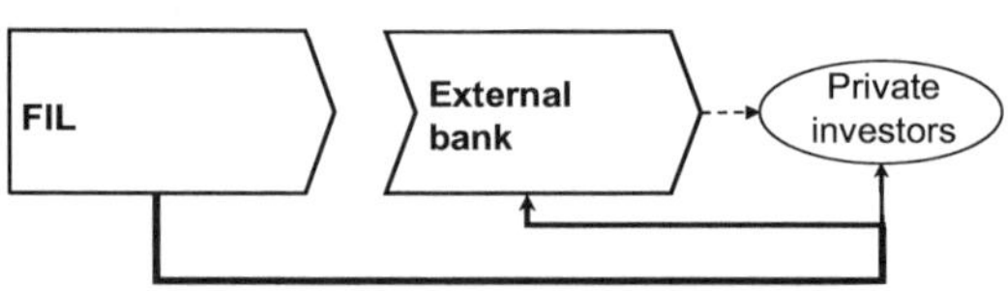

Key characteristic

- Focus mainly on reaching distributors but also end customers
- Blend of rational and emotional elements
- Use of outdoor and print as media channels
- Selective co-branding but with limited relationship specificity

Source: Author

Therefore, as outlined in Figure 35, in order to appropriately reach this target audience of distributing intermediaries and their staff as well as to cover the widespread segment of private investors, FIL runs a "branding" program in Germany that traditionally has relied [almost] exclusively on print media, with the daily [business] newspapers and the larger weekend papers being the main communication vehicle. Moreover, **FIL is increasingly turning to billboards and posters within the financial district in Frankfurt where most of the larger banks are located**. This media-mix appears to be suitable in a complementary way to increase awareness for FIL's product offering as well as to accentuate the benefits associated with these mutual funds. While billboards allow simple messages to be conveyed, the print medium is well-suited to communicating the product information in more detail. At the same time, such a mix of communication channel tends to allow FIL to keep its actual spending levels fairly moderate on these "branding" efforts. According to ACNielsen (2005), FIL's [above-the-line] expenditures have never topped EUR 5 million per year since 1999.

Regarding the actual content of these efforts, Jordan (2003, p. 23) argues that FIL in differentiation to German competitors pursues a strong product focus. In this regard, it becomes apparent that FIL highlights its asset management capabilities by pointing out that it is the largest independent asset management firm worldwide with distinctive skills for the activities along the product function for mutual funds. Persistently emphasizing the quality of its range of mutual funds, FIL leverages the leading position Fidelity as a whole has accomplished in the asset management sector. Moreover, it further shows that FIL attempts to increasingly blend these rather functional benefits with emotional appeal, as the recent "Schwarz-Rot-Geld" campaign in Germany demonstrates. This is expected to additionally strengthen the brand profile of FIL.

As far as the result of these measures is concerned, it becomes apparent that FIL has established a comparatively extensive brand capacity to cope most notably with latent issues of opportunistic tendencies but also with challenges related to the specificity inherent in the distribution activities. In more substantive terms, FIL is among the leading asset management brands in Germany, be it from the perspective of distributing intermediaries, or be it from the private investors' point of view. With regard to the perception of FIL's brand by distributors, while being viewed as the strongest brand in terms of awareness and reputation in the wider European context, Busch (2003, pp. 44-45) brings to light that FIL is ranked second and third with respect to awareness and reputation in Germany, respectively (please see Figure 36). This clearly underlines that **FIL has managed to accomplish a distinctive profile as an asset management firm within the distributing community. In addition to that, end customer research also indicates that FIL is within the group of the top 6 asset management brands in terms of [aided] awareness.**

Fig. 36: **BRAND STRENGTH OF FIL IN GERMANY**

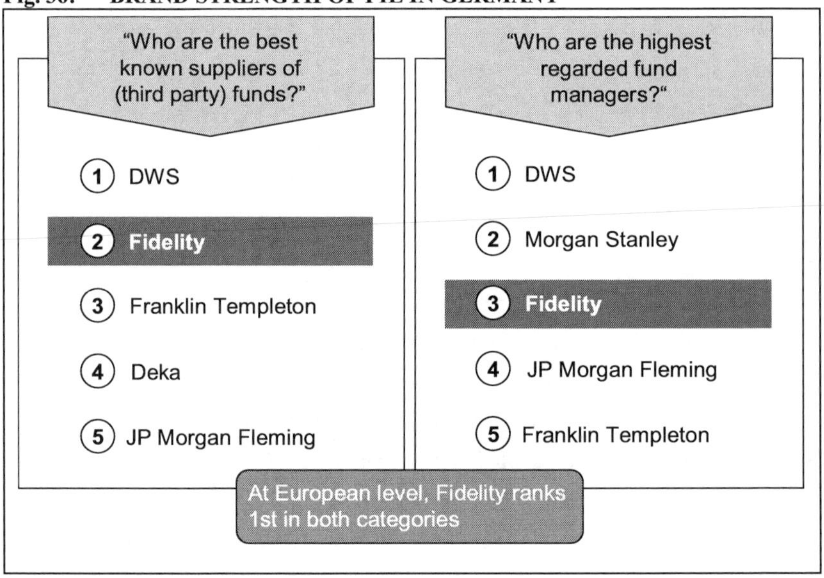

Source: Busch (2003, pp. 44-45)

This has considerable impact on the extent to which FIL is in a position to increase the pressure on distributing banks to take on the distribution function. It appears as if FIL's brand capacity is sufficiently strong to provide positive spill-over effects. These image-related benefits are expected to favor the external banks' endeavors to optimize their competitive positioning, thereby adequately serving their self-interest. In the light of FIL's brand strength in terms of awareness and its well-established reputation as one of the leading asset management firms, it seems as if FIL has established the structural prerequisites in order to curb latent negative side effects stemming from opportunistic tendencies.

Moreover, it further shows that private investors to a greater degree take notice of and consider FIL's mutual fund offering in their purchasing decisions. This indicates that the established capacity, at least to some extent, generates a pull-effect among end customers. Such a creation of demand not only provides potential economic benefits to both FIL and the banks [performing the distribution function], but also carries the chance to alleviate issues of specificity arising at the point-of-sale. With end customer increasingly being enabled to impose some form of control on the actual distribution services, the influence of banks and their staff seems somewhat limited to lure end customers away from FIL's product offering and, thus, to hold up the external asset management firm. Hence, it appears as if FIL's buildup of brand capacities also carries the potential to inhibit challenges related to "service firm specificity". As will be discussed later more comprehensively, **co-branding activities then will take a prominent role in further leveraging this capacity to serve the autonomous banks' competitive objectives**.

In summary, as "market" type of institutional arrangements extensively rely on the distributing banks' objectives to optimize their respective competitive positioning, it becomes evident that FIL intends to activate and maintain distributors' willingness to take on the distribution function by deploying these structure-shaping investments in "branding". It shows that this brand represents a prominent capacity in this design to account for latent issues of both specificity and opportunism. With the remarkable buildup in terms of awareness and reputation, it looks as if the required provisions are made to eventually trigger the advantages of increased scale associated with enlarged customer reach.

4.3.2.1.3 Setting up Sales Support Capacities to Secure Sales Success

The provision of "sales support" constitutes an additional measure of great functional relevance for accomplishing strong inflow streams. To improve distribution performance levels, "sales support" serves two main objectives. First, capacities in "sales support" aim to establish the cognitive prerequisites to adequately enable the external banks to perform the sales and advisory activities for mutual funds. In addition to this, "sales support" may also be positioned to serve banks' competitive interests and, thus, to induce and uphold their willingness to engage in "market"-type of agency-relationships. Therefore, investment decisions regarding "sales support" potentially constitute a further measure to properly account for the challenges stemming for the specificity inherent in the actual selling and advisory activities as well as the lurking opportunistic tendencies.

Fig. 37: SALES SUPPORT CAPACITIES FOCUSED ON DISTRIBUTORS' NEEDS

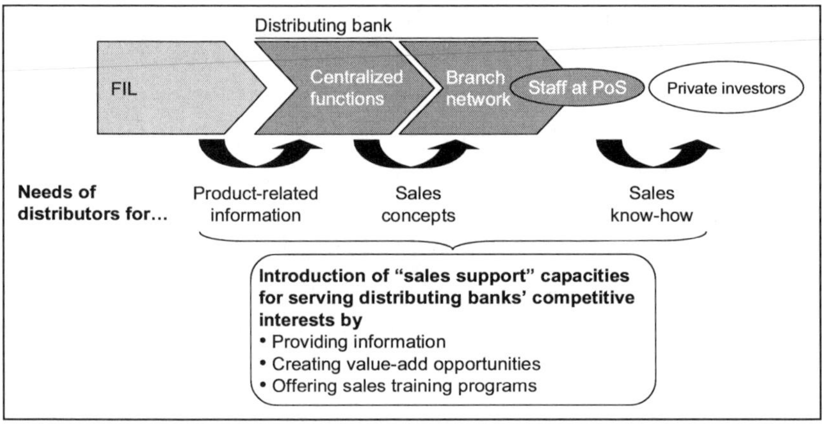

Source: adapted from Fidelity

In comparison to the other two case studies of the enquiry, it shows that FIL has set up "sales support" capacities with an explicit orientation on the different needs of distributing banks at the various interfaces and stages of its operations. As a sales manager stressed, a thorough understanding of the challenges confronting the distributing banks is imperative to eventually achieve strong inflows for FIL's product range.

Therefore, leveraging its vast "sales support" know-how acquired in the UK as well as in the US, FIL designs its "sales support" capacities in such a way to adequately account for this range of diverse needs. In more precise terms, as illustrated in Figure 37, FIL has set up capacities in three different but interrelated fields tailored to the typical informational needs at the different organizational interfaces not only to the distributing bank but also within the bank itself. In that respect, with the overriding function of serving the banks' competitive objectives, **FIL has implemented structural capacities**

- **to provide product-related information**,
- **to offer assistance in the derivation of sales stimulation concepts** [that at least in principle favor the creation of value-added to the distributing bank], and
- **to offer some form of sales training for banks' sales staff operating directly at the point-of-sale**.

In order to favor an appropriate interaction with autonomous banks in these managed agency-relationships, all this is accompanied by an increase in and stronger channel orientation of FIL's sales and marketing staff. Hence, by introducing these complementary ways to support the actual distributing function, FIL aims to make structural provisions to actively secure mutually beneficial sales success.

In more detail, similar to the other two asset management firms of this enquiry, FIL turns to a variety of vehicles to secure the regular delivery of **product-related information** to distributing banks. This includes a range of publications covering quantitative data of FIL's product portfolio as well qualitative information. For example, the so-called Chartbook brings to light detailed information for each mutual fund. Equally important, as it is increasingly the distributing bank that specifies the type of information to be delivered, FIL has introduced "sales support" capacities in order to be able to respond appropriately to these informational requests in a customized manner. Concerning the actual way of making these capacities available to the distributing bank, FIL mainly turns to electronic media in addition to the conventional ways of hard copies and road shows. Overall, having capacities in place to equip the distributing bank [and particularly its centralized functions] with information concerning past investment performance or the underlying investment focus, the purpose is to establish a deeper understanding of FIL's mutual fund offering. **The intention is to enable the external**

bank from a purely informational point of view to perform the distribution function for FIL's mutual fund range. Thus, these capacities have the potential to mitigate issues related in particular to the specificity inherent in the distribution function.

Additionally, and this is something that has only been observed in this case study in such an explicit form, **FIL also builds up capacities to assist the external bank and most notably its centralized functions in devising comprehensive sales concepts**. These concepts carry the opportunity for the autonomous distributors to take on a more differentiated positioning vis-à-vis distributing rivals. As one sales manager summarized, through making use of the know-how generated through serving more than 19 million investors around the globe, FIL has been able to elaborate proven concepts that potentially favor the creation of value-added for the external bank. In more specific terms, these programs intend to help distributors in further improving the acquisition of end customers and the subsequent development of the relationship, which also includes successful retention. Thus, by establishing the prerequisites to assist actual sales and advisory activities in this way, **the aim is to reinforce the external banks' perception that it is in line with their own competitive objectives to enter into a distribution arrangement with FIL**. The buildup of this kind of capacity is then expected to inhibit, at least to some extent, opportunistic tendencies.

Furthermore, FIL also puts in place capacities to be able to **provide sales training programs to the banks' sales staff who directly interact with private investors** as well to run joint **sales events** to present a specific product offering to the banks' customers. One main purpose of these capacities is to ensure that the sales concepts eventually reach the point-of-sale and, thus, favor the realization of the agents' competitive objectives. As far as the training programs are concerned, they give FIL the chance to build the required skill-set on the part of banks' sales staff by making them familiar with the so-called investment story for specific mutual funds of FIL's product range, highlighting and explaining the key advantages related to these investment products. Moreover, these sessions allow FIL to present rather general type of routines and methods on how to appropriately handle advisory challenges arising at the point-of-sale in the course of interaction with private investors. Therefore, **this capacity aims to**

provide relevant sales know-how to put the banks' sales staff in an adequate position from a more qualification point of view to successfully complete the sales activities. However, from a genuinely comparative perspective, in particular in contrast to the case study of "partnership", it seems as if these training programs[26] overall take place in a slightly more one-sided way rather than in a highly participative manner.

In summary, it cannot be denied that FIL has a comprehensive set of integrated capacities of "sales support" in place to account for challenges arising from specificity and opportunism. It shows that FIL seeks not only to appropriately enable external banks to perform the distribution function but also assists them by various means to attain a more competitive positioning, highlighting the managed character of the agency-relationships.

4.3.2.1.4 Systemic Configuration as Context

After having brought to light in which way FIL intends to outline the structural set-up of its "market" type of institutional arrangements for the distribution function in Germany, the purpose again is to clarify how this kind of systemic configuration operates in relation to the optimization objective. Thus, as far the internal fit problem is concerned, the ambition is to ascertain in which way this design of ["screening"], "contract design", "branding", and "sales support" and their interplay puts FIL in a position to cope with the latent negative side effects related to its organizational choice.

Following from the preceding discussion, once again it becomes clear that the systemic configuration as such primarily sets the frame within which process-related measures are applied in order to guide the actual distribution activities. In other words, also in this organizational design some additional, process-related instruments are needed to cope with situational demands arising with the organizational choice through either direct or indirect intervention. Hence, also in the case of FIL, the systemic configuration

---

26 In this context, a further positive side effect of having capacities to provide sales training programs is that these tend to transfer, in fact, relationship-specific know-how and, thus, potentially create some sort of lock-in effect on the part of autonomous banks. Hence, gaining direct access to the banks' sales increases the chance to continuously maintain their' willingness to take on this function.

represents the necessary rather than the sufficient condition to improve net inflows. In this regard, one sales manager pointed out that a strong brand helps to get access to distribution networks and, thus, favors the generation of inflow streams but it does not necessarily guarantee the improvement of distribution performance levels.

Taking the systemic configuration as a context-setting device, it shows that given a rather restrictive transfer of [product-related] property rights to the distributing bank, the decentralized agency-relationship essentially becomes shaped as a "market" type of distribution arrangement, despite the use of elements of a relational contract. Thus, contrary to the case study in which the asset management firm offers participative decentralization when turning to external banks for the distribution function, elements of trust and the self-interest to cooperate, at least in general, are not expected to take the most prominent role within the wider coordination activities along the value chain. Instead, **in the light of such a discrete allocation of responsibilities along the value chain, the coordination mechanism to a greater extent centers on the respective competitive interests with an explicit profit-optimizing orientation**. This, in turn, highlights the need for instruments that secure a sufficient harmonization of interests between FIL and the distributing banks to prevent the execution of the exit option by powerful agents as they own the relationship to private investors.

Therefore, from a comparative point of view, it shows that **FIL management deliberately builds up extensive capacities to serve as well as to eventually realize respective competitive interests**, thereby aligning the underlying motives related to "market"-type of distribution arrangements. As outlined, the brand capacity established in the German market carries the chance to provide differentiating spill-over effects. This is expected to allow the distributing bank to realize an improved competitive positioning. Moreover, by way of "branding", private investors are increasingly put in a position to impose some form of control on the distribution activities to limit the scope for issues related to the specificity inherent in these services. Additionally, a comprehensive set of integrated "sales support" capacities is in place to deliver product-related information, to build qualification, and to create value-added for the distributing bank. On the one hand, these capacities provide the opportunity to adequately enable the distributing banks in terms of information as well as qualifications, in this way making provision to adequately account for the lurking negative side effects of specificity. On the other hand, those prerequisites to realize value-added also aim at strengthening the notion among autonomous banks that it is to their own competitive and ultimately economic advantage to perform sales and advisory activities for FIL's product range. Hence, **this elaboration on these capacities brings forwards that it seems as if FIL adequately accounts for the lurking negative side effects of both opportunistic tendencies and specificity**.

However, even if the discussion on markets points out that the coordination mode of "market" may even contain steering elements, **this systemic configuration highlights very much the, in fact, managed character of the agency-relationships**. Whereas classic forms of markets predominately fall back on the price mechanism to coordinate economic activities, it will be shown for this case study that **this structural set-up paves the way for the application of process-related measures to intervene in the agents' sales and advisory activities in an indirect manner but also in an increasingly direct fashion**. While this is clearly inconsistent with an ideal type of market, it underlines that FIL in fact designs some managed form of "market" to bolster inflow streams for its mutual fund range. On the basis of this systemic configuration, in the following section the enquiry will turn to the process-related measures FIL operates in order to realize the aspired improvement in distribution performance levels.

4.3.2.2 Process-Related Measures of "Market"

At this point of the enquiry, the aspiration is to show which process-related measures FIL purposively employs to guide the external banks' behavior in order to realize the aspired improvement in inflows. With regard to the second fit problem, the goal is now to ascertain to what extent these process-related measures in the context of this "market"-type of systemic configuration allow FIL to adequately bring the latent challenges related to "service firm specificity" and "opportunism" under control.

As already pointed out, given the discrete assignment of responsibilities along the value chain to produce and market mutual funds, **the coordination mechanism for the decentralized agency-relationship relies to a considerable extent on the competitive**

interests and the inherent [short-term] orientation on maximizing profits. As indicated above, beyond the employment of indirect interventional measures it will become apparent that, based on information exchange, FIL purposively also turns to some form of rather direct, ad-hoc intervention as a move to appropriately serve these competitive interests. It will show that in some of its agency-relationships FIL feeds forward some more direct guidance for the sales and advisory activities to assist external distributors and their staff to realize the [mutual] advantages inherent in decentralized arrangements.

Therefore, from a functional point of view, FIL's purpose in putting in place process-related capacities is then to further contribute to the realization of the distributing banks' competitive objectives. Contrary to the case study of "partnership" with its far-reaching assignment of [product-related] property rights and the offer of fairly extensive participation, the mobilization of self-interest in this case study is addressed much more by bringing into play the prospects and measures to accomplish a more competitive positioning [already in the short term], which favors the [more immediate] maximization of profits. It is this blend of a discrete allocation of responsibilities, some form of goal-setting, and most notably the distinctive capacities in "branding" and "sales support" that intents to trigger the desired levels of self-interest to perform the distribution function. **Yet, by motivating distributing banks in this way, it appears as if the asset management firm remains prone to the danger of being replaced if a competing asset management firm offers a more appealing package to come to an even further improved competitive positioning in the short term**.

As mentioned before, FIL falls back on instruments to guide the distributing banks' behavior in a direct as well as indirect manner. In this regard, as for the other two case studies, the enquiry will distinguish between **information-processing means** and rather **motivational means**. As far as the direct intervening measures are concerned, these procedures are primarily discussed within the group of information-processing means as they are not only based on the exchange of information but also, in their very essence, mainly involve information-related instruments. In the following section, besides the context-setting variables, this enquiry will also touch on "relational exchange", "monitoring", and "incentive scheme" to bring to light how FIL intends to overcome the gap in distribution performance levels vis-à-vis the larger domestic competitors in Germany.

4.3.2.2.1 Information-Processing Means for Process-Intervention

The enquiry's goal is now to elaborate on the information-processing means FIL applies in its decentralized agency-relationships in Germany. In the light of the systemic configuration, this discussion will now point out that in different but interrelated ways FIL aims to improve distribution performance levels. As summarized in Figure 38, it will show that FIL leverages, in particular, the "sales support" capacities to run the information-processing means in a more customized manner and on a rather continuous basis. In this regard,

- FIL first of all manages an atmosphere that potentially favors the **formulation of instructions** in support of the actual distribution function.
- Secondly, within this wider procedure of providing information FIL runs sales trainings to transfer know-how to **build qualification** on the part of the distributing banks' sales force.
- Thirdly, it shows that FIL also introduces procedures to **receive feedback/ information** from autonomous banks on how distribution performance levels are evolving. With the permission of the external bank, this transparency is then leveraged by FIL to engage more directly in the distribution function.

This integrated procedure of indirectly as well as directly guiding the external banks' distribution activities underlines that FIL is keen on addressing the negative side effects lurking in such decoupled structures also by way of information-processing means.

Fig. 38: OVERVIEW OF INFORMATION-PROCESSING MEANS IN "MARKET"

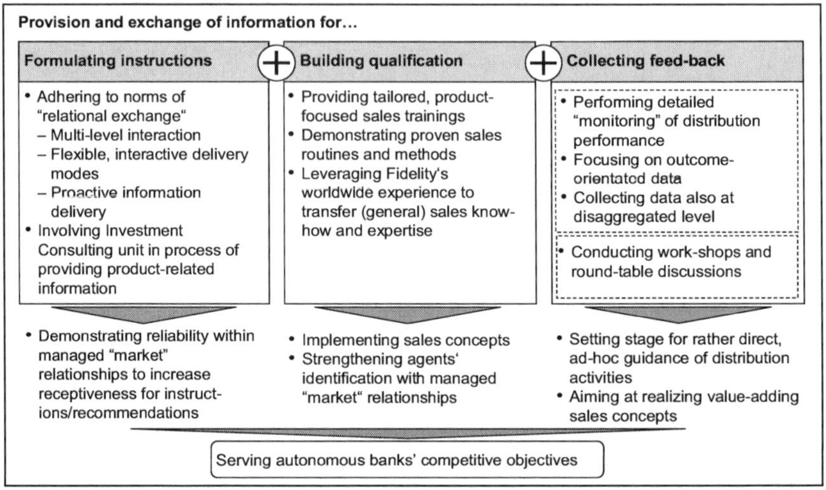

Source: Author

I) Formulating instructions

First of all, similar to the other case study dealing with decentralized arrangements for the distribution function, it shows that processes of providing information between the asset management firm and the distributing bank take place across a number of organizational levels. In other words, **FIL puts great emphasis on thorough multi-level interaction to deliver information to external banks**. The adoption of this norm of "relational exchange" indicates that information is not only exchanged between FIL and the autonomous banks at upper levels of management but also at the operational levels.

As far as the interactive exchange at the upper level for most of its agency-relationships is concerned, one sales manager pointed out that meetings between management committee members are held at least on an annual basis if not at a higher frequency. These meetings have the opportunity for FIL's and the respective bank's senior management to discuss and to resolve encountered difficulties, to set or refine performance level targets, and to outline action plans in order to eventually enjoy soaring inflow streams. Another sales manager stressed that this **involvement of senior management is critical for realizing the mutual benefits related to "market"-type of arrangements. These kind of agency-relationships need to have top management backing in order to be adequately introduced in the bank's branch network**. In addition to this interaction at upper levels, relationship managers are responsible for the more frequent, continuous provision and exchange of information at the operational level. In the light of the sales stimulation concepts introduced with the wider "sales support" capacities as well as the joint activities in "branding", these interactions predominately involve personnel from respective sales and marketing departments. With this multi-level interaction between FIL and the distributor, FIL aims to get the autonomous banks more deeply engaged in efforts to capture the [mutual] advantages related to this decentralized way of producing and marketing mutual funds to private investors.

Yet, concerning the regular provision of information at the operational level, asset management firms in general are increasingly facing the functionally relevant challenge that external distributors across the board increasingly prefer to deal directly with members of portfolio management teams to receive the relevant information first hand (Sector Analysis 2003b, p. 41). As illustrated above, the activities of the production function for mutual funds tend to be separated internally between the investment management units and the marketing and sales department. In general, the latter is primarily of charge for handling the interaction at the interface to distributors, which also includes the application of information-processing means. However, to adequately respond to this segment-wide growing demand to improve the quality and accuracy of product-related information, FIL management purposively implemented the so-called **Investment Consulting unit** in Germany at the beginning of 2004. This unit together with the marketing and sales teams now handles most of the interaction at the rather operational level. As one sales manager remarked this response has been highly appreciated by the external banks performing the distribution function on behalf of FIL.

The potential benefits to FIL of having this division in addition to the sales and marketing teams involved in the provision of information appear to be twofold. First of all, with the Investment Consulting unit assumed to possess the required technical know-how, FIL finds itself in a more credible position to meet the [rather purely product-focused] informational needs of the bank's respective so-called Fund-Selection-Unit. These Fund-Selection-Units of banks take the critical role of systematically screening the mutual fund offerings of the banks' [external] product providers in order to establish a so-called recommendation list. **From FIL's point of view, this recommendation list is of great relevance to strengthen inflow streams, as it tends to indirectly guide the behavior of banks' sale staff at the point-of-sale in their sales and advisory activities**. Secondly, the introduction of the Investment Consulting unit allows FIL's investment management teams to primarily focus on their main task, which is the management of mutual funds' assets.

With regard to the actual process by which the relevant sales information is delivered to external banks, FIL does not only fall back on one-way traffic to provide the sales material and information. As for the other two case studies of this enquiry, FIL is increasingly turning to more interactive formats. In the light of the trend towards on-demand-modes of information delivery, one sales manager pointed out that FIL is also increasingly relying on customized electronic mails to provide product-related information in addition to the standardized hard copies. By reacting to changes in information needs of the external banks in this way, **FIL demonstrates considerable levels of flexibility**. In turn, the application of this prominent norm of "relational exchange", at least in principle, is expected to trigger the same type of behavior on the part of the external banks.

Furthermore, **FIL goes to great lengths to adhere to the norm of sharing or delivering information in a proactive manner in its "market"-type of distribution arrangements in Germany**. The autonomous banks taking on the distribution function on behalf of FIL can expect to be informed about unforeseen developments that may affect their operations as soon as they start to surface. As also seen in the other case study of "partnership", FIL applies this norm of "relational exchange" most notably for two fields of information that are regarded as being of critical importance to external banks. In more precise terms, FIL delivers information proactively, in particular when fundamental issues emerge with regard to the investment performance of specific mutual funds and if key personnel within portfolio management teams are about to be replaced. Regarding the latter, one sales manager pinpointed the change of the portfolio manager for one of its blockbuster products at the beginning of 2004. The sales manager explained that before actually taking over the posting, the new portfolio manager was introduced to the distributing banks. This proactive approach allowed external banks to get to know the new person in charge, which helped FIL to maintain high levels of inflow streams for this specific mutual fund following the replacement of the previous portfolio manager.

All this shows that **FIL intends to establish an identity as a reliable exchange partner in the "market" type of distribution relationships with this design of providing relevant information and material.** Moreover, with the deliberate application of these norms of "relational exchange", it seems as if FIL is setting the stage to make external banks more attentive to the advice of sales concepts and trainings. In more precise terms, by adhering to multi-level interaction, flexible and proactive delivery of information, the autonomous bank is assumed to be more receptive to recommendations and instructions on how to perform the distribution function. From all this, it appears as if FIL finds itself in a more appropriate position to indirectly guide the external banks' selling activities, in this way coming to an adequate handling of the latent challenges of specificity and opportunism. Thus, the adoption of these norms potentially favors the formulation of instructions to the autonomous banks in support of their aspired competitive interests, which, in turn, is expected to facilitate FIL's prime objective of improving its distribution performance levels in Germany.

II) Building qualification

As indicated in the elaboration of the capacities in "sales support" as part of the systemic configuration, FIL also leverages the wider process of delivering information to transfer its expert knowledge to distributing banks to establish the relevant skill-set on the part of their sales staff operating at the point-of-sale. Given that Fidelity as a whole serves more than 19 millions investors around the world, it seems as if FIL is in a more than adequate position to have developed proven routines and methods for successfully marketing mutual funds. Sharing these experiences and expertise with the distributing banks potentially facilitates their efforts to accomplish a further improvement in their advisory services at large and, thus, to attain a more competitive positioning. Hence, from FIL's point of view, building qualification carries the opportunity to improve inflow streams by bringing the issues of specificity and opportunistic tendencies under control.

With regard to the extent to which FIL is able to offer this sales training to banks' sales staff, one sales manager emphasized that 3 of the larger autonomous banks performing the distribution function on behalf of FIL in Germany have agreed to grant comprehensive access for those qualification-building measures. Thus, although in some "market"-type of agency-relationships the autonomous banks refuse the external asset management firm far-reaching access to their sales staff to carry out this training, **FIL has managed to run these expertise-upgrading training programs in key agency-relationships**. Having the much sought direct contact to the sales staff who interact directly with private investors, FIL takes this chance to point out the proven actions to cope with the challenges FIL itself has encountered in other distribution channels and/or in other countries at the point-of-sale. In more detail, as one sales manager remarked, this sales training may center around a detailed presentation for a specific mutual fund, explaining the investment story and singling out the key selling points how this mutual fund suits the specific needs of private investors. Alternatively, these programs may take a broader focus, putting forward rather general methods on how to successfully perform distribution services for mutual funds. Irrespective of the type of sales training, being provided in a preparatory way with this kind of information, the banks' sales staff are predicted to be in a better position to independently handle difficulties emerging in the process of performing advisory services to private investors.

Hence, the demonstration of routines and methods tends to assist the external banks in realizing their competitive interests and, thus, contributes to the harmonization of goals between FIL and the autonomous banks. By indirectly guiding the banks' distribution activities in this way, FIL finds itself in an appropriate position to support autonomous banks in carrying the value-adding sales-stimulation concepts into their widespread branch networks. At the same time, even in the context of a "market"-type of arrangement, this buildup of qualification on the part of the banks' sales staff then also entails the chance to strengthen identification with FIL as external product provider and possibly even the internalization of its mutual fund offering. Ultimately, this is assumed to bolster FIL's distribution performance.

III) Collecting feedback

Complementing this use of the information-processing means to formulate instructions as well as to build qualification, FIL also turns to information-related procedures to collect some form of feedback from autonomous banks. As will be outlined, it is in particular one process of collecting information that is of critical functional relevance to FIL to achieve the aspired improvement in inflow streams. **The collection of data on banks' actual selling performance for FIL's product range takes a prominent part in FIL's design of the information-related processes**. Even though FIL also provides distributing banks with the opportunity to submit opinions and constructive ideas on how to raise the agency-relationships' overall proficiency, from a comparative perspective, it cannot be denied that this takes place in a less systematic manner. In the following section, therefore, the purpose is to elucidate in which way the design of these feed-back procedures allows FIL to guide the autonomous banks' distribution activities for its product range to improve the "cash inflow stream".

In general, the collection of data on performance levels as some form of "monitoring" hands the principal the chance to control for issues stemming from information asymmetry, most notably aberrant activities on part of the agent (Jensen and Meckling 1976, p. 307). As far as the design of **"monitoring"** is concerned, similar to the other two case studies, FIL focuses on outcome-oriented data. FIL concentrates on net inflow figures and the total volume of AuM in order to assess the actual distribution behavior. However, **FIL receives access to performance figures of a remarkably disaggregated nature,** which is in strong contrast to the case study of "partnership". One sales manager remarked that, given the extensive set of integrated "sales support" capacities [including the sales concepts], in some of its distribution arrangements FIL obtains a breakdown of performance data at the level of the banks' branches for FIL's product range. Moreover, there is a tendency that this sort of information is made available to FIL on a weekly basis. All this indicates that the autonomous banks deliberately give FIL the chance to dive into this disaggregated data to identify issues related to opportunistic tendencies and specificity. These are considered to be harmful not only to FIL's objective of bridging its performance gap but also to the banks' interests in truly realizing a more competitive positioning vis-à-vis distributing rivals.

Being provided with data of this kind, running "monitoring" processes allows FIL to perform a comparatively thorough benchmarking of the banks' respective distribution networks to identify those branches that appear to have difficulties in raising cash inflow streams from private investors for FIL's mutual fund offering. Thus, the purpose of this information exchange is not merely to give rewards to the autonomous bank as a whole or to single branches, but to introduce a fairly systematic controlling procedure, which sets the stage for some direct, rather ad-hoc type of guidance. In more specific terms, in the light of the Letter of Intent which tends to include some form of pledge in terms of distribution performance targets as well as the sales stimulation concepts, **this procedure is leveraged to enter into a dialogue with the respective autonomous bank on how to actually realize the mutual benefits inherent in the agency-relationship**.

Hence, taking a comparative perspective, **"monitoring"** of outcomes is designed in a way to actually guide the autonomous banks by feeding forward some direct assistance to reap the competitive benefits associated with decentralized arrangements. Thus, in case of an unsatisfactory development, the autonomous bank together with FIL tends to agree on some sort of intervention to be performed by FIL's sales teams [rather to redefine the terms of the contract for the "market" exchange]. As one sales manager explained, such an involvement can take the form of some more tailored sales training specifically for those branches, which appear to face impediments in raising strong inflows for FIL's mutual fund offering. This is then expected to favor FIL's ambition to bolster its own distribution performance levels as it provides the chance to more explicitly address issues of specificity and opportunism.

Regarding the extent to which this exchange of information is also leveraged to launch learning processes, one sales manager remarked, that so far a standardized and systematic way of collecting and processing distributing banks' suggestions and comments on how to create value-added is not in place. Nonetheless, FIL regularly invites banks performing the distribution function on behalf of FIL to round-table symposiums to discuss and share opinions regarding various topics and developments in the asset management sector in general and in particular with respect to the agency-relationships. Yet, quite in line with the very idea of a "market"-type of arrangement it seems that the main purpose at least until recently is not to systematically initiate interactive learning processes or to trigger continuous search-behavior on the part of external distributors in support of the "market" relationship. Therefore, **for this case study it appears as if there is a tendency that the detection of value-added opportunities is not based on joint-identification efforts but rather rests primarily on individual endeavors and experiences**. Still, value-added opportunities are of the greatest functional relevance in order to arrive at the aspired strengthening of inflows via a "market" type of structure, as FIL's sales stimulation concepts indicate. However, the process of identifying them jointly itself has so far been considered as playing only a minor role.

Overall, information-based processes are not only employed to formulate instructions and recommendations on how to perform distribution activities, or to transfer expertise in support of the advisory service. It shows that, even in the light of strong reliance on competitive self-interest [and, thus, on sufficient levels of self-monitoring], information-related procedures also cover the collection of information on the quality of the respective agency-relationships in order to perform some kind of "monitoring". In this regard, it becomes strikingly apparent that with the considerable transparency on distribution performance levels, which allows the principal to target more accurately issues of specificity and opportunism, an additional attempt is made to realize the mutual benefits of decoupled arrangements to produce and market mutual funds to private investors. The purpose of setting the stage to guide the distribution activities in a more direct, ad-hoc type of intervention is to further harmonize the banks' competitive objectives and FIL's own aspiration of increasing inflow streams. Thus, this procedure aims to further mobilize the self-interest of autonomous banks to perform the distribution function on behalf of FIL. However, as this sort of rather direct guidance is somewhat inconsistent with the genuine normative model of "market", **the employment of such**

measures indicates that FIL is potentially running the danger of giving up some of the efficiency advantages typically associated with decentralization.

4.3.2.2.2 Motivational Means for Process-Intervention

Regarding the internal fit problem, the discussion so far has outlined that in the context of the choice for some "market" type of arrangement, FIL has set up a systemic configuration to account for negative side effects related to specificity and opportunistic tendencies. Moreover, it has been put forward that to bridge the gap in distribution performance, FIL also falls back on information-processing means to facilitate the coordination within the arrangement. All this then indicates that though FIL's structure and process for its arrangements seem to be in line with the fundamental ideas of a market, it takes the form more of a managed or relational type of "market". In other words, while the design departs in some aspects from the classic type of market, which by its genuine definition relies on the "invisible" hand to coordinate economic activities, FIL in a consistent manner still attempts to bring into play and serve the competitive interests of autonomous distributors. Therefore, the purpose now is to clarify the additional measures the principal employs to further activate the desired distribution behavior on the part of the agents in order to achieve the aspired strengthening of cash inflow streams.

As outlined in the discussion on the systemic configuration, it is the restrictive assignment of [product-related] property rights resulting in a fairly discrete set-up of the value chain that considerably demarcates the frame in which activities are coordinated. **This rather limited transfer of [product-related] property rights to the distributing agents, in turn, accentuates the critical pressure on the principal to appropriately serve the agents' competitive interests**. Thus, the principal has to succeed particularly in favoring their rather short-term oriented profit-optimizing objectives to avoid being replaced by some competing asset management firms and to secure the adequate dovetailing of activities to successfully market mutual funds to private investors. In response to this imminent need to serve the agents' competitive interests, it has been outlined that it comes to the application of information-related means to mobilize and guide the agents' sales and advisory activities. However, as will be elaborated, FIL also attempts to trigger the advantages of "market"-type of arrangements through the explicit use of rather motivational means, despite relying on the self-interest of autonomous banks to optimize their product offering.

For this case study of a "market"-type of distribution arrangement, it shows, as outlined in Figure 39, that FIL most notably turns to opportunities from running actions in support of the actual distribution services to further activate the self-interest among external banks to perform the distribution function. As will be explained, these actions tend to involve considerable interaction between the principal and the respective agent and, therefore, will be referred to as **joint actions** in the following discussion. However, from a comparative point of view, there is the tendency that these joint actions in this case study exhibit a slightly less participative character than those discussed in the case of "partnership". In addition to these joint actions, FIL also provides **incentives** with the purpose of indirectly exerting influence on the distribution activities. All this then already points out that **FIL makes the attempt to promote and enforce the banks' willingness in a rather positive way**.

I) Engaging into joint actions

By way of undertaking activities together with the agent, Heide and John (1990, p. 24) argue that the principal is generally in a position to influence the agent's behavior and, thus, to inhibit opportunistic tendencies. As far as joint actions in this case study are concerned, it shows that once again the systemic configuration with the extensive buildup of capacities considerably lays the ground for the means by which FIL intends to trigger the desired levels of motivation on the part of external banks. In the light of the fairly discrete set-up of responsibilities along the value chain, it turns out that **the focus of these joint actions is mainly in support of the actual sales and advisory activities**, which is in slight contrast to the other two case studies. Therefore, the joint actions primarily aim to serve the banks' central competitive and economic benefits by leveraging the extensive buildup of distinctive capacities in "sales support" and "branding". In turn, this underlines that the strengthening of the distributors' role integrity

Fig. 39: OVERVIEW OF MOTIVATIONAL MEANS IN "MARKET"

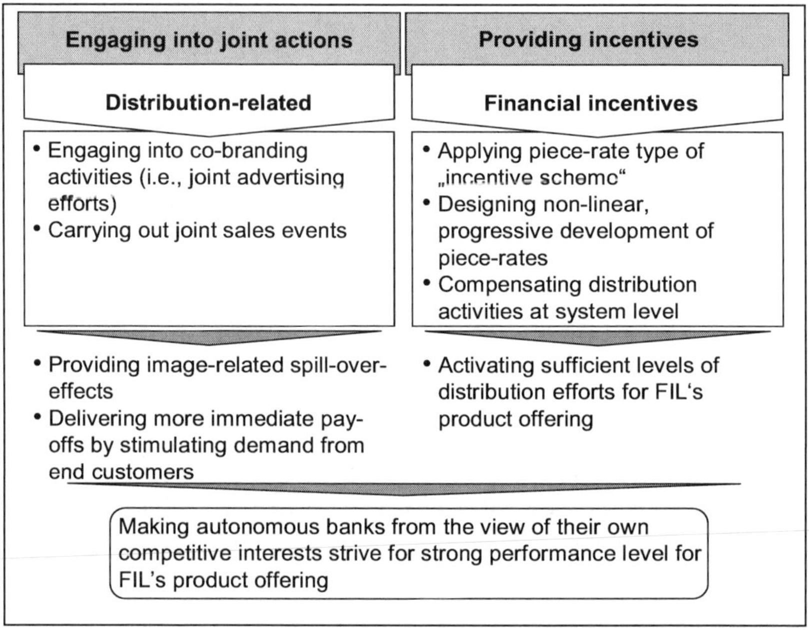

Source: Author

by offering extensive participation [in product-related decision-making processes] for motivating purposes plays only a minor role. However, there is no doubt that FIL also engages in a variety of discussions with external banks concerning product-focused questions such as product concepts and product designs.

Along those lines, FIL together with a number of selected distributing banks in Germany individually decides to plan, prepare, and carry out **joint advertising efforts** in various media channels, most notably in newspapers and magazines. These efforts involve **co-branding** to highlight the advanced degree of decentralization to produce and market mutual funds to private investors. In the light of FIL's extensive brand capacity, such co-branding activities are assumed to facilitate the provision of image-related benefits that in turn favor the distributing bank in attaining a more differentiated and, thus, enhanced competitive positioning. Hence, these **benefits related to co-branding activities include the chance to activate as well as maintain adequate levels of distribution efforts, as they are assumed to align the autonomous banks' competitive self-interest with FIL's ambition to improve its distribution performance levels**.

However, in the light of the "market"-type of arrangement, it shows that the parties to the exchange design this effort in a way to immunize themselves against opportunistic tendencies. **These "branding" activities are essentially of a multilateral character rather than of a bilateral nature, indicating that the parties to the distribution arrangement tend to deliberately abstain from significantly increasing dependence on a single transaction party** (Heide and John 1988, pp. 24-25). There is a tendency that not only FIL but in fact all asset management firms [with access to the distribution networks of respective banks] together with the bank engage in a single joint advertising effort. Thus, while this way of co-branding potentially provides image-related benefits to the respective autonomous bank, the switching costs (Monteverde and Teece 1982, pp. 206-207) to all parties turn out to be relatively moderate as the number of participants increases. In other words, this design tends to limit the ramifications of opportunistic tendencies.

In addition to those activities, FIL together with a number of distributing banks in Germany also engages in joint actions focusing more intensively on the actual point-of-sale to target in more tailored fashion the mutual benefits associated with the "market"-type of distribution arrangements. Generally, such actions may include the **placement of joint advertising in the banks' branches**. Furthermore, one sales manager pointed out that FIL and the respective bank may also set up and stage **sales events** to explain the product offering in more detail to the banks' end customers, thereby emphasizing the suitability of specific products to meet private investors' particular needs. One sales manager highlighted that these forms of joint actions entail the chance to trigger stronger demand from end customers and, thus, deliver immediate pay-offs. In principle, these activities increase the awareness among private investors for the banks' extended mutual fund offering and their endeavors to meet the growing demand for a more differentiated product choice. This is expected to strengthen the relationship between the respective bank and its customers. Ultimately, this increased customer orientation is assumed to benefit the autonomous bank in enjoying soaring cash inflow streams for mutual funds in general, but also for FIL' product offering.

Following on from this, it becomes evident that FIL aspires to mobilize the banks' self-interest to perform the sales and advisory activities by engaging most notably in distribution-related joint actions. These joint actions mainly aim to serve the banks' competitive interests to ensure desired levels of motivation, thereby bringing issues related to lurking opportunistic tendencies under control. Hence, it looks as if the focus of these activities under the regime of this "degree of decentralization" is primarily on the provision of more tangible and immediate, competitive-enhancing benefits to autonomous banks to incite their sustained willingness. In this regard, it also quite clear that role integrity and commitment on the part of the distributing banks induced through product-related joint actions is only of minor relevance for coping with issues of opportunism in the "market"-type of agency-relationships.

II) Providing incentives

As indicated above, in addition to those joint actions, by means of an **"incentive scheme",** further attempts are made to indirectly exert influence on the banks' distribution activities. As Katz (1971, p. 571) argues, the use of rewards assumes a critical condition to motivate the desired organizational behavior. Thus, at least in general, the principal is able to harmonize interest and to limit aberrant behavior on the part of agents by providing appropriate incentives. As far as these are concerned within FIL's design of its "market"-type of distribution arrangements, it turns out that FIL primarily relies on **financial, performance-related incentives** to guide the autonomous banks' distribution activities in an indirect manner. Once again it shows that the "incentive scheme" is based on the "monitoring" of outcome-orientated data and tends to be mostly of a rewarding character. Moreover, these incentives are primarily provided at the system-level of the respective agency-relationship.

In more specific terms, as pointed out in the discussion on the "contract design" within the structural set-up, distributors are entitled to receive some form of compensation for performing the sales and advisory activities. Generally, the actual level of **reimbursement** is calculated bottom-up considering the respective distribution performance for each single mutual fund for which the external bank as a whole has taken on the distribution function. [At the product-level] the compensation includes not only [**a proportion of] the load fee**, private investors are charged when they purchase a specific mutual fund, but also a **share of the management fee**, which represents the main revenue stream related to the offering of mutual funds. The absolute management fee is a function of the total AuM the autonomous bank has raised for a respective mutual fund. This implies that the bank's absolute level of compensation increases with the total volume it has raised from its customers. Hence, it shows that FIL aims to mobilize the banks' self-interest through applying a **piece-rate type of compensation** that rewards higher distribution performance levels.

Further underscoring its rewarding character, the "incentive scheme" generally includes a **non-linear slope in piece-rates**. In more precise terms, the actual percentage of the management fee transferred to the external bank tends to increase with the total level of AuM raised from private investors surpassing certain, agreed-upon thresholds. Hence, the absolute compensation to the distributing bank rises progressively with growing sales figures. Therefore, it shows that by providing financial incentives in such a staged way, FIL attempts to make the distributing banks, from the view of their own profit maximizing interests, to strive for strong distribution performance levels for FIL's product offering. Hence, this "incentive scheme" aims to indirectly exert influence on the behavior of the external bank through harmonizing the respective objectives. Concerning the concrete [percentage-] level, one sales manager remarked that vis-à-vis other asset management firms, FIL offers a competitive "incentive scheme", meeting more or less the segment-wide standard in Germany.

Moreover, in line with a far-reaching degree of decentralization, the **"incentive scheme" predominantly provides financial incentives at the system-level of the institutional arrangements**. In other words, as one sales manager explained, it remains in the scope of the autonomous bank to decide on how and to what extent this compensation is passed on to single divisions and/or to the actual sales staff performing the sales and advisory activities. With regard to the functional relevance of such an "incentive scheme" for improving its distribution performance levels, it shows that within this particular distribution channel segment [product-related] property rights are transferred only to a limited extent to the staff operating at the point-of-sale. In essence, the salary of the sales personnel directly interacting with private investors tends to include only a relatively small proportion of distribution-performance-related pay. Therefore, in the face of this somewhat watered-down reach of these financial incentives, as for the other case studies, it seems as if their employment aims to mainly maintain rather than intensively mobilize the external banks' interest to perform the distribution function for mutual funds. Along these lines, one sales manager stressed the limits of financial incentives in the distribution channel segment of banks. The sales manager argued that the **fee split needs to be competitive to get access to the distribution networks, but it is not viewed as a decisive measure to eventually realize inflow streams on a sustained basis**.

In summary, this discussion has brought to light that besides information-processing means FIL also deliberately falls back on motivating means in its "market" type of institutional arrangement to address the latent opportunistic tendencies. Hence, despite considerably relying on the autonomous banks' competitive objectives and their profit-maximizing interests, FIL employs further measures to guide the external banks' behavior through harmonizing interests. FIL most notably engages in joint actions in support of the actual distribution activities and also provides incentives. As outlined, these activities, which involve interaction with the external banks, primarily aim to favor their objectives of achieving stronger pay-offs and, thus, more tangible, competitive benefits. This kind of motivating assistance is expected to favor FIL's efforts to improve the "cash inflow stream" for its product range. Regarding the "incentive scheme", this discussion has put forward that FIL largely relies on financial rewards. However, with these incentives only reaching staff operating at the point-of-sale in a fairly diluted manner in this particular distribution channel segment, their efficacy to mobilize motivation to actively perform the distribution activities for FIL's mutual fund offering appears to be somewhat limited.

4.3.2.3 Towards the Efficacy of the Design of "Market"

For the internal fit problem, it is the consistency between the chosen "degree of decentralization" and the design of the institutional arrangement to coordinate activities that is critical to actually accomplish the optimization objective. Hence, according to the enquiry's framework of analysis, the design of the institutional arrangements needs to be set up in a consistent way to favor the generation of the aspired efficiency-enhancing effects. In this regard, the preceding elaboration has pointed out that even though deviating from the classic definition of "market" as organizational choice, **FIL's design appears to be set up in a consistent way to serve the distributors' competitive interests in some form of a managed and relational "market" arrangement, given the extensive use of process-related measures.**

The second fit problem accentuates the optimization-relevant requirement that the design appropriately accounts for the situational demands related to the specificity and lurking opportunistic tendencies. In this respect, the choice of "market" with its fairly discrete and specialized set-up along the value chain predominantly relies on the self-interest of parties to the exchange in optimizing their competitive positioning rather than on their genuine self-interest to cooperate. Therefore, according to the second fit problem, the design in terms of structure and process needs to aim at securing not only the autonomous banks' willingness to take on the distributing role on behalf of FIL but also their ability to actually accomplish the competitive objectives. In other words, to be in line with the fundamental idea of "market"-type of arrangements, the design has to establish the prerequisite that trigger and reinforce the notion of autonomous agents that is in their very own [short-term] profit-maximizing interest to perform sales activities for the principal's product offering. In this regard, by serving those considerations, the intention of the design's build-up is primarily to provoke the desired levels of self-steering behavior on the part of the distributing agents. However, given the considerable specificity inherent in the distribution function and the accentuated role of [short-term] competitive considerations, such a design remains extensively prone to the lack of ability and willingness on the part of the autonomous banks and their sales personnel spread across a large branch network. Therefore, the principal will have to turn to not only a context-setting systemic configuration but also to process-related measures. This then highlights a move away from a classic, spot-type of "market" exchange between anonymous parties towards a managed agency-relationship in a more relational setting.

Against this background, it important to find out that also in the case of FIL it is the introduction of the structural set-up with extensive and distinctive capacities that demarcates the frame within which it comes to the employment of process-related instruments. As elaborated, it shows that FIL turns not only to information-processing means but also to rather motivating measures to guide the autonomous banks' distribution activities. Regarding the **information-related procedures**, the purpose is to enable the external banks and their sales staff to appropriately advise FIL's product offering. By also encouraging their continuous willingness to perform the distribution services, FIL's aim is to strengthen the inflow stream for its product offering on a sustainable basis:

- By adhering to norms of "**relational exchange**" for providing relevant information to external banks FIL aspires to establish and secure an identity as a reliable exchange party, thereby reinforcing its position to articulate recommendations and instructions on how to carry out the distribution function
- By running procedures within its "**sales support**" to build qualification on the part of the external bank and its sales force, the attempt is made to ensure the necessary skills and know-how at the point-of-sale. These training efforts not only focus on specific mutual funds of FIL's product range but also on proven sales routines and methods as part of sales stimulation concepts to favor the autonomous banks' endeavors to attain a more differentiated and, thus, enhanced competitive positioning
- The regular exchange of information mainly focuses on feeding back performance-related information for "**monitoring**" purposes. It appears as if the procedure is designed in a way that allows FIL to run some quite thorough and detailed controlling of the actual distribution efforts performed by external banks
- Given this kind of informational exchange, the way is paved for some rather direct, ad-hoc type of assistance. In case of unsatisfactory performance evolvements that put the banks' objectives and FIL's own aspiration in danger, with the permission of the autonomous bank, FIL then feeds forward tailored support directly to single branches to bolster performance levels.

Hence, this **hands-on type of design of information-processing means** not only lays out the informational ground to enable the external banks but also mobilize the distributors' motivation to take on the distribution function on behalf of FIL. Moreover, with respect to the internal fit problem, it has become evident that in a simultaneous manner FIL also deliberately employs rather **motivational means** to further harmonize interests. This indicates that the mere provision of information is possibly not sufficient to secure continuous willingness and a strong inflow stream. Therefore, to fortify the notion on the part of external banks that is in line with their own competitive objectives to take on the distribution function for FIL's mutual fund offering, this enquiry brings to light the following points:

- FIL aims to offer image-related benefits to distributing banks by way of joint advertising efforts. Given that FIL is one of the leading brands in the asset management sector, this co-branding of producing and marketing mutual funds to private investors offers the chance for banks to enjoy differentiating spill-over effects
- Furthermore, FIL also attempts to trigger pay-offs and, thus, to provide more tangible economic benefits by engaging in activities in a rather immediate support of the sales and advisory activities at the actual point-of-sale, leveraging its extensive capacities for "branding" and "sales support". There is an [empirical] tendency that these activities entail the chance to stimulate strong demand from end customers for FIL's product offering, which is not only beneficial to FIL but also to the distributing bank
- Last but not least, FIL employs an **"incentive scheme"** that predominately provides financial, performance-related incentives at the system-level of the "market" relationship. This revenue-sharing primarily aims to account for the profit orientation of autonomous bank as a whole rather than to mobilize the banks' sales personnel operating at the point-of-sale

As outlined, it is the systemic configuration that brings into play the respective competitive objectives as the key underlying motive coordinating economic actions. To adequately meet these objectives the enquiry brings to light, that **the principal falls back on information-related means in conjunction with motivating measures to trigger**

the desired levels of self-interest of autonomous agents. In this regard, it shows that it is the interplay of not only providing information and mobilizing motivation but also of indirect and more direct, ad-hoc type of guidance that tends to reinforce the agents' attitude that it is to their own competitive benefit to actively take on the distribution function on behalf of this specific principal.

However, as already indicated, the discussion on FIL's design also argues that this set-up of structure and process is actually different from the classic definition of a "market". The deliberate application of process-related measures by FIL, which may even involve some form of direct intervention, points out that the mere reliance on competitive self-interest is possibly insufficient in the German context to improve distribution performance on a sustainable basis. Therefore, it seems as if FIL has deliberately opted to design a consistent type of managed "market" coordination-mode in order to account for the challenges related to the "service firm specificity" and "opportunism". Yet, although the employment of these process-based means tends to be efficacious in bringing these issues under control and facilitates improved inflows streams [already in the short term], it carries the danger of giving up [some of the] efficiency-enhancing effects typically associated with such an advanced "degree of decentralization".

Such a design of a managed "market" type of institutional arrangement for organizing the distribution function entails substantial [transaction] costs. These costs occur not only in terms of the structure-shaping investments in "branding" and "sales support", but most notably in running the process-related measures to exert influence on the agents' activities [to safeguard the capacities' efficacy]. In this respect, there can be no doubt that the application of situational, more direct interventional measure gives further rise to transaction costs. At the same time, however, it reduces the [short-term] risk of a lack in the agents' ability and/or willingness to take on the distribution function. Hence, in the light of the classical trade-off between efficiency and risks, it is in particular this move to offer and to carry out the rather direct, ad-hoc guidance that favors trimming down the danger of "hold-up". Along these lines then, as the upcoming discussion on the results will point out, whether a managed and relational "market" will bring about the aspired improvement of distribution performance levels is, in particular, driven by the quality of overall design, in terms of the structure with extensive capacities as well as the processes to appropriately leverage these to guide autonomous agents. This indicates that, also in this far-advanced "degree of decentralization", the set-up of the single action variables for governing the decoupled arrangement are critical to bridge the performance gap.

However, even with an internal design that is fairly consistent with that of a managed "market", this empirical study may face a situation in which the design may give rise to efficiency-concerns in terms of the actual out-of-pocket expenses for running the wide range of process-related measures and for serving the agents' [short-term] self-interests. This is assumed to take a critical optimizing-relevant role to successfully coordinate activities under the regime of such an advanced "degree of decentralization". Therefore, as far as the main optimization objective is concerned, this organizational design is then viewed to have the potential to bring about the desired strengthening of distribution performance levels. With its strong focus on mobilizing and securing the agents' competitive interests, this particular design in terms of both structure and process appears to be efficacious in handling the latent negative side effects. In the light of the considerably expanded customer reach, this specific way of organizing the distribution function bears the potential secure the desired improvement of "cash inflow stream". Yet, to what extent this approach also allows the principal to economize on the potentially increased scale will now be discussed in more detail.

4.3.3 Efficacy of Choice and Design of "Market"

Having discussed both fit problems concerning the institutional arrangement for the distribution function so far in a rather isolated but still interrelated way, the purpose now is to assess in a more cumulative manner to what extent distribution performance levels are enhanced. Therefore, the question to clarify is how choice and design in a simultaneous way favor the arrangement's efficacy in overcoming the perceived performance gap. In view of the overriding optimization objective, the aspiration is to elucidate in which way the chosen "degree of decentralization" and the buildup of the design positively impact the generation of "cash inflow stream". Therefore, the ambition is to ascertain if it comes to an adequate consideration of not only the "market dynamics" but also the challenges related to "opportunism" and "service firm specificity" inherent in the distribution function. From a wider normative perspective, by performing this integrated assessment, the enquiry aims to assess whether the external adjustments in combination with the internal design lead to the strengthening of the arrangement's efficacy to accomplish an improved "cash inflow stream".

Fig. 40: SIMULTANEOUS ASSESSMENT OF CHOICE AND DESIGN OF "MARKET"

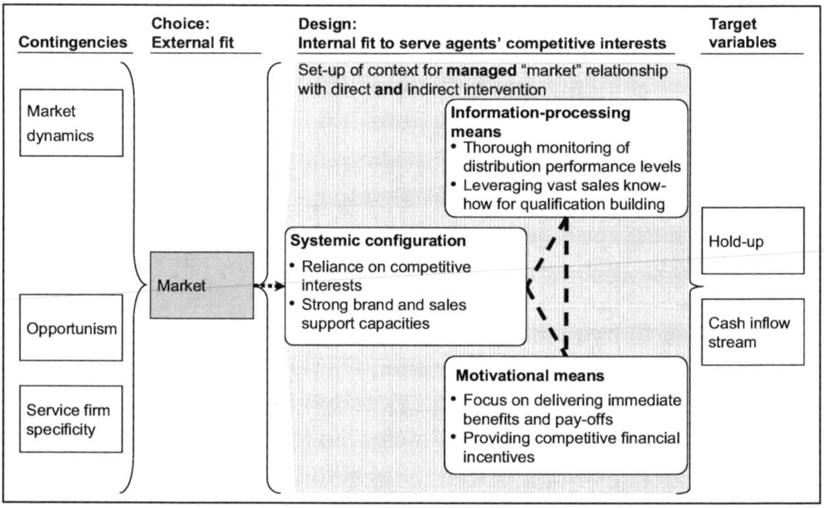

Source: Author

As far as this central choice and design problem is concerned, performing this assessment for the case of FIL is not easy as the implementation of choice and design in Germany still appears to be in a transitory period. Nevertheless, this elaboration on FIL's choice and designing decisions should be adequate to carry out the intended evaluation. Assessing FIL's approach against the criterion of classic contingency theory that requires sufficient consistency among the various components of the choice and design problem to accomplish efficiency-enhancing effects, this enquiry argues that FIL's choice carries some deficiencies which have implications for the largely consistent design of the agency-relationships.

In more specific terms, as summarized in Figure 40, this enquiry notes that driven by its founding culture, FIL makes the attempt to bridge the performance gap in Germany through turning to "market"-type of institutional arrangements. This is underlined by the rather restrictive assignment of [product-related] property rights and, thus, a fairly discrete allocation of responsibilities along the value chain. However, in the light of the remarkable application of process-related means, there can be no doubt that FIL, in fact, is running some managed type of "market", clearly indicating a departure from the normative model of "market". Therefore, **it appears as if the external adjustments to the distribution arrangement are somewhat incoherent in the face of the contingencies in Germany at the beginning of this century**. From a simultaneous assessment, when aiming at selling mutual funds through the distribution channel segment of banks it seems as if an organizational choice [and design] of the classic coordination model of "market" does not appropriately account for the challenges related to "opportunism" and "service firm specificity". As already elaborated above, an invisible hand of market control so far has not been fully established by the demand side for mutual funds, highlighting that **it is up to the asset management firm to actively compensate for the limited competitive forces in order to serve distributors' competitive interests**. As observed in this case study, **through adaptation in the internal design of the agency-relationship, the principal intends to adequately account for these impediments**. However, it requires some form of a corrective move in the internal design [towards a more managed relationship in terms of structure and processes], which gives rise to concerns that the principal has to give up [some of the] efficiency advantages related to such a far-reaching decentralization.

Nevertheless, this enquiry also stresses that given FIL's extensive capacities with the strong focus on both bringing into play and serving the autonomous banks' competitive objectives, there is a tendency to regard FIL's design as adequate for triggering an improvement in "cash inflow stream", vis-à-vis competing asset management firms at least in the imminent future. Hence, this assessment argues that while FIL's approach may trigger advantages associated with the expanded customer reach in the short to mid term. To what extent this is sustainable from a rather long-term perspective remains to be seen.

Fig. 41: DEVELOPMENT OF NET INFLOWS OF FIL RELATIVE TO MARKET TREND

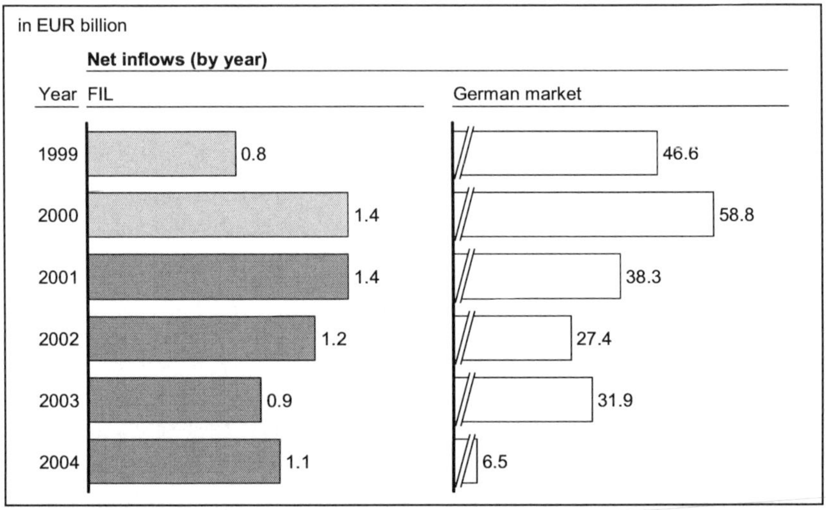

Source: Fidelity, BVI (2005)

Along these lines, concerning the efficacy of the managed "market" type of institutional arrangement, it becomes evident that FIL in Germany is enjoying comparatively strong distribution performance levels:

- FIL has been able to substantially increase the total AuM in Germany since the beginning of this century. AuM raised from private investors has grown significantly from EUR 5.2 billion in 2000 to EUR 9.3 billion to 2004
- While the recent recovery of global markets has contributed to this positive development, as illustrated in Figure 41, it is in particular the distribution performance that is driving this growth. In difficult market conditions with net inflows at the market level having evaporated considerably, FIL managed to raise a fairly constant stream of positive "cash inflow stream" throughout the beginning of this century
- Against the background of FIL's strategic aim of increasingly selling its mutual fund offering through the banking channel, FIL has succeeded in accomplishing this reorientation, as it is this particular channel segment that is spurring FIL's

recent positive development. Since 2001, each year the banking channel has contributed 70 percent or more to the "cash inflow stream" for FIL's product range

- Consequently, by 2004 this particular channel segment accounted for the largest share of the total AuM FIL has raised from private investors. In more precise terms, while the banking channel's contribution was only 7 percent in 1997, it rose to 54 percent in 2004

To what extent these "market" type of institutional arrangements have put FIL in the position to at least narrow or even bridge the noticed performance deficit vis-à-vis local competitors, it becomes apparent that since 2001 the gap to the leading asset management firms [in terms of AuM] has diminished more or less. As illustrated in Figure 42, in 2004 FIL's "cash inflow stream" in Germany is actually stronger than those of two domestic rivals. Diving into those figures, thereby taking a closer look at the development of the product-segment of **equity-based mutual funds**, the area in which FIL is mainly active, FIL has gained considerable ground since the beginning of this century vis-à-vis domestic asset management firms. **Since 2000, FIL has managed to gain market share in this particular segment due to a constant, segment-leading "cash inflow stream"**, moving up from seventh to fifth place in the ranking [in terms of AuM]. However, it also shows that it is not so much a striking improvement of FIL's distribution performance levels but rather the weakness of domestic competitors that has led to increasing similarity in performance levels. Thus, in this regard, it appears as if the managed "market" type distribution arrangements with autonomous banks allows FIL at least to maintain its overall performance levels in a challenging "market dynamics" and, thus, to overcome the difference compared with incumbent competitors. Hence, it looks as if the strong emphasis of FIL's choice and design on serving the agents' competitive objectives is considered as efficacious in leading to comparatively strong distribution performance at least in the short term.

Fig. 42: DEVELOPMENT OF NET INFLOW FIGURES RELATIVE TO DOMESTIC COMPETITORS

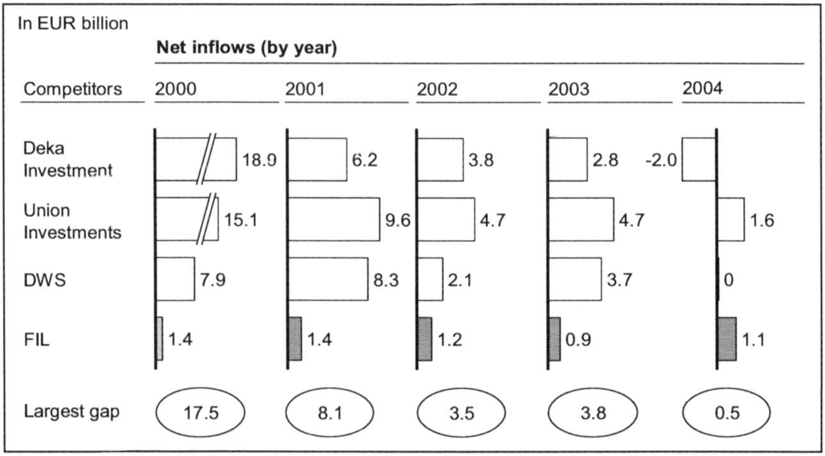

Source: Fidelity, BVI (2005)

However, despite this positive trend, from a comparative perspective, this enquiry also argues that **it seems as if FIL's structure and process entail shortcomings, implying that FIL's foregoes further efficiency-enhancing potential**. As mentioned before, this elaboration indicates that in the light of the incongruent organizational choice, FIL has to give up efficiency advantages inherent in decentralized arrangements in order to [actively] secure inflow streams into its mutual funds. Moreover, in the light of the so-far limited cooperation of a genuine kind between FIL and the autonomous banks that goes beyond the scope of the initial exchange to market mutual funds to private investors, it appears as if not all organizational options for strengthening distribution performance levels have been fully explored yet. Therefore, as a concluding remark, despite the already positive development FIL enjoys, this enquiry argues that FIL's unarguably extensive capacities tend to be underutilized with this organizational choice. The enquiry holds the view that, by increasing levels of participation along the value chain, there is further growth potential for FIL in the German private investor market.

Fig. 43: SUMMARY OF CASE STUDY ON FIL IN GERMANY

Organizational Choice	• Throughout the 1990s FIL enjoys positive development since entering German market in 1992 mainly through "market" type of arrangements with IFAs • However, FIL management notices gap to leading local competitors and considers the channel segment of banks to be most promising for bridging difference • In line with Fidelity's wider founding culture, FIL management clings to its traditional choice and aims at establishing "market" type of institutional arrangements with German banks
Organizational Design	• FIL falls back on a menu of contracts to assign [product-related] property rights in fairly restrictive kind, bringing into play competitive interests to coordinate activities along the specialized set-up of the value-chain • This coordination form is accompanied by strong capacities in brand and sales support to set the context for application of more process-related measures, highlighting the managed and relational character of the "market" relationships • Within the information-processing means, thorough monitoring and qualification building take a central role and may even entail rather direct, ad-hoc guidance of distribution activities to strengthen distribution performance • Within motivational means to harmonize interests, FIL is in the position to leverage its strong brand to offer image-related spill-over effects as well as to set free immediate pay-offs through stimulation of demand from end customers
Target Variables	• Despite difficult market conditions in Germany, FIL managed to continue its expansion via "market" type of arrangements with autonomous banks • Gap in distribution performance levels is bridged or narrowed to major local competitors • However, extensive efforts to manage "market" relationship hint at inconsistent fit relations and give rise to concerns that efficiency-advantages may not be fully unleashed

Source: Author

4.4 Summary of Case Studies

To conclude this chapter, the enquiry will now shortly summarize the salient [functional-relevant] findings for each of the three case studies in a comparative manner. From an empirical point of view, this résumé is meant to pave the way for the upcoming discussion towards the identification of an optimized distribution system in order to adequately address the enquiry's central research questions and its propositions.

Following the enquiry's overriding objective to clarify with which adaptations to their distribution systems [in terms of organizational choice and design] asset management firms can secure a best possible response to changing "market dynamics", this enquiry has established some staged, rather step-wise structure in its framework of analysis. This framework is applied to study agency-relationships between asset management firms [principal] and banks [agent] to market mutual funds to private investors under different governance regimes. In line not only with the classic NIE spectrum of institutional arrangements but also with the more recent developments in the German market for organizing these agency-relationships, this enquiry distinguishes between "hierarchy" [the case of DekaBank], "partnership" [the case of Julius Bär Asset Management] , and "market" [the case of Fidelity Investments].

As far as the organizational adaptations are concerned, the enquiry's study reveals that in the face of the "market dynamics" in Germany, **each of the asset management firms refrains from transformational adjustments to the organizational choice in terms of the "degree of decentralization". Instead, in rather small incremental but deliberate steps, respective management focuses mainly on introducing changes to the organizational design to strengthen the "cash inflow stream"**. Regarding the design of the different organizational choices, the empirical study brings to light that the **case studies exhibit [systematic] variation along the systemic configuration, information-processing means, and motivational means**, which highlights the considerable differences across the single variables conceptualized in the enquiry's framework of analysis.

Fig. 44: COMPARATIVE SUMMARY OF SYSTEMIC CONFIGURATION

Degree of decentralization (increasing from Hierarchy to Market)

	Hierarchy	Partnership	Market
Screening	• No screening performed to clarify motives of distributing owners	• Information exchange within negotiation phase used to verify distributors' motives	• Menus of contracts used to give distributors chance to make pledges and to signal commitment
Contract design	• Full transfer of property rights to distributors but resulting in diluted allocation within group of in-house distributors (due to ownership model)	• Far-reaching transfer of [product-related] property rights to distributing partner for offering scope for considerable participation along value chain	• Restrictive transfer of property rights to distributors underlining discrete allocation of responsibilities along value chain
Branding	• Extensive branding efforts targeting mainly end customers • Provision of image-related benefits to in-house distributors through specific design of brand communication	• No distinctive profile as asset management due limited branding efforts therewith lacking prerequisite for providing wide image-related spill-over effects to distributors	• Focused brand-building to mainly reach distributors but also end customers • Strong emphasis on asset management capabilities in brand communication
Sales Support	• Catalogue of comprehensive sales support in place to assist distributors in sales and advisory activities • Centralized units in place to stage sales trainings and events	• Extensive sales support available with focus on tailored information provision and build-up of qualification on part of distributors' sales staff	• Sales support capacities arranged according to different needs of distributors • Provision of sales concepts to serve competitive interests of distributors

Source: Author

Regarding the **systemic configuration**, as known from the detailed discussion of each case study, the "contract design" with its transfer of property rights plays a central role in setting up the fundamental coordination mode between principal and agent. Following some "screening" efforts, this allocation of property rights tends to be accompanied by further structure-shaping capacities in "branding" and "sales support" to establish the required cognitive and motivational prerequisite to account for the side-constraints related to "service firm specificity" and "opportunism". Along the summary, outlined in Figure 44, this enquiry emphasizes the following key findings:

- For the enquiry's case study of a **"hierarchy"**-type of relationship, considerable difficulties emerge to establish a type-consistent internal design. Despite the full transfer of property rights to the group of distributors as a whole as an attempt to manifest their [backward] integration, the resulting allocation of these rights appears to be considerably diluted within the group of distributors. Therefore, despite considerable "branding" efforts and centralized capacities for "sales support," this particular arrangement seems to suffer from some structure-driven deficit in the commitment of the distributing members in the "hierarchy". As mentioned, it appears as if the principal is facing some self-blocking situation to secure at least standard role behavior.
- In line with a consistent design of a **"partnership"**-type of coordination mode, the principal in the enquiry's second case study offers considerable scope for participation to distributors to promote their self-interest to cooperatively take on the distributing role. By focusing on building qualification rather than to merely transfer product information, capacities in "sales support" are designed in a way to additionally raise the agents' identification with the agency-relationship. However, inconsistent with a "partnership"-type of relationship, it looks as if this principal is not [always] able to offer prospects of image-related spill-over effects to further facilitate self-induced [extra] role behavior on the part of distribution partners. Due to limited "branding" efforts, no distinctive profile as an asset management firm is established in Germany.
- Corresponding to a **"market"**-type of institutional arrangement, the principal only transfers property rights to a relatively restricted extent to distributing agents, thereby relying on their [short-term] competitive interest to perform the

distribution function. To further mobilize and serve these interests, this asset management firm with great care engages in focused brand-building measures to carve out a strong reputation as an asset management firm not only in the mindset of distributors but also of private investors. However, the principal does not exclusively rely on the invisible hand of the "market" to achieve a strong "cash inflow stream", indicating that competitive forces are not sufficiently strong to bring the choice-specific side-constraints under control. Rather in contradiction to a "market"-type of coordination mode, this asset management firm also starts to provide "sales support" in the form of sales concepts to actively serve the distributors' competitive interests, in this way opening the door to some more direct [process-related] guidance of the distribution activities. This underlines the, in fact, managed and relational character of the "market"-orientated agency-relationships.

These designs of the systemic configuration demarcate the frame for introducing and running more on-going, process-related measures to bring distribution systems to full strength. As far as the **information-processing means** are concerned, from a comparative point of view it shows that based on the systemic configuration in each case study, the main focus appears to [systematically] vary with which approach the principal attempts to establish mainly the cognitive prerequisites for strong distribution performance levels. Along the summary in Figure 45, the enquiry brings to light the following points:

- In the **"hierarchy"**-type of institutional arrangement, the formulation of plans and [input-orientated] instructions mainly takes place via bureaucratically-shaped processes, most notably via a number of institutionalized committees. This is accompanied by regular provision of information, which also includes efforts to transfer the required skill-set to the distributors' sales staff operating in direct interaction with private investors. Quite in line with a "hierarchy"-type of coordination mode, these processes also involve considerable "monitoring" activities at comparatively disaggregated levels, while [joint] learning processes and proactive information delivery play rather a minor role in guiding the distribution behavior.

Fig. 45: COMPARATIVE SUMMARY OF INFORMATION-PROCESSING MEANS

	Degree of decentralization		
	Hierarchy	**Partnership**	**Market**
Relational exchange	• Running institutionalized committees with multi-level interaction for formulation of plans and instructions • Performing flexible and regular provision of information • Running "strategy circles" and workshops to exchange information	• Securing multi-level interaction to get distribution partners actively involved in relationship • Ensuring flexible and proactive information delivery to create trust-based atmosphere • Running systematic/ extensive two-way communication processes to trigger search-behavior and value guidance	• Running multi-level interaction to secure distribution success • Ensuring flexible and proactive information to emphasize reliability • Conducting round-table discussions for information exchange
Sales Support	• Providing tailored, product-focused sales trainings • Transferring required skill-set to carry out distribution activities for fund offering	• Providing tailored, product-focused sales trainings • Demonstrating proven sales methods to build qualification, thereby raising and identification	• Providing tailored, product-focused sales trainings • Leveraging own sales know-how for introducing sales concepts serving distributors' competitive interests
Monitoring	• Collecting outcome-data at disaggregated level • Performing detailed controlling of distribution results	• Receiving outcome-data at system-level • Relying on self-monitoring of distributing partners	• Starting to obtain access to outcome-data beyond system-level • Maintaining discrete allocation of responsibilities but applying monitoring-insights for direct, ad-hoc type of guidance

Source: Author

- For the **"partnership"**-type of agency-relationship, the information-processes are designed in such a way not only to enable the distributing partners to appropriately take on the assigned property rights but also to promote a positive attitude towards the relationship and behavior beyond the line of duty. In accordance with the very idea of "partnership", considerable focus rests on the buildup of qualifications through the demonstration of proven sales routines as well as on systematic two-way communication to trigger search-behavior and some form of value guidance. In line with a "partnership"-type of coordination mode as well, the principal does not allocate resources to engage in "monitoring" of distribution outcomes beyond the system-level. Instead, in the light of the assumed agents' self-interest to cooperate, the principal considerably relies on self-monitoring of agents to secure a relationship-strengthening improvement in distribution performance levels.
- In the managed **"market"**-type of institutional arrangement, the information-processing means predominantly focus on serving the distributors' competitive interests. Norms of "relational exchange" are designed in a way to essentially support the introduction of sales concepts, which aim to help distributors in strengthening their competitive positioning vis-à-vis distributing rivals. Based on its own sales know-how picked up in other markets, the principal intends to assist the distributing agents in acquiring, developing, and retaining their customer base. Further highlighting the managed character of the [still] "market"-type of agency-relationships, the principal is starting to obtain access to performance-outcome data beyond the system-level to selectively intervene in the actual distribution activities.

Besides these information-processing means, asset management firms also turn to a variety of **motivational means** as further attempts to activate the desired role behavior on the part of distributing agents. As summarized in Figure 46, from a comparative point it shows once again that there are considerable differences in the way the principals seek to overcome the choice-specific side-constraints, related in particular to challenges of "opportunism". In this regard, key findings are:

- In the **"hierarchy"**-type of agency-relationships, the principal traditionally has relied on system-rewards in its "incentive scheme" to secure distributing members' standard role behavior. Yet, it becomes apparent that the asset management firm additionally has started to introduce some performance-related components in the "incentive scheme" at the system-level to more directly reward strong distribution efforts. While these attempts pinpoint difficulties in the traditional approach to secure at least standard role behavior [due to the diluted distribution of property rights within the group of distributors], they also indicate the inconsistency in the organizational design of "hierarchy" observed in this case study.
- In accordance with far-reaching transfer of property rights in **"partnership"**-type of agency-relationships, the offer to distributing agents to participate along a variety of activities [particularly in questions regarding the product design itself] operates as an important means to strengthen their identification with the relationship and to motivate extra [distribution] role behavior. This is backed up by some performance-related pay at the system-level and the staging of some sales events to further promote their willingness to cooperate. However, it shows that due the limited buildup of "branding" capacities the principal is only to some extent able to offer image-related spill-over effects to distributors via bilateral co-branding activities. It seems that the design misses an important motivational lever to guarantee long-term binding effects.
- In line with the very idea of **"market"**-type of institutional arrangements, the principal particularly aims to meet the [short-term] profit-maximizing interests of the distributors. For this case study on a managed "market", it shows that the asset management firm runs sales events to rather immediately stimulate demand from end customers and participates in mainly multilateral co-branding activities to allow the distributor to gain a more differentiated competitive positioning. Last but not least, performance-related pay is placed at the system-level to essentially make autonomous banks, from the view of their own competitive interests, strive for a strong "cash inflow stream" for the principal's product offering.

Fig. 46: COMPARATIVE SUMMARY OF MOTIVATIONAL MEANS

Degree of decentralization →

	Hierarchy	Partnership	Market
Relational Exchange		• Offering participation in questions regarding product design in accordance with transfer of property rights to strengthen identification	
Sales Support	• Organizing sales event to create demand from end customers for mutual fund offering	• Developing sales events to create demand from end customers thereby raising identification with relationship	• Running sales evens to secure rather immediate payoffs, thereby serving competitive interests of distributors
Branding	• Adjusting product name to particular distributor in advertisements at point-of-sales to raise sales staff's identification	• Engaging into bilateral co-branding efforts to offer image-related spill-over effects	• Participating in multilateral co-branding activities to support distributors' aim for differentiation
Incentive scheme	• Providing system-rewards but introducing also performance-pay at system-level • Staging tournaments to reach distributors' sales staff	• Offering performance-pay at system-level to strengthen distributors' willingness to cooperate	• Offering performance-pay at system-level to meet profit-maximizing interests of distributors

Source: Author

With regard to the **"cash inflow stream"** the respective principals have been able to generate for their mutual fund range, this enquiry is able to observe sustained trends for the different coordination modes. For the case studies analyzed, this empirical study finds:

- In the **"hierarchy"**-type of institutional arrangement the generation of inflow streams into the mutual fund offering becomes increasingly difficult, despite the enormous distribution power of the distributing members of the "hierarchy" as a whole. As Figure 46 outlines, since the emergence of critically evolving inflow figures in 2001, distribution performance levels have in fact continued to deteriorate. By 2004, this negative trend has reached such an extent that the principal is even confronted with outflows for its product offering.
- The principal in the **"partnership"**-type of agency-relationships is also facing considerable obstacles to accomplish at least positive distribution performance levels in Germany. While enjoying strong growth at the global level with this form of a coordination mode, the empirical study shows that, in the German context, the principal overall has had to accept outflows for its mutual fund offering since 2003. However, by diving into these overall negative figures, it becomes apparent that when the principal is in a position to adequately serve the distributors' competitive interests the "partnership"-type of agency-relationships tend in fact to contribute a positive inflow stream.
- Under the regime of a **"market"**-orientated institutional arrangement, this particular principal has been able to more or less maintain its distribution performance levels, despite challenging "market dynamics" in the German asset management sector. It shows that this asset management firm has managed a constant positive inflow, in particular, into its equity-based mutual funds. This has allowed the principal to gain further ground vis-à-vis domestic competitors in this mutual fund segment.

Fig. 47: COMPARATIVE SUMMARY OF "CASH INFLOW STREAM"

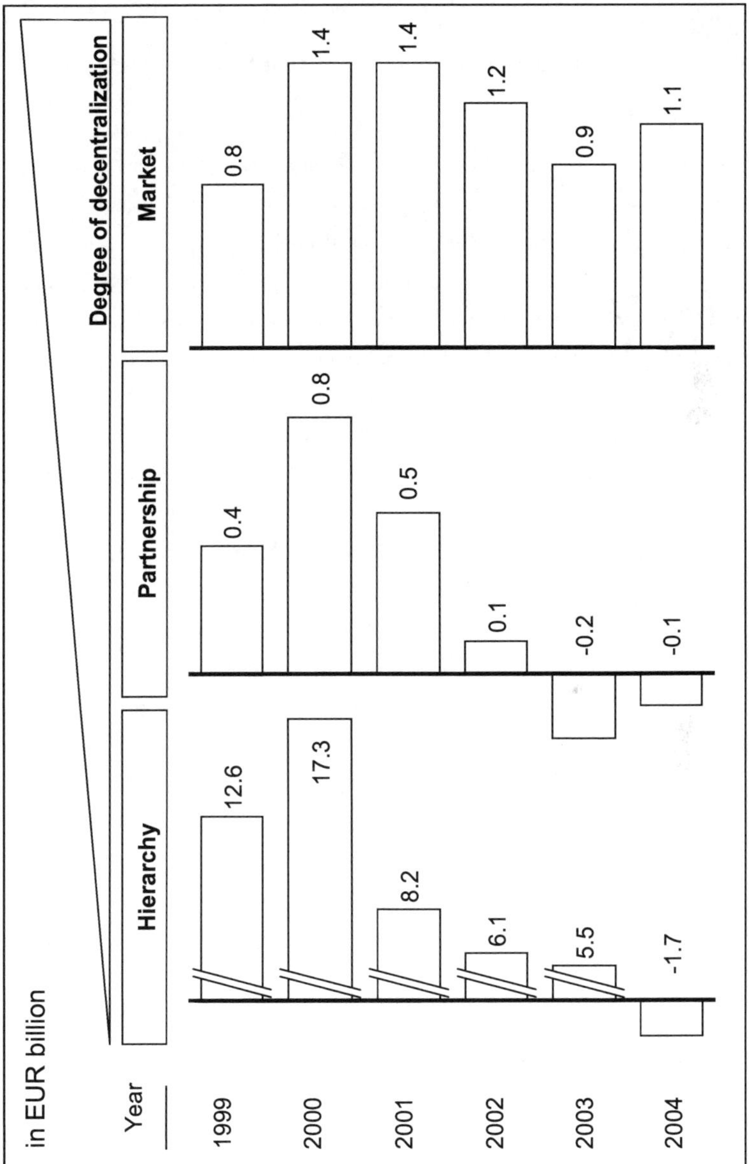

Source: DekaBank Annual Reports, Julius Bär Annual Reports, Fidelity

Chapter 5: Towards Identifying an Optimized Distribution System

Previous research on the drivers of inflow streams for mutual funds has mainly centered on product-related characteristics, such as past investment performance or price components. Questions regarding the organizational choice and design for marketing mutual funds to private investors have been mainly treated as a black-box so far. With the aspiration to shed light on this blind spot, this enquiry largely draws on NIE-arguments of strategic marketing as well as perspectives from the realm of organizational design theories for the derivation of an appropriate framework of analysis. By applying a comparative multi-case study methodology, this empirical study is confident of securing an adequate level of external validity for its findings. From a sampling point of view, although inspired by the NIE-typical distinction, this enquiry claims to be able to capture the representative spectrum mirroring the significant developments in the German private investor market by focusing the analysis on the elaboration of case studies of "hierarchy", "partnership", and "market". Thus, through applying this comparative type of research methodology as strictly as possible, **the enquiry is confident of arguing that the diverging results on the framework's task variables can be ascribed to a systematic variation in the organizational choice and design, against a somewhat uniform context**. This essentially favors this study's ambition to translate the empirical findings into general guidelines on how to accomplish optimized distribution systems for mutual funds in Germany. Hence, in the light of the enquiry's practical-normative perspective, the intention is now to establish optimization-relevant guiding principles for the choice and design problem confronting asset management firms from a rather meta-theoretical point of view.

As discussed in considerable detail, the overriding objective of this enquiry is to clarify with which adaptations to the institutional arrangement for marketing mutual funds to private investors, asset management firms secure a best possible response to the "market dynamics" at the turn of the century. This entails not only questions regarding an optimal organizational choice in terms of the "degree of decentralization" but also on how to design the chosen coordination mode to account for side-constraints related to "opportunism" and "service firm specificity" arising with the organizational choice. Therefore, as far as the implications to management are concerned, this discussion towards identifying an optimized distribution system on the basis of the comparative institutional analysis will, first of all, turn to the choice problem before outlining guiding principles for the designing decisions. This will be followed by the clarification of the institutional arrangement's overall efficacy regarding the optimization objective and the relative functional importance of the framework's fit-requirements. Last of all, this enquiry will conclude by putting forward a perspective on the theoretical implications of this empirical investigation, thereby outlining opportunities for further research.

5.1 The Optimal Organizational Choice

Regarding the development of a decision-making model to optimize distribution systems, this enquiry is inclined to argue that a choice in favor of **an advanced "degree of decentralization" provides asset management firms with the opportunity to regain distribution performance levels**. In the face of the fundamental "market dynamics" since the beginning of this century, with the asset management sector exhibiting hardly any growth and distributing banks showing diminishing loyalty to their in-house asset management firms, such a choice appears to offer the best possible chance to improve the "cash inflow stream" on a sustainable basis. However, a trend towards an advanced "degree of decentralization" does not bring about the prospect of translating expanded customer reach into a "cash inflow stream" in an unconditioned manner. Also in this enquiry's decision-making context, **there is no such thing as a free lunch**. With any decision regarding the organizational choice being exposed to various side-constraints, this enquiry considers more explicitly the challenges related to "opportunism" and "service firm specificity". In this view, it becomes apparent that control through the invisible hand of the "market" is not genuinely present in the German context. Although private investors increasingly demand more choice in the mutual fund assortment offered by distributing banks, they, in general, still lack the education to truly impose control on the actual sales and advisory activities performed by distributors' personnel at the point-of-sale. **Hence, quite in line with classic NIE reasoning, there is the tendency to conclude that the optimal organizational solutions rest** not on a "market"-type of institutional arrangement but rather **on a "partnership"-type of agency-relationship between asset management firm and distributing bank**. Such an intermediary approach appears the most efficacious in triggering the advantages of decentralization, while efficiently curbing the latent negative side effects.

This argumentation finds considerable support across the case studies, in particular when a more long-term perspective is adopted. A "partnership"-type institutional arrangement with its far-reaching delegation of property rights to distributing partners seems comparatively more efficacious in strengthening their commitment and identification with the relationship as a whole. In contrast to the rather discrete allocation of responsibilities along the value chain for producing and marketing mutual funds to private investors under the regime of "market" or "hierarchy", it is most notably the offer of participation that sets the stage to activate extra role behavior on the part of the agents [in the sense of extended search-behavior in support of the agency-relationship]. With such self-induced willingness to cooperate being established, the [joint] identification of value-creation opportunities to raise the proficiency of the relationship takes a much more prominent role in the interaction between principal and agent. This is expected to eventually translate into an increased likelihood of capturing market share in difficult market conditions. Furthermore, given the agents' self-interest to advance the relationship as a whole to higher performance levels, this enquiry shows, the principal's need to control the agents' activities then focus mainly on indirect guidance, absorbing only relatively few resources [i.e., personnel] to continuously manage the distribution systems. In other words, to market mutual funds to private investors, **it looks as if a choice in favor of a "partnership"-type of institutional arrangement may result in relatively low transaction costs in comparison to alternative coordination modes**. These costs may even further decline in the long term if the agents' identification with the relationship is truly manifested. However, in order to enjoy these optimizing effects, the principal also needs to adequately serve the competitive interests of the, in fact, quite powerful distributing partners as they own the relationship to end customers. Thus, if profit considerations, in other words, rents are not sufficiently met in the short term as well as in the long term, the principal will run the risk of not bringing a "partnership"-type of distribution system to full strength, meaning that a sustainable improvement in the "cash inflow stream" is unlikely.

In this regard, the comparison along the different choices of the "degree of decentralization" then reveals that a **"market"-type of institutional arrangement** [almost per se] is supposed to deliver superior performance outcomes at least in the short term. Yet, given the latent negative ramifications of "opportunism" and the "service firm specificity" and the limited presence of market control in Germany, **it looks as if it is largely up to the principal to actively ensure that the distribution system is producing adequate performance levels**. Thus, being exposed to this need to continuously manage and adjust the "market"-type of agency-relationship, it seems that the principal has to give up some of the advantages traditionally associated with such far-reaching decentralization. In order words, **the view is that the principal is facing comparatively high transaction costs under the regime of some form of a "market" to secure a strong "cash inflow stream" into its product range**. Hence, adopting some more long-term orientation, this enquiry is confident to conclude that this "degree of decentralization" to market mutual funds to private investors in Germany can hardly be considered as the most efficient organizational solution from the standpoint of an asset management firm. From a genuinely comparative point of view, a mere reliance on market forces, without fundamentally raising the agents' identification and [search] behavior in support of the relationship, appears inadequate to optimize distribution performance levels on a sustainable basis.

Concerning the rather traditional organizational choice in Germany for arranging the specialized set-up to produce and market mutual funds, this enquiry reveals that a choice in favor of a "hierarchy"-type of coordination mode tends to require considerable coordination efforts for the asset management firm. This already holds true to secure just standard role behavior on the part of distributing members. In the light of common backward integration of distributors into asset management operations in Germany, these distributors not only own the relationship to end customers but also enjoy considerable decision-making freedom on how to structure their product offering. With large number of outside-options [i.e., external asset management firms] available to distributors and willing to serve their [short-term] profit-maximizing interests, this enquiry shows that substantial resources are already needed only to keep distributing members within the "hierarchy". Therefore, speaking in more theoretical terms, **while a "hierarchy"-type of coordination mode already by its definition tends to entail high out-of-pocket expenses to run the system, it appears as if the "market dynamics" give further rise to these transaction costs**. This, in turn, encourages this enquiry to conclude that this coordination mode seems rather inefficient vis-à-vis a "partnership"-type of institutional arrangement for improving the "cash inflow stream" on a sustainable level.

Following on from all this, **there are indications that a "partnership"-type of institutional arrangement represents the optimal organizational choice for marketing mutual funds to private investors in Germany**. However, in view of the staged approach within the enquiry's framework of analysis, **the optimizing effect of the choice of the "degree of decentralization" is assumed to be moderated by decisions concerning the design of the chosen coordination mode**. Therefore, after having elaborated on the optimal external fit in the wake of the "market dynamics" in Germany, this discussion now turns to the internal adjustments in order to appropriately mitigate issues of "opportunism" and "service firm specificity".

5.2 The Optimal Organizational Design

The theoretical background of NIE rather implicitly assumes institutional arrangements are set up in a choice-consistent way. This, however, is not assumed as given in the design-theoretical perspective of this enquiry's framework of analysis. Instead, it explicitly requires the internal design of the agency-relationship to be consistent with the chosen "degree of decentralization" to activate the advantages related to the organizational choice. Therefore, to set the stage for an overall assessment of institutional arrangements, it is essential to consider how the design of the agency-relationship is set up alongside the choice-decision. The enquiry's framework argues that it is of decisive functional relevance as to what extent the principal is able to establish a type-consistent pattern of steering measures on the basis of the chosen "degree of decentralization" [with its underlying transfer of property rights]. Therefore, the key matter of interest is whether and in which way the principal is able to establish the necessary cognitive and motivational prerequisites [in terms of the systemic configuration and processes] on the part of distributing agents to guide a strong "cash inflow stream" into the principal's product offering. In other words, as far as the development of a decision-making model is concerned, **the optimizing-relevant point is if the design is able to secure the ideal type of behavior of agents, despite the side-constraints arising with organizational choice**.

Along those lines, for the outline of the decision-making model, it is essential to specify the conditions under which the principal meets the optimizing-relevant internal fit-requirement. In accordance with the literature on alternative modes for the coordination of economic activities, this study turns to the different "archetypes" of "hierarchy", "partnership", and "market" across its case studies. Therefore, as far as the analysis of the internal fit is concerned, based on the different choice-decisions of the "degree of decentralization," a systematic variation in the organizational design becomes visible regarding the attempts to exert influence on the agency-relationship. As laid out, following the different degrees of transferring property rights, the fundamental emphasis in structuring and running the institutional arrangements aims to bring into play the incentive-effect of membership and ownership, far-reaching scope for participation, or the mere profit-maximizing interests of distributing agents, respectively.

In this regard, for the enquiry's case study on **"hierarchy"**, attempts to implement a backward-type of vertical integration are accompanied by considerable structure-shaping investments to establish necessary cognitive and motivational conditions on the part of distributing members. As these investments in "branding" and "sales support" are key prerequisites for setting the stage for an ideal type of performance outcome, their design seems to be in line with requirements of this "degree of decentralization". In accordance with classic NIE arguments, extensive "branding" efforts with a focus on reaching private investors exhibit a comparatively strong relationship-specific character. Moreover, a comprehensive catalogue of "sales support" is in place to assist the distributing members in successfully executing sales and advisory activities. Yet, this empirical study also brings to light that, **already with the set-up of the systemic configuration, some self-blocking situation is created, which consequently gives rise**

to inconsistencies in the application of central steering measures. Although the internal design of the agency-relationship still intends to rely on the "visible hand" of administrative control, authority, and formal decision-making procedures to control for challenges related to "opportunism" and "service firm specificity", the principal is not always able to run information-processing means and motivational measures in a consistent way with the coordination mode of "hierarchy". For instance, there are indications that the transparency on performance outcomes and the underlying "monitoring" efforts cannot be fully leveraged to request and enforce adaptations in the role behavior of in-house distributors in order to increase distribution performance levels on a sustainable basis.

For the enquiry's case study on the **"market"**-type of institutional arrangement, the basic intention is to turn to some discrete allocation of responsibilities along the value chain of mutual funds to optimize distribution performance levels. In this regard, quite in line with NIE propositions, it shows that strong, but relationship-unspecific "branding" efforts become a crucial lever to activate the motivation of external distributors to enter into and maintain such a decoupled agency-relationship. It is essential that the principal carves out a strong and distinctive image as an asset management firm to activate willingness among external banks to take on the role as distributor for the principal's product offering. **The established profile can then potentially be leveraged as a central steering measure to encourage adequate behavior on the part of distributors**. As "Branding" represents a key vehicle to serve the distributors' wider competitive interests, it mobilizes distributors to make use of the principal's mutual fund offering in their sales and advisory activities. It shows that by means of relationship-specific co-branding the principal is able to support external distributors in attaining a more differentiating competitive positioning vis-à-vis distributing rivals. Therefore, to adequately serve these considerations and to activate some form of bonding effects, "branding" efforts need to penetrate, in particular, those communication channels with which the principal is able to reach not only end customers but also simultaneously gate-keepers and opinion-leaders.

However, to ensure the desired role behavior on the part of distributors, it becomes apparent that **"branding" efforts are necessary but not sufficient**. The "invisible hand" of market control overall is not firmly imposed by private investors on the distributors' sales and advisory activities. In general, private investors lack the financial literacy and information to truly understand the complexity of mutual funds and the related sales and advisory activities, making it rather difficult for them to thoroughly assess the quality of both the mutual fund offering and the service activities of competing distributors. Furthermore, the willingness among private investors to switch financial advisors remains rather low, implying that the potential competitive benefits to banks may, in fact, not fully materialize when they take on the distributing role for external asset management firms with a distinctive brand. In other words, due to the lack of a fully established demand side, competitive forces are not sufficiently strong to properly tame latent negative side effects related to "opportunism" and "service firm specificity". This, in turn, indicates that an exclusive reliance on "branding" and competitive considerations appears inappropriate to make external distributors push the principal's mutual fund offering to end customers and, thus, to improve the "cash inflow stream" on a sustainable basis.

In this context, it therefore becomes evident that **the principal runs into the predicament of actively controlling and guiding a "market"-type of agency-relationship to actually secure strong distribution performance levels**, while adhering to a discrete allocation of responsibilities along the value chain. Therefore, it shows that the design contains considerable structure shaping investments in "sales support" as well as process-related means, which can even involve some rather direct intervention in the sales and advisory activities. Highlighting the managed [and relational] character of the agency-relationships, **the principal leverages its own understanding of end customers to deploy extensive "sales support" capacities [in terms of sales concepts** but also in terms of personnel] to help distributors in acquiring, developing, and retaining private investors. In the course of bringing these capacities into play within the on-going support/ active management of the distribution function, the principal even collects performance outcome data of considerable depth to perform far-reaching "monitoring". The detailed transparency on the results of sales and advisory activities is made available by the agent to allow the principal to selectively guide and intervene in the distribution behavior. This underlines, that to a large degree, it is up to the principal to actively ensure the generation of a "cash inflow stream" at the point-of-sale. **All this clearly highlights the departure of the internal design from an ideal type of "market" as institutional arrangement. However, it also becomes evident that, in a relatively consistent manner, the attempt is made to actively compensate for the lack of genuine "market" conditions, thereby serving autonomous distributors' [short-term] profit-maximizing interests in order to secure desired role behavior.**

While the expected raise in the "cash inflow stream" is clearly to the benefit of both, it shows that **it is this active role of the principal in securing the distributors' sales success that is the critical condition for ensuring the desired role behavior**. By managing the generation of the "cash inflow stream" in such an active fashion to consistently compensate for the absence of strong competitive forces, the distributors' [short-term] profit-maximizing interests tend to be adequately served. They not only receive a considerable share of an enhanced revenue stream [driven by a sustained improvement in distribution performance levels] but also enjoy efficiency advantages [due to the comprehensive support of the principal to handle the specificity inherent in selling and advising mutual funds]. With this active role, the principal then seems able to curb issues that may otherwise flare up, in particular [short-term orientated] opportunistic tendencies of distributing intermediaries in setting up and exploiting the "market"-type of institutional arrangements. However, there can be no doubt that the activation of the desired distribution behavior and the realization of a sustained "cash inflow stream" only come at relatively high transaction costs for the principal. This underlines the fact that asset management firms have to give up or cannot fully capture the efficiency potentials [rents] typically associated with decentralization in the face of the absence of a well-functioning "market".

As far as the case study on the **"partnership"**-type of institutional arrangements is concerned, the offer to participate and the underlying far-reaching transfer of property rights fundamentally sets the tone for the internal design of the agency-relationship. In this regard, once again it shows that the design of structure-shaping investments represents a critical lever to allow adequate handling of side-constraints related to "opportunism" and "service firm specificity". For the capacities of **"sales support"** to be in line with very idea of a "partnership" it is essential that these **aim at enabling distributors and their sales staff not only from a pure informational standpoint but also from a more qualification-related point of view**. Therefore, as observed in the case study of "partnership", the design of "sales support" to a relatively strong extent has to focus on the buildup of qualifications of the distributors' personnel operating at the point-of-sale by way of sharing of proven sales routines and methods. The intention is to appropriately empower them to cope in a flexible manner with possible interferences arising in the course of interaction with end customers. This way of enabling, rather than a mere transfer of product-related information, is expected to favor successfully handling of the complexity along the "process of truth" when advising mutual funds to private investors.

In addition to the offer to participate, this design of "sales support" essentially paves the way for a prominent role of norms of "relational exchange" within the information-related processes. Corresponding with the ideal type of a "partnership", besides flexibility, multilevel interaction, and proactive information delivery, in particular the **systematic two-way communication represents a critical lever to efficiently mitigate challenges of "opportunism" and "service firm specificity"**. Since **this type of information exchange** tends to stimulate distributors' search-behavior and identification with the agency-relationship as a whole, **it is in fact a decisive prerequisite to count on the agents' self-interest to appropriately monitor their own behavior and performance levels in support of the "partnership"**. This activation of extra role behavior then potentially puts the principal in a position to guide the partners' sales and advisory activities at the point-of-sale in a mainly indirect manner. From a comparative point of view, it shows that this rather indirect guidance favors the principal in not having to surrender the efficiency advantages [cooperation-rents] of decentralization, whereas for other coordination modes substantial resources are required to continuously exert influence on distribution behavior to strengthen performance levels.

With regard to the motivational measures within the enquiry's case study on "partnership", a blend of different levers is applied to induce the distributors' willingness to cooperate on a sustainable basis. A truly performance-related "incentive scheme" [at the system-level of the agency-relationship] assumes a central, functional-relevant role in securing motivation on the part of external partners to take on the sales and advisory activities on behalf of the asset management firm. However, such a **competitive "incentive scheme" represents only a necessary rather than a sufficient condition** to enhance distribution performance levels on a sustainable basis. In this regard, it shows that, in particular, **joint actions [as a norm of "relational exchange"] between principal and agent represent a highly relevant lever to mobilize the desired role behavior**. Whereas joint actions in distribution-related areas, such as joint sales events, are an effective means to serve distributors' rent considerations, the introduction of joint actions in rather product-related areas tend to fundamentally reinforce the partners' role integrity as well as their search behavior in support of the agency-relationship. As this tends to curb side-constraints emerging with a more advanced "degree of decentralization", these joint actions constitute crucial levers to carve out an internal design that is consistent with the coordination mode of "partnership".

However, while the capacities in "sales support" and the design of information-processing means and motivational measure are all fairly in line with an ideal type of "**partnership**", it also becomes evident that **a highly relevant structural lever is missing** to secure the sustained willingness of distributors to cooperate. For the enquiry's case study on the "partnership"-type of institutional arrangement, it shows that **structure-shaping investments in "branding" are hardly made at all**, implying that this means for controlling distribution behavior is not adequately established. At least in the context of this enquiry, it appears as if the principal, only to a limited degree, is able to offer prospects of differentiating, image-related spill-over effects, which support agents in strengthening their competitive positioning vis-à-vis distributing rivals. From the empirical analysis, the design lacks structural prerequisites to truly provide these benefits to the larger number of [potential] distributing banks. As a consequence, the principal faces considerable obstacles to raise the attractiveness of such a collaborative coordination mode from the distributors' point of view. Therefore, given this deficiency in meeting the critical condition of adequately addressing distributors' competitive interests and rent considerations, **the analyzed design is in fact partially inconsistent with an ideal type of "partnership"**. As observed, this limited brand strength [at least in the German context] essentially gives rise to a situation in which the principal, only to a limited extent, is able to introduce "partnership"-type of coordination modes for marketing mutual funds to private investors in Germany. Hence, despite the otherwise consistent attempts to bring into play and reinforce extra role behavior [in the sense of search-behavior in support of the institutional arrangement as a whole], this partial inconsistency in the internal design brings about negative ramifications regarding the agency-relationships' overall efficacy in achieving a strong "cash inflow stream".

Across the three case studies, it shows that setting up an internal design, which is consistent with the ideal type of the chosen "degree of decentralization" is a complex, multi-faceted task. From the empirical analysis, there can be no doubt that a consistent design is essential to handle the side-constraints of "opportunism" and "service firm specificity" arising with respective organizational choice. It further shows that **it is especially the consistency of the design of the systemic configuration [with its transfer of property rights and the placement of investments] that is critical to activate the ideal type of behavior** on the part of agents and to pave the way for strong performance levels [given the external contingencies]. Any shortcomings in the systemic configuration of the internal design can only be rectified to a limited degree by the application of information-processing means and motivational measures.

5.3 Overall Efficacy of Institutional Arrangements and the Relative Importance of Fit-Requirements

After having discussed the optimal organizational choice and the optimal design for marketing mutual funds to private investors in Germany in a fairly isolated manner, the enquiry now turns to a summary of the overall efficacy of the respective institutional arrangements. To combine the intermediate results concerning optimal choice and design of institutional arrangements, the purpose now is to outline from a more integrated perspective in which way the handling of the two fit requirements secures best possible outcomes regarding the optimization of distribution systems. Therefore, this enquiry is now going to assess the institutional arrangements' overall efficacy in generating a sustained improvement in the "cash inflow stream". In essence, the intention is to position the empirical results in terms of practical and applicable decision-making criteria for the optimization problem of this enquiry.

As the enquiry's framework of analysis is structured in a way that the decision-making regarding the organizational choice is somewhat separated from the decision-making with respect to the internal organizational design, it has conceptualized two different fit requirements. By distinguishing between fit and misfit along the choice and the design decision, four combinations are essentially conceivable. In more detail, a distribution system may display congruence of the organizational choice with the optimizing-relevant contingencies and also consistency of the internal design with the chosen ideal type. Alternatively, the choice decision can be more or less congruent while the design exhibits inconsistencies, or vice versa. An institutional arrangement may even display some form of mismatch along both central decisions. **On the grounds of the empirical results across the enquiry's case studies it is then of greatest interest to ascertain the relative weight of these fit-requirements and their interrelation with regard to the distribution system's efficacy in generating a strong "cash inflow stream"**. As derived along the structure of the enquiry's framework of analysis, this study pursues most notably some form of an **extended configuration hypothesis:** there is the assumption that **external fit in conjunction with internal fit leads to the optimization of the distribution system**, implying an additive interrelation between choice and design regarding the overall efficacy.

From an empirical point of view, each of the case studies brings to light some form of deficits along those two fit-requirements. Across the selected case studies, this enquiry deals with different pairs of fit with misfit and even a constellation of mismatches along both decisions. In fact, the empirical results are quite complex, making it somewhat difficult to unambiguously single out the relative efficacy of the different steps in the decision-making with regard to the optimization of the framework's target variables. Nevertheless, on the basis of the results, this enquiry is still able to adequately

Fig. 48: EFFICACY OF INSTITUTIONAL ARRANGEMENTS AND RELATIVE IMPORTANCE OF FIT-REQUIREMENTS

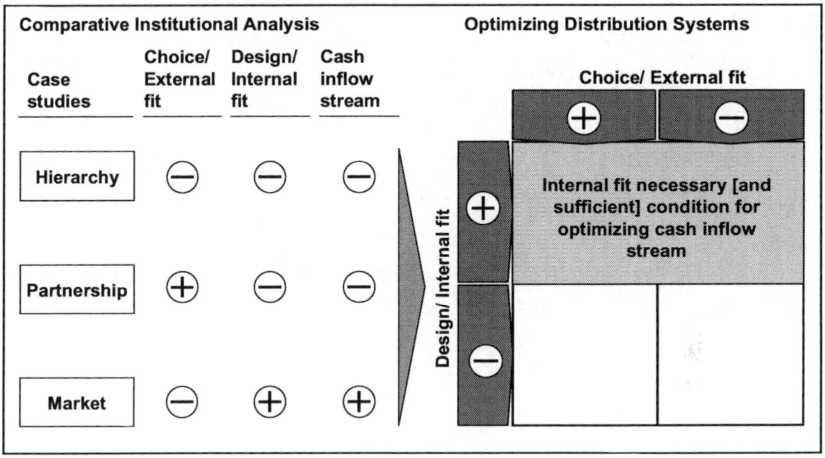

Source: Author

address both of its propositions. As summarized in Figure 48, by combining the respective choice and design decisions to an overall assessment of the efficacy, this enquiry brings to light:

- for its case study on **"hierarchy"** that this coordination mode not only represents an incongruent choice in the face of the "market dynamics" [**external fit:** –] but, in fact, also shows signs of inconsistencies in the internal design against the ideal type of the chosen "degree of decentralization" [**internal fit:** –]. While the incompleteness in internal design leads to severe deficiencies to generate a strong "cash inflow stream", it appears as if already the organizational choice in favor of an integrated coordination mode that, considerably relies on the "visible hand" of control and procedures, is inadequate to achieve a sustained boost in the distribution system's proficiency. Taking then both decisions in combination, it does not come as a surprise to see that the "cash inflow stream" has, in fact, continued to deteriorate to such an extent that it leaves the principal with outflows **["cash inflow stream":** –]. Therefore, all this indicates that inconsistency in the design adds to the negative ramifications of an unsuitable organizational choice with regard to the enquiry's target variables.

- for its case study on **"market"** that this "degree of decentralization" is basically inappropriate to boost distribution performance levels in the absence of effective market control [**external fit:** –]. Regarding the internal design, this enquiry then encounters some form of paradox. While relying on a discrete allocation of responsibilities along the value chain, the principal deliberately departs from a true "market" type of institutional arrangement to design a managed "market" agency-relationship. By consistently accounting for the absence of a fully established demand side, at least in the short term, the principal is then able to serve the general competitive ambitions of distributors and, in particular, their [short-term] profit-maximizing interests in a remarkably consistent manner [**internal fit:** +]. As far as the impact on the enquiry's target variables is concerned, it is this consistency in the active management of relationships to secure distributors' [short-term] profit-maximizing interests that so far ensures a relatively strong "cash inflow stream" [**"cash inflow stream":** +], even in difficult market conditions. Hence, the achieved distribution performance levels indicate that the consistency of the internal design, in fact, outshines the shortcomings of the organizational choice regarding the generation of the "cash inflow stream". However, as this move towards an extensively active management of the agency-relationships requires comparatively high resources, it essentially shows that the incongruence of the initial choice ultimately puts the principal at risk of giving up [transferring] the efficiency advantages typically related to decentralization.
- for its case study on **"partnership"** that this organizational choice is in fact quite appropriate in response to the "market dynamics" to secure a sustained improvement in the "cash inflow stream" [**external fit:** +]. In those agency-relationships in which the principal is able to activate and maintain the desired [extra] role behavior on part of distributors, there are signs that the principal enjoys a steady, positive "cash inflow stream", without having to deploy enormous resources to intervene in the actual sales and advisory activities. However, this study also reveals that the internal design lacks a critical vehicle to

adequately serve the competitive considerations of larger distributing banks for mutual funds in Germany. Therefore, the shortcomings in "branding" pinpoint an inconsistency with severe consequences [**internal fit:** –]. The somewhat blurred profile as an asset management firm causes considerable difficulties in triggering self-interest among the larger distributors to enter and remain in such a participation-orientated institutional arrangement. Hence, with regard to the combined effect of choice and design, it seems as if the inconsistent design tends to spoil the positive potential of a congruent choice. The "cash inflow stream" continues to decline [**"cash inflow stream":** –] and, in fact, has become negative. Following from this overall efficacy assessment combining the choice decision with the decision on the internal design, **this enquiry cannot reject its two propositions.**

Regarding the first proposition, which claims that both fit requirements are of functional relevance to come to an optimization of distribution systems [extended configuration hypothesis], across the case studies it shows that external fit as well as internal fit have a positive impact on the framework's target variable. As this highlights the **assumed additive interrelation between a congruent organizational choice and a consistent organizational design, this proposition cannot be rejected**. However, as far as the relative weights of these fit requirements are concerned, this enquiry is confident to suggest some further refinements to this proposition. Across the case studies, it becomes evident that **the internal fit has a more imminent impact on the target variable than the external fit**. In other words, [from a short-term perspective] there are indications that an internally consistent design already constitutes a sufficient condition to achieve strong distribution performance levels. On the contrary, based on the empirical results this enquiry argues that [from a short-term perspective] a congruent organizational choice is neither sufficient nor necessary to secure a relatively strong "cash inflow stream". Nevertheless, with a long-term orientation, to accomplish an optimal solution to organize distribution systems, it is essential that the institutional arrangement for marketing mutual funds private investors meets the internal as well as the external fit requirement. All this clearly underlines: rather than single levers, it is **the choice <u>and</u> the design of the institutional arrangement that are a key factor of success in achieving a sustained improvement in the "cash inflow stream".**

In this regard, there are also good reasons as to why this enquiry cannot reject its second proposition. This propositions claims a "partnership"-type of institutional arrangement – if set up in consistence with the ideal type across the range of design variables – is superior in dealing with latent negative side effects of "opportunism" and "service firm specificity" in the face of the "market dynamics" to come to an improved "cash inflow stream". This comparative institutional analysis brings to light that this "degree of decentralization" tends to establish the relevant cognitive and motivational conditions for optimizing performance levels, without absorbing as many resources as observed in the managed "market" agency-relationship or in the "hierarchy" to continuously manage the system. As only the ideal type of "partnership" is genuinely able to establish and rely on extra role behavior on the part of distributing agents, it appears to be the only organizational solution that favors a relatively smooth adaptability of the relationship as whole. In contrast to this, in the managed "market" relationship [due to limited strength of competitive forces] as well as in the "hierarchy"-type of institutional arrangement, it requires substantial resources to actively ensure adaptations in distribution behavior to strengthen the "cash inflow stream". Hence, without neglecting the fact that other organizational choices may enjoy strong performance levels [at least in the short term], **this empirical investigation is confident to argue that, in the German context, a consistent design of a "partnership"-type of coordination mode, in the long term, offers the best possible way to realize an optimization of distribution systems for mutual funds**.

Consequently, as a guiding principle to the enquiry's decision-making problem, against the given background a "partnership" approach constitutes better-practice to accomplish a sustained boost in the "cash inflow stream". In this regard, this enquiry then also advises management of asset management firms to focus with great care on the consistency of the design with the ideal type in order to eventually come to the aspired performance levels. In line with the argumentation in the realm of design theory, it is most notably this consistency of the choice of the "degree of decentralization" that to a considerable extent ensures the success of the distribution system.

5.4 Theoretical Implications

In the view of these empirical results, the intention is now to shortly outline the theoretical implications of this enquiry, thereby suggesting promising routes for further research. To outline how to optimize the "cash inflow stream" for mutual funds, this enquiry has investigated the choice and the design of distribution systems for marketing mutual funds to private investors. In order to shed light on this subject of enquiry from this organizational perspective, a research area on which academic literature has so far remained rather silent, this effort has turned to the comparative multi-case study research method. Although this comparative institutional analysis is influenced profoundly by the theoretical concepts underlying NIE, its **framework of analysis represents an attempt to move considerably beyond the classic scope of NIE arguments**. This extension rests largely on the fact that the derivation of the framework and its application explicitly include arguments from the wider realm of organizational theories, most notably from the structural contingency theory. The resulting system perspective provides the enquiry with the chance not only to investigate the organizational choice but also to decompose and examine decisions on the design of the chosen coordination mode more overtly. In this respect, this enquiry is then able to follow suggestions of recent marketing literature to treat [specific] investments endogenously in order to study strategic decisions on how to arrange distribution channels. In this way, from a pragmatic point of view, this study is not only able to address central propositions of NIE but also to offer further insights into a research area, which is currently considered to be of high priority in marketing literature (Ghosh and John 2005, p. 335). That is, in particular, the interest to understand the importance of governance choices to firm performance.

From a theoretical point of view, this enquiry is able to bring to light a variety of implications. As far as the **placement of productive investments** is concerned, in line with the well-known classic propositions of NIE, this study shows that **levels of specificity are purposively defined in correspondence with the degree of decentralization**. It becomes apparent that, in rather integrated institutional arrangements, investments are placed with a high relationship-specific character. On the contrary, for more advanced degrees of decentralization, investments are made in a mainly relationship-unspecific manner and are tailored to particular exchange relationships only in a selective manner.

It further shows that if strong investments most notably in the area of "branding" [and "sales support"] are designed appropriately, they tend to be highly productive in supporting the initiation and structure of agency-relationships and, thus, pave the way for the realization of aspired performance levels. There are clear signs that such **investments carry the chance to balance dependence in the interaction**, rather than to give further rise to coordination challenges related to behavioral assumptions and the complexity inherent in the delegated service activities. On the grounds of this empirical result, this enquiry suggests further investigation of the effect of the designing of "branding" [as the means of communicating relevant and differentiating capabilities] to control for inefficiencies stemming from coordination issues along the value chain. In this view, **"branding" can then represent an interesting marketing vehicle to combine arguments from the RBV with the NIE** in order to study the optimization of proficiency levels for decentralized distribution systems for financial services.

However, even if it comes to a strong placement of investments as well as an adequate alignment with the governance choice, there are still considerable differences in performance levels across the three case studies. By operationalizing not only the choice but also the decisions on the design of institutional arrangements, this enquiry is able to explain these variations, at least to some extent. In this way, this study is able to provide suggestions in which way governance modes impact firm performance. As brought to light, it is most notably the consistency of the internal design with the chosen coordination mode, rather than the external organizational adjustments, that to a considerable degree drives strong performance levels. With classic NIE propositions assuming that each [generic] mode of governance is defined as an internally consistent syndrome of attributes (Williamson 2002, p. 175), a governance choice is expected to rather automatically entail a consistent design of the institutional arrangement. Yet, this enquiry clearly underlines **a mere consideration of the choice is not sufficiently sophisticated to elucidate why firms enjoy strong performance or not**. As a matter of fact, it is the organizational design that may substantially moderate the proficiency of the institutional arrangement. Hence, an analysis of institutional arrangements only at the global level will not bring about the desired insights. It seems as if **there is a need to more explicitly include system-perspectives in the theoretical background of NIE** to address the widely known criticism regarding "ad-hoc theorization" in NIE-based reasoning. On the basis of this enquiry, to further sharpen investigations on how to arrange optimal governance modes, additional research is needed to more prominently incorporate the interplay of structure and processes for a given organizational choice into the classic argumentation of NIE.

In the context of shaping a decision-making model, this enquiry applies some step-wise procedures, based on the staged structure of the framework of analysis, to address multiple fit-requirements. In this regard, the conflicting demands of the internal and external orientation have become very apparent. Given the contradictory forces at work in the enquiry's framework, with "market dynamics" essentially suggesting decentralized systems whereas latent hazards related to "opportunism" and "service firm specificity" indicate the superiority of rather integrated arrangements, this enquiry has attempted to assess the relative weights of these different fits on the grounds of logical reasoning against the empirical results. While able to illustrate an additive interrelation between external and internal fit, this study also brings to light a compensating effect in the interaction of the multiple fit-requirements (Remer 2001, pp. 370). At least in the short-term, the [in]consistency of internal design tends to have a more imminent impact on the target variable than the external organizational choice. However, as academic literature provides no formalized approach to shed light on the interplay between [contradicting] fits, this enquiry then remains somewhat limited in absorbing and establishing a full grasp of the interdependence between external and internal adjustments. Therefore, **further research is necessary to specify the different ways of interaction [i.e., linear, non-linear, recursive] between multiple fit-requirements** in order to pave the way for a more systematic investigation of these highly relevant managerial challenges.

In the face of the methodology applied, there can be no doubt that this enquiry is somewhat limited in generalizing its results. Yet, this enquiry has still been able to illustrate the functional relevance of organizational choice and design for marketing mutual funds to private investors. In this respect, the empirical study has covered a large number of different variables in considerable depth. On the ground of its empirical results, this enquiry suggests the application of a different research design with possibly a more focused scope to further strengthen the generalization of the empirical findings. In the light of this empirical study, the use of a larger sample and some more quantitative methodology appears to be an attractive avenue for additional research to demonstrate that it is not only the choice but also the design of the distribution system that drives the success or failure of asset management firms in realizing optimal distribution performance levels for their mutual fund offering.

Appendix

Appendix A: Operationalization of Variables

Variable	Operationalization
Market dynamics	• Decline in operational performance (AuM, inflows) in comparison to market trend/ main competitors
Opportunism	• Limited willingness and commitment among distributing banks to sell mutual funds of external asset management firms
Service firm specificity	• Levels of professional skills, know-how and customization required for performing product-specific and customer-specific distribution activities
Degree of decentralization	• Type of coordination mechanism (Hierarchy, Partnership, or Market)
Monitoring	• Focus (outcome – behavior) and intensity (system-level – branch/individual-level; frequency) of controlling banks
Screening	• Focus and intensity of identifying motivation and ability on part of distributing banks
Incentive scheme	• Types of rewards to harmonize interests (system-rewards, performance pay, non-monetary rewards; system-level – branch/individual-level)
Relational exchange	• Types and intensity of multi-level interaction, flexibility, proactive information-sharing, two-way communication, and joint actions (product-related – distribution related) along value chain
Contract design	• Degree of assignment of property rights to distributing banks
Branding	• Focus (end-customers – distributors) and intensity of brand investments • Relationship-specific character (co-branding)
Sales Support	• Focus (information – qualification) and intensity of predefining desired behavior on the part of distributing banks • Relationship-specific character (trainings)
Hold up	• Experienced intensity of willingness and commitment to cooperate and to sell asset management firms products
Cash inflow stream	• Cash inflow stream generated through [external] distributing banks (in monetary terms)

Appendix B: Interview-Guide

OVERARCHING INTERVIEW GUIDE

General perspectives

- How does your organization organize and manage the relationship to [external] banks (in Germany)?
- What kind of difficulties have you experienced in the course of a relationship with an [external] distributor? What are the most common forms of hold-up or opportunistic behaviour on part of [external] banks?
- From your perspective, what have been most effective measures to solve interruptions or problems within relationships to distributors? How can a steady inflow stream be generated through [external] distributors?

Discussion on framework of analysis

- With your experience, how effective is a systematic **screening** of potential distributors to control for possible hold-up problems? Why? Do you and how do perform the qualification of potential distributors?
- How important is a detailed **contract** in limiting potential opportunistic behaviour on part of [external] distribution channels? How do you design contracts and the associated negotiations to secure cooperation in the course of the relationship?
- Given your experience, how effective are certain types of **compensation schemes** in controlling opportunism? What are prominent examples of effective (i.e. successful) designs of contracts and compensation schemes?
- What does your organization focus on when **monitoring** the [external] distributors' activities? What are the effects of the monitoring process?
- What range of actions does your organization take to establish an atmosphere of **relational exchange** with your [external] distributors? Are there prominent examples where strong emphasize on relational exchange has resulted in more stabilized relationships?
- How is your **brand** perceived in Germany? Does your brand create a sufficiently strong pull-effect among end customers? With your experience, does your brand balances the dependence between your organization and [external] banks?
- What kind of **sales support** does your organization offer to enable distributors? Which aspects determine the level of sales support you provide? What are prominent examples where sales support led to enhanced cooperation and subsequently to steady inflow streams?

Appendix C: Overview of Specific Information Needs

INFORMATION NEEDS DEFINED ALONG FRAMEWORK OF ANALYSIS

1. **Introduction and key facts***
2. **Screening**
3. **Contract design**
4. **Incentives**
5. **Monitoring**
6. **Relational exchange**
7. **Branding**
8. **Sales Support**
9. **Level of hold-up**

* includes gathering of dependent variable "Inflow stream" for each [external] distributor

① INTRODUCTION AND KEY FACTS (1/3)

Use of [external] distributors – *Source: General Management, Sales Management*

- Since when does your asset management firm use [external] distributors to sell its products? In which country and with which distributor did your asset management firm enter into an sales-agreement for the very first time? What was the underlying rationale for this move?
- How many [external] distributors does your asset management firm currently use? (by category of distributor: banks, insurance companies, IFA networks, etc.)
- In how many countries does your asset management firm currently use [external] distributors?
- Since when does your asset management firm use [external] distributors in Germany? Who was the first distributor your asset management firm entered into an agreement with? What was the underlying rationale for this move?
- How many [external] distributors does your asset management firm currently use in Germany? (by category of distributor: banks, insurance companies, IFA networks, etc.)

① INTRODUCTION AND KEY FACTS (2/3)

Assets under Management, Inflows – *Source: Controlling, General Management*

- How much AuM does your asset management firm currently manage?
- What is the split of AuM between the Retail and Institutional segment? Of the Retail AuM, what is the split between the in-house private banking channel and [external] distributors?
- Of the Retail AuM gathered through [external] distributors, in what form are these AuM generated? (i.e., FoF, PLF, branded, etc.)
- Of the Retail AuM gathered through [external] distributors, how much are generated in each country?
- Of the Retail AuM gathered through [external] distributors in Germany, in what from are these AuM generated? (i.e., FoF, PLF, branded, etc.) How much AuM are generated by each distributor?
- Question 1-5 with regard to inflows (gross, net)

① INTRODUCTION AND KEY FACTS (3/3)

Products – *Source: Sales Management, Controlling*

- How many Retail products (Mutual Funds) does your asset management firm offer in Germany? What is the product range (by product type: i.e., Equity, Fixed Income, Money Market, etc.) your asset management firm offers in Germany?
- What are the best (branded) sellers in Germany of the your asset management firm product/fund range?
- In general, what type of (branded) products are most commonly sold through [external] banking distribution channels?

Your operations in Germany – *Source: General Management, Sales Management*

- Since when does your asset management firm operate an office in Germany?
- What is the role/function of the German office of your asset management firm with regard to the operation in Germany? Are German distributors serviced out of the German office or from the central headquarters? How are these activities coordinated?

② SCREENING (1/2)

Screening/qualification activities – *Source: General Management, Sales Management*

- In general, what is usually the first step in the process to initiate a distribution agreement with a German bank for (branded) sales of your products/funds?
- Who does usually take the first step? Your asset management firm or the distributor/bank?
- Is information usually exchanged between the distributor and your asset management firm to allow for up-front assessment of attractiveness of potential agreement? What kind of information is presented/exchanged? Does your asset management firm explicitly ask for certain types of information to perform some form of qualification effort?
- How does your asset management firm identify potential distributors? What kind of activities does your asset management firm perform to identify potential distributors? How standardized are these activities? What kind of criteria are applied to identify potential distributors (i.e., banks)? What areas does your asset management firm attempt to qualify when screening potential distributors? How regular are these activities performed?

② SCREENING (2/2)

Screening/qualification activities – *Source: General Management, Sales Management*

- Are distributors invited to some form of beauty-contest? Has your asset management firm participated in some form of beauty-contest initiated by distributing banks?
- Does your asset management firm grant some form of selectivity to its distributors? Does your asset management firm demand/require any kind of selectivity from its distributors? (i.e., demand status of "preferred provider")
- What kind of resources has your asset management firm deployed to identify potential distributors?

③ CONTRACT DESIGN

Negotiation activities and contract structure – *Source: General Management, Sales Management*

- In general, what is the process to negotiate distribution agreements between your asset management firm and a German bank?
- How long do negotiations usually take to finalize the (branded) sales agreement between your asset management firm and a German bank? How many rounds of negotiations are usually held before reaching the agreement? What is usually the focus of the negotiations between your asset management firm and the distributor?
- What are the resources that your asset management firm deploys for the negotiation and finalization of an agreement with a distributor?
- How many different types of (standardized) sales agreements (for branded sales) does your asset management firm have? How complete are these sales agreements?
- What is the structure and the content of the agreement between your asset management firm? Do agreements primarily focus on the terms of the exchange? Do contracts outline the intended process/interaction between parties? Do contracts define/propose roles for each party that go beyond the original sales agreement? Do contracts pose any kind of continuity expectations?

④ INCENTIVE SCHEME

Design of incentive scheme to distributors –
Source: General Management, Sales Management

- What kind of compensation schemes does your asset management firm offer to its distributors? How are these compensation schemes (fee-tables) designed? (e.g. fixed schemes, variable schemes, lump-sums, etc.)? At which organizational level do your provide incentives to your distributors?
- What factors are included to determine the distributor's compensation? (i.e., AuM-level, inflows, product type, product performance, etc.)
- Which compensation schemes are the most frequently used with German distributors? Do certain compensation schemes (fee-splits) find greater acceptance among distributors?

⑤ MONITORING

Controlling activities and processes – ***Source: Sales Management, Controlling***

- How does your asset management firm monitor/control the selling performance of [external] distributors?
- What is the scope of monitoring activities (i.e. focus on outcome and/or behaviour)? Which criteria are applied to assess the performance of [external] distributors?
- Has your asset management firm put in place any standardized tools to monitor/control/manage/direct the selling efforts made by distributors? (e.g., distributor profitability)
- Do ([external]) distributor provide detailed information (requested) to facilitate specific monitoring of behaviour/activities/outcomes?
- How many resources has your asset management firm deployed to monitor/control the activities of [external] distributors?

⑥ RELATIONAL EXCHANGE

Activities to establish atmosphere of mutual cooperation –
Source: General Management, Sales Management

- What kind of activities does your asset management firm perform to demonstrate importance of relationship with distributor? What kind of measures has your asset management firm engaged into to facilitate relationship-building, good faith, trust and solidarity?
- At the beginning of a relationship with a distributor, what is the common understanding with regard to continuity expectations?
- How flexible does your asset management firm react to any kind of enquiries/requests made by distributors?
- Does your asset management firm engage into any kind of
  - proactive sharing of information and communication enhancing activities?
  - multilevel interaction?
  - mutual coordination/cooperation that goes beyond the original exchange?

  How are each of these activities organized?
- How many resources has your asset management firm deployed to establish an atmosphere of relational exchange?

⑦ BRANDING

Branding activities – ***Source: Sales Management, Marketing Department***

- What kind of end customer branding efforts does your asset management firm perform? (in Germany) (i.e., ATL: TV, Print, Radio, Outdoor, BTL)
- What is the level of brand investments of your asset management firm in Germany?
- Does your asset management firm coordinate any branding activities with its distributors in the German market?
- Does your asset management firm coordinate any branding activities with [external] distributors in Germany?
- What is the current level of brand strength of your asset management firm (in Germany)? (i.e., level of brand awareness, funnel performance)

⑧ SALES SUPPORT

Services provided to support distributors' sales activities –
Source: Sales Management, Marketing Department

- What kind of marketing support does your asset management firm offer to its distributors (i.e. road shows, marketing material, product brochures, posters, etc.)? What kind of different levels of sales support does your asset management firm offer to its distributors? What are the underlying drivers for different levels?
- What kind of activities/programs does your asset management firm provide to train sales staff of distributors? How flexible/standardized are these training programs? What kind of information tools has your asset management firm put in place to secure a regular and on-time update of distributors (e.g., IT-based information tools, dedicated websites, fact-sheets, etc.)
- Who is handling interaction with distributors? Has your asset management firm put in place dedicated personnel to manage client interaction/relationship?
- How is the process of administrating the relationship (i.e. fund ordering, settlement, etc.) with distributors organized? What kind of infrastructure has been put in place?
- How much resources has your asset management firm deployed to provide sales support to its distributor?

⑨ LEVEL OF HOLD-UP

Lack of cooperation/coordination – ***Source: General Management, Sales Management***

- How often do negotiations between your asset management firm and potential distributors breakdown before an initial agreement is reached? What are the reasons for breakdown?
- How often are distribution agreements with distributors unexpectedly renegotiated? (i.e., fee split arrangements) How long do these renegotiations take? What is the focus of these renegotiations?
- How much resources has your asset management firm deployed for these renegotiations?
- How often have relationships with distributors broken down despite an agreement in place?
- How many agreements/relationships do not generate any new AuM for your asset management firm? What is the underlying reason? How many agreements/relationships have been terminated/broken down in the last 3 years?

References

Akerlof, George (1970): "The Market for "Lemons": Quality Under Uncertainty and the Market Mechanism", Quarterly Journal of Economics, **84** (August): pp. 488-500.

Alchian, Armen and Harold Demsetz (1972): "Production, Information Costs, and Economic Organization", American Economic Review, **62** (5): pp. 777-795.

Anderson, Erin (1985): "The Salesperson as Outside Agent or Employee: A Transaction Cost Analysis", Marketing Science, **4** (3): pp. 234-254.

Anderson, Erin (1988): "Transaction Costs as Determinants of Opportunism in Integrated and Independent Sales Forces", Journal of Economic Behavior and Organization, **9** (May): pp. 247-264.

Anderson, Erin and Anne Coughlan (1987): "International Market Entry and Expansion via Independent or Integrated Channels of Distribution", Journal of Marketing, **51** (January): pp. 71-82.

Anderson, Erin and Richard Oliver (1987): "Perspective on Behavior-Based Versus Outcome-Based Salesforce Control Systems", Journal of Marketing, **51** (October): pp. 76-88.

Anderson, Erin and David Schmittlein (1984): "Integration of the Sales Force: An Empirical Examination", RAND Journal of Economics, **15** (3): pp. 385-395.

Anderson, Erin and Barton Weitz (1992): "The Use of Pledges to Build and Sustain Commitment in Distribution Channels", Journal of Marketing Research, **29** (February): pp. 18-24.

Anderson, James and James Narus (1990): "A Model of Distributor Firm and Manufacturer Firm Working Partnership", Journal of Marketing, **54** (January): pp. 42-58.

Argyres, Nicholas (1996): "Evidence on the Role of Firm Capabilities in Vertical Integration Decisions", Strategic Mangement Journal, **17** (2): pp. 129-150.

Artz, Kendall and Thomas Brush (2000): "Asset Specificity, Uncertainty and Relational Norms: An Examination of Coordination Costs in Collaborative Strategic Alliances", Journal of Economic Behavior and Organization, **41** (4): pp. 337-362.

Axelrod, Robert (2005): Die Evolution der Kooperation (6th ed.). München, Oldenbourg.

Balk, Thomas (2001): "Offener Fondsvertrieb: Banken als Gewinner?" bank und markt, **30** (Januar): pp. 18-21.

Balzer, Arno and Georg Jakobs (2005): "Wieder auf Kurs", Manager-Magazin, **35:** pp. 122-127.

Barber, Brad; Terrance Odean and Lu Zheng (2005): "Out of Sight, Out of Mind: The Effects of Expenses on Mutual Fund Flows", Journal of Business, **78** (6): pp. 2095-2120.

Barberis, Nicolas and Richard Thaler (2003): "A Survey of Behavioral Finance". Handbook of the Economics of Finance. G. Constantinides, M. Harris and R. Stulz, Eds. Amsterdam, Elsevier: pp. 1053-1128.

Barney, Jay (1991): "Firm Resources and Sustained Competitive Advantages", Journal of Management, **17** (1): pp. 99-120.

Barney, Jay (1999): "How a Firm's Capabilities Affect Boundary Decisions", Sloan Management Review, **40** (September): pp. 137-146.

Barzel, Yoram (1982): "Measurement Cost and the Organization of Markets", Journal of Law and Economics, **25** (April): pp. 27-48.

Bauer, Hans; Nicola Sauer and Stefan Werbick (2002): "Erfolgsfaktoren von Investmentfonds aus Nachfragersicht", Working Paper M69 des Instituts für Marktorientierte Unternehmensführung der Universität Mannheim, University of Mannheim.

Baum, Klaus-Jürgen (2005): "Fondsvertrieb: Der Kunde will die Wahl", bank und markt, **34** (Januar): pp. 23-25.

Baumgarth, Carsten (2004): "Co-Branding". Handbuch Markenführung. M. Bruhn, Ed. (2nd ed.). Stuttgart, Schäffer-Poeschel: pp. 235-259.

Beaujean, Marc; Jonathan Davidson and Stacey Madge (2006): "The "Moment of Truth" in Customer Service", The McKinsey Quarterly (1): pp. 63-73.

Bergen, Mark; Shantanu Dutta and Orville Walker (1992): "Agency Relationships in Marketing: A Review of the Implications and Applications of Agency and Related Theories", Journal of Marketing, **56** (July): pp. 1-24.

Bergstresser, Daniel and James Poterba (2002): "Do After-Tax Returns Affect Mutual Fund Inflows", Journal of Financial Economics, **63** (3): pp. 381-414.

Besanko, David; David Dranove and Mark Shanley (2000): Economics of Strategy (2nd ed.). New York, NY, John Wiley & Sons.

Bleeke, Joel and David Ernst (1991): "The Way to Win in Cross-Border Alliances", Harvard Business Review, **69** (6): pp. 127-135.

Bleeke, Joel and David Ernst (1995): "Is Your Strategic Alliance Really a Sale?" Harvard Business Review, **73** (1): pp. 97-105.

Boerner, Christopher and Jeffrey Macher (2001): "Transaction Cost Economics: An Assessment of Emprical Research in the Social Sciences", Whitepaper, Georgetown University, Washington, *http://faculty.msb.edu/jtm4/Papers/JLEO.pdf*, (23.03.2006).

Böhme, Markus (1997): Die Zukunft der Universalbank im Zeitalter von Informationstechnik und Finnanzinnovation - Strategie, Organisation und Shareholder Value. Wiesbaden, Universitätsverlag.

Bonoma, Thomas (1985): "Case Research in Marketing: Opportunities, Problems, and a Process", Journal of Marketing Research, **22** (May): pp. 199-208.

Boos, Hans-Christian (2001): "Fondsvertrieb: Abschied von Exklusiv-Modellen", bank und markt, **30** (Dezember): pp. 27-29.

Bradach, Jeffrey and Robert Eccles (1989): "Price, Authority, and Trust: From Ideal Types to Plural Forms", Annual Review of Sociology, **15** (August): pp. 97-118.

Brown, James; Chekitan Dev and Dong-Lin Lee (2000): "Managing Marketing Channel Opportunism: The Efficacy of Alternative Governance Mechanisms", Journal of Marketing, **64** (April): pp. 51-65.

Bryman, Alan (1988): Quantity and Quality in Social Research. London, Unwin Hyman.

Busch, Henning (2003): "Der Standort Deutschland aus der Sicht eines ausländischen Fondsanbieter". Asset Management - Investmentkonzepte, Produkte, Vertriebswege und Standortfrage der Fondsbranche. I. Westphal; C. Horstkotte and K. Ripper, Eds. (2nd ed.). Stuttgart, Schäffer-Poeschel: pp. 31-48.

Busse, Caspar (2005): "Die DKB ist unverkäuflich", Süddeutsche Zeitung, p. 27, 08.10.2005

BVI (2005): "Anlagen zur Jahres-PK 2005: Bilanz 2004", Frankfurt a. Main, 20.01.2005, *http://www.bvi.de/export/sites/internet/de/infocenter/presse/pressemitteilungen/2005/pk200105_folien/pk200105_folien.pdf*, (23.03.2006).

BVI (2006): "Anleger kaufen Investmentsfonds am liebsten bei Banken bzw. Sparkassen", Frankfurt a. Main, 06.01.2006, *http://www.bvi.de/export/sites/internet/de/infocenter/presse/pressemitteilungen/2006/pm060106/pm060106.pdf*, (23.03.2006).

Cameron, Doug (2002): "Deutsche/Amvescap "open" plan", Financial Times FM, p. 2, 29.04.2002

Cashman, George and Daniel Deli (2004): "Locating Decision Rights: Evidence from the Mutual Fund Industry", Whitepaper, Arizona State University, *http://www.fma.org/Chicago/Papers/LocatingDecisionRightsEvidencefromtheMutualFundIndustry.pdf*, (23.03.2006).

Caspar, Mirko; Achim Hecker and Tatjana Sabel (2002): "Markenrelevanz in der Unternehmensführung - Messung, Erklärung und empirische Befunde für B2B-Märkte", McKinsey&Company/ Marketing Centrum Münster, Arbeitspapier Nr. 4, Düsseldorf.

Celly, Kirti and Gary Frazier (1996): "Outcome-Based and Behavior-Based Coordination Efforts in Channel Relationships", Journal of Marketing Research, **33** (May): pp. 200-210.

Chandler, Alfred jr. (1962): Strategy and Structure. Cambridge, MA, MIT Press.

Chen, Joesph; Harrison Hong; Ming Huang and Jeffrey Kubik (2004): "Does Fund Size Erode Mutual Fund Performance? The Role of Liquidity and Organization", American Economic Review, **94** (5): pp. 1276-1302.

Chen, Joseph; Harrison Hong and Jeffrey Kubik (2005): "Outsourcing Mutual Fund Management: Firm Boundaries, Incentives and Performance", Whitepaper, University of Princeton, *http://www.princeton.edu/~hhong/Outsourcing08-05.pdf*, (23.03.2006).

Chevalier, Judith and Glenn Ellision (1997): "Risk taking by mutual funds as a response to incentives", Journal of Political Economy, **105** (6): pp. 1167-1200.

Chevalier, Judith and Glenn Ellision (1999): "Career concerns of mutual fund managers", Quarterly Journal of Economics, **114** (2): pp. 389-432.

Child, John (1972): "Organizational structure, environment and performance: The role of strategic choice", Sociology, **6** (1): pp. 1-22.

Coase, Ronald (1937): "The Nature of the Firm", Economica, **4** (16): pp. 386-405.

Conner, Kathleen and C. K. Prahalad (1996): "Resource-Based Theory of the Firm: Knowledge versus Opportunism", Organization Science, **7** (5): pp. 477-501.

Corsten, Hans (2001): Dienstleistungmanagement (4th ed.). München, Oldenbourg.

Coughlan, Anne; Erin Anderson; Louis Stern and Adel El-Ansary (2001): Marketing Channels (6th ed.). Upper Saddle River, NJ, Prentice Hall.

Cripps, Elizabeth (2005): "The Benefits of Getting the Experts In", Professional Wealth Management (34): pp. 13-18.

Crocker, Keith and Scott Masten (1991): "Pretia ex machina? Prices and Process in Long-Term Contracts", Journal of Law and Economics, **34** (April): pp. 69-99.

Crosby, Lawrence; Kenneth Evans and Deorah Cowles (1990): "Relationship Quality in Services Selling: An Interpersonal Influence Perspective", Journal of Marketing, **54** (July): pp. 68-81.

Davies, Paul (2005): "Challenges for funds appear on many fronts", Financial Times FM, p. 3, 21.02.2005.

Dechow, Moritz (2003): Wettbewerb von Aktieninvestmentfonds im Distributionskanal Discount Brokerage. Bern, Haupt.

Delery, John and D. Harold Doty (1996): "Modes of Theorizing in Strategic Human Resource Management: Tests of Universalistic, Contingency, and Configurational Predictions", Academy of Management Journal, **39** (4): pp. 802-835.

Del Guercio, Diane and Paula Tkac (2001): "Star Power: The Effect of Morningstar Ratings on Mutual Fund Flows", Working Paper 2001-15, Federal Reserve Bank of Atlanta.

De Ruiter, Wim and Thomas Koch (1991): "Leistungsförderung im Vertrieb durch Incentives". Handbuch Anreizsysteme. G. Schanz, Ed. Stuttgart, C.E. Poeschel**:** pp. 1025-1036.

DeVaus, David (2001): Research Design in Social Research. London, Sage.

Dixit, Avinash and Barry Nalebuff (1991): Thinking Strategically: The Competitive Edge in Business, Politics, and Everyday Life. New York, NY, Norton.

Donaldson, Lex (1987): "Strategy and structural adjustment to regain fit and performance: In defence of contingency theory", Journal of Management Studies, **24** (1): pp. 1-24.

Donaldson, Lex (1995): American Anti-Management Theories of Organization. Cambridge, Cambridge University Press.

Donaldson, Lex (1996a): For Positivist Organization Theory. London, Sage.

Donaldson, Lex (1996b): "The Normal Science of Structural Contingency Theory". Studying Organization. S. Clegg and C. Hardy, Eds. London, Sage: pp. 51-70.

Doney, Patricia and Joseph Cannon (1997): "An Examination of the Nature of Trust in Buyer-Seller Relationships", Journal of Marketing, **61** (April): pp. 35-51.

Doty, Harold; William Glick and George Huber (1993): "Fit, Equifinality, and Organizational Effectiveness: A Test of Two Configurational Theories", Academy of Management Journal, **30** (December): pp. 1196-1250.

Drazin, Robert and Andrew Van de Ven (1985): "Alternative Forms of Fit in Contingency Theory", Administrative Science Quarterly, **30** (December): pp. 514-539.

Dwyer, F. Robert; Paul Schurr and Sejo Oh (1987): "Developing Buyer-Seller Relationships", Journal of Marketing, **51** (April): pp. 11-27.

Dyer, Jeffrey (1997): "Effective Interfirm Collaboration: How Firms Minimize Transaction Costs and Maximize Transaction Value", Strategic Mangement Journal, **18** (7): pp. 535-556.

Ebers, Mark and Wilfried Gotsch (1999): "Institutionenökonomische Theorien der Organisation". Organisationstheorien. A. Kieser, Ed. (3rd ed.). Stuttgart, Kohlhammer: pp. 199-251.

Eccles, Robert and Harrison White (1988): "Price and Authority in Inter-Profit Center Transactions", American Journal of Sociology, **94** (Supplement): pp. 17-51.

Eisenhardt, Kathleen (1989): "Building Theories from Case Study Research", Academy of Management Journal, **14** (4): pp. 532-550.

Erramilli, M. Krishna and C. P. Rao (1993): "Service Firms' International Entry-Mode Choice: A Modified Transaction-Cost Analysis Approach", Journal of Marketing, **57** (July): pp. 19-38.

Fant, Franklin and Edward O'Neal (2000): "Temporal Changes in the Determinants of Mutual Funds Flows", Journal of Financial Research, **23** (3): pp. 353-371.

Fein, Adam and Erin Anderson (1997): "Patterns of Credible Commitments: Territory and Brand Selectivity in Industrial Distribution Channels", Journal of Marketing, **61** (April): pp. 19-34.

Ferber, Michael (2003): "Fidelity bricht Vertriebsstruktur auf", Handelsblatt, p. 24, 28.01.2003.

Ferber, Michael and Ingo Narat (2002): "Fidelity will in die deutsche Top-Liga", Handelsblatt, p. 26, 05.12.2002.

Frühauf, Markus (2002): "Bei der offenen Archetiktur liegen die Tücken in der Umsetzung", Die Börsen-Zeitung, p. 18, 21.09.2002.

Furubotn, Eirik and Svetozar Pejovich (1974): The Economics of Property Rights. Cambridge, MA, Ballinger.

Furubotn, Eirik and Rudolf Richter (1991): "The New Institutional Economics: An Assessment". The New Institutional Economics. E. Furubotn and R. Richter, Eds. College Station, TX, Texas A&M University Press: pp. 1-32.

Galbraith, Jay (2002): Designing Organizations: An Executive Guide to Strategy, Structure, and Process. San Francisco, CA, Jossey-Bass.

Ghosh, Mrinal and George John (1999): "Governance Value Analysis and Marketing Strategy", Journal of Marketing, **63** (Special Issue): pp. 131-145.

Ghosh, Mrinal and George John (2005): "Strategic Fit in Industrial Alliances: An Empirical Test of Governance Value Analysis", Journal of Marketing Research, **42** (August): pp. 346-357.

Glaser, Barney and Anselm Strauss (1967): The Discovery of Grounded Theory: Strategies for Qualitative Research. Chicago, Aldine.

Göbel, Elisabeth (2002): Neue Institutionenökonomik. Stuttgart, Lucius & Lucius.

Granovetter, Mark (1985): "Economic Action and Social Structure: The Problem of Embeddedness", American Journal of Sociology, **91** (November): pp. 481-510.

Grinblatt, Mark and Sheridan Titman (1998): Financial Markets and Corporate Strategy. Boston, MA, Irwin/McGraw-Hill.

Grossman, Sanford and Oliver Hart (1986): "The Costs and Benefits of Ownership: A Theory of Vertical and Lateral Ownership", Journal of Political Economy, **94** (4): pp. 691-719.

Gundlach, Gregory; Ravi Achrol and John Mentzer (1995): "The Structure of Commitment in Exchange", Journal of Marketing, **59** (January): pp. 78-92.

Hackethal, Andreas and Reinhard Schmidt (2005): "Structural Change in the German Banking System?", Working Paper Series: Finance & Accounting No. 147, Johann Wolfgang Goethe Universität Frankfurt, *http://www.wiwi.uni-frankfurt.de/schwerpunkte/finance/wp/888.pdf,* (02.05.2007).

Handelsblatt (2004): "Commerzbank verkauft mehr Fremdfonds", p. 25, 16./17.01.2004.

Hart, Oliver (1995): Firms, Contracts and Financial Structure. Oxford, Oxford University Press.

Hart, Oliver and John Moore (1990): "Property Rights and the Nature of the Firm", Journal of Political Economy, **98** (December): pp. 1119-1158.

Hayek, Friedrich (1945): "The Use of Knowledge in Society", American Economic Review, **35** (September): pp. 519-530.

Heide, Jan (1994): "Interorganizational Governance in Marketing Channels", Journal of Marketing, **58** (January): pp. 71-85.

Heide, Jan (2003): "Plural Governance in Industrial Purchasing", Journal of Marketing, **67** (October): pp. 18-29.

Heide, Jan and George John (1988): "The Role of Dependence Balancing in Safeguarding Transaction-Specific Assets in Conventional Channels", Journal of Marketing, **52** (January): pp. 20-35.

Heide, Jan and George John (1990): "Alliances in Industrial Purchasing: The Determinants of Joint Action in Buyer-Supplier Relationships", Journal of Marketing Research, **27** (February): pp. 24-36.

Heide, Jan and George John (1992): "Do Norms Matter in Marketing Relationships?" Journal of Marketing, **56** (April): pp. 32-44.

Heinemann, Friedrich; Michael Schröder; Martin Schüler; Claudia Stirböck and Peter Westerheide (2003): "Towards a Single European Market in Asset Management", Studie des Zentrum für Europäische Wirtschaftforschung, Universität Mannheim.

Held, Martin and Hans Nutzinger (2003): "Perspektiven einer Allgemeinen Institutionenökonomik". Ökonomischer und soziologischer Insitutionalismus. M. Schmid and A. Maurer, Eds. Marburg, Metropolis: pp. 117-137.

Hellstern, Gerd-Michael and Hellmut Wollmann (1983): Evaluierungsforschung. Basel, Birkhäuser.

Henselek, Hilmar (1996): Das Management von Unternehmenskonfigurationen. Wiesbaden, Gabler.

Hill, Charles (1990): "Cooperation, Opportunism and the Invisible Hand: Implications for Transaction Cost Theory", Academy of Management Journal, **15** (3): pp. 500-513.

Hill, Wilhelm; Raymond Fehlbaum and Peter Ulrich (1994): Organisationslehre. Bern, Haupt.

Hollis, Martin (1994): The Philosophy of Social Science. Cambridge, Cambridge University Press.

Holmstrom, Bengt (1979): "Morald Hazard and Observability", Bell Journal of Economics, **10** (Spring): pp. 74-91.

Holmstrom, Bengt and Jean Tirole (1991): "Transfer Pricing and Organizational Form", Journal of Law, Economics, and Organization, **7** (2): pp. 201-228.

Huber, Martin; Stéphane Leroy and Maxime Saada (2003): "The Liabilities of Europe's Asset Managers", The McKinsey Quarterly (Special Edition: The Value in Organization): pp. 9-12.

Hughes, Duncan (2002): Asset Management in Theory and Practice. Canterbury, The Chartered Insitute of Bankers.

Jacobides, Michael and Lorin Hitt (2005): "Losing Sight of the Forest for the Trees? Productive Capabilities and Gains from Trade as Drivers of Vertical Scope", Strategic Management Journal, **26** (13): pp. 1209-1227.

Jacobides, Michael and Sidney Winter (2005): "The Co-Evolution of Capability and Transaction Costs: Explaining the Institutional Structure of Production", Strategic Management Journal, **26** (5): pp. 395-413.

Jacques, Elliot (1990): "In praise of hierarchy", Harvard Business Review, **68** (1): pp. 127-133.

Jain, Prem and Joanna Wu (2000): "Truth in Mutual Fund Advertising: Evidence on Future Performance and Fund Flows", Journal of Finance, **55** (2): pp. 937-958.

Jap, Sandy (1999): "Pie-Expansion Efforts: Collaboration Processes in Buyer-Supplier Relationships", Journal of Marketing Research, **36** (November): pp. 461-475.

Jenkins, Patrick (2005): "German funds are losing to foreigners on home ground", Financial Times FM, p. 3, 21.03.2005.

Jensen, Michael and William Meckling (1976): "Theory of the Firm: Managerial Behavior, Agency Costs and Ownership Structure", Journal of Financial Economics (3): pp. 305-360.

Jensen, Michael and Kevin Murphy (2004): "Renumeration: Where we've been, how we got to here, what are the problems, and how to fix them", ECGI Working Paper Series in Finance 44/2004, http://ssrn.com/abstract=561305 (23.03.2006).

John, George and Barton Weitz (1988): "Forward Integration into Distribution: An Empirical Test of Transaction Cost Analysis", Journal of Law, Economics, and Organization, **4** (2): pp. 337-355.

John, George and Barton Weitz (1989): "Salesforce Compensation: An Empirical Investigation of Factors Related to Use of Salary Versus Incentive Compensation", Journal of Marketing Research, **26** (February): pp. 1-14.

Johnson, Bradford; James Manyika and Lareina Yee (2005): "The Next Revolution in Interactions", The McKinsey Quarterly (4): pp. 21-33.

Johnston, Russel and Paul Lawrence (1988): "Beyond vertical integration - the rise of the value-adding partnership", Harvard Business Review, **66** (4): pp. 94-101.

Jordan, Jenny (2001): "Fondswerbung und Zielgruppen stärker differenzieren", bank und markt, **30** (Dezember): pp. 22-26.

Jordan, Jenny (2003): "Fondsgesellschaften: Wege zum eigenen Profil", bank und markt, **32** (September): pp. 23-27.

Joskow, Paul (1987): "Contract Duration and Relationship-Specific Investments: Empirical Evience from Coal Market", American Economic Review, **77** (1): pp. 168-185.

Jost, Peter -J. (2001a): Die Spieltheorie in der Betriebswirtschaftslehre. Stuttgart, Schäffer-Poeschel.

Jost, Peter-J. (2001b): Die Prinizipal-Agenten-Theorie in der Betriebswirtschaftslehre. Stuttgart, Schäffer-Poeschel.

Kaas, Klaus-Peter and Tobias Schneider (2002): "Ermittlung von Kundenpräferenzen bei Investmentfonds mit Conjoint-Measurement", Jahrbuch der Absatz- und Verbrauchsforschung, **48** (1): pp. 28-46.

Kammlott, Christian; Matija Denise Mayer-Fiedrich and Dirk Schiereck (2005): "Die deutsche Sparkassen-Finanzgruppe als Anbieter von Beteiligungskapital – Status Quo und Fiktion zum öffentlichen Auftrag", Zeitschrift für KMU und Entrepreneurship, **53** (2): pp. 87-109.

Katz, Daniel (1971): "The motivational basis of organizational behavior". Current Perspectives in Social Psychology. E. Hollander and R. Hunt, Eds. New York, NY, Oxford University Press: pp. 131-146.

Kaufmann, Patrick and Francine Lafontaine (1994): "Costs of Control: The Source of Economic Rents for McDonald's Franchisees", Journal of Law and Economics, **37** (2): pp. 417-453.

Kay, John (1993): Foundations of Corporate Success. Oxford, Oxford University Press.

Keller, Kevin Lane (2003): Strategic Brand Management: Building, Measuring and Managing Brand Equity (2nd ed.). Upper Saddle River, NJ, Pearson Education.

Kepper, Gaby (1994): Qualitative Marktforschung: Methoden, Einsatzmöglichkeiten und Beurteiltungskriterien. Wiesbaden, Deutscher Universitäts-Verlag.

Kieser, Alfred and Peter Welgenbach (2003): Organisation (4th ed.). Stuttgart, Schäffer-Poeschel.

Kirmani, Amna and Akshay Rao (2000): "No Pain, No Gain: A Critical Review of the Literature on Signaling Unobservable Product Quality", Journal of Marketing, **64** (April): pp. 66-79.

Klein, Benjamin; Robert Crawford and Armen Alchian (1978): "Vertical Integration, Appropriable Rents, and the Competitive Contracting Process", Journal of Law and Economics, **21** (October): pp. 297-326.

Klein, Benjamin and Keith Leffler (1981): "The Role of Market Forces in Assuring Contractual Performance", Journal of Political Economy, **89** (4): pp. 615-641.

Klein, Peter (1999): "New Institutional Economics". Encyclopedia of Law and Economics. B. Bouckaert and G. de Geest, Eds. Northampton, MA: pp. 456-489.

Klein, Saul; Gary Frazier and Victor Roth (1990): "A Transaction Cost Analysis Model of Channel Integration in International Markets", Journal of Marketing Research, **27** (May): pp. 196-208.

Koch, Jochen (2005): "Markt und Organisation? - Eine Dekonstruktion". Institutionenökonomik als Managementlehre? Managementforschung 15. B. Schauenberg; G. Schreyögg and J. Sydow, Eds. Wiesbaden, Gabler: pp. 185-227.

Koch, Rainer (1985): "Methodologische Entwicklungen in der Verwaltungswissenschaft", Verwaltungs-Archiv, **76** (3): pp. 247-275.

Kogut, Bruce and Udo Zander (1996): "What Firms do? Coordination, Identity, Learning", Organization Science, **7**: pp. 502-518.

Kotler, Philip and Friedhelm Bliemel (1999): Marketing Management (9th ed.). Stuttgart, Schäffer-Poeschel.

Krahnen, Jan; Frank Schmid and Erik Theissen (1997): "Performance and Market Share. Evidence from the German Mutual Fund Industry", Working Paper of Center for Financial Studies 97/01, Johann Wolfgang Goethe Universität Frankfurt.

Kramer, Wolfgang (2004): "Ratings im Fondmarketing: kein Ersatz für Beratung", bank und markt, **33** (Januar): pp. 21-22.

Kraus, Jan-Hendrik (2004): Preissetzung im Aktienfondgeschäft: Eine empirische Analyse des Kauf- und Preisverhaltens privater Fondsinvestoren mit Hilfe der Conjoint-Analyse. Hamburg, Dr. Kovac.

Lal, Rajiv (1990): "Improving Channel Coordination Through Franchising", Marketing Science, **9** (4): pp. 299-318.

Lal, Rajiv and Richard Staelin (1986): "Salesforce Compensation Plans in Environment with Asymmetric Information", Marketing Science, **5** (3): pp. 179-198.

Langer, Robert (2003): "Trends und Erfolgsfaktoren des Retailvertriebs in Deutschland". Asset Management - Investmentkonzepte, Produkte, Vertriebswege und Standortfragen der Fondsbranche. I. Westphal; C. Hortskotte and K. Ripper, Eds. Stuttgart, Schäffer-Poeschel: pp. 87-102.

Lazear, Edward and Sherwin Rosen (1981): "Rank-Order Tournements as Optimum Labor Contracts", Journal of Political Economy, **89** (5): pp. 841-864.

Lee, Thomas (1999): Using Qualitative Methods in Organizational Research. London, Sage.

Lehmann, Axel (1998): "Servicemarketing in der Versicherungswirtschaft - Bausteine und Entwicklungstendenzen". Handbuch Dienstleistungsmarketing. A. Meyer, Ed. Stuttgart, Schäffer-Poeschel: pp. 1726-1734.

Macneil, Ian (1980): The New Social Contract: An Inquiry into Modern Contractual Relations. New Haven, CT, Yale University Press.

Madhok, Annop (2002): "Reassessing the Fundamentals and Beyond: Ronald Coase, the Transaction Cost and Resource-Based Theories of the Firm and the Insitutional Structure of Production", Strategic Mangement Journal, **23** (6): pp. 535-550.

Maier, Michael (1998): "Finanz-Dienstleitungen im Privatkundengeschäft: Dynamik im Markt und Marketing". Handbuch Dienstleistungs-Marketing. A. Meyer, Ed. Stuttgart, Schäffer-Poeschel: pp. 1667-1685.

McGuinness, Tony (1991): "Markets and managerial hierarchies". Markets, Hierachies and Network. G. Thompson; J. Frances; R. Levacic and J. Mitchell, Eds. London, Sage: pp. 66-81.

McKinsey&Company (2003): Will the goose keep laying golden eggs? The fifth annual survey on the profitability of European Asset Management. London.

McMeeken, Roxane (2005): "Hunt for the Perfect Combination", Professional Wealth Management (31): pp. 29-32.

Meffert, Heribert and Christoph Burmann (2000): "Markenbildung und Markenstrategien". Handbuch Produktmanagement. S. Albers and A. Herrmann, Eds. Wiesbaden, Gabler: pp. 167-187.

Menon, Anil and P. Rajan Varadarajan (1992): "A Model of Marketing Knowledge Use within Firms", Journal of Marketing, **56** (October): pp. 53-71.

Miles, Raymond and Charles Snow (1984): "Fit, Failure and the Hall of Fame", California Management Review, **26** (3): pp. 10-28.

Milgrom, Paul and John Roberts (1992): Economics, Organization & Management. Upper Saddle River, NJ, Prentice Hall.

Mintzberg, Henry (1979): The Structuring of Organizations. Englewood Cliffs, NJ, Prentice Hall.

Mintzberg, Henry (1981): "Organization Design: Fashion or Fit?", Harvard Business Review, **59** (1): pp. 103-116.

Mishra, Debi; Jan Heide and Stanton Cort (1998): "Information Asymmetry and Levels of Agency Relationships", Journal of Marketing Research, **35** (August): pp. 277-295.

Mohr, Jakki and Robert Spekmann (1994): "Characteristics of Partnership Success: Partnership Attributes, Communication Behavior, and Conflict Resolution Techniques", Strategic Management Journal, **15** (2): pp. 135-152.

Monteverde, Kirk and David Teece (1982): "Supplier switching costs and vertical integration in the automobile industry", Bell Journal of Economics, **13** (1): pp. 206-213.

Murray, Janet and Masaaki Kotabe (1999): "Sourcing Strategies of U.S. Service Companies: A Modified Transaction-Cost Analysis", Strategic Management Journal, **20** (9): pp. 791-809.

Narat, Ingo (2003): "Die Zukunft in der Anlagebranche: Konsolidierung und Arbeitsteilung". Asset Management - Investmentkonzepte, Produkte, Vertriebswege und Standortfragen der Fondsbranche. I. Westphal; C. Horstkotte and K. Ripper, Eds. (2nd ed.). Stuttgart, Schäffer-Poeschel: pp. 261-272.

Narat, Ingo and Anke Remzer (2005): "Ausländische Fonds rollen den Markt auf", Handelsblatt, p. 21, 10.03.2005.

Nickerson, Jack and Brian Silverman (2003): "Why firms want to organize efficiently and what keeps them from doing so: Evidence form the for-hire trucking industry", Administrative Science Quarterly, **48** (3): pp. 433-465.

Noordewier, Thomas; George John and John Nevin (1990): "Performance Outcomes of Purchasing Arrangements in Industrial Buyer-Vendor Relationships", Journal of Marketing, **54** (October): pp. 80-93.

North, Douglas (1995): "Five Propositions about Institutional Change". Explaining Social Institutions. J. Knight and I. Sened, Eds. Ann Arbor, The University of Michigan Press: pp. 15-26.

Olsen, Eric; Stanley Slater and G. Tomas Hult (2005): "The Performance Implications of Fit Among Business Strategy, Marketing Organization Strcuture and Strategic Behavior", Journal of Marketing, **69** (July): pp. 49-65.

Osborn, Richard and Christopher Baughn (1990): "Forms of Interorganizational Governance for Multinational Alliances", Academy of Management Journal, **33** (3): pp. 503-519.

Osterloh, Margit and Bruno Frey (2000): "Motivation, Knowlegde Transfer, and Organizational From", Organization Science, **11** (5): pp. 538-550.

Otto, Susanne (2003): "Bauchladen ade - Vertrieb von Fremdfonds setzt nun auf langfristige Partnerschaften", Frankfurter Allgemeine Zeitung (Sonderbeilage), p. 3, 27.05.2003

Ouchi, William (1980): "Markets, Bureaucracies, and Clans", Administrative Science Quarterly, **25** (1): pp. 129-141.

Oxley, Joanne (1997): "Appropriability hazards and governance in strategic alliances: A transaction cost approach", Journal of Law, Economics, and Organization, **13** (2): pp. 387-409.

Penrose, Edith (1959): The Theory of the Growth of the Firm. Oxford, Blackwell.

Picot, Arnold and Peter Hardt (1998): "Make-or-Buy-Entscheidungen". Handbuch Dienstleistungs-Marketing. A. Meyer, Ed. Stuttgart, Schäffer-Poeschel: pp. 625-646.

Picot, Arnold; Ralf Reichwald and Rolf Wigand (2003): Die grenzlosen Unternehmung - Information, Organisation und Management (5th ed.). Wiesbaden, Gabler.

Pisano, Gary (1990): "Using Equity Participation to Support Exchange: Evidence from the Biotechnology Industry", Journal of Law, Economics, and Organization, **5** (1): pp. 109-126.

Powell, Walter (1990): "Neither Market nor Hierarchy: Network forms of organization", Research in Organizational Behavior, **12**: pp. 295-336.

Prahalad, C. K. and Gary Hamel (1990): "The Core Competence of the Corporation", Harvard Business Review, **68** (3): pp. 79-91.

Promethee (2002): "Bridging the funds divide", Paris, *http://164.109.168.129/Publications/ bridging.pdf*, (23.03.2006).

Rathmann, Christina (2004): "Sparkassen und Genossen öffnen ihr Vertriebsnetz", Börsen-Zeitung, p. 2, 23.03.2004.

Remer, Andreas (2001): "Management im Dilemma - von den konsistenten zur kompensatorischen Managementkonfiguration", Die Unternehmung, **55** (6): pp. 353-375.

Rindfleisch, Aric and Jan Heide (1997): "Transaction Cost Analysis: Past, Present, and Future Applications", Journal of Marketing, **61** (October): pp. 30-54.

Rokkan, Aksel; Jan Heide and Kenneth Wathne (2003): "Specific Investments in Marketing Relationships: Expropriation and Bonding Effects", Journal of Marketing Research, **40** (May): pp. 210-224.

Saussier, Stephanie (2000): "Transaction Costs and Contractual Incompleteness: The Case of Électricité de France", Journal of Economic Behavior and Organization, **42** (2): pp. 189-206.

Scherff, Dyrk (2003): "Fonds aus dem Supermarkt", Frankfurter Allgemeine Sonntagszeitung, p. 41, 25.05.2003

Schrader, Stephan (1993): "Kooperation". Ergebnisse empirischer betriebswirtschaftlicher Forschung. J. Hauschildt and O. Grün, Eds. Stuttgart, Schäffer-Poeschel: pp. 221-254.

Sector Analysis (2003a): The State of Open Architecture in the European Fund Industry. London.

Sector Analysis (2003b): Insights into Third Party Fund Buying Behaviour in Europe. London.

Shelanski, Howard and Peter Klein (1995): "Empirical Research in Transaction Cost Economics: A Review and Assessment", The Journal of Law, Economics, and Organization, **11** (2): pp. 335-361.

Shiller, Robert (2000): Irrational Exuberance. Princeton, NJ, Princeton University Press.

Siggelkow, Nicolaj (1999): "Expense Shifting: An Empricial Study of Agency Costs in the Mutual Fund Industry", Working Paper, University of Pennsylvannia, Philadelphia, *http://fic.wharton.upenn.edu/fic/papers/99/9909.pdf*, (23.03.2006).

Simon, Herbert (1957): Models of man: social and rational; mathematical essays on rational human behavior in social setting. New York, NY, Wiley.

Simon, Herbert (1959): Administrative Behavior: A Study of Decision-Making Processes in Administrative Organization (2nd ed.). New York, NY, MacMillan.

Sirri, Erik and Peter Tufano (1998): "Costly Search and Mutual Fund Flows", Journal of Finance, **53** (5): pp. 1589-1622.

Skypala, Pauline (2004): "Experts warn against the blind use of open architecture", Financial Times FM, p. 3, 22.11.2004.

Skypala, Pauline (2005): "Bank admit need for service approach", Financial Times FM, p. 6, 07.11.2005.

Sopp, Richard (2005): ""Guided Architecture" as Wettbewerbsvorteil", bank und markt, **34** (Januar): pp. 26-28.

Spence, Magnus (2004): "Measuring Distribution Costs in European Retail Asset Management", Financial Research Corporation, Boston, MA.

Spence, Michael (1973): "Job Market Signalling", Quarterly Journal of Economics, **87** (3): pp. 355-374.

Staehle, Wolfgang (1999): Management - Eine verhaltenswissenschaftliche Perspektive (8th ed.). München, Vahlen.

Stake, Robert (1994): "Case Studies". Handbook of Qualitative Research. N. Denzin and Y. Lincoln, Eds. Thousand Oaks, CA, Sage: pp. 236-247.

Stauss, Bernd (2004): "Dienstleistungsmarken". Handbuch Markenführung. M. Bruhn, Ed. Stuttgart, Schäffer-Poeschel: pp. 95-118.

Steiner, Manfred and Christoph Bruns (2002): Wertpapiermanagement (8th ed.). Stuttgart, Schäffer-Poeschel.

Stiglitz, Joseph (1975): "Incentives, Risk and Information: Notes towards a Theory of Hierarchy", Bell Journal of Economics, **6** (2): pp. 552-579.

Stump, Rodney and Jan Heide (1996): "Controlling Supplier Opportunism in Industrial Relationships", Journal of Marketing Research, **33** (November): pp. 431-441.

Sydow, Jörg (1991): "On the Management of Strategic Networks", Arbeitspapier Nr. 67/91, Freie Universität Berlin.

Sydow, Jörg (1992): Strategische Netzwerke: Evolution und Organisation. Wiesbaden, Gabler.

Teece, David; Gary Pisano and Amy Shuen (1997): "Dynamic Capabilities and Strategic Management", Strategic Mangement Journal, **18** (7): pp. 509-533.

Telser, Lester (1980): "A Theory of Self-Enforcing Agreements", Journal of Business, **53** (1): pp. 27-44.

Vorhies, Douglas and Neil Morgan (2003): "A Configuration Theory Assessment of Marketing Organization Fit with Business Strategy and Its Relationship with Marketing Performance", Journal of Marketing, **67** (January): pp. 100-115.

Walker, Gordon and David Weber (1984): "A Transaction Cost Approach to Make-or-Buy Decisions", Administrative Science Quarterly, **29**: pp. 373-391.

Wathne, Kenneth and Jan Heide (2000): "Opportunism in Interfirm Relationships: Forms, Outcomes, and Solutions", Journal of Marketing, **64** (October): pp. 36-51.

Wathne, Kenneth and Jan Heide (2004): "Relationship Governance in a Supply Chain Network", Journal of Marketing, **68** (January): pp. 73-89.

Wernerfelt, Birger (1984): "A Resource-Based View of the Firm", Strategic Mangement Journal, **5** (2): pp. 171-180.

Whinston, Michael (2001): "Assessing the Property Rights and Transaction Cost Theories of Firm Scope", AEA Papers and Proceedings, **91** (2): pp. 184-188.

Williamson, Oliver (1975): Markets and Hierarchies: Analysis and Antitrust Implications. New York, NY, The Free Press.

Williamson, Oliver (1985): The Economic Institutions of Capitalism. New York, NY, The Free Press.

Williamson, Oliver (1991a): "Comparative Economic Organization: The Analysis of Discrete Strcutural Alternatives", Administrative Science Quarterly, **36**: pp. 269-296.

Williamson, Oliver (1991b): "Strategizing, Economizing, and Economic Organization", Strategic Management Journal, **12** (8): pp. 75-94.

Williamson, Oliver (1996): "Transaktionskostenökonomik". Ökonomische Theorie der Institutionen. H. Dietl; C. Erlei; M. Erlei and M. Leschke, Eds. Band 3.

Williamson, Oliver (1998): "Transaction Cost Economics: How it works; Where it is headed", De Economist, **146** (1): pp. 23-58.

Williamson, Oliver (1999): "Strategy Research: Governance and Competence Perspective", Strategic Management Journal, **20** (12): pp. 1087-1108.

Williamson, Oliver (2002): "The Theory of the Firm as Governance Structure: From Choice to Contract", Journal of Economic Perspectives, **16** (3): pp. 171-195.

Wittkowski, Bernd (2003): "Zeitenwende im Fondsgeschäft", Börsen-Zeitung, p. 8, 06.03.2003.

Wolf, Joachim (2000): Der Gestaltansatz in der Management- und Organisationslehre. Wiesbaden, Gabler.

Wolf, Joachim (2003): Organisation, Management, Unternehmensführung. Wiesbaden, Gabler.

Wolff, Birgitta (1999): "Zum methodischen Status von Verhaltensannahmen in der Neuen Institutionenökonomik". Institutionenökonomik und Neuer Institutionalismus. T. Edeling; W. Jann and D. Wagner, Eds. Opladen, Leske + Budrich**:** pp. 133-146.

Wolff, Birgitta (2005): "Internationales Management aus der Perspektive der Neuen Institutionenökonomik". Institutionenökonomik als Managementlehre? Managementforschung 15. B. Schauenberg; G. Schreyögg and J. Sydow, Eds. Wiesbaden, Gabler**:** pp. 107-143.

Wollmann, Hellmut (2000): "Evaluierung und Evaluierungsforschung von Verwaltungspolitik und -moderinisierung: Zwischen Analysepontential und -defizit". Evaluationsforschung. R. Stockmann, Ed. Opladen, Leske & Budrich**:** pp. 195-231.

Yin, Robert (1994): Case Study Research: Design and Methods. Thousand Oaks, CA, Sage.

Zaheer, Akbar and N Venkatraman (1995): "Relational Governance as an Interorganizational Strategy: An Empirical Test of the Role of Trust in Economic Exchange", Strategic Mangement Journal, **16** (6): pp. 373-392.

Zajac, Edward; Matthew Kraatz and Rudi Bresser (2000): "Modeling the Dynamics of Strategic Fit: A Normative Approach to Strategic Change", Strategic Mangement Journal, **21** (4): pp. 429-453.

Company Information/ Internal Documents

DekaBank (1999): "Annual Report", *http://www.dekabank.de/download/de/bank/geschaefts bericht_1999.pdf*, (23.03.2006).

DekaBank (2000): "Annual Report", *http://www.dekabank.de/download/de/bank/geschaefts bericht_2000.pdf*, (23.03.2006).

DekaBank (2001): "Annual Report", *http://www.dekabank.de/download/de/bank/geschaefts bericht_2001.pdf*, (23.03.2006).

DekaBank (2002): "Annual Report", *http://www.dekabank.de/download/de/bank/geschaefts bericht_2002.pdf*, (23.03.2006).

DekaBank (2003): "Annual Report", *http://www.dekabank.de/download/de/bank/geschaefts bericht_2003.pdf*, (23.03.2006).

DekaBank (2004): "Annual Report", *http://www.dekabank.de/download/de/bank/geschaefts bericht_2004.pdf*, (23.03.2006).

Fidelity Investments (2004a): "Jahrespressekonferenz 2004", Frankfurt a. Main, 06.02.2004.

Fidelity Investments (2004b): "Introduction into Fidelity", Kronburg, 09.06.2004.

Fidelity Investments (2004c): "Verändertes Anlageverhalten bringt Chancen im Fremdfondsgeschäft", Frankfurt a. Main, 29.09.2004.

Julius Bär (1999): "Annual Report", *http://www.juliusbaer.ch/runappl.cfm/Kurzbericht %201999?wm=a%28133%29&dp=a%28dl%29d%281444%29&ext=.*, (23.03.2006).

Julius Bär (2000): "Annual Report", *http://www.juliusbaer.ch/runappl.cfm/GB00_KB_D_Klein? wm=a%28133%29&dp=a%28dl%29d%281445%29&ext=.*, (23.03.2006).

Julius Bär (2001): "Annual Report", *http://www.juliusbaer.ch/runappl.cfm/GB01_KB_D?wm= a%28133%29&dp=a%28dl%29d%281446%29&ext=.*, (23.03.2006).

Julius Bär (2002): "Annual Report", *http://www.juliusbaer.ch/runappl.cfm/Geschaeftsbericht? wm=a%28133%29&dp=a%28dl%29d%281447%29&ext=.*, (23.03.2006).

Julius Bär (2003): "Annual Report", *http://www.juliusbaer.ch/runappl.cfm/2003_ar_de_Annual Report?wm=a%28133%29&dp=a%28dl%29d%281448%29&ext=.*, (23.03.2006).

Julius Bär (2004a): "Annual Report", *http://www.juliusbaer.ch/runappl.cfm/2004_ar_de_jb-holding?wm=a%28133%29&dp=a%28dl%29d%281716%29&ext=.*, (23.03.2006).

Julius Bär (2004b): "Werbewirkungs-Analyse Julius Bär Finanzgruppe", Zurich, May 2004.

Julius Bär Asset Management (2003): "Building Solid Relationships Between Third-Party Distributors and Fund Managers", Munich, 01.04.2003.

Julius Bär Asset Management (2004): "Service Landscape Review", Zurich, May 2004.